ANNUAL EDIT

United States History

Volume 1—Colonial Through Reconstruction

Twentieth Edition

EDITOR

Robert James Maddox (Emeritus)
Pennsylvania State University
University Park

Robert James Maddox, distinguished historian and professor emeritus of American history at Pennsylvania State University, received a BS from Fairleigh Dickinson University in 1957, an MS from the University of Wisconsin in 1958, and a PhD from Rutgers in 1964. He has written, reviewed, and lectured extensively, and is widely respected for his interpretations of presidential character and policy.

 **Higher Education**

Boston   Burr Ridge, IL   Dubuque, IA   New York   San Francisco   St. Louis
Bangkok   Bogotá   Caracas   Kuala Lumpur   Lisbon   London   Madrid   Mexico City
Milan   Montreal   New Delhi   Santiago   Seoul   Singapore   Sydney   Taipei   Toronto

The McGraw-Hill Companies

Mc Graw Hill **Higher Education**

ANNUAL EDITIONS: UNITED STATES HISTORY, VOLUME 1, TWENTIETH EDITION

Published by McGraw-Hill, a business unit of The McGraw-Hill Companies, Inc., 1221 Avenue of the Americas, New York, NY 10020.

Some ancillaries, including electronic and print components, may not be available to customers outside the United States.

Annual Editions® is a registered trademark of The McGraw-Hill Companies, Inc.
Annual Editions is published by the **Contemporary Learning Series** group within the McGraw-Hill Higher Education division.

1 2 3 4 5 6 7 8 9 0 QPD/QPD 0 9 8

ISBN 978–0–07–339761–0
MHID 0–07–339761–X
ISSN 0733–3560

Managing Editor: *Larry Loeppke*
Senior Managing Editor: *Faye Schilling*
Developmental Editor: *Jade Benedict*
Editorial Assistant: *Nancy Meissner*
Production Service Assistant: *Rita Hingtgen*
Permissions Coordinator: *Leonard Behnke*
Senior Marketing Manager: *Julie Keck*
Marketing Communications Specialist: *Mary Klein*
Marketing Coordinator: *Alice Link*
Project Manager: *Sandy Wille*
Design Specialist: *Tara McDermott*
Senior Administrative Assistant: *DeAnna Dausener*
Senior Production Supervisor: *Laura Fuller*
Cover Graphics: *Kristine Jubeck*

Compositor: Laserwords Private Limited
Cover Image: Royalty-Free/CORBIS

Library in Congress Cataloging in Publication Data
Main entry under title: Annual Editions: United States History Vol. 1: Colonial Through Reconstruction. 20e.
  1. United States—History—Periodicals. 2. United States—Historiography—Periodicals. 3. United States—Civilization—Periodicals. I. 1. Maddox, Robert James, *comp.* II Title: United States History, Vol. 1: Colonial Through Reconstruction.
658'.05

www.mhhe.com

Editors/Advisory Board

Members of the Advisory Board are instrumental in the final selection of articles for each edition of ANNUAL EDITIONS. Their review of articles for content, level, currentness, and appropriateness provides critical direction to the editor and staff. We think that you will find their careful consideration well reflected in this volume.

Preface

In publishing ANNUAL EDITIONS we recognize the enormous role played by the magazines, newspapers, and journals of the public press in providing current, first-rate educational information in a broad spectrum of interest areas. Many of these articles are appropriate for students, researchers, and professionals seeking accurate, current material to help bridge the gap between principles and theories and the real world. These articles, however, become more useful for study when those of lasting value are carefully collected, organized, indexed, and reproduced in a low-cost format, which provides easy and permanent access when the material is needed. That is the role played by ANNUAL EDITIONS.

The writing of history has changed dramatically since the first edition of this anthology. A look at the table of contents will show that individuals and groups previously ignored or down-played are now being given much fuller attention. The westward expansion of this nation, for instance, usually was depicted as a triumphant migration that overcame great obstacles to "settle" the frontier. But what whites considered a process of civilization was to Native Americans a disastrous invasion of their lands. Some tribes were demoralized by the destruction of buffalo herds upon which their cultures and sustenance rested. Most Native Americans were finally herded onto reservations where they became little more than wards of the federal government. Attempts to tell the story from their standpoint, as in the article "How the West was Lost," enrich our understanding of the past.

A similar process has taken place with regard to the treatment of Women, Blacks, and others who were marginalized in conventional histories. Earlier accounts, when they treated such groups at all, tended to focus attention on notable leaders rather than the rank and file members. This was understandable as source material about prominent figures was more readily available. The development of history "from the bottom up" has produced a great deal of writing about the lives of ordinary people as exemplified by several essays in this volume. The tendency towards inclusion has to be applauded.

Another recent development in writing about the past has been an emphasis on viewing issues within broader contexts as opposed to those obtained in one or another colony or in the United States as a whole during its early national period. One essay included in this edition, for example, analyzes the American Civil War and its aftermath as it played out on the "world stage." Events that previously were treated in isolation are now presented within the framework of how they influenced or were influenced by other people and other nations. "Transnational history," as it has been called, can provide insights previously lacking in conventional histories.

There has been a downside. A deplorable tendency in recent historical writing has been the practice of enlisting the past to promote specific agendas, however admirable those agendas might be. "Objective" history is impossible to attain, of course, because each of us carries intellectual baggage that pushes us towards one interpretation rather then another. But efforts to create a "usable past" often have resulted in gross distortions of the historical record.

It is tempting for both authors and readers to analyze and judge the past from the standpoint of present-day knowledge and assumptions. How easy it is to criticize people born in the 18th Century, for instance, on the grounds that the ideas they held and the practices they followed have since become discredited. Who could believe in witchcraft? Who could defend slavery? Who could see "the natural order of things" in the relegation of women and other groups to second-class citizenship? The fact is that many intelligent and reasonable people in earlier times held such beliefs. Treating our predecessors with contempt because they did not hold the beliefs that many of us now take for granted can be comforting because it assures us of our own intellectual and moral superiority. One should keep in mind, however, many of today's "truths" will seem equally wrong-headed to people looking back at us hundreds of years from now, assuming we do not destroy the planet before then.

Annual Editions: United States History, Volume I is designed for non-specialized survey courses. We have attempted to present a fair sampling of articles that incorporate newer approaches to the study of history as well as more traditional ones. The sources from which these essays have been taken for the most part are intended for the general reader: they require no particular expertise to understand them and they avoid the dreadful jargon that permeates so much of modern academic writing.

This volume contains a number of features designed to aid students, researchers, and professionals. These include a *topic guide* for locating articles on specific subjects; the *table of contents, abstracts* that summarize each essay, with key concepts in bold italics. Articles are organized into four units, each preceded by an overview that provides a background for informed reading of the articles, emphasizes critical issues, and presents *challenge questions.*

Every revision of *Annual Editions: United States History, Volume I* replaces about fifty percent of the previous articles with new ones. We try to update and improve the quality of the sections, and we would like to consider alternatives that we may have missed. If you find an article that you think merits inclusion in the next edition, please send it to us (or at least send us the citation, so that the editor can track it down for consideration). We welcome your comments about the readings in this volume, and a postage-paid reader response card is included in the back of the book for your convenience. Your suggestions will be carefully considered and greatly appreciated.

Robert James Maddox

Robert James Maddox
Editor

Contents

F THE PILGRIMS AT PLYMOUTH, MASS. DEC. 22°

UNIT 1
The New Land

The concepts in bold italics are developed in the article. For further expansion, please refer to the Topic Guide.

UNIT 2
Revolutionary America

The concepts in bold italics are developed in the article. For further expansion, please refer to the Topic Guide.

UNIT 3
National Consolidation and Expansion

The concepts in bold italics are developed in the article. For further expansion, please refer to the Topic Guide.

The concepts in bold italics are developed in the article. For further expansion, please refer to the Topic Guide.

UNIT 4
The Civil War and Reconstruction

The concepts in bold italics are developed in the article. For further expansion, please refer to the Topic Guide.

The concepts in bold italics are developed in the article. For further expansion, please refer to the Topic Guide.

Correlation Guide

The *Annual Editions* series provides students with convenient, inexpensive access to current, carefully selected articles from the public press. **Annual Editions: United States History, Volume 1: Colonial through Reconstruction** is an easy-to-use reader that presents articles on important topics in the study of United States History. For more information on *Annual Editions* and other *McGraw-Hill Contemporary Learning Series* titles, visit www.mhcls.com.

This convenient guide matches the units in **Annual Editions: United States History, Volume 1** with the corresponding chapters in one of our best-selling McGraw-Hill History textbooks by Davidson et al.

Annual Editions: United States History, Volume 1, 20/e	**Nation of Nations: A Narrative History of the American Republic: Volume 1: to 1877, 6/e, by Davidson et al.**
Unit 1: The New Land	**Chapter 1:** The First Civilizations of North America
	Chapter 2: Old Worlds, New Worlds (1400–1600)
	Chapter 3: The First Century of Settlement in the Colonial South (1600–1750)
	Chapter 4: The First Century of Settlement in the Colonial North (1600–1700)
Unit 2: Revolutionary America	**Chapter 5:** The Mosaic of Eighteenth-Century America (1689–1771)
	Chapter 6: Toward the War for American Independence (1754–1776)
	Chapter 7: The American People and the American Revolution (1775–1783)
	Chapter 9: The Early Republic (1789–1824)
Unit 3: National Consolidation and Expansion	**Chapter 10:** The Opening of America (1815–1850)
	Chapter 11: The Rise of Democracy (1824–1840)
	Chapter 12: The Fires of Perfection (1820–1850)
	Chapter 14: Western Expansion and the Rise of the Slavery Issue (1820–1850)
Unit 4: The Civil War and Reconstruction	**Chapter 15:** The Union Broken (1850–1861)
	Chapter 16: Total War and the Republic (1861–1865)
	Chapter 17: Reconstructing the Union (1865–1877)

Topic Guide

This topic guide suggests how the selections in this book relate to the subjects covered in your course. You may want to use the topics listed on these pages to search the Web more easily.

On the following pages a number of Web sites have been gathered specifically for this book. They are arranged to reflect the units of this *Annual Edition*. You can link to these sites by going to the student online support site at *http://www.mhcls.com/online/*.

ALL THE ARTICLES THAT RELATE TO EACH TOPIC ARE LISTED BELOW THE BOLD-FACED TERM.

African Americans
6. The Root of the Problem
9. Slavery in the North
11. Dirty Little Secret
26. African Americans in the Early Republic
28. From Detroit to the Promised Land
31. Free at Last
33. New York City's Secession Crisis
34. Lincoln and the Constitutional Dilemma of Emancipation
35. A Gallant Rush for Glory
38. The American Civil War, Emancipation, and Reconstruction on the World Stage

American Revolution
11. Dirty Little Secret
13. God and the Founders
14. The Rocky Road to Revolution
15. A Day to Remember: July 4, 1776
16. Washington Takes Charge
18. Evacuation Day

Business
27. Liberty Is Exploitation

Civil War
33. New York City's Secession Crisis
34. Lincoln and the Constitutional Dilemma of Emancipation
35. A Gallant Rush for Glory
38. The American Civil War, Emancipation, and Reconstruction on the World Stage

Constitution
19. The Necessity of Refusing My Signature

Culture
1. America's First Immigrants
2. 1491
5. The Birth of America
6. The Root of the Problem
8. American Indians, Witchcraft, and Witch-hunting
13. God and the Founders
25. Women in the Early Republic
26. African Americans in the Early Republic

Declaration of Independence
15. A Day to Remember: July 4, 1776

Environment
2. 1491
4. America, the Atlantic, and Global Consumer Demand, 1500–1800
23. The Revolution of 1803

Exploration
1. America's First Immigrants
2. 1491

3. How Cruel Were the Spaniards?
5. The Birth of America

First Continental Congress
13. God and the Founders

Government
13. God and the Founders
15. A Day to Remember: July 4, 1776
19. The Necessity of Refusing My Signature
21. The Best of Enemies
29. Andrew Jackson Versus the Cherokee Nation
34. Lincoln and the Constitutional Dilemma of Emancipation
38. The American Civil War, Emancipation, and Reconstruction on the World Stage

Hamilton, Alexander
21. The Best of Enemies

Immigration
1. America's First Immigrants

Jackson, Andrew
24. Saving New Orleans
29. Andrew Jackson Versus the Cherokee Nation

Jefferson, Thomas
15. A Day to Remember: July 4, 1776
21. The Best of Enemies
23. The Revolution of 1803

Labor
27. Liberty Is Exploitation

Laffite, Jean
24. Saving New Orleans

Lincoln, Abraham
34. Lincoln and the Constitutional Dilemma of Emancipation

Louisiana Purchase
23. The Revolution of 1803

Mason, George
19. The Necessity of Refusing My Signature

Native Americans
1. America's First Immigrants
2. 1491
3. How Cruel Were the Spaniards?
5. The Birth of America
8. American Indians, Witchcraft, and Witch-Hunting
10. Were American Indians the Victims of Genocide?
36. How the West Was Lost

Internet References

The following Internet sites have been carefully researched and selected to support the articles found in this reader. The easiest way to access these selected sites is to go to our student online support site at *http://www.mhcls.com/online/*.

AE: United States History, Volume 1

The following sites were available at the time of publication. Visit our Web site—we update our student online support site regularly to reflect any changes.

General Sources

American Historical Association (AHA)
http://www.historians.org

This site is an excellent source for data on just about any topic in American history. All affiliated societies and publications are noted, and AHA and its links provide material related to myriad fields of history.

American Studies Web
http://www.georgetown.edu

Links to a wealth of Internet resources for research in American studies, from agriculture and rural development, to government, to race and ethnicity, are provided on this eclectic site.

Harvard's John F. Kennedy School of Government
http://www.ksg.harvard.edu

Starting from this home page, click on a huge variety of links to information about American history, politics, and government, including material related to debates of enduring issues.

History Net
http://www.thehistorynet.com/

Supported by the National Historical Society, this site provides information on a wide range of topics. The articles are of excellent quality, and the site has book reviews and even special interviews. It is also frequently updated.

Library of Congress
http://www.loc.gov

Examine this Web site to learn about the extensive resource tools, library services/resources, exhibitions, and databases available through the Library of Congress in many different subfields of government studies.

Smithsonian Institution
http://www.si.edu

This site provides access to the enormous resources of the Smithsonian, which holds some 140 million artifacts and specimens for "the increase and diffusion of knowledge." Learn about American social, cultural, economic, and political history from a variety of viewpoints here.

UNIT 1: The New Land

Early America
http://earlyamerica.com/earlyamerica/index.html

Explore the "amazing world of early America" through early media data at this site. Topics include Pages of the Past, Lives of Early Americans, Notable Women of Early America, Milestone Events, and many more.

1492: An Ongoing Voyage/Library of Congress
http://lcweb.loc.gov/exhibits/1492/

Displays examining the causes and effects of Columbus's voyages to the Americas can be accessed on this Web site. "An Ongoing Voyage" explores the rich mixture of societies coexisting in five areas of this hemisphere before European arrival. It then surveys the polyglot Mediterranean world at a dynamic turning point in its development.

The Mayflower Web Page
http://www.mayflowerhistory.com

The Mayflower Web Page represents thousands of hours of research, organization, and typing; it grows daily. Visitors include everyone from kindergarten students to history professors, from beginning genealogists to some of the most noted genealogists in the nation. The site is a merger of two fields: genealogy and history.

UNIT 2: Revolutionary America

The Early America Review
http://www.earlyamerica.com/review/

Explore the Web site of *The Early America Review,* an electronic journal of fact and opinion on the people, issues, and events of eighteenth-century America. The quarterly is of excellent quality.

House of Representatives
http://www.house.gov

This home page of the House of Representatives will lead to information about current and past House members and agendas, the legislative process, and so on.

National Center for Policy Analysis
http://www.public-policy.org/web.public-policy.org/index.php

Through this site, click onto links to read discussions of an array of topics that are of major interest in the study of American history, from regulatory policy and privatization to economy and income.

Supreme Court/Legal Information Institute
http://supct.law.cornell.edu/supct/index.html

Open this site for current and historical information about the Supreme Court. The archive contains a collection of nearly 600 of the most historical decisions of the Court.

U.S. Senate
http://www.senate.gov

The U.S. Senate home page will lead to information about current and past Senate members and agendas, legislative activities, committees, and so on.

The White House
http://www.whitehouse.gov/

Visit the home page of the White House for direct access to information about commonly requested federal services, the White House Briefing Room, and all of the presidents and vice presidents. The "Virtual Library" provides an opportunity to search White House documents, listen to speeches, and view photos.

www.mhcls.com/online/

The World of Benjamin Franklin
http://www.fi.edu/franklin/

Presented by the Franklin Institute Science Museum, "Benjamin Franklin: Glimpses of the Man" is an excellent multimedia site that lends insight into Revolutionary America.

UNIT 3: National Consolidation and Expansion

Consortium for Political and Social Research
http://www.icpsr.umich.edu

At this site, the inter-university Consortium for Political and Social Research offers materials in various categories of historical social, economic, and demographic data. Presented is a statistical overview of the United States beginning in the late eighteenth century.

Department of State
http://www.state.gov

View this site for an understanding into the workings of what has become a major U.S. executive branch department. Links explain what the Department does, what services it provides, what it says about U.S. interests around the world, and much more information.

Mystic Seaport
http://amistad.mysticseaport.org/

The complex Amistad case is explored in a clear and informative manner on this online educational site. It places the event in the context of the issues of the 1830s and 1840s.

Social Influence Website
http://www.workingpsychology.com/intro.html

The nature of persuasion, compliance, and propaganda is the focus of this Web site, with many practical examples and applications. Students of such topics as the roles of public opinion and media influence in policy making should find these discussions of interest.

University of Virginia Library
http://www.lib.virginia.edu/exhibits/lewis_clark/

Created by the University of Virginia Library, this site examines the famous Lewis and Clark exploration of the trans-Mississippi west.

Women in America
http://xroads.virginia.edu/~HYPER/DETOC/FEM/

Providing the views of women travelers from the British Isles, France, and Germany on the lives of American women, this valuable site covers the years between 1820 and 1842 and is informative, stimulating, and highly original.

Women of the West
http://www.wowmuseum.org/

The home page of the Women of the West Museum offers several interesting links that include stories, poems, educational resources, and exhibits.

UNIT 4: The Civil War and Reconstruction

The American Civil War
http://sunsite.utk.edu/civil-war/warweb.html

This site provides a wide-ranging list of data on the Civil War. Some examples of the data that are available are: army life, the British connection, diaries/letters/memos, maps, movies, museums, music, people, photographs, and poetry.

Anacostia Museum/Smithsonian Institution
http://www.si.edu/archives/historic/anacost.htm

This is the home page of the Center for African American History and Culture of the Smithsonian Institution, which is expected to become a major repository of information. Explore its many avenues.

Abraham Lincoln Online
http://www.netins.net/showcase/creative/lincoln.html

This is a well-organized, high-quality site that will lead to substantial material about Abraham Lincoln and his era. Discussions among Lincoln scholars can be accessed in the Mailbag section.

Gilder Lehrman Institute of American History
http://www.digitalhistory.uh.edu/index.cfm?

Click on the links to various articles presented through this Web site to read outstanding, first-hand accounts of slavery in America through the period of Reconstruction.

Secession Era Editorials Project
http://history.furman.edu/~benson/docs/dsmenu.htm

Newspaper editorials of the 1800s regarding events leading up to secession are presented on this Furman University site. When complete, this distinctive project will offer additional features that include mapping, statistical tools, and text analysis.

We highly recommend that you review our Web site for expanded information and our other product lines. We are continually updating and adding links to our Web site in order to offer you the most usable and useful information that will support and expand the value of your Annual Editions. You can reach us at: *http://www.mhcls.com/annualeditions/*.

UNIT 1
The New Land

Unit Selections

1. **America's First Immigrants,** Evan Hadingham
2. **1491,** Charles C. Mann
3. **How Cruel Were the Spaniards?,** Iris H. W. Engstrand
4. **America, the Atlantic, and Global Consumer Demand,** Carole Shammas
5. **The Birth of America,** Lewis Lord
6. **The Root of the Problem,** Orlando Patterson
7. **Blessed and Bedeviled,** Helen Mondloch
8. **American Indians, Witchcraft, and Witch-Hunting,** Matthew Dennis
9. **Slavery in the North,** Shane White
10. **Were American Indians the Victims of Genocide?,** Guenter Lewy

Key Points to Consider

• What new evidence is there that American Indians may have come to the Western Hemisphere at a much earlier time than previously thought?

• Discuss the article "How Cruel Were the Spaniards?" Does the author make a convincing case that those Spaniards who came to the New World as missionaries, farmers, and ranchers have been unfairly lumped with their predecessors, the Conquistadors?

• What is meant by the phrase "Atlantic world economic community?" One of the most important categories of goods traded during the period 1500–1800 was "groceries." Discuss some of the products that fall under this classification.

• Analyze the problems faced by the early settlers in Jamestown, and how they attempted to cope. In what ways did they plant "the seeds of the nation's spirit?" What significance did the introduction of slavery have?

• Discuss slavery in the North. How did it resemble and how did it differ from slavery in the South? What types of work did Northern slaves do?

• Some historians have likened the treatment of American Indians to Adolf Hitler's destruction of European Jews during World War II. Is this valid? What are the similarities, what are the differences?

Student Web Site
www.mhcls.com/online

Internet References
Further information regarding these Web sites may be found in this book's preface or online.

Early America
http://earlyamerica.com/earlyamerica/index.html
1492: An Ongoing Voyage/Library of Congress
http://lcweb.loc.gov/exhibits/1492/
The Mayflower Web Page
http://www.mayflowerhistory.com

THE LANDING OF THE PILGRIMS AT PLYMOUTH, MASS. DEC. 22ᴺᴰ1620.

The MAYFLOWER left Delft Haven in Holland Sept 6ᵗʰ1620, and after a boisterous passage of Sixty three days anchored within Cape Cod, in her cabin the first Republican Government in America was solemnly inaugurated. That vessel thus became truly the "Cradle of Liberty" rocked on the free waves of the Ocean.

Europeans had been fascinated with the "New World" long before they were able to mount expeditions to actually go there. Artists and writers imagined all sorts of exotic plants and animals, and depicted human inhabitants as ranging from the most brutal savages to races of highly advanced peoples. These latter were reputed to have constructed cities of great splendor, where fabulous treasures of precious metals and jewels lay for the taking. The "age of exploration" had to await the sufficient accumulation of capital to finance expeditions and the advanced technology to make them feasible. Motives were mixed in undertaking such ventures: the desire to explore the unknown, national rivalries, the quest for routes to the Far East, converting the heathens to Christianity, and pure greed. Spain and Portugal led the way, followed by France and England.

The "new world," of course, was new only to Europeans. The inhabitants had lived here for a long time without even knowing (let alone caring) that Europe existed. Estimates are that there were from 80 to 100 million people living in the Western Hemisphere at the time the explorations began. In the region that became the United States there were no powerful empires such as those developed by the Aztecs in Mexico or the Incas in Peru. There were, however, fairly sophisticated settlements such as the small town of Cahokia, located near present-day St. Louis, Missouri. European incursions proved catastrophic for peoples of whatever stage of civilization. Not only did some of the explor-

ers treat indigenous peoples with great brutality, they brought with them a variety of deadly diseases against which natives had no defenses. The expansion of Europe, therefore, came at the expense of millions of unfortunates in the new world.

For years the conventional wisdom was that what we call "Native Americans" emigrated here from Asia across the Bering land bridge to Alaska. The article, "America's First Immigrants," shows that this view has been challenged by archaeologists who have found a settlement dating from at least 1,000 years before this migration was supposed to have occurred. "1491" discusses population estimates and what is known about their societies, and suggests that they had a far larger impact on the environment than previously suspected. Much has been written about the Spanish "Conquistadors," and their frequently brutal treatment of indigenous peoples. "How Cruel Were the Spaniards?" does not minimize their behavior, put points out that those who came later as farmers, ranchers, and missionaries do not deserve the opprobrium heaped upon their predecessors. "America, the Atlantic, and Global Consumer Demand, 1500–1800," discusses the period from the standpoint of what the author calls the "Atlantic world economic community" rather than from the traditional view of competing mercantile empires.

The English arrived late in the process. Some of them were searching for precious metals and jewels, as had their Spanish counterparts. Others came to settle permanently, either to escape religious persecution or merely to build new lives for themselves. "The Birth of America" tells the harrowing experiences of those who settled Jamestown in 1607. They had to cope with climate, disease, Indians, and struggles among themselves. "The Root of the Problem" points out that only a few years later about 20 black slaves were sold to the colonists. At first they worked under approximately the same conditions as did white indentured servants. After about 1660, however, when it became cheaper to buy slaves than indentured servants, Virginia was on its way to becoming a slave society.

The idea that witches existed was commonly held in New England during the 17th Century, as it was elsewhere. The Salem Witch Trials have received great attention by historians, who differ among themselves as to the roots of this phenomenon. What is less known is that many Native Americans held similar ideas. "American Indians, Witchcraft, and Witch-Hunting" describes some of these beliefs. Ironically, the likenesses between them drove the two cultures farther apart rather than uniting them.

Accounts of the South before the Civil War inevitably describe the institution of slavery and all of its baneful effects on whites and blacks alike. Slavery in the North during the same period, if discussed at all, usually is mentioned just in passing. "Slavery in the North" helps rectify this myopia, and points out that two of the bloodiest slave insurrections took place in New York City during the 18th Century.

No one denies that European exploration and conquest had devastating consequences for native peoples. Some have gone beyond this recognition to claim that the treatment of Native Americans can be compared with the Holocaust visited upon Jews by the Nazis. "Were American Indians the Victims of Genocide?" denies this accusation. The author points out that German annihilation of the Jews was deliberately conceived and executed. Europeans committed many atrocities in the New World, but by far the greatest cause of fatalities came from contagious diseases against which the Indians had no immunity. Given the state of medical knowledge at the time, the Europeans themselves had no idea of the diseases they carried with them.

America's First Immigrants

You were probably taught that the hemisphere's first people came from Siberia across a long-goneland bridge. Now a sea route looks increasingly likely, from Asia or even Europe.

EVAN HADINGHAM

About four miles from the tiny cattle town of Florence, Texas, a narrow dirt road winds across parched limestone, through juniper, prickly pear and stunted oaks, and drops down to a creek. A lush parkland of shade trees offers welcome relief from the 100-degree heat of summer. Running beside the creek for almost half a mile is a swath of chipped, gray stone flakes and soil blackened by cooking fires—thousands of years of cooking fires. This blackened earth, covering 40 acres and almost six feet thick in places, marks a settlement dating back as far as the last ice age 13,000 years ago, when mammoths, giant sloths and saber-toothed cats roamed the North American wilderness.

Since archaeologists began working here systematically seven years ago, they have amassed an astonishing collection of early prehistoric artifacts—nearly half a million so far. Among these are large, stone spearheads skillfully flaked on both sides to give an elegant, leaf-shaped appearance. These projectiles, found by archaeologists throughout North America and as far south as Costa Rica, are known as Clovis points, and their makers, who lived roughly 12,500 to 13,500 years ago, are known as Clovis people, after the town in New Mexico near where the first such point was identified some seven decades ago.

A visit to the Gault site—named after the family who owned the land when the site was first investigated in 1929—along the cottonwood- and walnut-shaded creek in central Texas raises two monumental questions. The first, of course, is, Who were these people? The emerging answer is that they were not simple-minded big-game hunters as they have often been depicted. Rather, they led a less nomadic and more sophisticated life than previously believed.

The second question—Where did they come from?—lies at the center of one of archaeology's most contentious debates. The standard view holds that Clovis people were the first to enter the Americas, migrating from Siberia 13,500 years ago by a now-submerged land bridge across the Bering Strait. This view has been challenged recently by a wide range of discoveries, including an astonishingly well-preserved site in South America predating the supposed migration by at least 1,000 years.

Researchers delving into the origins question have sought to make sense of archaeological finds far and wide, from Canada, California and Chile; from Siberia; and even, most controversially, from France and Spain. The possibility that the first people in the Americas came from Europe is the boldest proposal among a host of new ideas. According to University of Texas at Austin archaeologist Michael Collins, the chief excavator of the Gault site, "you couldn't have a more exciting time to be involved in the whole issue of the peopling of the Americas. You can't write a paper on it and get it published before it's out of date. Surprising new finds keep rocking the boat and launching fresh waves of debate."

In 1932, an American archaeologist identified distinctive spearheads associated with mammoth skeletons near Clovis, New Mexico. The discovery supported an emerging realization that humans lived with now-extinct ice age creatures in North America.

For prehistoric people, one of the chief attractions of the Gault site was a knobby outcrop of a creamy white rock called chert, which conceals a fine, gray, glasslike interior. If struck expertly with a stone or antler tool, the rock fractures in predictable ways, yielding a Clovis point. In the end, each spearhead has distinctive grooves, or "flutes," at the base of each face and was fastened to a wooden shaft with sinew and resin.

Ancient pollen and soil clues tell archaeologists that the climate in Clovis-era Texas was cooler, drier and more tolerable than today's summertime cauldron. Vast herds of mammoths, bison, horses and antelope ranged on the grasslands south-east of Gault, and deer and turkeys inhabited the plateau to the west. Along the creek, based on bones found at the site, Clovis hunters also preyed on frogs, birds, turtles and other small animals.

This abundance of food, coupled with the exceptional quality of the chert, drew people to Gault in large numbers. Unlike the majority of Clovis sites, which are mostly the remains of temporary camps, Gault appears to have been inhabited over long periods and thus contradicts the standard view that Clovis people were always highly mobile, nomadic hunters. Michael Collins says that of the vast quantity of artifacts found at the site, many are tool fragments, left behind by people who'd stuck around long enough to not only break their tools but also to salvage and rework them. The researchers also unearthed a seven by seven foot square of gravel—perhaps the floor of a house—and a possible well, both signs of more than a fleeting presence.

Another clue was concealed on a 13,000-year-old Clovis blade about the size of a dinner knife. Under a magnifying lens, the blade's edge is glossy, rounded and smooth. Marilyn Shoberg, a stone tool analyst on the Gault team who has experimented with replicas, says the blade's polish probably came from cutting grass. This grass could have been used for basketry, bedding, or thatching to make roofs for huts.

Among the most unusual and tantalizing finds at the Gault site are a hundred or so fragments of limestone covered with lightly scratched patterns. Some resemble nets or basketry, while a few could be simple outlines of plants or animals. Although only a dozen can be securely dated to Clovis times, these enigmatic rocks are among the very few surviving artworks from ice age America.

"What this site tells us is that Clovis folks were not specialized mammoth hunters constantly wandering over the landscape," says Collins. "They exploited a variety of animals, they had tools for gathering plants and working wood, stone and hide, and they stayed through the useful life of those tools. All these things are contrary to what you'd expect if they were highly nomadic, dedicated big-game hunters." Yet this unexpected complexity sheds only a feeble glimmer on the more contentious issue of where the Clovis people came from and how they got here.

In the old scenario, still popular in classrooms and picture books, fur-clad hunters in the waning moments of the last ice age, when so much seawater was locked up in the polar ice caps that the sea level was as much as 300 feet lower than today, ventured across a land bridge from Siberia to Alaska. Then, pursuing big game, the hunters trekked south through present-day Canada. They passed down a narrow, 1,000-mile-long treeless corridor bounded by the towering walls of retreating ice sheets until they reached the Great Plains, which teemed with prey. The human population exploded, and the hunters soon drove into extinction some 35 genera of big animals (see box on page 6). All of these were supposedly dispatched by the Clovis point, a Stone Age weapon of mass destruction.

Digging at the Gault site in central Texas, according to project director Michael Collins, has almost doubled the number of Clovis artifacts excavated in North America. Researchers there have also uncovered evidence of ice age art.

For more than half a century, this plausible, "big-game" theory carried with it an appealing, heroic image. As James Adovasio of Mercyhurst College puts it in his book *The First Americans,* it was as if the ice sheets had parted "like the Red Sea for some Clovis Moses to lead his intrepid band of spear-toting, mammoth-slaying wayfarers to the south." But recent discoveries are indicating that almost everything about the theory could be wrong. For one thing, the latest studies show that the ice-free corridor didn't exist until around 12,000 years ago—too late to have served as the route for the very first people to come to America.

Clovis people buried caches of tools. Some stashed points were crafted from exotic stone; others seem too big and thin to have functioned as weapons. One cache was found with a child's bones, suggesting that burying tools could be a ritual act.

Perhaps the strongest ammunition against the old scenario comes from Monte Verde, an archaeological site on a remote terrace, which is today some 40 miles from the Pacific in southern Chile. Here, about 14,500 years ago, a hunting-and-gathering band lived year-round beside a creek in a long, oval hide tent, partitioned with logs. Archaeologist Tom Dillehay of Vanderbilt University began probing Monte Verde in 1977, unearthing the surface of the ancient encampment, complete with wood, plants and even remains of food, all preserved under a layer of waterlogged peat. Dillehay recovered three human footprints, two chunks of uneaten mastodon meat and possibly even traces of herbal medicine (indicated by nonfood plants still used by healers in the Andes). The dating of these extraordinary finds, at least 1,000 years before the earliest Clovis sites in North America, aroused skepticism for two decades until, in 1997, a group of leading archaeologists inspected the site and vindicated Dillehay's meticulous work.

No such triumph has emerged for any of the dozen or so sites in North America claimed to predate Clovis. But among the most intriguing is a rock overhang in Pennsylvania called Meadowcroft, where a 30-year campaign of excavation suggests that hunters may have reached the Northeast 3,000 or 4,000 years before the Clovis era.

Saber-toothed cats prowled North America for millions of years. For some reason, they died out about 13,000 years ago.

Meanwhile, genetics studies are pointing even more strongly to an early entry into the continent. By analyzing the mitochondrial DNA of living Native Americans, Douglas Wallace, a geneticist at the University of California at Irvine, and his colleagues have identified five distinct lineages that stretch back like family trees. Mitochondria are the cells' energy factories. Their DNA changes very little from one generation to the next, altered only by tiny variations that creep in at a steady and predictable rate. By counting the number of these variations in related lineages, Wallace's team can estimate their ages. When the team applied this technique to the DNA of Native Americans, they reached the stunning conclusion that there were at least four separate waves of prehistoric migration into the Americas, the earliest well over 20,000 years ago.

If the first Americans did arrive well before the oldest known Clovis settlements, how did they get here? The most radical theory for the peopling of the New World argues that Stone Age mariners journeyed from Europe around the southern fringes of the great ice sheets in the North Atlantic. Many archaeologists greet this idea with head-shaking scorn, but the proposition is getting harder to dismiss outright.

Dennis Stanford, a Clovis expert at the Smithsonian Institution's Department of Anthropology who delights in prodding his colleagues with unconventional thinking, was a longtime supporter of the land bridge scenario. Then, with the end of the cold war came the chance to visit archaeological sites and museums in Siberia—museums that should have been filled with tools that were predecessors of the Clovis point. "The result was a big disappointment," says Stanford. "What we found was nothing like we expected, and I was surprised that the technologies were so different." Instead of a single leaf-shaped Clovis spearhead, ice age Siberian hunters made projectiles that were bristling with rows of tiny razor-like blades embedded in wooden shafts. To Stanford, that meant no Siberian hunters armed with Clovis technology had walked to the Americas.

Meanwhile, Bruce Bradley, a prehistoric stone tool specialist at Britain's University of Exeter, had noticed a strong resemblance between Clovis points and weapons from ice age Europe. But the idea that the two cultures might be directly connected was heretical. "It certainly wasn't part of the scientific process at that point," Bradley says. "There was no possibility, forget it, don't even think about it." Bradley eventually pursued it to the storerooms of the Musée National de Préhistoire in Les Eyzies-de-Tayac in southwest France, where he pored through boxes of local prehistoric stone tools and waste flakes. "I was absolutely flabbergasted," he recalls. "If somebody had brought out a box of this stuff in the United States and set it down in front of me, I'd have said, 'Man, where did you get all that great Clovis stuff?'" But the material was the work of a culture called the Solutrean that thrived in southwest France and northern Spain during the coldest spell of the ice age, from around 24,000 to 19,000 years ago.

Thousands of years before their successors created the masterworks of Lascaux and Altamira, Solutrean-age artists began painting vivid murals in the depths of caves such as Cougnac and Cosquer. They made delicate, eyed sewing needles out of bone, enabling them to stitch tightfitting skin garments to repel the cold. They devised the *atlatl,* or spear thrower, a hooked bone or wood handle that extends the reach of the hunter's arm to multiply throwing power. But their most distinctive creation was a stone spearhead shaped like a laurel leaf.

Apart from the absence of a fluted base, the Solutrean laurel leaf strongly resembles the Clovis point and was made using the same, highly skillful flaking technique. Both Clovis and Solutrean stone crafters practiced controlled overshot flaking, which involved trimming one edge by striking a flake off the opposite side, a virtuoso feat of handiwork rarely seen in other prehistoric cultures. To Bradley, "there had to be some sort of historic connection" between the Solutrean and Clovis peoples.

Dennis Stanford and Bruce Bradley say that similarities between Clovis and Solutream finds are overwhelming.

Critics of the theory point to a yawning gap between the two peoples: roughly 5,000 years divide the end of Solutrean culture and the emergence of Clovis. But Stanford and Bradley say that recent claims of pre-Clovis sites in the southeastern United States may bridge the time gap. In the mid-1990s at Cactus Hill, the remains of an ancient sand dune overlooking the Nottoway River on Virginia's coastal plain, project director Joseph McAvoy dug down a few inches beneath a Clovis layer and uncovered simple stone blades and projectile points associated with a hearth, radiocarbon dated to some 17,000 to 19,000 years ago. This startlingly early date has drawn skeptical fire, but the site's age was recently confirmed by an independent dating technique. Stanford and Bradley suggest that the early people at Cactus Hill were Clovis forerunners who had not yet developed the full-blown Clovis style. They are convinced that many more sites like Cactus Hill will turn up on the East Coast. But the burning question is, Did these ice age Virginians invent the Clovis point all by themselves, or were they descendants of Solutreans who brought the point with them from Europe?

Many archaeologists ridicule the notion that people made an arduous, 3,000-mile journey during the bleakest period of the ice age, when the Atlantic would have been much colder and stormier than today. Stanford believes that traditional Inuit technology suggests otherwise; he has witnessed traditional seagoing skills among Inupiat communities in Barrow, Alaska. Inupiat hunters still build large skin-covered canoes, or *umiaks,* which enable them to catch seals, walrus and other sea

Hunted to Extinction?

At the end of the last ice age, 35 genera of big animals, or "megafauna," went extinct in the Americas, including mammoths, mastodons, giant ground sloths, giant beavers, horses, short-faced bears and saber-toothed cats. Archaeologists have argued for decades that the arrival of hunters wielding Clovis spear points at around the same time was no coincidence. Clovis hunters pursued big game—their signature stone points are found with the bones of mammoths and mastodons at 14 kill sites in North America. Experiments carried out with replica spears thrust into the corpses of circus elephants indicate that the Clovis point could have penetrated a mammoth's hide. And computer simulations suggest that large, slow-breeding animals could have easily been wiped out by hunting as the human population expanded.

But humans might not be entirely to blame. The rapidly cycling climate at the end of the ice age may have changed the distribution of plants that the big herbivores grazed on, leading to a population crash among meat-eating predators too. New research on DNA fragments recovered from ice age bison bones suggests that some species were suffering a slow decline in diversity—probably caused by dwindling populations—long before any Clovis hunters showed up. Indigenous horses are now thought to have died out in Alaska about 500 years before the Clovis era. For mammoths and other beasts who did meet their demise during the Clovis times, many experts believe that a combination of factors—climate change plus pressure from human hunters—drove them into oblivion.

Amid all the debate, one point is clear: the Clovis hunter wasn't as macho as people once thought. Bones at the Gault site in central Texas reveal that the hunters there were feeding on less daunting prey—frogs, birds, turtles and antelope—as well as mammoth, mastodon and bison. As the late, renowned archaeologist Richard (Scotty) MacNeish is said to have remarked, "Each Clovis generation probably killed one mammoth, then spent the rest of their lives talking about it."

and medium-sized game with a similar, limited range of raw materials—stone, bone, ivory, antler, wood and sinew. They're going to come up with similar solutions."

More tellingly, in Straus' view, is that he can find little evidence of seafaring technology in the Solutrean sites he has dug in northern Spain. Although rising sea levels have drowned sites on the ice age coastline, Straus has investigated surviving inland cave sites no more than a couple of hours' walk from the beach. "There's no evidence of deep-sea fishing," says Straus, "no evidence of marine mammal hunting, and consequently no evidence, even indirect, for their possession of seaworthy boats."

And David Meltzer, an archaeologist at Southern Methodist University and a critic of the European-origins idea, is struck more by the differences between the Solutrean and Clovis cultures than their similarities—particularly the near-absence of art and personal ornaments from Clovis. Still, he says, the controversy is good for the field. "In the process of either killing or curing" the theory, "we will have learned a whole lot more about the archaeological record, and we'll all come out smarter than we went in."

Besides crossing the land bridge from Asia and traveling to ice age America from Europe by boat, a third possible entryway is a sea route down the west coast. Using maritime skills later perfected by the Inuit, prehistoric south Asians might have spread gradually around the northern rim of the Pacific in small skin-covered boats. They skirt the southern edge of the Bering land bridge and paddle down the coast of Alaska, dodging calving glaciers and icebergs as they pursue seals and other marine mammals. They keep going all the way to the beaches of Central and South America. They arrive at Monte Verde, inland from the Chilean coast, some 14,500 years ago. Each new generation claims fresh hunting grounds a few miles beyond the last, and in a matter of centuries these first immigrants have populated the entire west coast of the Americas. Soon the hunters start moving inland and, in the north, their descendants become the Clovis people.

Clovis people may well have reached North America via sea route. Seals and other marine prey may have sustained them until they found New World hunting grounds.

Many archaeologists now accept the west coast theory as a likely solution to the origin of the earliest Americans. On Prince of Wales Island in southeastern Alaska, inside the aptly named On Your Knees Cave, University of South Dakota paleontologist Timothy Heaton and University of Colorado at Boulder archaeologist E. James Dixon recovered an accumulation of animal bones from the last ice age. When mile-high ice sheets still straddled the interior of the continent 17,000 years ago, ringed seals, foxes and seabirds made their home on the island. "Humans could easily have survived there," Heaton says.

The ultimate evidence for the western sea route would be the discovery of pre-Clovis human remains on the coast. No

mammals that abound along the frozen edges of the pack ice. When twilight arrives or storms threaten, the hunters pull their boats up on the ice and camp beneath them. Ronald Brower of the Inupiat Heritage Center in Barrow says, "There's nothing that would have prevented . . . people from crossing the Atlantic into the Americas 19,000 years ago. It would be a perfectly normal situation from my perspective."

A different critique of the out-of-Europe theory dismisses the resemblance between Solutrean and Clovis points. Many archaeologists suggest that similarities between Clovis and Solutrean artifacts are coincidental, the result of what they call convergence. "These were people faced with similar problems," says Solutrean expert Lawrence Straus of the University of New Mexico. "And the problems involved hunting large-

such luck. Dixon and Heaton have found human jaw fragments and other remains in the On Your Knees Cave, but those date to about 11,000 years ago—too recent to establish the theory. And what may be the oldest-known human remains in North America—leg bones found on Santa Rosa Island, off the California coast—are from 13,000 years ago, the heart of the Clovis era. Still, those remains hint that by then people were plying the waters along the Pacific Coast.

If the trail of the very earliest Americans remains elusive, so, too, does the origin of the Clovis point. "Although the technology needed to produce a Clovis point was found among other cultures during the ice age," says Ken Tankersley of Northern Kentucky University, "the actual point itself is unique to the Americas, suggesting that it was invented here in the New World." If so, the spearhead would be the first great American invention—the Stone Age equivalent of the Swiss Army Knife, a trademark tool that would be widely imitated. The demand for the weapon and the high-quality stone it required probably encouraged Clovis people to begin long-distance trading and social exchanges. The spearhead may also have delivered a new level of hunting proficiency and this, in turn, would have fueled a population spurt, giving Clovis people their lasting presence in the archaeological record.

Sheltering from the broiling heat under the cottonwoods at Gault, Michael Collins told me of his conviction that the Clovis people who flocked to the shady creek were not pioneers but had profited from a long line of forebears. "Clovis represents the end product of centuries, if not millennia, of learning how to live in North American environments," he said. "The Clovis culture is too widespread, is found in too many environments, and has too much evidence for diverse activities to be the leavings of people just coming into the country." Collins reminded me that his team has investigated less than 10 percent of the enormous site. And archaeologists have barely scratched the surface of a handful of other Gault-size, Clovis-era sites—Williamsburg, in Virginia, for instance, or Shoop, in Pennsylvania. "One thing you can be sure," he said, beaming, "there'll be great new discoveries just around the corner."

EVAN HADINGHAM is the senior science editor of the PBS series NOVA and the author of books on prehistory.

1491

Before it became the New World, the Western Hemisphere was vastly more populous and sophisticated than has been thought—an altogether more salubrious place to live at the time than, say, Europe. New evidence of both the extent of the population and its agricultural advancement leads to a remarkable conjecture: the Amazon rain forest may be largely a human artifact.

CHARLES C. MANN

The plane took off in weather that was surprisingly cool for north-central Bolivia and flew east, toward the Brazilian border. In a few minutes the roads and houses disappeared, and the only evidence of human settlement was the cattle scattered over the savannah like jimmies on ice cream. Then they, too, disappeared. By that time the archaeologists had their cameras out and were clicking away in delight.

Below us was the Beni, a Bolivian province about the size of Illinois and Indiana put together, and nearly as flat. For almost half the year rain and snowmelt from the mountains to the south and west cover the land with an irregular, slowly moving skin of water that eventually ends up in the province's northern rivers, which are sub-subtributaries of the Amazon. The rest of the year the water dries up and the bright-green vastness turns into something that resembles a desert. This peculiar, remote, watery plain was what had drawn the researchers' attention, and not just because it was one of the few places on earth inhabited by people who might never have seen Westerners with cameras.

Clark Erickson and William Balée, the archaeologists, sat up front. Erickson is based at the University of Pennsylvania; he works in concert with a Bolivian archaeologist, whose seat in the plane I usurped that day. Balée is at Tulane University, in New Orleans. He is actually an anthropologist, but as native peoples have vanished, the distinction between anthropologists and archaeologists has blurred. The two men differ in build, temperament, and scholarly proclivity, but they pressed their faces to the windows with identical enthusiasm.

Indians were here in greater numbers than previously thought, and they imposed their will on the landscape. Columbus set foot in a hemisphere thoroughly dominated by humankind.

Dappled across the grasslands below was an archipelago of forest islands, many of them startlingly round and hundreds of acres across. Each island rose ten or thirty or sixty feet above the floodplain, allowing trees to grow that would otherwise never survive the water. The forests were linked by raised berms, as straight as a rifle shot and up to three miles long. It is Erickson's belief that this entire landscape—30,000 square miles of forest mounds surrounded by raised fields and linked by causeways—was constructed by a complex, populous society more than 2,000 years ago. Balée, newer to the Beni, leaned toward this view but was not yet ready to commit himself.

Erickson and Balée belong to a cohort of scholars that has radically challenged conventional notions of what the Western Hemisphere was like before Columbus. When I went to high school, in the 1970s, I was taught that Indians came to the Americas across the Bering Strait about 12,000 years ago, that they lived for the most part in small, isolated groups, and that they had so little impact on their environment that even after millennia of habitation it remained mostly wilderness. My son picked up the same ideas at his schools. One way to summarize the views of people like Erickson and Balée would be to say that in their opinion this picture of Indian life is wrong in almost every aspect. Indians were here far longer than previously thought, these researchers believe, and in much greater numbers. And they were so successful at imposing their will on the landscape that in 1492 Columbus set foot in a hemisphere thoroughly dominated by humankind.

Given the charged relations between white societies and native peoples, inquiry into Indian culture and history is inevitably contentious. But the recent scholarship is especially controversial. To begin with, some researchers—many but not all from an older generation—deride the new theories as fantasies arising from an almost willful misinterpretation of data and a perverse kind of political correctness. "I have seen no evidence that large numbers of people ever lived in the Beni," says Betty

J. Meggers, of the Smithsonian Institution. "Claiming otherwise is just wishful thinking." Similar criticisms apply to many of the new scholarly claims about Indians, according to Dean R. Snow, an anthropologist at Pennsylvania State University. The problem is that "you can make the meager evidence from the ethnohistorical record tell you anything you want," he says. "It's really easy to kid yourself."

More important are the implications of the new theories for today's ecological battles. Much of the environmental movements is animated, consciously or not, by what William Denevan, a geographer at the University of Wisconsin, calls, polemically, "the pristine myth"—the belief that the Americas in 1491 were an almost unmarked, even Edenic land, "untrammeled by man," in the words of the Wilderness Act of 1964, one of the nation's first and most important environmental laws. As the University of Wisconsin historian William Cronon has written, restoring this long-ago, putatively natural state is, in the view of environmentalists, a task that society is morally bound to undertake. Yet if the new view is correct and the work of humankind was pervasive, where does that leave efforts to restore nature?

The Beni is a case in point. In addition to building up the Beni mounds for houses and gardens, Erickson says, the Indians trapped fish in the seasonally flooded grassland. Indeed, he says, they fashioned dense zigzagging networks of earthen fish weirs between the causeways. To keep the habitat clear of unwanted trees and undergrowth, they regularly set huge areas on fire. Over the centuries the burning created an intricate ecosystem of fire-adapted plant species dependent on native pyrophilia. The current inhabitants of the Beni still burn, although now it is to maintain the savannah for cattle. When we flew over the areas, the dry season had just begun, but mile-long lines of flame were already on the march. In the charred areas behind the fires were the blackened spikes of trees—many of them one assumes, of the varieties that activists fight to save in other parts of Amazonia.

After we landed, I asked Balée, Should we let people keep burning the Beni? Or should we let the trees invade and create a verdant tropical forest in the grasslands, even if one had not existed here for millennia?

Balée laughed. "You're trying to trap me, aren't you?" he said.

Like a Club between the Eyes

According to family lore, my great-grandmother's great-grandmother's great-grandfather was the first white person hanged in America. His name was John Billington. He came on the *Mayflower*, which anchored off the coast of Massachusetts on November 9, 1620. Billington was not a Puritan; within six months of arrival he also became the first white person in America to be tried for complaining about the police. "He is a knave," William Bradford, the colony's governor, wrote to Billington, "and so will live and die." What one historian called Billington's "troublesome career" ended in 1630, when he was hanged for murder. My family has always said the he was framed—but we *would* say that, wouldn't we?

A few years ago it occurred to me that my ancestor and everyone else in the colony had voluntarily enlisted in a venture that

brought them to New England without food or shelter six weeks before winter. Half the 102 people on the *Mayflower* made it through to spring, which to me was amazing. How, I wondered, did they survive?

In his history of Plymouth Colony, Bradford provided the answer: by robbing Indian houses and graves. The *Mayflower* first hove to at Cape Cod. An armed company staggered out. Eventually it found a recently deserted Indian settlement. The newcomers—hungry, cold, sick—dug up graves and ransacked houses, looking for underground stashes of corn. "And sure it was God's good providence that we found this corn," Bradford wrote, "for else we know not how we should have done." (He felt uneasy about the thievery, though.) When the colonists came to Plymouth, a month later, they set up shop in another deserted Indian village. All through the coastal forest the Indians had "died on heapes, as they lay in their houses," the English trader Thomas Morton noted. "And the bones and skulls upon the several places of their habitations made such a spectacle" that to Morton the Massachusetts woods seemed to be "a new found Golgotha"—the hill of executions in Roman Jerusalem.

To the Pilgrims' astonishment, one of the corpses they exhumed on Cape Cod had blond hair. A French ship had been wrecked there several years earlier. The Patuxet Indians imprisoned a few survivors. One of them supposedly learned enough of the local language to inform his captors that God would destroy them for their misdeeds. The Patuxet scoffed at the threat. But the Europeans carried a disease, and they bequeathed it to their jailers. The epidemic (probably of viral hepatitis, according to a study by Arthur E. Spiess, an archaeologist at the Maine Historic Preservation Commission, and Bruce D. Spiess, the director of clinical research at the Medical College of Virginia) took years to exhaust itself and may have killed 90 percent of the people in coastal New England. It made huge differences to American history. "The good hand of God favored our beginnings," Bradford mused, by "sweeping away great multitudes of the natives . . . that he might make room for us."

By the time my ancestor set sail on the *Mayflower*, Europeans had been visiting New England for more than a hundred years. English, French, Italian, Spanish, and Portuguese mariners regularly plied the coastline, trading what they could, occasionally kidnapping the inhabitants for slaves. New England, the Europeans saw, was thickly settled and well defended. In 1605 and 1606 Samuel de Champlain visited Cape Cod, hoping to establish a French base. He abandoned the idea. Too many people already lived there. A year later Sir Ferdinando Gorges—British despite his name—tried to establish an English community in southern Maine. It had more founders than Plymouth and seems to have been better organized. Confronted by numerous well-armed local Indians, the settlers abandoned the project within months. The Indians at Plymouth would surely have been an equal obstacle to my ancestor and his ramshackle expedition had disease not intervened.

Faced with such stories, historians have long wondered how many people lived in the Americas at the time of contact. "Debated since Columbus attempted a partial census on Hispaniola in 1496," William Denevan has written, this "remains one of the great inquiries of history." (In 1976 Denevan assembled and edited an entire book on the subject, *The Native Population of the Americas in 1492.*) The first scholarly estimate of the indigenous population was made in 1910 by James Mooney, a distinguished ethnographer at the Smithsonian Institution. Combing through old documents, he concluded that in 1491 North America had 1.15 million inhabitants. Mooney's glittering reputation ensured that most subsequent researchers accepted his figure uncritically.

That changed in 1966, when Henry F. Dobyns published "Estimating Aboriginal American Population: An Appraisal of Techniques With a New Hemispheric Estimate," in the journal *Current Anthropology*. Despite the carefully neutral title, his argument was thunderous, its impact long-lasting. In the view of James Wilson, the author of *The Earth Shall Weep* (1998), a history of indigenous Americans, Dobyns's colleagues "are still struggling to get out of the crater that paper left in anthropology." Not only anthropologists were affected. Dobyns's estimate proved to be one of the opening rounds in today's culture wars.

Dobyns began his exploration of pre-Columbian Indian demography in the early 1950s, when he was a graduate student. At the invitation of a friend, he spent a few months in northern Mexico, which is full of Spanish-era missions. There he poked through the crumbling leather-bound ledgers in which Jesuits recorded local births and deaths. Right away he noticed how many more deaths there were. The Spaniards arrived, and then Indians died—in huge numbers at incredible rates. It hit him, Dobyns told me recently, "like a club right between the eyes."

It took Dobyns eleven years to obtain his Ph.D. Along the way he joined a rural-development project in Peru, which until colonial times was the seat of the Incan empire. Remembering what he had seen at the northern fringe of the Spanish conquest, Dobyns decided to compare it with figures for the south. He burrowed into the papers of the Lima cathedral and read apologetic Spanish histories. The Indians in Peru, Dobyns concluded, had faced plagues from the day the conquistadors showed up—in fact, before then: smallpox arrived around 1525, seven years ahead of the Spanish. Brought to Mexico apparently by a single sick Spaniard, it swept south and eliminated more than half the population of the Incan empire. Smallpox claimed the Incan dictator Huayna Capac and much of his family, setting off a calamitous war of succession. So complete was the chaos that Francisco Pizarro was able to seize an empire the size of Spain and Italy combined with a force of 168 men.

Smallpox was only the first epidemic. Typhus (probably) in 1546, influenza and smallpox together in 1558, smallpox again in 1589, diphtheria in 1614, measles in 1618—all ravaged the remains of Incan culture. Dobyns was the first social scientist to piece together this awful picture, and he naturally rushed his findings into print. Hardly anyone paid attention. But Dobyns was already working on a second, related question: If all those people died, how many had been living there to begin with? Before Columbus, Dobyns calculated, the Western Hemisphere held ninety to 112 million people. Another way of saying this is that in 1491 more people lived in the Americas than in Europe.

His argument was simple but horrific. It is well known that Native Americans had no experience with many European diseases and were therefore immunologically unprepared—"virgin soil," in the metaphor of epidemiologists. What Dobyns realized was that such diseases could have swept from the coastlines initially visited by Europeans to inland areas controlled by Indians who had never seen a white person. The first whites to explore many parts of the Americas may therefore have encountered places that were already depopulated. Indeed, Dobyns argued, they must have done so.

Peru was one example, the Pacific Northwest another. In 1792 the British navigator George Vancouver led the first European expedition to survey Puget Sound. He found a vast charnel house: human remains "promiscuously scattered about the beach, in great numbers." Smallpox, Vancouver's crew discovered, had preceded them. Its few survivors, second lieutenant Peter Puget noted, were "most terribly pitted . . . indeed many have lost their Eyes." In *Pox Americana* (2001), Elizabeth Fenn, a historian at George Washington University, contends that the disaster on the northwest coast was but a small part of a continental pandemic that erupted near Boston in 1774 and cut down Indians from Mexico to Alaska.

Because smallpox was not endemic in the Americas, colonials, too, had not acquired any immunity. The virus, an equal-opportunity killer, swept through the Continental Army and stopped the drive into Quebec. The American Revolution would be lost, Washington and other rebel leaders feared, if the contagion did to the colonists what it had done to the Indians. "The small Pox! The small Pox!" John Adams wrote to his wife, Abigail. "What shall We do with it?" In retrospect, Fenn says, "One of George Washington's most brilliant moves was to inoculate the army against smallpox during the Valley Forge winter of '78." Without inoculation smallpox could easily have given the United States back to the British.

So many epidemics occurred in the Americas, Dobyns argued, that the old data used by Mooney and his successors represented population nadirs. From the few cases in which before-and-after totals are known with relative certainty, Dobyns estimated that in the first 130 years of contact about 95 percent of the people in the Americas died—the worst demographic calamity in recorded history.

Dobyns's ideas were quickly attacked as politically motivated, a push from the hate-America crowd to inflate the toll of imperialism. The attacks continue to this day. "No question about it, some people want those higher numbers," says Shepard Krech III, a Brown University anthropologist who is the author of *The Ecological Indian* (1999). These people, he says, were thrilled when Dobyns revisited the subject in a book, *Their Numbers Become Thinned* (1983)—and revised his own estimates upward. Perhaps Dobyns's most vehement critic is David Henige, a bibliographer of Africana at the University of Wisconsin, whose *Numbers from Nowhere* (1998) is a landmark in the literature of demographic fulmination. "Suspect in 1966, it is no less suspect nowadays," Henige wrote of Dobyns's work. "If anything, it is worse."

When Henige wrote *Numbers From Nowhere,* the fight about pre-Columbian populations had already consumed forests' worth of trees; his bibliography is ninety pages long. And the dispute shows no sign of abating. More and more people have jumped in. This is partly because the subject is inherently fascinating. But more likely the increased interest in the debate is due to the growing realization of the high political and ecological stakes.

Inventing by the Millions

On May 30, 1539, Hernando de Soto landed his private army near Tampa Bay, in Florida. Soto, as he was called, was a novel figure: half warrior, half venture capitalist. He had grown very rich very young by becoming a market leader in the nascent trade for Indian slaves. The profits had helped to fund Pizarro's seizure of the Incan empire, which had made Soto wealthier still. Looking quite literally for new worlds to conquer, he persuaded the Spanish Crown to let him loose in North America. He spent one fortune to make another. He came to Florida with 200 horses, 600 soldiers, and 300 pigs.

From today's perspective, it is difficult to imagine the ethical system that would justify Soto's actions. For four years his force, looking for gold, wandered through what is now Florida, Georgia, North and South Carolina, Tennessee, Alabama, Mississippi, Arkansas, and Texas, wrecking almost everything it touched. The inhabitants often fought back vigorously, but they had never before encountered an army with horses and guns. Soto died of fever with his expedition in ruins; along the way his men had managed to rape, torture, enslave, and kill countless Indians. But the worst thing the Spaniards did, some researchers say, was entirely without malice—bring the pigs.

According to Charles Hudson, an anthropologist at the University of Georgia who spent fifteen years reconstructing the path of the expedition, Soto crossed the Mississippi a few miles downstream from the present site of Memphis. It was a nervous passage: the Spaniards were watched by several thousand Indian warriors. Utterly without fear, Soto brushed past the Indian force into what is now eastern Arkansas, through thickly settled land—"very well peopled with large towns," one of his men later recalled, "two or three of which were to be seen from one town." Eventually the Spaniards approached a cluster of small cities, each protected by earthen walls, sizeable moats, and deadeye archers. In his usual fashion, Soto brazenly marched in, stole food, and marched out.

After Soto left, no Europeans visited this part of the Mississippi Valley for more than a century. Early in 1682 whites appeared again, this time Frenchmen in canoes. One of them was Réné-Robert Cavelier, Sieur de la Salle. The French passed through the area where Soto had found cities cheek by jowl. It was deserted—La Salle didn't see an Indian village for 200 miles. About fifty settlements existed in this strip of the Mississippi when Soto showed up, according to Anne Ramenofsky, an anthropologist at the University of New Mexico. By La Salle's time the number had shrunk to perhaps ten, some probably inhabited by recent immigrants. Soto "had a privileged glimpse" of an Indian world, Hudson says. "The window opened and slammed shut. When the French came in and the record opened up again, it was a transformed reality. A civilization crumbled. The question is, how did this happen?"

Swine alone can disseminate anthrax, brucellosis, leptospirosis, trichinosis, and tuberculosis. Only a few of Hernando de Soto's pigs would have had to wander off to infect the forest.

The question is even more complex than it may seem. Disaster of this magnitude suggests epidemic disease. In the view of Ramenofsky and Patricia Galloway, an anthropologist at the University of Texas, the source of the contagion was very likely not Soto's army but its ambulatory meat locker: his 300 pigs. Soto's force itself was too small to be an effective biological weapon. Sicknesses like measles and smallpox would have burned through his 600 soldiers long before they reached the Mississippi. But the same would not have held true for the pigs, which multiplied rapidly and were able to transmit their diseases to wildlife in the surrounding forest. When human beings and domesticated animals live close together, they trade microbes with abandon. Over time mutation spawns new diseases: Avian influenza becomes human influenza, bovine rinderpest becomes measles. Unlike Europeans, Indians did not live in close quarters with animals—they domesticated only the dog, the llama, the alpaca, the guinea pig, and here and there, the turkey and the Muscovy duck. In some ways this is not surprising: the New World had fewer animal candidates for taming than the Old. Moreover, few Indians carry the gene that permits adults to digest lactose, a form of sugar abundant in milk. Non-milk-drinkers, one imagines, would be less likely to work at domesticating milk-giving animals. But this is guesswork. The fact is that what scientists call zoonotic disease was little known in the Americas. Swine alone can disseminate anthrax, brucellosis, leptospirosis, taeniasis, trichinosis, and tuberculosis. Pigs breed exuberantly and can transmit diseases to deer and turkeys. Only a few of Soto's pigs would have had to wander off to infect the forest.

Indeed, the calamity wrought by Soto apparently extended across the whole Southeast. The Coosa city-states, in western Georgia, and the Caddoan-speaking civilization, centered on the Texas-Arkansas border, disintegrated soon after Soto appeared. The Caddo had had a taste for monumental architecture: public plazas, ceremonial platforms, mausoleums. After Soto's army left, notes Timothy K. Perttula, an archaeological consultant in Austin, Texas, the Caddo stopped building community centers and began digging community cemeteries. Between Soto's and La Salle's visits, Perttula believes, the Caddoan population fell from about 200,000 to about 8,500—a drop of nearly 96 percent. In the eighteenth century the tally shrank further, to 1,400. An equivalent loss today in the population of New York City would reduce it to 56,000—not enough to fill Yankee Stadium. "That's one reason whites think of Indians as nomadic hunters," says Russell Thornton, an anthropologist at the University of California at Los Angeles. "Everything else—all the heavily populated urbanized societies—was wiped out."

Could a few pigs truly wreak this much destruction? Such apocalyptic scenarios invite skepticism. As a rule, viruses, microbes, and parasites are rarely lethal on so wide a scale—a pest that wipes out its host species does not have a bright evolutionary future. In its worst outbreak, from 1347 to 1351, the European Black Death claimed only a third of its victims. (The rest survived, though they were often disfigured or crippled by its effects.) The Indians in Soto's path, if Dobyns, Ramenofsky, and Perttula are correct, endured losses that were incomprehensibly greater.

One reason is that Indians were fresh territory for many plagues, not just one. Smallpox, typhoid, bubonic plague, influenza, mumps, measles, whooping cough—all rained down on the Americas in the century after Columbus. (Cholera, malaria, and scarlet fever came later.) Having little experience with epidemic diseases, Indians had no knowledge of how to combat them. In contrast, Europeans were well versed in the brutal logic of quarantine. They boarded up houses in which plague appeared and fled to the countryside. In Indian New England, Neal Salisbury, a historian at Smith college, wrote in *Manitou and Providence* (1982), family and friends gathered with the shaman at the sufferer's bedside to wait out the illness—a practice that "could only have served to spread the disease more rapidly."

Indigenous biochemistry may also have played a role. The immune system constantly scans the body for molecules that it can recognize as foreign—molecules belonging to an invading virus, for instance. No one's immune system can identify all foreign presences. Roughly speaking, an individual's set of defensive tools is known as his MHC type. Because many bacteria and viruses mutate easily, they usually attack in the form of several slightly different strains. Pathogens win when MHC types miss some of the strains and the immune system is not stimulated to act. Most human groups contain many MHC types; a strain that slips by one person's defenses will be nailed by the defenses of the next. But, according to Francis L. Black, an epidemiologist at Yale University, Indians are characterized by unusually homogeneous MHC types. One out of three South American Indians have similar MHC types; among Africans the corresponding figure is one in 200. The cause is a matter for Darwinian speculation, the effects less so.

In 1966 Dobyns's insistence on the role of disease was a shock to his colleagues. Today the impact of European pathogens on the New World is almost undisputed. Nonetheless, the fight over Indian numbers continues with undiminished fervor. Estimates of the population of North America in 1491 disagree by an order of magnitude—from 18 million, Dobyns's revised figure, to 1.8 million, calculated by Douglas H. Ubelaker, an anthropologist at the Smithsonian. To some "high counters," as David Henige calls them, the low counters' refusal to relinquish the vision of an empty continent is irrational or worse. "Non-Indian 'experts' always want to minimize the size of aboriginal populations," says Lenore Stiffarm, a Native American-education specialist at the University of Saskatchewan. The smaller the numbers of Indians, she believes, the easier it is to regard the continent as having been up for grabs. "It's perfectly acceptable to move into unoccupied land," Stiffarm says. "And land with only a few 'savages' is the next best thing."

"Most of the arguments for the very large numbers have been theoretical," Ubelaker says in defense of low counters. "When you try to marry the theoretical arguments to the data that are available on individual groups in different regions, it's hard to find support for those numbers." Archaeologists, he says, keep searching for the settlements in which those millions of people supposedly lived, with little success. "As more and more excavation is done, one would expect to see more evidence for dense populations than has thus far emerged." Dean Snow, the Pennsylvania State anthropologist, examined Colonial-era Mohawk Iroquois sites and found "no support for the notion that ubiquitous pandemics swept the region." In his view, asserting that the continent was filled with people who left no trace is like looking at an empty bank account and claiming that it must once have held millions of dollars.

The low counters are also troubled by the Dobynsian procedure for recovering original population numbers: applying an assumed death rate, usually 95 percent, to the observed population nadir. Ubelaker believes that the lowest point for Indians in North America was around 1900, when their numbers fell to about half a million. Assuming a 95 percent death rate, the pre-contact population would have been 10 million. Go up one percent, to a 96 percent death rate, and the figure jumps to 12.5 million—arithmetically creating more than two million people from a tiny increase in mortality rates. At 98 percent the number bounds to 25 million. Minute changes in baseline assumptions produce wildly different results.

"It's an absolutely unanswerable question on which tens of thousands of words have been spent to no purpose," Henige says. In 1976 he sat in on a seminar by William Denevan, the Wisconsin geographer. An "epiphanic moment" occurred when he read shortly afterward that scholars had "uncovered" the existence of eight million people in Hispaniola. *Can you just invent millions of people?* he wondered. "We can make of the historical record that there was depopulation and movement of people from internecine warfare and diseases," he says. "But as for how much, who knows? When we start putting numbers to something like that—applying large figures like ninety-five percent—we're saying things we shouldn't say. The number implies a level of knowledge that's impossible."

Nonetheless, one must try—or so Denevan believes. In his estimation the high counters (though not the highest counters) seem to be winning the argument, at least for now. No definitive data exist, he says, but the majority of the extant evidentiary scraps support their side. Even Henige is no low counter. When I asked him what he thought the population of the Americas was before Columbus, he insisted that any answer would be speculation and made me promise not to print what he was going to say next. Then he named a figure that forty years ago would have caused a commotion.

To Elizabeth Fenn, the smallpox historian, the squabble over numbers obscures a central fact. Whether one million or 10 million or 100 million died, she believes, the pall of sorrow that engulfed the hemisphere was immeasurable. Languages, prayers, hopes, habits, and dreams—entire ways of life hissed away like steam. The Spanish and the Portuguese lacked the germ theory of disease and could not explain what was happening (let alone stop it). Nor can we explain it; the ruin was too long ago and too all-encompassing. In the long run, Fenn says, the consequential finding is not that many people died but that many people once lived. The Americas were filled with a stunningly diverse assortment of peoples who had knocked about the continents for millennia. "You have to wonder," Fenn says. "What were all those people *up* to in all that time?"

Buffalo Farm

In 1810 Henry Brackenridge came to Cahokia, in what is now southwest Illinois, just across the Mississippi from St. Louis. Born close to the frontier, Brackenridge was a budding adventure writer; his *Views of Louisiana,* published three years later, was a kind of nineteenth-century *Into Thin Air,* with terrific adventure but without tragedy. Brackenridge had an eye for archaeology, and he had heard that Cahokia was worth a visit. When he got there, trudging along the desolate Cahokia River, he was "struck with a degree of astonishment." Rising from the muddy bottomland was a "stupendous pile of earth," vaster than the Great Pyramid at Giza. Around it were more than a hundred smaller mounds, covering an area of five square miles. At the time, the area was almost uninhabited. One can only imagine what passed through Brackenridge's mind as he walked alone to the ruins of the biggest Indian city north of the Rio Grande.

To Brackenridge, it seemed clear that Cahokia and the many other ruins in the Midwest had been constructed by Indians. It was not so clear to everyone else. Nineteenth-century writers attributed them to, among others, the Vikings, the Chinese, the "Hindoos," the ancient Greeks, the ancient Egyptians, lost tribes of Israelites, and even straying bands of Welsh. (This last claim was surprisingly widespread; when Lewis and Clark surveyed the Missouri, Jefferson told them to keep an eye out for errant bands of Welsh-speaking white Indians.) The historian George Bancroft, dean of his profession, was a dissenter: the earthworks, he wrote in 1840, were purely natural formations.

Bancroft changed his mind about Cahokia, but not about Indians. To the end of his days he regarded them as "feeble barbarians, destitute of commerce and of political connection." His characterization lasted, largely unchanged, for more than a century. Samuel Eliot Morison, the winner of two Pulitzer Prizes, closed his monumental *European Discovery of America* (1974) with the observation that Native Americans expected only "short and brutish lives, void of hope for any future." As late as 1987 *American History: A Survey,* a standard high school textbook by three well-known historians, described the Americas before Columbus as "empty of mankind and its works." The story of Europeans in the New World, the book explained, "is the story of the creation of a civilization where none existed."

Alfred Crosby, a historian at the University of Texas, came to other conclusions. Crosby's *The Columbian Exchange: Biological Consequences of 1492* caused almost as much of a stir when it was published, in 1972, as Henry Dobyns's calculation of Indian numbers six years earlier, though in different circles. Crosby was a standard names-and-battles historian who became frustrated by the random contingency of political events. "Some trivial thing happens and you have this guy winning the presidency instead of that guy," he says. He decided to go deeper. After he finished his manuscript, it sat on his shelf—he couldn't find a publisher willing to be associated with his new ideas. It took him three years to persuade a small editorial house to put it out. *The Columbian Exchange* has been in print ever since; a companion, *Ecological Imperialism: The Biological Expansion of Europe, 900–1900,* appeared in 1986.

Human history, in Crosby's interpretation, is marked by two world-altering centers of invention: the Middle East and central Mexico, where Indian groups independently created nearly all of the Neolithic innovations, writing included. The Neolithic Revolution began in the Middle East about 10,000 years ago. In the next few millennia humankind invented the wheel, the metal tool, and agriculture. The Sumerians eventually put these inventions together, added writing, and became the world's first civilization. Afterward Sumeria's heirs in Europe and Asia frantically copied one another's happiest discoveries; innovations ricocheted from one corner of Eurasia to another, stimulating technological progress. Native Americans, who had crossed to Alaska before Sumeria, missed out on the bounty. "They had to do everything on their own," Crosby says. Remarkably, they succeeded.

When Columbus appeared in the Caribbean, the descendants of the world's two Neolithic civilizations collided, with overwhelming consequences for both. American Neolithic development occurred later than that of the Middle East, possibly because the Indians needed more time to build up the requisite population density. Without beasts of burden they could not capitalize on the wheel (for individual workers on uneven terrain skids are nearly as effective as carts for hauling), and they never developed steel. But in agriculture they handily outstripped the children of Sumeria. Every tomato in Italy, every potato in Ireland, and every hot pepper in Thailand came from this hemisphere. Worldwide, more than half the crops grown today were initially developed in the Americas.

Maize, as corn is called in the rest of the world, was a triumph with global implications. Indians developed an extraordinary number of maize varieties for different growing conditions, which meant that the crop could and did spread throughout the planet. Central and Southern Europeans became particularly dependent on it; maize was the staple of Serbia, Romania, and Moldavai by the nineteenth century. Indian crops dramatically reduced hunger, Crosby says, which led to an Old World population boom.

In the Aztec capital Tenochtitlán the Spaniards gawped like hayseeds at the side streets, ornately carved buildings, and markets bright with goods from hundreds of miles away.

Along with peanuts and manioc, maize came to Africa and transformed agriculture there, too. "The probability is that the population of Africa was greatly increased because of maize and other American Indian crops," Crosby says. "Those extra people helped make the slave trade possible." Maize conquered Africa at the time when introduced diseases were leveling Indian societies. The Spanish, the Portuguese, and the British were alarmed by the death rate among Indians, because they wanted to exploit them as workers. Faced with a labor shortage, the Europeans turned their eyes to Africa. The continent's quarrelsome societies helped slave traders to siphon off millions of people. The maize-fed population boom, Crosby believes, let the awful trade continue without pumping the well dry.

Back home in the Americas, Indian agriculture long sustained some of the world's largest cities. The Aztec capital of Tenochtitlán dazzled Hernán Cortés in 1519; it was bigger than Paris, Europe's greatest metropolis. The Spaniards gawped like hayseeds at the wide streets, ornately carved buildings, and markets bright with goods from hundreds of miles away. They had never before seen a city with botanical gardens, for the excellent reason that none existed in Europe. The same novelty attended the force of a thousand men that kept the crowded streets immaculate. (Streets that weren't ankle-deep in sewage! The conquistadors had never heard of such a thing.) Central America was not the only locus of prosperity. Thousands of miles north, John Smith, of Pocahontas fame, visited Massachusetts in 1614, before it was emptied by disease, and declared that the land was "so planted with Gardens and Corne fields, and so well inhabited with a goodly, strong and well proportioned people . . . [that] I would rather live here than any where."

Smith was promoting colonization, and so had reason to exaggerate. But he also knew the hunger, sickness, and oppression of European life. France—"by any standards a privileged country," according to its great historian, Fernand Braudel—experienced seven nationwide famines in the fifteenth century and thirteen in the sixteenth. Disease was hunger's constant companion. During epidemics in London the dead were heaped onto carts "like common dung" (the simile is Daniel Defoe's) and trundled through the streets. The infant death rate in London orphanages, according to one contemporary source, was 88 percent. Governments were harsh, the rule of law arbitrary. The gibbets poking up in the background of so many old paintings were, Braudel observed, "merely a realistic detail."

The Earth Shall Weep, James Wilson's history of Indian America, puts the comparison bluntly: "the western hemisphere was larger, richer, and more populous than Europe." Much of it was freer, too. Europeans, accustomed to the serfdom that thrived from Naples to the Baltic Sea, were puzzled and alarmed by the democratic spirit and respect for human rights in many Indian societies, especially those in North America. In theory, the sachems of New England Indian groups were absolute monarchs. In practice, the colonial leader Roger Williams wrote, "they will not conclude of ought . . . unto which the people are averse."

Pre-1492 America wasn't a disease-free paradise, Dobyns says, although in his "exuberance as a writer," he told me recently, he once made that claim. Indians had ailments of their own, notably parasites, tuberculosis, and anemia. The daily grind was wearing; life-spans in America were only as long as or a little longer than those in Europe, if the evidence of indigenous graveyards is to be believed. Nor was it a political utopia—the Inca, for instance, invented refinements to totalitarian rule that would have intrigued Stalin. Inveterate practitioners of what the historian Francis Jennings described as "state terrorism practiced horrifically on a huge scale," the Inca ruled so cruelly that one can speculate that their surviving subjects might actually have been better off under Spanish rule.

I asked seven anthropologists, archaeologists, and historians if they would rather have been a typical Indian or a typical European in 1491. Every one chose to be an Indian.

I asked seven anthropologists, archaeologists, and historians if they would rather have been a typical Indian or a typical European in 1491. None was delighted by the question, because it required judging the past by the standards of today—a fallacy disparaged as "presentism" by social scientists. But every one chose to be an Indian. Some early colonists gave the same answer. Horrifying the leaders of Jamestown and Plymouth, scores of English ran off to live with the Indians. My ancestor shared their desire, which is what led to the trumped-up murder charges against him—or that's what my grandfather told me, anyway.

As for the Indians, evidence suggests that they often viewed Europeans with disdain. The Hurons, a chagrined missionary reported, thought the French possessed "little intelligence in comparison to themselves." Europeans, Indians said, were physically weak, sexually untrustworthy, atrociously ugly, and just plain dirty. (Spaniards, who seldom if ever bathed, were amazed by the Aztec desire for personal cleanliness.) A Jesuit reported that the "Savages" were disgusted by handkerchiefs: "They say, we place what is unclean in a fine white piece of linen, and put it away in our pockets as something very precious, while they throw it upon the ground." The Micmac scoffed at the notion of French superiority. If Christian civilization was so wonderful, why were its inhabitants leaving?

Like people everywhere, Indians survived by cleverly exploiting their environment. Europeans tended to manage land by breaking it into fragments for farmers and herders. Indians often worked on such a grand scale that the scope of their ambition can be hard to grasp. They created small plots, as Europeans did (about 1.5 million acres of terraces still exist in the Peruvian Andes), but they also reshaped entire landscapes to suit their purposes. A principal tool was fire, used to keep down underbrush and create the open, grassy conditions favorable for game. Rather than domesticating animals for meat, Indians retooled whole ecosystems to grow bumper crops of elk, deer, and bison. The first white settlers in Ohio found forests as open as English parks—they could drive carriages through the woods. Along the Hudson River the annual fall burning lit up the banks for miles on end; so flashy was the show that the Dutch in New Amsterdam boated upriver to goggle at the blaze like children at fireworks. In North America, Indian torches had their biggest impact on the Midwestern prairie, much or most of which was created and maintained by fire. Millennia of exuberant burning shaped the plains into vast buffalo farms. When Indian societies disintegrated, forest invaded savannah in Wisconsin, Illinois, Kansas, Nebraska, and the Texas Hill Country. Is it possible that the Indians changed the Americas more than the invading Europeans did? "The answer is probably yes for most regions for the next 250 years or so" after Columbus. William Denevan wrote, "and for some regions right up to the present time."

Amazonia has become the emblem of vanishing wilderness—an admonitory image of untouched Nature. But the rain forest itself may be a cultural artifact—that is, an artificial object.

When scholars first began increasing their estimates of the ecological impact of Indian civilization, they met with considerable resistance from anthropologists and archaeologists. Over time the consensus in the human sciences changed. Under Denevan's direction, Oxford University Press has just issued the third volume of a huge catalogue of the "cultivated landscapes" of the Americas. This sort of phrase still provokes vehement objection—but the main dissenters are now ecologists and environmentalists. The disagreement is encapsulated by Amazonia, which has become *the* emblem of vanishing wilderness—an admonitory image of untouched Nature. Yet recently a growing number of researchers have come to believe that Indian societies had an enormous environmental impact on the jungle. Indeed, some anthropologists have called the Amazon forest itself a cultural artifact—that is, an artificial object.

Green Prisons

Northern visitors' first reaction to the storied Amazon rain forest is often disappointment. Ecotourist brochures evoke the immensity of Amazonia but rarely dwell on its extreme flatness. In the river's first 2,900 miles the vertical drop is only 500 feet. The river oozes like a huge runnel of dirty metal through a landscape utterly devoid of the romantic crags, arroyos, and heights that signify wilderness and natural spectacle to most North Americans. Even the animals are invisible, although sometimes one can hear the bellow of monkey choruses. To the untutored eye—mine, for instance—the forest seems to stretch out in a monstrous green tangle as flat and incomprehensible as a printed circuit board.

The area east of the lower-Amazon town of Santarém is an exception. A series of sandstone ridges several hundred feet high reach down from the north, halting almost at the water's edge. Their tops stand drunkenly above the jungle like old tombstones. Many of the caves in the buttes are splattered with ancient petroglyphs—renditions of hands, stars, frogs, and human figures, all reminiscent of Miró, in overlapping red and yellow and brown. In recent years one of these caves, La Caverna da Pedra Pintada (Painted Rock Cave), has drawn attention in archaeological circles.

Wide and shallow and well lit, Painted Rock Cave is less thronged with bats than some of the other caves. The arched entrance is twenty feet high and lined with rock paintings. Out front is a sunny natural patio suitable for picnicking, edged by a few big rocks. People lived in this cave more than 11,000 years ago. They had no agriculture yet, and instead ate fish and fruit and built fires. During a recent visit I ate a sandwich atop a particularly inviting rock and looked over the forest below. The first Amazonians, thought, must have done more or less the same thing.

In college I took an introductory anthropology class in which I read *Amazonia: Man and Culture in a Counterfeit Paradise* (1971), perhaps the most influential book ever written about the Amazon, and one that deeply impressed me at the time. Written by Betty J. Meggers, the Smithsonian archaeologist, *Amazonia* says that the apparent lushness of the rain forest is a sham. The soils are poor and can't hold nutrients—the jungle flora exists only because it snatches up everything worthwhile before it leaches away in the rain. Agriculture, which depends on extracting the wealth of the soil, therefore faces inherent ecological limitations in the wet desert of Amazonia.

As a result, Meggers argued, Indian villages were forced to remain small—any report of "more than a few hundred" people in permanent settlements, she told me recently, "makes my alarm bells go off." Bigger, more complex societies would inevitably overtax the forest soils, laying waste to their own foundations. Beginning in 1948 Meggers and her late husband, Clifford Evans, excavated a chiefdom on Marajó, an island twice the size of New Jersey that sits like a gigantic stopper in the mouth of the Amazon. The Marajóara, they concluded, were failed offshoots of a sophisticated culture in the Andes. Transplanted to the lush trap of the Amazon, the culture choked and died.

Green activists saw the implication: development in tropical forests destroys both the forests and their developers. Meggers's account had enormous public impact—*Amazonia* is one of the wellsprings of the campaign to save rain forests.

Then Anna C. Roosevelt, the curator of archaeology at Chicago's Field Museum of Natural History, re-excavated Marajó. Her complete report, *Moundbuilders of the Amazon* (1991), was like the anti-matter version of *Amazonia*. Marajó, she argued, was "one of the outstanding indigenous cultural achievements of the New World," a powerhouse that lasted for more than a thousand years, had "possibly well over 100,000" inhabitants, and covered thousands of square miles. Rather than damaging the forest, Marajó's "earth construction" and "large, dense populations" had *improved* it: the most luxuriant and diverse growth was on the mounds formerly occupied by the Marajóara. "If you listened to Meggers's theory, these places should have been ruined," Roosevelt says.

Meggers scoffed at Roosevelt's "extravagant claims," "polemical tone," and "defamatory remarks." Roosevelt, Meggers argued, had committed the beginner's error of mistaking a site that had been occupied many times by small, unstable groups for a single, long-lasting society. "[Archaeological remains] build up on areas of half a kilometer or so," she told me, "because [shifting Indian groups] don't land exactly on the same spot. The decorated types of pottery don't change much over time, so you can pick up a bunch of chips and say, 'Oh, look, it was all one big site!' Unless you know what you're doing, of course." Centuries after the conquistadors, "the myth of El Dorado is being revived by archaeologists," Meggers wrote last fall in the journal *Latin American Antiquity,* referring to the persistent Spanish delusion that cities of gold existed in the jungle.

The dispute grew bitter and personal; inevitable in a contemporary academic context, it has featured vituperative references to colonialism, elitism, and employment by the CIA. Meanwhile, Roosevelt's team investigated Painted Rock Cave. On the floor of the cave what looked to me like nothing in particular turned out to be an ancient midden: a refuse heap. The archaeologists slowly scraped away sediment, traveling backward in time with every inch. When the traces of human occupation vanished, they kept digging. ("You always go a meter past sterile," Roosevelt says.) A few inches below they struck the charcoal-rich dirt that signifies human habitation—a culture, Roosevelt said later, that wasn't supposed to be there.

For many millennia the cave's inhabitants hunted and gathered for food. But by about 4000 years ago they were growing crops—perhaps as many as 140 of them, according to Charles R. Clement, an anthropological botanist at the Brazilian National Institute for Amazonian Research. Unlike Europeans, who planted mainly annual crops, the Indians, he says, centered their agriculture on the Amazon's unbelievably diverse assortment of trees: fruits, nuts, and palms. "It's tremendously difficult to clear fields with stone tools," Clement says. "If you can plant trees, you get twenty years of productivity out of your work instead of two or three."

Planting their orchards, the first Amazonians transformed large swaths of the river basin into something more pleasing to human beings. In a widely cited article from 1989, William Balée, the Tulane anthropologist, cautiously estimated that about 12 percent of the nonflooded Amazon forest was of anthropogenic origin—directly or indirectly created by human beings. In some circles this is now seen as a conservative position. "I basically think it's all human-created," Clement told me in Brazil. He argues that Indians changed the assortment and density of species throughout the region. So does Clark Erickson, the University of Pennsylvania archaeologist, who told me in Bolivia that the lowland tropical forests of South America are among the finest works of art on the planet. "Some of my colleagues would say that's pretty radical," he said, smiling mischievously. According to Peter Stahl, an anthropologist at the State University of New York at Binghamton, "lots" of botanists believe that "what the eco-imagery would like to picture as a pristine, untouched Urwelt [primeval world] in fact has been managed by people for millennia." The phrase "built

environment," Erickson says, "applies to most, if not all, Neotropical landscapes."

"Landscape" in this case is meant exactly—Amazonian Indians literally created the ground beneath their feet. According to William I. Woods, a soil geographer at Southern Illinois University, ecologists' claims about terrible Amazonian land were based on very little data. In the late 1990s Woods and others began careful measurements in the lower Amazon. They indeed found lots of inhospitable terrain. But they also discovered swaths of *terra preta*—rich, fertile "black earth" that anthropologists increasingly believe was created by human beings.

Terra preta, Woods guesses, covers at least 10 percent of Amazonia, an area the size of France. It has amazing properties, he says. Tropical rain doesn't leach nutrients from *terra preta* fields; instead the soil, so to speak, fights back. Not far from Painted Rock Cave is a 300-acre area with a two-foot layer of *terra preta* quarried by locals for potting soil. The bottom third of the layer is never removed, workers there explain, because over time it will re-create the original soil layer in its initial thickness. The reason, scientists suspect, is that *terra preta* is generated by a special suite of microorganisms that resists depletion. "Apparently," Woods and the Wisconsin geographer Joseph M. McCann argued in a presentation last summer, "at some threshold level . . . dark earth attains the capacity to perpetuate—even *regenerate* itself—thus behaving more like a living 'super'-organism than an inert material."

In as yet unpublished research the archaeologists Eduardo Neves, of the University of São Paulo; Michael Heckenberger, of the University of Florida; and other colleagues examined *terra preta* in the upper Xingu, a huge southern tributary of the Amazon. Not all Xingu cultures left behind this living earth, they discovered. But the ones that did generated it rapidly—suggesting to Woods that *terra preta* was created deliberately. In a process reminiscent of dropping microorganism-rich starter into plain dough to create sourdough bread, Amazonian peoples, he believes, inoculated bad soil with a transforming bacterial charge. Not every group of Indians there did this, but quite a few did, and over an extended period of time.

When Woods told me this, I was so amazed that I almost dropped the phone. I ceased to be articulate for a moment and said things like "wow" and "gosh." Woods chuckled at my reaction, probably because he understood what was passing through my mind. Faced with an ecological problem, I was thinking, the Indians *fixed* it. They were in the process of terraforming the Amazon when Columbus showed up and ruined everything.

Scientists should study the microorganisms in *terra preta*, Woods told me, to find out how they work. If that could be learned, maybe some version of Amazonian dark earth could be used to improve the vast expanses of bad soil that cripple agriculture in Africa—a final gift from the people who brought us tomatoes, corn, and the immense grasslands of the Great Plains.

"Betty Meggers would just die if she heard me saying this," Woods told me. "Deep down her fear is that this data will be misused." Indeed, Meggers's recent *Latin American Antiquity* article charged that archaeologists who say the Amazon can support agriculture are effectively telling "developers [that they] are entitled to operate without restraint." Resuscitating the myth of El Dorado, in her view, "makes us accomplices in the accelerating pace of environmental degradation." Doubtless there is something to this—although, as some of her critics responded in the same issue of the journal, it is difficult to imagine greedy plutocrats "perusing the pages of *Latin American Antiquity* before deciding to rev up the chain saws." But the new picture doesn't automatically legitimize paving the forest. Instead it suggests that for a long time big chunks of Amazonia were used nondestructively by clever people who knew tricks we have yet to learn.

Environmentalists want to preserve as much of the world's land as possible in a putatively intact state. But "intact" may turn out to mean "run by human beings for human purposes."

I visited Painted Rock Cave during the river's annual flood, when it wells up over its banks and creeps inland for miles. Farmers in the floodplain build houses and barns on stilts and watch pink dolphins sport from their doorsteps. Ecotourists take shortcuts by driving motorboats through the drowned forests. Guys in dories chase after them, trying to sell sacks of incredibly good fruit.

All of this is described as "wilderness" in the tourist brochures. It's not, if researchers like Roosevelt are correct. Indeed, they believe that fewer people may be living there now than in 1491. Yet when my boat glided into the trees, the forest shut out the sky like the closing of an umbrella. Within a few hundred years the human presence seemed to vanish. I felt alone and small, but in a way that was curiously like feeling exalted. If that place was not wilderness, how should I think of it? Since the fate of the forest is in our hands, what should be our goal for its future?

Novel Shores

Hernando de Soto's expedition stomped through the Southeast for four years and apparently never saw bison. More than a century later, when French explorers came down the Mississippi, they saw "a solitude unrelieved by the faintest trace of man," the nineteenth-century historian Francis Parkman wrote. Instead the French encountered bison, "grazing in herds on the great prairies which then bordered the river."

To Charles Kay, the reason for the buffalo's sudden emergence is obvious. Kay is a wildlife ecologist in the political-science department at Utah State University. In ecological terms, he says, the Indians were the "keystone species" of American ecosystems. A keystone species, according to the Harvard biologist Edward O. Wilson, is a species "that affects the survival and abundance of many other species." Keystone species have a disproportionate impact on their ecosystems. Removing them,

Wilson adds, "results in a relatively significant shift in the composition of the [ecological] community."

When disease swept Indians from the land, Kay says, what happened was exactly that. The ecological ancient régime collapsed, and strange new phenomena emerged. In a way this is unsurprising; for better or worse, humankind is a keystone species everywhere. Among these phenomena was a population explosion in the species that the Indians had kept down by hunting. After disease killed off the Indians, Kay believes, buffalo vastly extended their range. Their numbers more than sextupled. The same occurred with elk and mule deer. "If the elk were here in great numbers all this time, the archaeological sites should be chock-full of elk bones," Kay says. "But the archaeologists will tell you the elk weren't there." On the evidence of middens the number of elk jumped about 500 years ago.

Passenger pigeons may be another example. The epitome of natural American abundance, they flew in such great masses that the first colonists were stupefied by the sight. As a boy, the explorer Henry Brackenridge saw flocks "ten miles in width, by one hundred and twenty in length." For hours the birds darkened the sky from horizon to horizon. According to Thomas Neumann, a consulting archaeologist to Lilburn, Georgia, passenger pigeons "were incredibly dumb and always roosted in vast hordes, so they were very easy to harvest." Because they were readily caught and good to eat, Neumann says, archaeological digs should find many pigeon bones in the pre-Columbian strata of Indian middens. But they aren't there. The mobs of birds in the history books, he says, were "outbreak populations—always a symptom of an extraordinarily disrupted ecological system."

Throughout eastern North America the open landscape seen by the first Europeans quickly filled in with forest. According to William Cronon, of the University of Wisconsin, later colonists began complaining about how hard it was to get around. (Eventually, of course, they stripped New England almost bare of trees.) When Europeans moved west, they were preceded by two waves: one of disease, the other of ecological disturbance. The former crested with fearsome rapidity; the later sometimes took more than a century to quiet down. Far from destroying pristine wilderness, European settlers bloodily *created* it. By 1800 the hemisphere was chockablock with new wilderness. If "forest primeval" means a woodland unsullied by the human presence, William Denevan has written, there was much more of it in the late eighteenth century than in the early sixteenth.

Cronon's *Changes in the Land: Indians, Colonists, and the Ecology of New England* (1983) belongs on the same shelf as works by Crosby and Dobyns. But it was not until one of his articles was excerpted in *The New York Times* in 1995 that people outside the social sciences began to understand the implications of this view of Indian history. Environmentalists and ecologists vigorously attacked the anti-wilderness scenario, which they described as infected by postmodern philosophy. A small academic brouhaha ensued, complete with hundreds of footnotes. It precipitated *Reinventing Nature?* (1995), one of the few academic critiques of postmodernist philosophy written largely by biologists. *The Great New Wilderness Debate*

(1998), another lengthy book on the subject, was edited by two philosophers who earnestly identified themselves as "Euro-American men [whose] cultural legacy is patriarchal Western civilization in its current postcolonial, globally hegemonic form."

It is easy to tweak academics for opaque, self-protective language like this. Nonetheless, their concerns were quite justified. Crediting Indians with the role of keystone species has implications for the way the current Euro-American members of that keystone species manage the forests, watersheds, and endangered species of America. Because a third of the United States is owned by the federal government, the issue inevitably has political ramifications. In Amazonia, fabled storehouse of biodiversity, the stakes are global.

Guided by the pristine myth, mainstream environmentalists want to preserve as much of the world's land as possible in a putatively intact state. But "intact," if the new research is correct, means "run by human beings for human purposes." Environmentalists dislike this, because it seems to mean that anything goes. In a sense they are correct. Native Americans managed the continent as they saw fit. Modern nations must do the same. If they want to return as much of the landscape as possible to its 1491 state, they will have to find it within themselves to create the world's largest garden.

How Cruel Were the Spaniards?

Iris H. W. Engstrand

The Spanish word "conquistador" means "conqueror" and has been used loosely to describe Spaniards who came to the New World during the colonial period in search of wealth and Indian labor. Unfortunately, the word has been applied to Spaniards who came as missionaries to convert the natives to Christianity, as explorers to chart the coasts, as farmers to cultivate the soil, as ranchers to raise cattle and sheep, or even as naturalists to study the fauna and flora.[1]

Curiously, the English, French, Portuguese, Dutch, and Russians came for similar purposes, but have escaped the label of "conquerors." The English are usually remembered as colonists or settlers, while the French, Portuguese, and Dutch are often thought of as merchants or traders.[2] The Russians, as aggressive as they may have been against the Eskimos or Aleuts, are seldom referred to as "conquerors." It is the Spaniards—because of events surrounding the Spanish Inquisition, the notoriety of the so-called "Black Legend,"[3] and the widespread attention given to the conquest of the Aztecs and Incas—who became the avaricious "conquistadores." The cruelest deeds of individual Spaniards have become emblematic of a people and have been described in detail in various monographs, given ample space in general textbooks, and popularized in movies and television for American audiences stretching from Cape Horn to the Bering Strait. Even the spread of smallpox among Indians of the Northwest Coast has been attributed to Spaniards without supporting evidence.[4]

Were the Spanish conquistadores of the sixteenth century cruel? Of course. How would it be possible to conquer other peoples without acts of cruelty? But cruelty of one nation toward another, or one group of people toward another, must be evaluated in terms of time and place. One could ask, "Were the Indians of the sixteenth century cruel?" Of course. Some engaged in human sacrifice, slavery, infanticide, and other forms of human behavior that we regard today as "cruel." We could also ask about cruelty in modern times—the bombing of cities, the destruction caused by nuclear attacks, torture of political prisoners, and random shootings of innocent victims. A study of areas conquered by other Europeans, or methods of punishment throughout Europe from the sixteenth through the eighteenth centuries can also be helpful in understanding degrees of cruelty. Sailors, petty criminals, and even schoolboys were routinely flogged or subjected to treatment considered extremely cruel by today's standards. Even though comparisons cannot

give the answers, they can put our discussion into a broader framework. But because of space limitations it will be possible to give only a few examples to confirm or dispel the "conquistador image" as applied to all Spaniards of the colonial period.

From first contact in the Caribbean, Spaniards uprooted natives from their homelands, forced them to give up their treasures, and placed them in captivity. Spaniards who were victims of conquest by Muslims over much of their history, and common sailors who were struggling to find some kind of wealth after weeks of deprivation on board ship were not disposed to act kindly. Countless Indians died during the first years of contact, although mainly from disease. Other Spaniards in the Caribbean, like the Dominican priest Antonio de Montesinos, spoke out against mistreatment of Indians as early as 1511.[5]

When rumors of Indian riches on the mainland reached the Spanish headquarters in the West Indies, the men of the conquest followed their dreams of instant wealth. They soon found that the civilizations of both the Aztecs and the Incas were sedentary, wealthy, powerful, and in control of subjugated peoples. Centuries of warfare in the name of a "true" religion on the Iberian Peninsula—the well-known Reconquista—shaped the Spanish course of action. With the defeat of these New World empires, the conquistadores leveled pyramids and built churches in their place. With the arrival of priests and missionaries, they introduced the Catholic faith and set up schools and hospitals. This pattern of conquest continued, although with less fruitful economic gain, throughout the sixteenth century. Exploratory expeditions covered the southern part of the present United States from Florida to California, tolerating or eliminating Indians as Spaniards deemed necessary.[6] It must be kept in mind, however, that the English and French in early America also fought against natives when necessary and introduced them to gunpowder and distilled spirits, both of which were capable of destroying life and health.[7]

By the seventeenth and early eighteenth centuries, new circumstances prevailed within the areas of New Mexico and Texas that can serve as case studies and give a different viewpoint about the Spanish presence in America. No obvious wealth had been found in the southern regions of today's United States. Jesuits built missions in Sonora, southern Arizona, and Baja California while Franciscan missionaries moved into Florida, Georgia, New Mexico, and Texas.[8] From the beginning, however, the conflict between church and state—between missionaries protecting the natives and those wishing to exploit Indian lands and labor—led to a different kind of struggle.

The Spanish Crown, in its *Royal Orders for New Discoveries* of 1573, decreed that Indians should be taught "to live in a civilized manner, clothed and wearing shoes . . . given the use of bread and wine and oil and many other essentials of life—bread, silk, linen, horses, cattle, tools, and weapons, and all the rest that Spain has had. Instructed in the trades and skills with which they might live richly."[9] The Franciscans, as well as other missionaries, made tremendous sacrifices to carry out those instructions in some inhospitable areas. Some considered themselves an antidote to the cruel treatment leveled against natives by other Spaniards. In New Mexico, despite difficulties of distance, extremes of heat and cold, lack of material support, and struggles with civilian and military authorities, Franciscans founded eleven missions and baptized some ten thousand Indians in New Mexico by 1616. By 1629, numbers had increased to twenty-five missions, fifty priests, and over sixty thousand Indians by their count. As "politically incorrect" as these actions may seem to certain groups at present, we cannot judge missionary motivations by today's standards. Franciscans believed that conversion was necessary to save souls and assure a person's entry into heaven.

Nevertheless, nonreligious authorities wanted Indians to work in textile mills and leather factories, serve as soldiers against warring tribes, and otherwise work for the benefit of the government. Even though Europeans also worked long hours in fields, factories, and mines, Indians were unaccustomed to such structured servitude for foreign overlords.[10] Both church and state restricted Indian freedom, suppressed native customs and religion, and inadvertently introduced disease.[11] In New Mexico, these excesses led eventually to the most disastrous event in the province's colonial history—the Pueblo Revolt of 1680, in which the Indians succeeded in expelling the Spaniards from their territory for more than a decade.[12] Some Pueblo Indians in New Mexico had benefitted from Spanish occupation, however, and fled with them; others welcomed the Spaniards back. If Spaniards were cruel, not all Indians saw them that way. Like natives in other parts of the Spanish empire, the Pueblo Indians of New Mexico also found protection in the Hispanic legal system through the office of the *protector de indios*. The protector, whose duty was to "aid and defend" the natives against the Spaniards, often played a major role in guiding them through judicial procedures with varying degrees of success.[13]

The occupation of California little resembled earlier contacts in New Mexico because of differences in the nature of the Indians, the purposes of Spanish explorers, and the Spaniards' prospects for wealth or exploitation of natives in that remote setting. As early as 1542 Juan Rodríguez Cabrillo reported that on San Salvador [Catalina] Island, "a great number of Indians emerged from the bushes and grass, shouting, dancing, and making signs that they should land." The Spaniards "gave them beads and other articles, with which they were pleased."[14] In 1602 Sebastián Vizcaíno visited the same island and the natives "came alongside without the least fear and came on board our ships, mooring their own. . . . [Vizcaíno] received them kindly and gave them some presents."[15]

The next important contact did not take place until 1769, when the expedition of Captain Gaspar de Portolá and Father Junípero Serra arrived to found the first mission at San Diego. Lieutenant Pedro Fages of the Catalonian Volunteers reported on their friendly interchange with the natives, "We have made very good friends with them and we are never lacking some little rabbits, hares, and fish that they bring to us. We gave them some glass beads, but they value very highly any kind of cloth."[16]

By 1775 Franciscan missionaries had founded five missions in Alta California, and Juan Bautista de Anza from the presidio of Tubac, south of Tucson, Arizona, opened an overland route connecting the mission fields of Sonora and California. In late October 1775, however, several hundred nonmission Indians at San Diego revolted against the Spaniards, attacked and burned the mission, and killed the resident priest along with several others. Father Junípero Serra, who had sought protection for Indians against the exploitation by soldiers that apparently provoked the revolt, asked the viceroy for leniency for one of the Indians responsible. "Give him to understand, after a moderate amount of punishment, that he is being pardoned in accordance with our law, which commands us to forgive injuries; and let us prepare him, not for death, but for eternal life."[17]

In California, as throughout the Spanish empire, the Franciscans supported the rights of Indians when they conflicted with demands of Spanish settlers. In 1786 Father Francisco Palóu complained to the viceroy that the proximity of the civilian town of San José to Mission Santa Clara had caused harm to the Indians. There had been a mingling of mission and town herds of cattle, and the settlers' livestock had damaged the mission corn fields. Moreover, the settlers scandalized the Indians, committed adultery, and threatened those husbands who protested. They asked that a fixed boundary between the mission and town be drawn so that further conflict could be avoided. The matter, taken seriously by all concerned, was settled to the satisfaction of the missionaries and their charges in 1801.

The mission system remains a controversial topic among California historians. Some stress that Indians benefitted if they learned to live in settled communities, cultivate the soil, tend cattle and sheep, ride horses, weave cloth, and adapt to European ways. Others emphasize that native groups who had previously enjoyed independence were forcibly reduced to subject peoples, rigidly controlled by a foreign nation, and decimated by European diseases.[18] For their part, the Franciscans believed that Indians had to be separated from their aboriginal culture or they would not learn the ways of Christians. Missionaries used both rewards and punishments. Certainly individual friars were sometimes guilty of excesses in forms of punishment, but their motives were to improve the lives of their charges and give their souls salvation. In several ways, they subjected Indians to the same forms of discipline as they meted out to Spanish students in Franciscan schools.[19] With hindsight it might be said that Indians, who in the long run proved powerless to resist European encroachment upon their lands throughout the New World, may have been better off under Spanish missionaries than they would have been under civilians or the military forces of other conquering nations.[20]

Finally, it must be remembered that some Spaniards came to the New World to study rather than subjugate Indians. Spanish naturalists of the late eighteenth century sought to learn about native customs from a purely scientific viewpoint. They surveyed native villages much as a sociologist does today, taking note of natural resources, social customs, goods produced, food supplies, kinds of housing, religious beliefs, medicinal plants, and even musical instruments. This kind of investigation reflected the enlightened learning found in Europe during the eighteenth century.[21] Although defense of the empire and trade considerations were the Crown's motives in sponsoring these expeditions, the advancement of science played a major role.[22]

José Mariano Moziño, a naturalist/physician born in Mexico, lived with the Mowachaht Indians of Nootka Sound on Vancouver Island for more than four months in the spring and summer of 1792, learning the language and becoming familiar with their customs, religion, and history. A trained scientist, Moziño had no agenda to save souls or to achieve economic gains, and so he recorded the Mowachahts' customs as objectively as he could. He found it difficult, for example, to give their religion an adequate name but noted that "the natives recognize the existence of a God Creator, Preserver of all things" as well as "another malign deity, author of wars, of infirmities, and of death."[23] Dionisio Alcalá Galiano and Cayetano Valdés of the Spanish navy, in command of the exploring expedition of the *Sutil* and *Mexicana,* respectfully described the Indians in the area of Monterey, California, in their journal of 1792: "[The Indians] show signs of tenderness toward their children, and like sensitive people, they never leave them, not even in their most tiring occupations, but rather they are frequently seen loaded down with their little ones. They are loving mothers, and they are not indifferent nor unfaithful wives."[24]

How cruel then, were the Spaniards? If we are talking about the first Spaniards in many areas—adventurers, seekers of wealth at any cost, and illiterate fighters imbued with the idea that territories inhabited by pagan peoples were fair game—the conquistadores and their armies were cruel. Later land, mine, and factory owners were also cruel in terms of exploitation of native labor. Even missionaries, who had the purest of motives, often displaced, estranged, and forced Native Americans into resistance or outright rebellion. On the other hand, there were always those who protected Indians from these excesses, and there were often advantages to Spanish settlement in contrast to colonization by other European nations. Spaniards built schools and hospitals for Native Americans from the earliest days of the conquest and brought new crops, livestock, and tools.

In the long run, interactions between Spaniards and Indians have resulted, not in the annihilation of either group, but ultimately in the development of racially and ethnically merged peoples living in the Americas and a portion of what is now the United States. In the main, Spanish society absorbed Indians rather than excluded them. As historian Philip Wayne Powell wrote in 1971: "Spain's three centuries of tutelage and official concern for the welfare of the American Indian is a record not equaled by other Europeans in overseas government of peoples of lesser, or what were considered lesser, cultures. For all the mistakes, for all the failures, for all the crimes committed . . . in its overall performance Spain, in relation to the American Indian, need offer no apology to any other people or nation."[25]

We cannot go back and change history to suit present standards, but we can try to understand actions and motives by both players and recorders of past events. We can understand only what we know, and we can know only what we learn. But, most importantly, we can learn only by keeping an open mind and not falling victim to half-truths or prejudices developed over time.

Notes

1. As the result of an intense reexamination of Native American issues during the Columbus quincentennial, Spaniards underwent tremendous criticism for having been the first to exploit the resources of the New World, for mistreatment of indigenous peoples, and even for opening the way for other Europeans to follow in their footsteps. See, for example, Kirkpatrick Sale, *Conquest of Paradise* (New York: Knopf, 1990). An insightful summary of the issues can be found in Frederick P. Bowser, "Columbus Transformed (Again)," in *Columbus, Confrontation, Christianity: The European-American Encounter Revisited,* ed. Timothy O'Keefe (Los Gatos, CA: Forbes Mills Press, 1994), 211–28.

2. Even when the epithet pirate or privateer is given to those who preyed on Spanish shipping, harmful treatment of Spaniards does not seem to constitute cruelty.

3. A scathing denunciation of Spanish mistreatment of Indians during the earliest days of the conquest was written by the Dominican priest Bartólome de las Casas to force the Spanish sovereign Carlos V to promote laws to protect the native inhabitants. As a result, the New Laws of 1542, with safeguards for Indians, were passed but not always followed. The writings of Las Casas were quickly translated into English, Dutch, French, and German and used as anti-Catholic and anti-Spanish propaganda, becoming known as "The Black Legend." For a reevaluation of the Black Legend, see Nicolas Kanellos, *Thirty Million Strong: Reclaiming the Hispanic Image in American Culture* (Golden, CO: Fulcrum Publishing, 1998).

4. See Christon I. Archer, "Whose Scourge? Smallpox Epidemics on the Northwest Coast," in *Pacific Empires: Essays in Honour of Glyndwr Williams,* ed. by Alan Frost and Jane Sampson (Vancouver: UBC Press, 1999), 165–91.

5. See Lewis Hanke, *The Spanish Struggle for Justice in the Conquest of America* (Philadelphia: University of Pennsylvania Press, 1949), 17–18.

6. The expeditions of Francisco Vásquez de Coronado and Hernando de Soto committed unnecessarily cruel acts towards Indians during the early 1540s in their relentless search for gold and other riches. The Pacific explorers under Juan Rodríguez Cabrillo in 1542, on the other hand, attempted to deal with the natives on the basis of friendship.

7. Even the racist concept of "Manifest Destiny"—the popular belief in promoting nineteenth-century American westward expansion (i.e., conquest) at the expense of Native Americans and Hispanic settlers—has never received the same degree of criticism as that leveled against Spain during the discovery period. A number of writings of the mid 1800s extol the virtues of an "Anglo-Saxon" civilization in contrast to that of Spaniards, Indians, or "a mixed population." In contrast to this Anglo American attitude, runaway slaves could find freedom in

Spanish Florida, and the government of Mexico tried to prevent the introduction of slavery into Texas.

8. The Jesuits by this time were the most important teaching order in the Americas, and the Franciscans were well known for their hospitals and orphanages.

9. Quoted in David J. Weber, *The Spanish Frontier in North America* (New Haven: Yale University Press, 1992), 106.

10. Some Indians were effectively enslaved despite royal strictures against the practice.

11. For details of this era, see Donald Cutter and Iris H. W. Engstrand, *Quest for Empire: Spanish Settlement in the Southwest* (Golden, CO: Fulcrum Publishing, 1996), 73–116.

12. A new work on this subject designed for students is David J. Weber, ed., *What Caused the Pueblo Revolt of 1680?* (Boston: Bedford/St. Martin's, 1999).

13. See Charles R. Cutter, *The Protector de Indios in Colonial New Mexico, 1659–1821* (Albuquerque: University of New Mexico Press, 1986).

14. A summary account of Juan Rodríguez Cabrillo's voyage, quoted in Herbert E. Bolton, ed., *Spanish Exploration in the Southwest, 1542–1706* (1908; reprint, New York: Barnes and Noble, 1963), 23–24.

15. Journal of Sebastián Vizcaíno, quoted in Bolton, *Spanish Exploration*, 80–82.

16. Pedro Fages to José de Gálvez, 26 June 1769, MS GA 487, Huntington Library, San Marino, CA.

17. Antonine Tibesar, ed. and trans., *Writings of Junípero Serra*, 4 vols. (Washington, DC: American Academy of Franciscan History, 1955–1966), 2:7.

18. See David J. Weber, "Blood of Martyrs, Blood of Indians: Toward a More Balanced View of Spanish Missions in Seventeenth Century North America," in O'Keefe, ed., *Columbus, Confrontation, Christianity: The European-American Encounter Revisited,* 134–47.

19. For a legal defense of Native Americans, see Iris H. W. Engstrand, "Franciscan Missionary Practices in California During the Spanish Period," in O'Keefe, ed., *Columbus, Confrontation, Christianity,* 158–68.

20. Examples include the crushing of Pequot resistance by the English during the 1630s; the distribution of smallpox-infected blankets to the Indians at a peace conference in 1763 after attacks by Pontiac; and the forced resettlement of Cherokee, Creeks, and other Indians under Andrew Jackson, known as the Trail of Tears, during the 1830s.

21. Another aspect of the Enlightenment, however, was the idea of individual freedom, whereby a person was no longer subject to the dictates of church or state authorities. Private property, not communal living, was the ideal for some liberal thinkers—clearly in opposition to missionary goals of a cooperative society. See D. A. Brading, *The First America: The Spanish Monarchy, Creole Patriots, and the Liberal State, 1492–1867* (New York: Cambridge University Press, 1991).

22. See Iris H. W. Engstrand, "The Eighteenth Century Enlightenment Comes to Spanish California," *Southern California Quarterly,* 80 (Spring 1998): 3–30.

23. See José Mariano Moziño, *Noticias de Nutka: An Account of Nootka Sound in 1792,* ed. and trans. Iris H. W. Engstrand (Seattle: University of Washington Press, 1991).

24. Donald C. Cutter, *California in 1792: A Spanish Naval Visit* (Norman: University of Oklahoma Press, 1990), 144.

25. Philip Wayne Powell, *Tree of Hate: Propaganda and Prejudices Affecting United States Relations with the Hispanic World* (New York: Basic Books, 1971), 25.

Iris H. W. Engstrand, professor and chair of history at the University of San Diego, is the author of numerous books and articles on Spain's role in the New World, including *San Diego: California's Cornerstone* (1980); *Spanish Scientists in the New World* (1981); and *Quest for Empire: Spanish Settlement in the Southwest* (1996).

From *OAH Magazine of History,* Summer 2000. Copyright © 2000 by Organization of American Historians. Reprinted by permission via the Copyright Clearance Center.

America, the Atlantic, and Global Consumer Demand, 1500–1800

CAROLE SHAMMAS

The Atlantic migration of Europeans and Africans to America and the commercial activities associated with it created an economy that for the first time in history could be called global. For many years, historians have relied upon the word *mercantilism* to capture this international world. Over the last decade, as research has focused more intently on ties between early modern consumers, producers, and distributors in America, Europe, and Africa, the concept of an *Atlantic world* economic community has eclipsed the mercantilism paradigm. More recently, scholarly voices have cautioned against portraying the commerce of the Atlantic as a separate economic world unto itself and ignoring the true *globalism* of trade in the period. In discussing the evolving conceptualization of the early modern economy, it is important not only to recognize the commercial growth that occurred during the period, but also to take into account the demographic and environmental changes that were consequences of that growth.

The mercantilist explanation for what kept the early modern economy running is quite straightforward. The kingdoms of Spain, Portugal, Great Britain, and France as well as the Dutch Republic each sought to accumulate wealth through advantageous overseas trading arrangements and colonies, while thwarting the ambitions of their rivals to do the same. America played the role of colony. When I use the term America here, I do not just mean the thirteen colonies that bolted from the British Empire in 1776, but rather the entire Western hemisphere. For nearly all of the period under consideration, the area that became the U.S. had no separate identity. The thirteen colonies were neither the only colonies nor the only British colonies, and in the view of the rest of the world, none of the thirteen were considered as the most important in the New World. That honor would probably go to the sugar islands of the West Indies or, depending on the century, either the viceroyalty of Peru or New Spain, the main sites of silver mines. The scrappy, slave-trading, rum-running, smuggling-prone merchant communities that sprang up in towns like Boston, Newport, New York, Philadelphia, and Charleston might command center stage from the perspective of the national history of the U.S., but they contained just a small proportion of the cast of thousands who developed new markets in America.

Though the mercantilist paradigm was a global one, the most common visualization of it in U.S. history textbooks featured a map of Atlantic commerce. This map illustrated the "Triangular Trade" whereby eastern American colonies furnished raw materials, western Africa provided the labor force to produce the raw materials, and the imperial center, often referred to as the Mother Country, shipped manufactured goods to both. Historians pointed to inequities in this system as an important cause of the American Revolution.

Today, this schema has not so much been repudiated as reinterpreted. The most salient economic characteristic of the period remains the growth in overseas commerce, but the term mercantilism is now used infrequently and the marketplace desires of individuals—especially on the consumption side—receive much greater credit for effecting change. Students are encouraged to think less about European empires struggling for control of the major sea lanes and colonial bases to achieve favorable trading balances and more about the Atlantic as a meaningful economic entity where coastal inhabitants from all continents exchanged people and goods without always honoring imperial boundaries.[1]

To Atlantic scholars, it is not just a European or European transplant story. Transatlantic migrants were three times more likely to be from Africa than Europe during the period[2] and as a result historians now have to take account of the strategies of African kingdoms and institutions in the making of the slave trade.[3] Indian nations are not only relevant as providers of furs and skins and consumers of manufactures and alcohol but as the introducers of new agricultural commodities and, in some regions of America, a prime source of labor and cultural identity. The persistence with which colonists fixed their gaze across the Atlantic rather than across the American continent may have less to do with their attachment to Europe and more to do with the ability of Indian nations to contain colonial settlements to coastal areas, up until the latter eighteenth century.

The availability of land and natural resources in America enabled the collection or production of a wide variety of commodities—furs, lumber, cod, and wheat, for example. It was, however, the demand for two categories of goods that stands out as being most responsible for the continuing flow of capital, labor, and governmental military services across the Atlantic: groceries and silver.

Contemporaries called the tropical dietary items that acted as energizers and appetite appeasers for the population on either side of the Atlantic and in Asia *groceries*. They included tobacco, sugar, sugar byproducts such as molasses and rum, and caffeine drinks, namely tea, coffee, and cocoa. America became the prime site for growing all of these crops except for tea and the enslaved migrants from Africa became the prime cultivators. Tobacco and the beans to make cocoa were indigenous to America while others—coffee and sugar—were transferred over to take advantage of the low cost of land and the bound labor force. Because many of these plantation commodities were thought of as luxuries—that is, not essential for human survival—their central role in the expansion of the world economy has been often overlooked.[4] That is a misconception, however. By the late seventeenth century, the Dutch and the English dominated the carrying trade over the Atlantic. 74 percent of the value of imports coming into Amsterdam and more than 85 percent coming into London from colonies in America consisted of tobacco and sugar products.[5] Portraits, aristocratic and more middling class, as in the household shown here, often displayed the paraphernalia—tea service, porcelain tea cups, sugar bowls, clay pipes, snuff boxes—associated with the consumption of these tropical groceries. By the eighteenth century, the laboring classes also used these groceries on a regular basis.[6]

Initially, western European governments gave little encouragement to the consumption of such commodities. In fact royal authorities often disparaged their production and use, considering them either harmful or trivial. Instead, support for the commodities came from transatlantic merchant-planter alliances along with consumers living in maritime communities and urban centers. Once the revenues from the import duties began pouring into the treasury, however, the royals changed their minds. These seemingly frivolous raw materials altered the dietary habits of the Atlantic community and ultimately the world. They were responsible for the spread of the plantation complex,[7] a system of production that would become extremely controversial in the nineteenth-century U.S. Taking a specific commodity such as tobacco and tracing the diffusion of consumption and the transformation in production and distribution to meet demand has emerged as an important way to study Atlantic history in the early modern period.

Even the way historians portray the relationship between the commercial system and the American Revolution has been transformed by the Atlantic world approach. Americans reacted to the taxation of sugar products, tea, and British manufactured goods, it has been argued, as consumers. Colonists from disparate provinces with divergent interests could all relate to problems connected to the consumption of the empire's goods. Their mass consumption led to their mass mobilization: resisting the Sugar, Stamp, and Townshend Acts, boycotting tea, pledging nonimportation, and ultimately declaring independence.[8] Rather than viewing the American Revolution as the point at which the colonies threw off mercantilism and embraced economic liberalism,[9] students are now encouraged to regard the market principles of demand and supply as representing the colonial status quo. The colonists, in this telling of the story, mobilized in order to halt any heavy handed imperial state meddling that would turn back the clock.

The Atlantic world concept has much to recommend it as a way to understand the global economy in which the U.S. came to be a dominant player. The Atlantic as the supplier of population for America cannot be denied. Migration from other parts of the globe during these years amounted to little more than a trickle. The dramatic transformation of Atlantic commerce is also obvious. For thousands of years prior to the mid-fifteenth century, existing evidence suggests that nothing ventured far out into the Atlantic aside from a few Viking expeditions and occasional fishing vessels, while in the next three hundred years global commerce came to be directed and conducted from nations and cities bordering that ocean. And so it remained until the later twentieth century when the emergence of the Pacific Rim, the European Union, and NAFTA suggest that a realignment is now taking place.[10]

Where the Atlantic world paradigm falls short, in the view of some scholars, is in its poor integration of Asia, home to two-thirds of the world's population, into the early modern network of trade. They argue that western Europe and even parts of the Americas and Africa had relationships with Asia that were as or more important than their relationships with one another.[11] The choice then is whether we should think in terms of two separate worlds operating in this period, the Asian world and the demographically much smaller Atlantic world of which America was a part, or whether we should consider the east-west connection significant enough to argue for a fully integrated global economy.

Those arguing the latter position would point out that capturing the East Indian and Chinese market loomed much larger in the minds of Europeans than anything having to do with America or Africa and that America owed its "discovery" to that preoccupation. Columbus's and his sponsors' stated purpose was not the discovery of a New World but a north-west passage to the "Indies," by which they meant East Asia. Just as the first Portuguese attempts to sail around Africa had been sparked by the hope to establish trade with India, about the only reason for undertaking voyages to the Americas, until Cortes defeated the Aztecs in 1519, was to find East Asia. Even after Cortes's conquest, which led to an influx of sword wielding military adventurers seeking tribute, a northwest passage project proved much more attractive to merchant investors than any military expedition. The picture changed once again, however, with the discovery of rich silver mines in America. Silver is the other major product that most directly linked America with the global economy and, in terms of chronology, it came before the groceries associated with the plantation complex.

The old histories of mercantilism centered their story on the infusion of Spanish empire silver and gold, the rampant inflation in Europe it produced, and its role in the underdevelopment of Spain and its colonies. The new version of this story considers inflation less of a problem and concentrates on the enormity of Chinese demand for silver, which was needed both to expand its monetary system and to manufacture silver wares. Its willingness to offer advantageous terms of trade for those

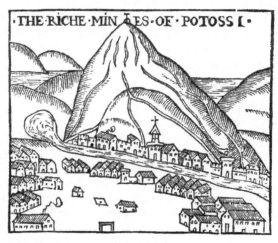

Figure 1 "The ritche mines of Potosi" from *The discouerie and conquest of the prouinces of Peru, and the nauigation in the South Sea, along that coast* [electronic resource] by Agustin de Zarate, (London: [John Charlewood, William How, and John Kingston for] Richard Ihones, Febru 6. 1581.)

sought-after commodities created a global commercial network in which America and Africa supplied the bullion and foodstuffs to pay for Asian commodities distributed largely in European ships.[12]

It was the mining of precious metals that kept European kings and commoners interested in the Americas during that awkward half century or so between the last conquistadors and the first big boom in sugar and tobacco cultivation that ushered in the American plantation complex. Not until the discovery of silver at Potosi in the Peruvian vice-royalty during the 1540s did the Spanish Crown, as distinct from private adventurers and religious orders, make a commitment to govern America directly. Forcing Indians to extract the valuable ore [see a contemporary's depiction of the Potosi community in Figure 1], every year the Spaniards shipped over 50 tons of silver abroad. They sent it across the Atlantic where their European creditors used it in the Chinese trade or they transported it across the Pacific to Manila, Spain's east Asian entrepôt. Why in the 1570s did Sir Francis Drake, the famous Elizabethan privateer, venture into the Pacific and circumnavigate the globe? Pure love of adventure? Or could the mines of Peru have had something to do with it? Without the lure of these Atlantic and Pacific fleets full of bullion most English, French, and Dutch exploration and colonization expeditions would never have materialized.

Western European nations granted monopolies to trading companies, the big businesses of the day, to compete for Asian commodities. Some were dietary products like Chinese tea and spices from what is now known as Indonesia, but others were manufactured goods such as Chinese porcelain and silk and Indian cotton cloth.[13] All of these goods became wildly popular in Europe and America. In fact, in 1720 the British government forbade the importation of cotton cloth because it weakened demand for light woolens, their major industrial product. The Chinese refused to allow western European trading companies to establish permanent facilities in their port cities, so western Europeans, first the Portuguese and then a wider international community, built a commercial center at Macao on the west banks of the Pearl, the river which leads to the Chinese port of Canton. Not until later in the nineteenth century did Hong Kong, on the east side of the Pearl River, overtake Macao. Both cities remained under the control of western Europeans until the end of the twentieth century. Manila, the Spanish entrepot, also spent most of its history as a colony. Originally, however, these outposts had been set up because it was the only way westerners could obtain Chinese products.

Consumer demand for East Indian commodities grew over the course of the eighteenth century. In an important departure from the past and one that foreshadowed nineteenth-century developments, Europeans learned how to mass produce "knock-offs" of east and south Asian cloth, furniture, and pottery. It was the manufacturing of Indian-like cotton fabric in Britain that launched the Industrial Revolution. After independence, as the American merchant community regrouped, those on the Atlantic seaboard began competing with their former partners for the lucrative China trade and manufacturing "knock-offs" of their own. Using Hawaii as an entrepot, the U.S. also expanded Pacific commerce.[14] By 1800 it was Britain's biggest competitor in the China trade and later in cotton cloth manufacturing.[15]

The three different approaches to understanding the place of pre-1800 America in the international economy each have their strengths and weaknesses. The mercantilism paradigm, emphasizing as it does imperial rivalries, is global in scope but relies almost exclusively on the machinations of European royal governments to explain commercial expansion and colonization. The proponents of the Atlantic world view assert that the use of said ocean as a highway for migrants, capital, and commodities represented the period's biggest change in world trade patterns and that consumer demand of the societies bordering the ocean had much to do with that change. Assuming, however, that a self-contained commercial system existed within the boundaries of that ocean, critics contend, means leaving out more than two-thirds of the consumers of the earth, including those in China, India, and southeast Asia, producers of some of the world's most sought-after commodities. Better integration of such important elements as the silver trade to China, the boom in Indian cotton textiles, and the commercial history of the settlements and islands of the Pacific is a task currently underway, even if the exact importance of each of these elements in the overall picture has yet to be ascertained.

Regardless of the approach, it seems clear that the economic order that took shape after the European discovery of America

Table 1　World Population (in Millions)

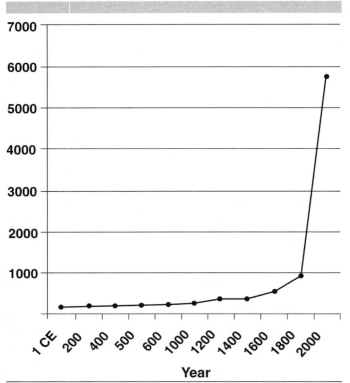

Source: Figures derived from Colin McEvedy and Richard Jones, *Atlas of World Population History* (New York: Penguin, 1978). 342.

redistributed unprecedented numbers of people to satisfy a growing global demand for its resources and products that in turn kept more labor and capital flowing in to the so-called new world. Overseas trade has been identified as the leading sector in economic growth during this period. Even in well established European nations, growth depended primarily on the expansion of the overseas trade sector.[16] A major impetus for the adoption of the U.S. Constitution was the belief that survival as a nation depended on overseas commerce and that its success required a strong central government.

If the origins of world economic growth are linked to this global commerce, other forms of growth that have been associated with the discovery of America appear to be more problematic. The sizeable Atlantic migration proved disastrous for the indigenous population, primarily because of its susceptibility to new diseases brought by invaders or simply merchants who did no more than trade from their sailing vessels anchored offshore.[17] Despite the staggering losses of Indian life in the Americas, the demographic record suggests growth in global population from the time of discovery onward. At first, as Table 1 shows, the ascent was modest and, although the detail here is not sufficient to indicate it, population numbers are believed to have stalled in the seventeenth century. Over the course of the eighteenth century, however, world population is estimated to have jumped by 50 percent, the slope slanting upward ever more steeply thereafter and continuing its dramatic ascent through the twentieth century.

In the Americas, succeeding generations of Atlantic migrants and their descendants enjoyed high fertility rates in their new low density environment. Concurrently, Europe's population,

despite the out-migration, began to climb, as did China's. Some of this "old world" growth has been attributed to the transfer of "new world" foodstuffs such as potatoes, sweet potatoes, peanuts, and corn (maize) as well as American sales of wheat and rice in European markets.[18] While in North America the bounty in foodstuffs and the accompanying high fertility never produced a Malthusian reaction, in certain parts of nineteenth-century Europe and in China it eventually did. The denser population put greater pressure on natural resources. The environmental repercussions of the human species spreading into previously uninhabited parts of the globe is a fascinating subject that deserves a great deal more attention. Nowhere might the investigation be more worthwhile than in America during the period under consideration here.

Notes

1. The April 2004 issue [volume 18 no. 3] of the *OAH Magazine of History,* entitled "The Atlantic World" and edited by Alison Games, takes this approach and focuses on three themes in the Atlantic: disease, commodities, and migration. The issue contains references to the many books and articles that have been written on early modern Atlantic communities in the past two decades.

2. James Horn and Philip D. Morgan, "Settlers and Slaves: European and African Migrations to Early Modern British America," Elizabeth Mancke and Carole Shammas, eds., *Creation of the British Atlantic World* (Baltimore: Johns Hopkins University Press, forthcoming).

3. John Thornton. *Africa and Africans in the Making of the Atlantic World, 1400–1800.* 2nd ed.(New York: Cambridge University Press, 1998).

4. Immanuel Wallerstein, *The Modern World System: Capitalist Agriculture and the Origins of the European World-Economy in the Sixteenth Century* (New York: Academic Press. 1974), 41–42.

5. Victor Enthoven. "An Assessment of Dutch Transatlantic Commerce, 1585–1817." *Riches from Atlantic Commerce: Dutch Transatlantic Trade and Shipping, 1585–1817,* edited by Johannes Postma and Victor Enthoven (Leiden: Brill. 2003), 438: Nuala Zahedieh, "Overseas Expansion and Trade in the Seventeenth Century," in Nicholas Canny, ed., *Oxford History of the British Empire: Origins of Empire* (Oxford: Oxford University Press, 1998), 410.

6. Carole Shammas, *The Preindustrial Consumer in England and America* (Oxford: Clarendon Press of Oxford University Press, 1990).

7. Philip D. Curtin, *The Rise and Fall of the Plantation Complex: Essays in Atlantic History* (New York: Cambridge University Press, revised ed. 1998). Sidney Mintz recounts this process in *Sweetness and Power: The Place of Sugar in Modern History* (New York: Viking Press. 1985).

8. T. H. Breen, *The Marketplace of Revolution: How Consumer Politics Shaped American Independence* (New York: Oxford University Press. 2004).

9. Economic liberalism is used here in its nineteenth-century sense of belief in market forces of demand and supply rather than governmental policies directing production and consumption.

10. The later twentieth century witnessed a significant geographic shift of world trade towards the Pacific Rim.

11. Peter A. Coclanis. "Drang Nach Osten: Bernard Bailyn. the World-Island, and the Idea of Atlantic History," *Journal of World History* 13 (2002): 169–182.

12. Dennis O. Flynn and Arturo Giratdez. "Cycles of Silver: Global Economic Unity through the Mid-Eighteenth Century," *Journal of World History* 13 (2002): 391–428, and Enthoven, "An Assessment of Dutch Transatlantic commerce," 435–6 refer to the Dutch use of American silver for East Indies trade.

13. John E. Wills, Jr., "European Consumption and Asian Production in the Seventeenth and Eighteenth Centuries," in John Brewer and Roy Porter eds. *Consumption and the World of Goods* (London: Routledge, 1993), 133–47.

14. David Igler, "Diseased Goods: Global Exchanges in the Eastern Pacific Basin, 1770–1850." *American Historical Review* 109 (2004): 693–719.

15. See the statistics in Louis Dermigny, *La Chine et L'Occident: Le Commerce a Canton au XVIIIe Siecle 1719-1833* tome 11 (Paris: S.E.V.P.E.N., 1964), 521-528, 532, 539, 735, and 744 that show the scope of America's entry into the tea trade from the 1780s on and also its supplying of silver and cotton.

16. Robert C. Allen, "Progress and Poverty in Early Modern Europe."*Economic History Review* 56 (2003): 431: Kevin H. O'Rourke and Jeffrey G. Williamson, "After Columbus: Explaining Europe's Overseas Trade Boom, 1500–1800." *Journal of Economic History* 62 (2002): 417–62. The latter article asks a number of good questions about the reasons for the boom in trade but lacks the evidence to prove its central contention that transport costs did not decline over the three hundred year period.

17. Igler, "Diseased Goods."

18. Flynn and Giraldez, "Cycles of Silver," concerning the effects of the transfer of maize, sweet potatoes, and peanuts over the Pacific.

Bibliographical Note

Classic treatments of the emergence of global trade include J. H. Parry's beautifully succinct *The Establishment of the European Hegemony 1415–1715. Trade and Exploration in the Age of the Renaissance* (New York: Harper and Row. Torchbooked., 1961), Immanuel Wallerstein's three comprehensive volumes on the modern world-system, *The Modern World-System: Capitalist Agriculture and the Origins of the European World-Economy in the Sixteenth Century; The Modern World-System II: Mercantilism and the Consolidation of the European World-Economy, 1600–1750;* and *The Modern World-System III, The Second Era of Great Expansion of the Capitalist World-Economy, 1730–1840s* (New York: Academic Press. 1974–1989), and Fernand Braudel's magisterial *Civilization and Capitalism III: The Perspective of the World,* tr. Sian Reynolds (Berkeley: University of California Press, 1992. orig. pub. in French 1979).

The *OAH Magazine of History* 18 (April 2004) issue edited by Alison Games is an excellent guide to the ever-growing literature on the Atlantic World approach particularly as it relates to the area that became the United States. The Atlantic Seminar at Harvard University maintains a web site, <http://www.fas.harvard.edu/~athantic/>, that features recent research in the field and has links to other sites of interest. In addition to the Thornton book on the African Atlantic cited above, the existing ship manifests recording the African migration across the Atlantic are now available for study on CD, David Eltis et al. *The Transatlantic Slave Trade: A Database on CD-Rom* (New York: Cambridge University Press, 1999). The most exhaustive examination of transatlantic commerce is for Spain in the sixteenth and seventeenth centuries, Huguette Chaunu and Pierre Chaunu, *Seville et l'Atlantique (1504–1640)* 8 vols. (Paris: Colin. 1955–1959). The phenomenal rise in consumer demand for groceries and the growth of the plantation complex is documented in Curtin, Mintz, Enthoven, Zahedieh, and Shammas mentioned above. For those seeking a regional breakdown of Anglo-American trade, see John J. McCusker and Russell R. Menard, *The Economy of British America 1607–1789* (Chapel Hill: University of North Carolina Press, 2nd ed. 1991). Breen's book, above, relates the American Revolution to the Atlantic trade boom.

The need to take a global rather than an Atlantic world perspective, as expressed in Coclanis' essay cited above, comes largely from studying the work on monetary flows, Asian commerce, and the Pacific Rim. Dennis O. Flynn, in the article he co-authored above and in a series of other books and articles, has made the strongest case that the demand for silver in China created an integrated global economy both Atlantic and Pacific. In addition to the works on Chinese commerce and products by Dermigny and Wills cited above, a number of volumes have recently appeared confirming the size, allure, and sophistication of Chinese, Indian, and southeast Asian production during the period 1500 to 1800. Coclanis' essay cites many of them. Kenneth Pomeranz and Steven Topik, *The World that Trade Created: Society. Culture, and the World Economy: 1400 to the Present* (Armonk, NY: M.E. Sharpe. 1999) is designed for a general audience that picks up on that theme among others.

Colin McEvedy and Richard Jones, *Atlas of World Population History* (New York: Penguin, 1978) remains the best source for world population figures. The USC-Huntington Library Institute for Early Modern Studies has a new web site <http://www.usc.edu/dept/LAS/history/emsi/> which offers online bibliographies with a world perspective on specific topics. Finally, <http://www.h-net.org> is the web address for H-Net which features numerous networks for different fields in history, among them h-world and h-atlantic. These networks offer teaching resources, discussions, and reviews.

CAROLE SHAMMAS holds the John R. Hubbard Chair in History at the University of Southern California. Her most recent book is *A History of Household Government in America* (2002).

I would like to thank the OAH/AP referees, and my colleagues John E. Wills Jr., Ayse Rorlich, and Darryl Holter for their comments and assistance in writing this essay.

The Birth of America

Struggling from One Peril to the Next, the Jamestown Settlers Planted the Seeds of the Nation's Spirit

LEWIS LORD

"Virginia, Earth's only Paradise!" So declared Michael Drayton, poet laureate of England, in a merry ballad marking the departure of three ships crammed with men anticipating fast fortunes in the New World. The prospective colonists set sail from London just before Christmas of 1606, bound for the Chesapeake Bay. It was the last Christmas most of them would ever know.

By the following August, when their Jamestown settlement was barely three months old, almost every day brought a new death.

September found half of those 105 original settlers in their graves. "Our men were destroyed with cruell diseases such as Swellings, Flixes, Burning Fevers, and by warres," a survivor reported, "but for the most part they died of meere famine."

Thirteen years before the Mayflower brought Pilgrims to Massachusetts, the Virginia colony served as England's toehold on a continent eventually inhabited and governed mostly by English-speaking people. History books list Jamestown, founded in 1607, as America's first permanent English settlement, and its 400th anniversary will be celebrated this year with festivals, exhibits, and commemorative coins, plus a springtime visit by Queen Elizabeth II. But that success in Virginia was not the piece of cake it first was billed to be. For years, Jamestown was a deadly fiasco, periodically in peril and ultimately revived and enriched by cultivation of a habit-forming weed and the toil of indentured whites and enslaved blacks.

In Europe's race to colonize the New World, England started late. For nearly a century after 1492, the English watched with envy as Spain dominated much of the hemisphere that Columbus discovered. In 1587, two decades after the Spanish settled St. Augustine in Florida, the English abandoned their insular ways and planted 110 men, women, and children on Roanoke Island off present-day North Carolina. When a supply ship returned later, all were gone. Even now, no one knows what became of that "Lost Colony."

Sir Walter Raleigh, the favorite courtier of Elizabeth I, reportedly lost 40,000 pounds on the venture. His reward, granted in advance, was knighthood and the Virgin Queen's permission to name the new land Virginia, in her honor. They envisioned Virginia as every place north of Mexico that the English could take and occupy.

Despite the costs and setbacks, pressures mounted for another expedition. English traders imagined colonists producing wine and olive oil, harvesting timber, and uncovering gold. Others saw Virginia as an ideal home for the poor. England's population was rising rapidly, but jobs were stagnant. Ministers noted that God ordered man to multiply and fill the Earth. What better place to do so than the vast and—as they perceived it—empty continent across the sea?

Pacific path. In 1606, several well-to-do Englishmen laid plans for what would become the Jamestown colony. With the blessings of James I, Elizabeth's successor, they formed the Virginia Company, a joint stock company in which investors, known as "adventurers," bought stock worth $3,000 a share in today's currency.

Encouraging investors and settlers alike was the popular notion that there existed on America's Atlantic coast a river within reach of the Pacific—the fabled short cut to Asia sought by Columbus and countless other explorers. Other Englishmen who bet their money or their lives may have seen the London play *Eastward Ho!* describing customs across the sea. It reported native Virginians gathering diamonds by the seashore and using chamber pots of pure gold.

In December of 1606, colonists and crew members squeezed into their three tiny ships docked in London. Within days of departure, men were bickering and seasick from storms and winds that left the Susan Constant, the Godspeed, and the Discovery anchored a month in the English Channel.

Collegiality remained in short supply as the expedition entered the Atlantic. On the flagship Susan Constant, an outspoken commoner named John Smith annoyed a higher-up and was accused of plotting insurrection. He was confined below deck, sentenced to death at the age of 27 once on shore.

Secret seven. On a stop at Nevis in the West Indies, Smith's foes stood ready to hang him. But the skipper delayed the execution, wanting more evidence before giving his passenger the rope. The young captain's luck improved further when the expedition entered the Chesapeake. The four-month ocean crossing ended with the voyagers dropping anchor on April 26, 1607, near the windswept dunes of a Virginia site they called Cape Henry. There the ship commanders opened a sealed box and pulled out a secret document: the company's instructions for starting a colony.

Read aloud was a list identifying seven members of a ruling council, the settlers who would run the colony. The first six names belonged to men of social prominence. The seventh was the bumptious prisoner in the hold. Unknowingly, someone in London had saved the man who, as much as anyone, would save Jamestown.

The company's other instructions could have been penned by a modern PR executive. Among the do's and don'ts: "Have Great Care not to Offend the naturals [the American Indians]." Don't show fear, weakness, or sickness. And, to keep investors investing and settlers settling, never mention anything unpleasant in letters sent home.

For the moment, there was nothing unpleasant to report. One man who went ashore marveled at the "faire meddowes and goodly tall Trees." But for the next 15 years, the English blundered their way from one calamity to another, beginning with the choice of where to settle. Seeking a spot easy to defend, the colonists picked a marshy peninsula 2 miles long and a mile wide that jutted into the river they named the James, 50 miles southeast of present-day Richmond. They erected a trading post, a storehouse, and a church, sprinkled the grounds with tents made of tattered sailcloth, and named the creation James Town.

No one sensed the lethal implications of the low site with its brackish water and mosquito-thick swamps. Nor did the settlers realize how much food had spoiled in the overlong voyage from London. Had they known, they might have used those days in May to plant a garden instead of scratching for gold. Nor did anyone dig a well, even though every low tide was "full of slime and filth." That summer half the colony died. "God (being angrie with us) plagued us with such famin and sicknes that the living were scarce able to bury the dead," Smith later wrote.

In the captain's view, God was "angrie" because too few of the settlers were willing to work. A third of the colonists were "gentlemen" who, by definition, did no manual labor. Some of the Jamestown gents no doubt did grab a shovel or ax, but many, in Smith's words, did nothing but "complain, curse, and despaire."

Faulty notions. All along, the danger of Indian attack competed with disease and hunger as the No. 1 threat to the colony's survival. On their first night in Virginia, two colonists were wounded by arrows shot by painted warriors hiding behind the Cape Henry dunes. Days later, however, colonists and Indians were dining together on corn bread and water, seemingly confirming the English notion that the natives lacked only a civilizing influence. Thus the settlement that sprouted at Jamestown did so without a protective wall of logs around it. Yet, within a month, hundreds of Indians attacked the outpost, killing two settlers. A strong wall was built quickly, forming a triangular fort.

The American Indians, the English believed, would quit being "savages"—their usual word for Indians—once they learned English manners. But Smith was convinced that Englishmen, too, had a lot to learn: The natives, he wrote, were "our enemies, whom we neither knew nor understood." The English even thought Indians were born white, with skin darkened by paints and dyes.

The Indians likewise guessed wrong about the English. Initially, they did not deem the settlers a threat. Powhatan, the region's powerful chief, expected the intruders to either die off or leave. When their numbers were small, he seemed pleased to swap furs and food for pots and tools. But as ship after ship brought new settlers, including a few women, the chief sensed ominous change. "Your coming hither is not for trade," he suspected, "but to invade my people, and possess my country."

Neither side felt secure. Some mornings found the Indians bringing corn to the settlement. On other days, they peppered the fort with arrows and picked off settlers who ventured outside its walls. In one instance, seven settlers in a boat spotted several native women on a riverbank. When the squaws returned their smiles, the men scrambled onto land, only to be confronted by warriors who had been hiding. Six of the seven managed to rush back to the boat. The straggler was stripped naked and tied to a stake, around which a fire was set. His tormentors used mussel shells to saw off his fingers and toes and skin him. He died as they danced around the flames.

Another ambush landed Smith in the most famous predicament of his life. While ashore during a trip up the Chickahominy River, he was surrounded and captured by hundreds of warriors.

Christmas of 1607 found him being led from village to village as a showpiece. Finally he was brought to a large lodge where a man in a raccoon-skin robe with the tails still attached was sitting. The man was Powhatan, chief of a confederacy of two dozen tribes and 200 villages spread over much of what is now eastern Virginia.

Smith in time would give two very different accounts of what occurred next. The first version, written soon after the event, had the two men discussing their intentions. The chief invited the captain "to live with him upon his river" and engage in trade, Smith wrote, and "this request I promised to performe." Smith, according to this account, then was set free. No role was mentioned for Powhatan's daughter Pocahontas, then 10 or 11 years old.

In the more celebrated record, penned many years later, Smith's head was placed on a stone and men with clubs were told "to beate out his braines." But "Pocahontas the King's dearest daughter . . . got his head in her armes, and laid her owne upon his to save him from death: whereat the Emperour was contented he should live."

Whatever Pocahontas's role, her father declared Smith his friend and set him free. That friendship, for a while, strengthened Smith's ability to barter for the food that time and again kept Jamestown from going under. With an eye on the benefits of trade, Powhatan seemed to crave peace. "Why should you take by force from us that which you can obtain by love?" the chief asked during one of the several visits Smith would make in the months ahead. "Why should you destroy us who have provided you with food?"

But the relationship between captain and chief was fickle. Whenever they met, Powhatan asked Smith to prove his friendship by leaving his pistol outside. Smith, wary of being overtaken, insisted it's OK for a friend to come armed. At one point, over the objections of Smith, the English gave Powhatan a copper crown. They were delighted when he allowed it to be placed on his head, because it meant he now was a subject of King James. Once the proud chief recognized the symbolism, he ordered another of his intermittent cutoffs in trade.

And kindness, Smith believed, was not to be wasted on savages. After his men beat back a waterborne ambush, he ordered the attackers' canoes destroyed. He relented when the Indians agreed to deliver 400 baskets of corn at harvest time. When they failed to keep their word, Smith started burning their houses. The natives quickly complied.

From his legendary close call at Powhatan's place, Smith returned to Jamestown and instantly found his life again at risk. For letting settlers be ambushed and killed, council leaders had decided he too should die. Suddenly, a supply ship from London arrived. Its commander, Christopher Newport, the same skipper who had saved Smith's neck in the West Indies, took charge and set the captain free.

No free meals. Five days after Newport's relief ship brought 80 fresh settlers into the colony, one of the newcomers accidentally set a fire that raced from one thatched structure to another, destroying almost the entire village plus the new provisions. Again, food from the Indians helped the settlers hang on till the next supply vessel appeared in the spring.

Summer 1608 found the colonists sick, lame, and complaining about the "silly president," the vain John Ratcliffe, for whom a presidential palace was being built. When Ratcliffe's term expired in September, Smith took over. He promptly scrapped the palace and dispensed a dose of military discipline. "He that will not worke shall not eate," Smith declared as he set the indolent to cutting timber and sawing boards for shelters that would help the colony endure the hard winter. Any toiler who cursed risked the penalty of cold water poured down his sleeve.

Fears of another disaster erupted with the discovery that the entire corn supply had been ruined, either from rotting or by rats. Smith halted all work in Jamestown and divided the colonists into three groups. He sent one bunch upriver to hunt game until the next supply ship arrived. Another went downriver to live on fish. The largest group got by on oysters from the Chesapeake shore.

But nothing Smith could do would give the Virginia Company what it wanted most: gold and a route to the Orient. That summer, the company ordered a new charter with "one able and absolute governor"—not a turn-taking president—serving as Jamestown's boss. Smith was demoted to running a remote lookout garrison. But before that change took effect, an accidental gunpowder explosion burned him so badly that he took a boat to England in October 1609, never to return.

Along with the leadership shakeup came a nine-ship expedition to Virginia, the largest yet, with 500 settlers on board. Since the new governor, Lord De La Warr (for whom Delaware is named), was not ready to leave, a deputy took command. Off the West Indies, a hurricane struck, sinking one ship. Seven of the eight remaining vessels limped into Jamestown just before Smith left for London.

As for the eighth ship, Sea Venture, Shakespeare would write his *Tempest* from accounts of its bout with the hurricane. For months, the flagship lay wrecked on Bermuda. From its ruin, survivors jury-rigged a new vessel. The deputy governor, Thomas Gates, was board in May 1610 as it sailed up the Chesapeake Bay. What he found was one of American history's most dreadful horrors.

Survivors called it "the Starving Time." Sensing weakness after Smith's departure, Powhatan had told his subjects to withhold corn. Food dwindled to nothing that winter, and diseases broke out. The famished ate horses and dogs, then cats and rats, and finally the leather of their boots. One man killed, salted, and ate his wife. Of the 500 colonists alive when Smith left in the fall, barely 60 lasted into spring.

Gates decided to shut the settlement and ship everyone to England. They were 15 miles down the James when up the river came a rowboat with wondrous news: The governor, Lord De La Warr, en route from England with 150 men and ample supplies, was in the bay. Three days after it perished, the Jamestown colony was alive again.

His lordship took a whiff of the town he revived, declared it "unwholesome," and ordered a cleanup. Yet troubles persisted. Like many, De La Warr took sick almost as soon as he arrived. Ten months later, he fled to England in search of a cure.

When his successor, Sir Thomas Dale, reached Jamestown in May 1611, the colonists were at "their daily and usuall workes, bowling in the streetes." To eradicate such idleness, the company imposed a severe set of rules solemnly entitled Lawes Divine, Morall and Martiall. The draconian regulations had drumbeats starting and ending each workday, with whippings for latecomers and early quitters. A single incident of blasphemy merited the lash. A second meant a needle through the tongue, and a third meant death. Execution was prescribed for thieves, runaways, and adulterers. Dale enforced the rules mercilessly, even having a pregnant seamstress lashed for making shirts too short.

Far more useful was Dale's decision to junk what amounted to communism. Since Jamestown's start, all land was held and worked in common, with rations distributed evenly from a central storehouse. There was no incentive for an individual to work harder. Dale assigned colonists plots and let them grow for their own benefit.

It was on one of those 3-acre plots that John Rolfe tinkered with tobacco and transformed Jamestown. The English regarded the tobacco grown in Virginia as much too coarse to compete in the growing world market with the sweet-tasting leaf the Spanish raised in the West Indies. Rolfe took Indies seed, combined it in 1612 with the local variety, and produced a leaf that was smooth to smoke and easy to raise.

In 1614, he sent his first shipment to England. Soon, London was importing tens of thousands of pounds of Virginia leaf a year. Virtually every clearing in the colony was planted with tobacco.

Rolfe also made a decision in his personal life that helped ease Jamestown's relationship with the Indians, which had deteriorated since Smith's exit. In dealing with natives, Smith relied on threats and an occasional hut-burning to show toughness. His successors favored massacres. In one nighttime attack, the English killed 15 men, burned their village, and captured and murdered their queen and her children. Indians responded with attacks of their own. Amid the strife, the English took a hostage—not an ordinary hostage, but Powhatan's daughter Pocahontas. The Indian attacks subsided. While the princess remained in custody, Rolfe got Dale's permission to marry her. In April 1614—the year he first sent tobacco to London—Rolfe and Pocahontas wed in the Jamestown church. In deference to his daughter, the chief would fight no more.

Thanks to Rolfe's tobacco and Powhatan's peace, Jamestown began to thrive, as did England's newer settlements along the

James. The colony's population doubled in 1619 when more than 1,200 settlers came ashore. Many paid their way and got 50 acres in return. But most were indentured servants who worked payless for years in exchange for eventual freedom and a share of profits or a piece of land. Ninety were "young and uncorrupt maids," sent as wives for settlers.

That year, amid the sudden prosperity, popular government made its start. The company told its governor to abolish arbitrary rule, usher in English common law and due process, and form a representative assembly. Paradoxically, that also was the year a ship docked at Jamestown with 20 men and women from Africa—the beginning of the slave trade.

When Powhatan died in 1618, the "married peace" died as well. His subjects were retreating to the west, yielding their cornfields to the tobacco-driven colonists. The new chief, Opechancanough, decided the English had encroached enough. On Good Friday of March 1622, his warriors surprised and massacred 347 settlers. The survivors swore to "destroy them who sought to destroy us." Armies of Englishmen torched Indian villages and cornfields and killed hundreds of men, women, and children. The eradication campaign would continue off and on for decades. By century's end, only a few hundred Indians remained in a region once inhabited by tens of thousands.

The Good Friday massacre also spelled the end of the Virginia Company. In 1624, James I dissolved the company and turned Virginia into a crown colony.

No longer were the settlers mere laborers toiling for a stock company. They became free citizens with power to seek landed estates for themselves and their heirs. From calamities and despair emerged a permanent colony, sustaining the aspirations of an early Jamestown ballad: "Wee hope to plant a nation / Where none before hath stood."

Elsewhere . . . Trouble in the Melting Pot

In 1626, the Dutch West India Company landed the whole island of Manhattan for just $24. Of course, there has never been a bargain in Manhattan that came without a catch. While the Dutch thought they'd bought the island, the Indians thought they'd merely sold rights to *share* it. New Netherland—with towns called Lang Eylant, Breuckelen, and Staten Eylant—prospered nevertheless, cashing in on Europeans' appetite for beaver hats and its budding slave trade. By 1664, slaves made up as much as one fifth of the population of what would become New York. Colonists also hailed from Germany, Scandinavia, and France. The melting-pot-to-be was not without troubles: Slave trade aside, director-general Peter Stuyvesant also suppressed Jews and had Quakers beaten.

Elsewhere . . . Idealism on Cape Cod

Thanksgiving and cranberry sauce were not the legacy the Pilgrims set out to leave when they landed on Cape Cod in November 1620. Communalism and godliness would have been more their speed; to avoid the materialism they'd detested in England, the Pilgrims determined to share work and land in the close quarters of a single tight-knit village. But the idealism quickly derailed as reality set in: In the village, soil was subpar, but when the Pilgrims dispersed to private farms, they found better land—and more of it. Unlike Jamestown colonists, Plymouth residents interpreted England's dominion flexibly, keeping the laws they liked (bestiality remained a crime) and relinquishing those they didn't (in England, the oldest son inherited all the land, but in Plymouth, his brothers got some, too).

Elsewhere . . . Mapping New France

It took Samuel de Champlain 29 trips across the Atlantic to found and secure the city of Quebec, and all he got for his trouble was what looked at first like the wimpiest of the European colonies: In 1627, Quebec (founded in 1608) had only 55 settlers, who had cleared only $1^1/_2$ acres of land. England had dissidents, but the French liked their country too much to leave. Lacking a regular influx of residents, Quebec distinguished itself in other ways. Champlain, who had first found the natives grotesque, eventually began joining them on the warpath; he even was given three Indian girls as a sign of friendship. The relationship paid off: What New France lacked in colonists, it made up for in cartographic knowledge; New France's holdings arced from Quebec down to New Orleans.

Elsewhere . . . A 40-Year Head Start

The first continuously settled American colony began as an act of war. In 1564, the French threatened Spain's monopoly in the Americas by founding a fort on the coast of Florida, smack in the middle of Spain's shipping route. Philip II was determined to fight back—with a whole new colony. So fleet captain Pedro Menéndez de Avilés marshaled craftsmen, professionals, and families. English pirates, disease, and the lack of a sound economy hurt. But then, profit was never St. Augustine's purpose. It was meant to be a military post and a center for religious conversions. Yet friars' prayers could not compete with English guns, and governors could not block an attack by Francis Drake in 1585. Spain gave St. Augustine to the United States in 1821.

The Root of the Problem

Jamestown gave birth to a contradiction—a democracy that was committed to slavery.

ORLANDO PATTERSON

Less than a dozen years after the founding of Jamestown, about 20 Africans from what is now Angola were sold to settlers of the fledgling colony. They found themselves in a raw, chaotic frontier society in which the English settlers were still trying to figure out the best way to survive and turn a profit.

In this unsettled, formative phase, the Africans worked side by side with white indentured servants whose physical hardships and treatment were largely similar to their own. Too much has been made of the fact that manumission, the formal emancipation from slavery, was open to the most resourceful of them, that a few of the manumitted prospered and that blacks and laboring whites interacted on intimate terms. This was typical of nearly all new multiethnic settlements in the Americas. The colony's élite remained committed to indentured white servitude as the backbone of the labor force until at least the middle of the 17th century because indentures were cheaper than African slaves. And since the élite viewed their indentured servants as lazy "salvages"—the very scum of English society not above cannibalism during periods of need and the women little better than prostitutes—it is hardly surprising that no one was especially bothered by the occasional mixed unions.

By the 1660s, the labor equation changed: increased supplies made it cheaper to buy African slaves than white indentures, and the former were also considered less rebellious. The turn toward black slavery did not reduce the inflow of white immigrants, as happened in the sugar islands. Instead, a large white population developed of small and even midsize farmers who relied on their own or nonslave white labor. As the black population grew and increasingly became the labor force of élite whites, both attitudes and laws changed. By 1662 the children of all slave women were declared slaves in perpetuity. Five years later, Christianity ceased to be an obstacle to enslavement, and by 1669 a master could legitimately kill his slave while inflicting punishment. At the same time, the distinction between slave status and indentured servitude was more sharply defined.

But there were two peculiar features of Jamestown's, and more broadly Virginia's, transition to a fully functioning slave society that were to have fateful consequences for black Americans. One

was the presumption, by the end of the 17th century, that a black person was a slave. The second was the hostility toward manumission and freed blacks generally, leading to laws requiring freed persons to leave the colony. In all the other slave societies of the hemisphere, including those of the French and British, manumission was not uncommon and resulted in the growth of significant freed nonwhite populations, some of them quite prosperous. Why did Virginia move away from this pattern, especially after its early similarity to other emerging slave regimes?

One reason was the distinctive demographic pattern that began to take shape by the last quarter of the 17th century. Virginia and the other Southern states were the only large-scale slave regimes in which white settlers, committed to the creation of a new social order, remained in the majority and thus had no incentive to create alliances with free blacks or mixed populations. The second reason is offered by Yale historian Edmund Morgan in his celebrated study of Virginia: the élite, fearful of an insurrectionary union of white servants and slaves, actively promoted racism and a racially exclusive popular democracy as a way of dividing and ruling black and white workers. By glorifying whiteness and restricting the electorate to whites, a bond of racial solidarity emerged between all classes of whites predicated on the permanent exclusion of blacks.

So emerged one of the great contradictions in the growth of American democracy. The region with the most vibrant democracy, and the largest electorate, was deeply committed to large-scale slavery and the strong conviction that there was no inconsistency between liberty and slavery. For black Americans the consequences were tragic and lasting. Jamestown's creation instilled in the broader culture the belief that African Americans, even though they were among the earliest arrivals, did not belong to the body politic and were to be permanently excluded from all basic rights of citizenship.

It became cheaper to buy African slaves than white indentured servants

The great achievement of the civil rights revolution was the dismantling of what the inheritors of Jamestown had instituted. Today a black woman fills one of the most powerful political offices after the presidency, and a black man holds serious promise of becoming the presidential candidate of the Democratic Party. Whatever the persisting problems of black Americans—many of which, like a fragile family life and the lack of inheritance, also originated in slavery—it is now incontestable that they belong to America as America belongs to them. In this, America stands far above all other multiethnic Western nations. Nonetheless, it cannot, and should never, be forgotten that the racial tragedy that began in Jamestown took more than 350 years to overcome.

PATTERSON is a sociology professor at Harvard University and author of *Slavery and Social Death: A Comparative Study.*

Blessed and Bedeviled

Tales of remarkable providences in puritan New England.

HELEN MONDLOCH

On October 31, 2001, Massachusetts Gov. Jane Swift signed a bill exonerating the last five souls convicted of witchcraft during the infamous Salem witch trials of 1692. Rectifying a few of history's wrongs on this Halloween day, the governor's conciliatory gesture was arguably ill-timed, given the frivolous revelry associated with this annual celebration of superstition and frights. In the real-life horror of the witch scare, at least 150 people were imprisoned, including a four-year-old girl who was confined for months to a stone dungeon. Twenty-three men and women, all of whom have now been cleared of their crimes, were hanged or died in prison, and one man was pressed (crushed) to death for his refusal to stand trial.

In probing the underpinnings of this tragic and incredible chapter of American history, New England observers past and present have agreed that the nascent Massachusetts Bay Colony provided a fertile ground for the devil's plagues. Among others, folklore scholar Richard Dorson, author of *America in Legend and American Folklore,* has argued that the frenzy culminating in the witch-hunt was fueled by legends that flourished among the Puritans, a populace that imagined itself both blessed and bedeviled. Of key importance was belief in phenomena called "providences" (more commonly called "remarkable providences"). These were visible, often terrifying, signs of God's will that forged themselves onto the fabric of daily life.

As Dorson explains, "Since, in the Puritan and Reformation concept, God willed every event from the black plague to the sparrow's fall, all events held meaning for errant man." The providences brought rewards or protection for the Lord's followers (generally the Puritans themselves) or vengeance upon His enemies. Sprung from European roots and embraced by intellectuals and common folk alike, they became the subject of a passionate story tradition that enlarged and dramatized events in the manner of all oral legends.

The pursuit of providences was greatly reinforced by those who felt compelled to record their occurrence, including John Winthrop, longtime theocratic governor of Massachusetts Bay Colony. Two prominent New England ministers, Increase Mather and his son Cotton, became the most zealous popularizers of such tales. In 1684 the elder Mather set forth guidelines for their documentation in *An Essay for the Recording of Illustri-*

ous Providences, a study that Cotton Mather would later extend in his own works. The Essay defined "illustrious" providences as the most extraordinary of divinely ordained episodes: "tempests, floods, earthquakes, thunders as are unusual, strange apparitions, or whatever else shall happen that is prodigious." The directives for recording the providences—a duty over which the elder Mather would preside in order to preserve the stories for all posterity—are likened by Dorson to methods observed by modern folklore collectors.

The flip side of the providences were the witchcrafts of the devil, who poised himself with a special vengeance against this citadel of God's elect. Where faith and fear converged, the tales of remarkable providences heightened both.

A 'City upon a Hill'

In his *Book of New England Legends and Folklore in Prose and Poetry* (1901), Samuel Adams Drake called New England "the child of a superstitious mother." Dorson acknowledges that folk legends in the colonies were "for the most part carbon copies of the folklore in Tudor and Stuart England." But in grafting themselves onto a New World setting, says Dorson, the old beliefs took on a special intensity in the realm of the Puritans.

Many have credited the Mathers with projecting and magnifying this Puritan zeal. Writing at the turn of the last century, historian Samuel McChord Crothers, quoted in B.A. Botkin's *Treasury of New England Folklore,* captured the fervency of the younger Mather, who became a principal driver of the witch-hunt:

> Even Cotton Mather could not avoid a tone of pious boastfulness when he narrated the doings of New England . . .
>
> . . . New England had the most remarkable providences, the most remarkable painful preachers, the most remarkable heresies, the most remarkable witches. Even the local devils were in his judgment more enterprising than those of the old country. They had to be in order to be a match for the New England saints.

Perhaps we can gain the proper perspective on the Puritans' passion when we consider the enormous pains they undertook to escape persecution in England and establish their new covenant across the sea. Upholding that covenant was now critical, as evidenced in the lofty proclamations of a sermon delivered in 1630 by John Winthrop. Excerpted in Frances Hill's *Salem Witch Trials Reader,* the governor's words resound with poignant irony given the events that rocked Salem sixty-two years later: "We shall be as a City upon a Hill, the eyes of all people . . . upon us; so if we shall deal falsely with our God in this work we have undertaken and to cause Him to withdraw His present help from us, we shall be made a story . . . through the world . . . and . . . we shall shame the faces of . . . God's worthy servants, and cause their prayers to be turned into curses upon us."

Clearly, the task of maintaining this sinless "City upon a Hill" wrought insecurity among the Puritans, and so, says Dorson, they "searched the providences for continued evidence of God's favor or wrath." As he reveals, popular legends spurred their confidence: "Marvelous escapes from shipwreck, Indian captivity, or starvation reassured the elect that the Lord was guarding their fortunes under His watchful eye."

Cotton Mather recorded many such episodes in his 1702 chronicle titled Magnalia Christi Americana: *The Ecclesiastical History of New England.* In one renowned tale, a spectral ship appeared to an ecstatic crowd of believers in New Haven harbor in 1647. Six months earlier the heavily freighted vessel was presumed lost, after it had sailed from that harbor and never returned. According to Mather's account, quoted by Botkin, the community lost "the best part of their tradable estates . . . and sundry of their eminent persons." Mather quotes an eyewitness who believed that God had now "condescended" to present the ship's ghostly image as a means of comforting the afflicted souls of the mourners, for whom this remarkable providence affirmed not only their fallen friends' state of grace but also their own.

The Puritans also gleaned affirmation from providences in which the Lord exacted harsh punishments on the enemies of His elect. According to Dorson, the Puritans apparently relished most these tales of divine judgment. Those scourged in the tales included Indians, Quakers, and anyone else deemed blasphemous or profane. In the *Magnalia,* Cotton Mather correlates providential offenses to the Ten Commandments. He cites the destruction of the Narragansett Indian nation by a group of white settlers as retribution for the Indians' foul contempt for the Gospel. Oral legends also relayed the fate of Mary Dyer, a Quaker who was sent to the gallows around 1659; Dyer was said to have given birth to a monster, a common curse meted out to nefarious women. Even members of the elect might be struck down by plague or fatal lightning bolts for lapses ranging from the omission of prayer to adultery and murder. The *Magnalia* narrates the doom suffered by various "heretics" who quarreled with village ministers or voted to cut their salaries.

In addition to these ancient themes of reward and punishment, the providence tales incorporated a host of familiar spectacles from an Old World tradition, including apparitions, wild tempests, and corpses that communicated with blood—all magnanimous instruments of an angry but just Lord. Like the spectral ship, apparitions offered hope and solved mysteries; the apparition of a murder victim often disclosed the identity of his killer, a belief that came into play during the witch trials. The age-old notion that a corpse bleeds at the murderer's touch also surfaced abundantly in the tales.

Increase Mather devoted a whole chapter of his *Essay* to thunder and lightning, perceiving in them signs of God's consternation over the advent of secularism in Massachusetts Bay Colony. Mather declared that thunder and lightning had been observed ever since "the English did first settle these American deserts," but warned that only in recent years had they wrought "fatal and fearful slaughters . . . among us." In the *Magnalia,* Cotton Mather, too, expounded on thunder, a phenomenon that the Harvard scholar and scientist, quoted in Dorson, astutely attributed to the "laws of matter and motion [and] . . . divers weighty clouds" in collision; lightning, he postulated, derived from "subtil and sulphureos vapours." Like his erudite father, however, Cotton maintained that God was the omnipotent "first mover" of these and other natural forces.

Tales of Witchcraft

Dorson explains that "providences issued from God and witch-crafts from the devil, and they marked the tide of battle between the forces of Christ and the minions of Satan." Tales of witchery had their own illustrious elements, including menacing poltergeists, enchantments, and innocent creatures who became possessed and tormented by wicked sorcerers.

He and others have argued that the widely circulated tales of remarkable providences, wherein the Puritans sealed their identity of chosenness, created a fertile climate for witch tales and the witch-hunt. According to Dorson, "Other Protestants in New York and Virginia, and the Roman Catholics in Maryland, spoke of witchery, but the neurotic intensity of the New England witch scare . . . grew from the providential aura the Puritans gave their colonial enterprise."

Cotton Mather himself, quoted in Dorson, described the devil's vengeful plot to "destroy the kingdom of our Lord Jesus Christ" in this region that had once been "the Devil's territories" (that is, inhabited by Indians). Both Mathers were implicated as early as the mid-eighteenth-century for promoting bloodlust over witchcraft with their recordings of providence tales. Thomas Hutchinson, governor of Massachusetts Bay in 1771–74, lamented the witch debacle in his *History of the Colony of Massachusetts Bay* (1765). According to Hill, who refers to the governor as a "man of the Enlightenment," Hutchinson's chronicle suggests "that there was widespread disapproval of hanging witches until the *Illustrious Providences and Memorable Providences* [Cotton's later work] . . . changed the climate of opinion."

Providence lore undoubtedly played a part in the actions of those who spearheaded the witch scare with their clamorous cries of demonic possession. The trouble began in January 1692 when two girls, Betty Parris, the nine-year-old daughter of Salem Village minister Samuel Parris, and her cousin Abigail Williams, age eleven, began experiencing spells of bizarre behavior. In these alarming episodes, the girls convulsed and ranted incoherently. Within a month other neighborhood girls began having similar spells; soon they all began accusing various members of the community of bewitching them.

The cause of these disturbing bouts—which would continue for ten months, until the last of the condemned was pulled down from the gallows—has been the topic of much scholarly speculation and simplistic analysis. Some have theorized, at least as an initiating factor, that the girls suffered from temporary mental illness engendered by eating ergot-infected rye (a theory to which the growing conditions and agricultural practices of the time lend credence, according to Hill). Others have postulated a conspiracy theory incorporating the fierce factionalism that emerged in large part over arguments related to the Reverend Parris' salary and living arrangements.

The most prevalent theory suggests that the girls' hysteria grew from feelings of paranoia and guilt at having dabbled in fortune-telling and other occult practices with Tituba, a native of Barbados who served as the Parris family's slave (and who later confessed, albeit under dubious circumstances, to having engaged in such activities with her young charges). Perhaps one falsehood led to another as the girls struggled to cover up their forbidden deeds; perhaps one or another girl actually believed, for a period, that she had been bewitched; perchance the girls also were pressured by their elders, who were eager to avoid scandal, to reveal the cause of their afflictions. Quite possibly, too, some combination of these factors set into motion the outbursts and subsequent accusations. In any case, as Hill argues, the girls very likely started out as victims of "human suggestibility" and at some point later became perpetrators of fraud.

This view is supported by the fact that the girls had been reared abundantly on tales of providences and demonic possession. In his popular *Memorable Providences,* quoted by Hill, Mather provided a detailed description of four children who suffered "strange fits, beyond those that attend an epilepsy," as a result of a wicked washerwoman's sorcery. In addition, Hill reveals that Puritans young and old "devoured" sensational pamphlets describing similar demonic episodes, a fact that is hardly surprising, she says, since secular reading was prohibited. In his account of the witch trials, Governor Hutchinson charges that the similarities between these well-known accounts of demonic possession and those of the "supposed bewitched at Salem . . . is so exact, as to leave no room to doubt the stories had been read by the New England persons themselves, or had been told to them by others who had read them."

One case in particular demonstrates the far-reaching influence of the providence legends: that of Giles Corey, who suffered an excruciating death by pressing for his refusal to stand trial for witchcraft. According to Dorson, as the executions mounted with dreadful fury, the fatal torture of this "sturdy, uncowed farmer" aroused the people's sympathy. Some wondered whether his only crime had been his stubborn silence. Public opinion shifted, however, thanks to the actions of Thomas Putnam, a prominent citizen and the father of twelve-year-old Anne Putnam, one of the principal accusers.

The elder Putnam wrote a letter to Samuel Sewall, one of the trial judges who would later become a famous diarist. The letter reported that on the previous night, Anne had witnessed the apparition of a man who had lived with Giles Corey seventeen years earlier. This "Natural Fool"—perhaps a mentally disabled man—had died suddenly in Corey's house; his ghost now claimed that Corey had murdered him by pressing him to death, causing "clodders of blood about his heart." The apparition reported, moreover, that Corey had escaped punishment for his crime by signing a pact with the devil, whose protective powers were now being usurped by a God who meted out His just desserts—that is, a ghastly punishment precisely matching the crime. Hence, Putnam's letter, now filed by Cotton Mather as an official court document, helped sanctify Corey's execution in the eyes of the citizenry.

By the fall of 1692 the witch crisis had begun to die down. Hill explains that the girls had apparently "overreached themselves by naming as witches several prominent people, including Lady Phipps, the wife of the governor." As the executions began drawing public criticism, Phipps dissolved the witch court and later granted reprieves to the remaining accused. Twelve years later, a sullen Anne Putnam, now twenty-four years old, stood before the congregation in Salem Village Church while the minister read aloud her apology, quoted in Hill, for the "great delusion of Satan" that had caused her to "bring upon . . . this land the guilt of innocent blood."

A Dark Legacy

With his strangely circular reasoning, Mather, reflecting on the witch crisis in a 1697 chronicle excerpted by Hill, shaped the tragedies into one great remarkable providence. Oblivious to any possibility of delusion or fraud, he attributed the calamities to God's wrath on New England, ignited by the "little sorceries" practiced by its youth as well as the "grosser" witchcrafts of those condemned: "Although these diabolical divinations are more ordinarily committed perhaps all over the world than they are in the country of New England, yet, that being a country devoted unto the worship and the service of the Lord Jesus Christ above the rest of the world, He signaled His vengeance against such extraordinary dispensations, as have not often been seen in other places."

While post-Enlightenment scholars have generally dismissed Mather's arguments as the rantings of a self-righteous fanatic, his thoughts and actions have left their mark on us. In 1953, the "Red Scare" of the McCarthy era inspired playwright Arthur Miller to re-create the Salem witch-hunt in *The Crucible.* Miller remarked in a 1996 *New Yorker* article, quoted by Hill, that the play's enduring relevance lies in its core subject: "human sacrifice to the furies of fanaticism and paranoia that goes on repeating itself forever."

In our own time, such furies seem painfully present. The era of remarkable providences leaves as its dark legacy a number of lessons not easily reckoned. Now, as the world grapples with the bane of terrorism, Hill's analysis of the Salem trials strikes a contemporary nerve: "The more a group idealizes itself, its own values, and its god, the more it persecutes both other groups and the dissenters in its midst."

Today the American government is repeatedly challenged to implement policies that will prevent the current conflict from turning into a witch-hunt. Moreover, our democratic principles still face the perennial threat of an arrogant religious impulse that has never totally died out. Even now, those among us who boldly stake their claim to the mind of God—like the self-appointed prophets who construed the events of last September 11 as a kind of remarkable providence—risk the resurrection of demons similar to the forces that once ravaged a New England community. The calamities of 1692 entreat us to conquer those demons by loving our neighbor and consigning the will of Providence to the realm of mystery.

Additional Reading

B.A. Botkin, ed., *A Treasury of New England Folklore,* Crown Publishers, Inc., New York, 1967.

Richard Dorson, *American Folklore,* University of Chicago Press, Chicage, 1967.

——, *America in Legend: Folklore from the Colonial Period to the Present,* Pantheon Books, New York, 1973.

Samual Adams Drake, *A Book of New England Legends and Folklore in Prose and Poetry,* Little, Brown, 1901.

Frances Hill, *The Salem Witch Trials Reader,* DeCapo Press, Boston, 2000.

Increase Mather, *An Essay for the Recording of Remarkable Providences,* Scholars' Facsimiles and Reprints, Inc., Delmar, N.Y., 1977. Reprint of the 1684 edition printed by J. Green for J. Browning, Boston.

HELEN MONDLOCH is a freelance writer and frequent contributor to the Culture section.

American Indians, Witchcraft, and Witch-hunting

MATTHEW DENNIS

To paraphrase historian David D. Hall, "the people[s] of seventeenth-century New England lived in an enchanted universe. Theirs was a world of wonders".[1] As much as English settlers, Native New Englanders (and Native Americans generally) inhabited worlds of wonder, milieus peopled with extraordinary beings and marked by supernatural phenomena. Witchcraft, among other remarkable beliefs and practices, was an integral part of their worldview, as common among Natives as among European newcomers.

Since the advent of American colonization itself, European commentators have emphasized the cultural differences between American Natives and European colonists, often equating Indian difference with inferiority. Yet, at least in retrospect, the similarities among these contending peoples are striking. A few recent scholars have even argued persuasively that such similarities—not differences, certainly not any "racial" distinction—set European colonists and Native Americans at odds as they competed for the same thing: American land and resources. Yet a shared belief in witchcraft—no more than a similar ambition to live abundant lives in the North American landscape—hardly brought the two peoples together. At least in one important respect, Indian supernaturalism, particularly claims of direct, personal revelation, made Natives suspect in the eyes of colonists and helped persuade English settlers that Indians liberally practiced the dark arts. Hostile colonists characterized the Natives' homeland as "wilderness," a "devil's den." They saw the Indians' natural religion as diabolical, understood Native shamans as witches, and demeaned Native practitioners as slaves of Satan. Consider, for example, the descriptions of the missionary Thomas Mayhew Jr. regarding the Wampanoags of Martha's Vineyard in 1652.

> When the Lord first brought me to these poor Indians on the *Vinyard,* they were mighty zealous and earnest in the Worship of False gods and Devils, . . . The Devil also with his Angels had his Kingdom among them; . . . by him they were often hurt in their Bodies, distracted in their Minds, wherefore they had many meetings with their *Pawwaws* [shaman or chief religious practitioner], (who usually had a hand in their hurt) to pacifie the Devil by their sacrifice, . . . The *Pawwaws* counted their lmps their Preservers, had them treasured up in their friends.[2]

Perhaps most disconcerting about this description is that Mayhew, who spoke the Wampanoag language, was himself a knowledgeable and not particularly hostile observer.

The religious contest between Puritans and Indians—or between Europeans and Native Americans generally in the colonial period—was not principally a battle of modernity against primitivism, or reason vs. revelation (let alone "superstition"). It was a contest of power (even magic), and in the minds of Europeans it pit a stronger god against a weaker one. Against Christ, Indian gods—and devils—were simply overmatched. This providential view of triumphant European colonization would continue to set the tone for European American understanding of Indian religion in subsequent eras.

While colonial representations of Indian witchcraft gave the narrative of American colonization a mythic quality—made it an epic contest of life and death, good vs. evil—Native people believed *themselves* to be the primary victims of witchcraft. Devastating epidemics decimated Native populations, white encroachment depleted game and took away their land, and periodic warfare brought violent death and turned Native worlds upside down. Such crises could be interpreted as providentially by Indians as they were by European Christians—that the catastrophe was induced, in part, by witchery—and Indians sought solutions both in religious tradition and innovation. Although Indians continued to face physical and cultural dislocation in the two centuries following the colonial period, they have survived, and among some "traditionalists," belief in witchcraft endures today (as it does among some Christians), as a means of understanding a world in which, for them, evil exists and bad things happen.

Such contemporary beliefs vary considerably among the diverse American Indian communities of our own time and are not easily summarized. Reconstructing the nature of witchcraft beliefs among those who lived hundreds of years ago is even more difficult. Nonetheless, it is possible to get a sense of Native witchcraft and witch-hunting from the imperfect historical and ethnographic records historians and anthropologists have amassed. The Five, later Six, Nations of the Iroquois, who resided in central and western New York during the colonial period, offer an exemplary case. Here we must distinguish between the "witchcraft" attributed to Indians by ignorant or biased white observers—misrepresentations of misunderstood

Native rites and beliefs, which had nothing to do with any diabolical force—and the witchcraft that Indians believed actually troubled their existence, an indigenous craft uniformly regarded by them as nefarious and dangerous.

According to the Jesuit missionary and ethnographer, Father Joseph-François Lafitau, who lived among the Iroquois early in the eighteenth century, "the men and women who cast spells [sorcerers] are regarded . . . as *agotkon* or spirits because of the traffic which people think that they have with the spirits or tutelary geniuses. . . . [T]hose who cast spells have no other aim than to harm and work harm." These "evil ones" are "the authors of their curses and witchcraft".[3] *Agotkon, utgon,* or *otkon,* for the Iroquois, was the evil power or force that witches personified, as they mobilized *orenda;* or power, for evil rather than benevolent purposes to injure others, even their own kin. Both female and male witches inspired near universal fear among Iroquoians, and those suspected of such maleficence were hated and avoided. Although Lafitau decried native shamans as *jongleurs* ("jugglers" or charlatans), unlike Puritan commentators he nonetheless distinguished shaman practices from those of witches, who inspired considerable antipathy among the Iroquois.

Witches' afflictions threatened the mental and physical health of individuals and entire communities. Iroquois men and women struggled to discern whether the injuries, illnesses, and misfortunes that periodically beset them resulted from natural processes or sinister magic. When natural remedies failed to produce results, and when rituals to uncover hidden wishes of the soul through the examination of dreams failed to have their therapeutic effect, it became clear that witchcraft lurked nearby. In a society based on consensus and the avoidance of outward expressions of conflict, Iroquois men and women repressed their aggression, but such feelings could still simmer below the surface, waiting for opportunities to express themselves. Witchcraft offered a covert, wicked means to assault antagonists within Iroquois communities, to indulge one's sense of resentment, rivalry, jealousy, even hatred in secret ways. Behind affectations of serenity or stoicism could lay intense feelings and emotions; disgruntled persons could silently cultivate enmity for years and might be driven, ultimately, to seek the help of witches to punish their enemies or to indulge in the black arts themselves. Fear of witches certainly encouraged circumspection and repression of aggressive acts among the Iroquois, but it also bred endemic suspicion.

Such was the danger of witchcraft that the Iroquois, like English Puritans, would "not suffer a witch to live." They sanctioned the execution of witches, as quickly as the act could be carried out, and they exempted witch-killing from the rules of kin-based revenge and atonement. In 1653, the Jesuit missionary Francesco Gioseppe Bressani wrote about the Hurons, who were culturally similar to the Iroquoians, "the confidence of the Savages in the multiplicity of spells and witchcraft went so far, that upon mere suspicion they often killed and burned even their fellow-countrymen, without any other accuser or judge than a dying man, who said that he had been bewitched by such a one, who was killing him . . . ".[4] A witch discovered among one's own lineage or clan, after all, could be more dangerous than one operating from afar—he or she could become a cancer within.

Fear of witches, diabolical sorcery, and witch-hunting was gendered among the Iroquois, but in ways more complicated than we might expect. Wherever antagonisms tended to surface in seventeenth- and eighteenth-century Iroquois culture, witchcraft might be implicated. Frustrated men, for example, might seek aid in hunting, fishing, or trading activities, to counteract bad luck in such enterprises, and some could be so driven to distraction that they crossed over to the dark side, seeking the services of witches. Some may have become witches themselves; others procured magical charms—considered living, non-human persons of great power—which required careful handling. Those who failed to propitiate them, by feeding, talking, singing, or listening to them, could endanger themselves and their families, as dishonored charms could "turn on" and "eat" their holders. Similarly, women (or men) sometimes resorted to witchcraft as well as legitimate magic in the interest of love, which might have enticed them to cross the line separating the benign from the malignant.

In general, in contrast to European and colonial witch-hunting, those suspected, accused, and executed among the Iroquois were no more apt to be women than men. It is suggestive, for example, that perhaps the most venerable witch among the Iroquois was Atotarho, the powerful male shaman and sorcerer of the Iroquois political creation myth. A hideous figure, twisted in mind and body, with writhing snakes for hair, Atotarho had nearly destroyed the cultural hero Hiawatha with his nefarious magic before the great Iroquois Peacemaker pacified him and transformed him into a benevolent leader. Iroquois communities repeatedly accused Jesuit missionaries of committing acts of malevolence, often attributing to them the contagion that swept through Iroquoia in the seventeenth century. The Jesuit Isaac Jogues, for example, who proselytized among the Mohawks in 1646, came to be considered a sorcerer and a witch. Jogues's alleged witchcraft cost him his life. Iroquois men and women practiced and suffered witchcraft equally; it was a male as well as female art.

If conscientious religious practice ensured Native people health and prosperity, witchcraft's malignant object was to challenge and frustrate the divine order and to afflict suffering on its victims. As the accusation against a Jesuit missionary above suggests, Indians often associated sickness with witchcraft. Who or what caused loved ones to sicken and die, and what force precipitated the unprecedented misery of epidemic disease that destroyed entire villages and nations? For many, the logical answer was witchcraft. And witchcraft was implicated in the disasters Native people experienced in the late colonial and early national periods as well, when the American Revolution and its aftermath brought new rounds of death, disruption, and dislocation to the Iroquois and numerous other Indian people. As Natives struggled to reconstitute themselves and survive, visionaries emerged among their leaders who offered charters for the future which blended tradition and innovation. Many such prophets—the Seneca Handsome Lake, for example, and the Shawnee Tenskwatawa—distinguished themselves as adept in identifying witches. Witch-hunting sometimes played a critical role in these postcolonial Native revivals; identification and prosecution of alleged witches destroyed those deemed responsible for the chaos (collaborating leaders who sold land, for example), and continued purges of witches—many of whom dissented or frustrated the prophets' reforms—helped to forge a Native solidarity based on fear but designed to resist the pressures of white encroachment.

The new, nineteenth-century worlds of Native Americans—even those designed by Indian prophets to remain "traditional"—were hybrid creations. While many of those worlds continued to be haunted by witchcraft, the nature of that witchcraft (like Native religion generally) evolved and accommodated or adjusted to the intrusions of outsiders. For the Iroquois (and perhaps other Indians), witchcraft seems to have been feminized—increasingly witches tended be women, following the prophet Handsome Lake's subordination of women to men in the new social order he prescribed. Witch-hunting, which flourished in the first decades of the nineteenth century and became sporadic thereafter, paradoxically represented both continuity with traditional Iroquois beliefs and practices and a departure from ancient ways toward a more Christian, misogynous understanding of witchcraft. Oddly, as white Americans distanced themselves from the unsavory past represented by the Salem "witch" trials of 1692, one Iroquois leader, the Seneca orator Red Jacket, appropriated and invoked Salem in order to legitimate Native beliefs and protect Iroquois sovereignty. During an inconclusive murder trial of a Seneca man accused of executing a witch, Red Jacket exclaimed:

> What! Do you denounce us as fools and bigors, because we still believe that which you yourselves believed two centuries ago? Your black-coats thundered this doctrine from the pulpit, your judges pronounced it from the bench, and sanctioned it with the formalities of law; and you would now punish our unfortunate brother for adhering to the faith of *his* fathers and of yours! Go to Salem! Look at the records of your own government, and you will find that hundreds have been executed for the very crime which has called forth the sentence of condemnation against this woman, and drawn down upon her the arm of vengeance. What have our brothers done more than the rulers of your people have done? And what crime has this man committed, by executing, in a summary way, the laws of his country, and the command of the Great Spirit?[5]

The defendant was ultimately freed, though he admitted his deed, and the Iroquois resourcefully continued to defend their lives, culture, land, and sovereignty, with varied success. The Iroquois, like other Native people, generally did not attempt to imitate Puritan forefathers as they sought to survive as Indians. But in their troubled modern history, some Native Americans remained convinced that their distress, both internal and external, emanated from witchery.

Notes

1. David D. Hall, *Worlds of Wonder, Days of Judgement: Popular Religious Beliefs in Early New England,* (Cambridge, MA: Harvard University Press, 1989), 71.

2. "Tears of Repentance: Or, a Further Narrative of the Progress of the Gospel amongst the Indians in New England," Massachusetts Historical Society, *Collections,* 3d ser., 4 (1834): 201–202.

3. Joseph François Lafitau, *Customs of the American Indians Compared to the Customs of Primitive Times,* no. 49, 2 vols. ed. and trans. William N. Fenton and Elizabeth Moore (Toronto: Champlain Society, 1974–1977 [first publ., 1724]), 1, 241.

4. *The Jesuit Relations and Allied Documents,* 73 vols. trans and ed. Reuben Gold Thwaites (Cleveland: Burrows Brothers, 1896–1901), vol. 39, 27.

5. William L. Stone, *The Life and Times of Red-Jacket, or Sa-Go-Ye-Wat-Ha; Being the Sequel to the History of the Six Nations* (New York; Wiley and Putnam, 1841), 320–21.

Selected Bibliography

Blanchard, David. "Who or What's a Witch? Iroquois Persons of Power." *American Indian Quarterly* 6 (1982): 218–37.

Cave, Alfred A. "The Failure of the Shawnee Prophet's Witch-Hunt," *Ethnohistory* 42 (1995): 445–75.

Dennis, Matthew, "Sericca Possessed; Colonialism, Witchcraft, and Gender in the Time of Handsome Lake," In *Spellbound: Women and Witchcraft in America,* ed. 121–43. Wilmington, DE: SR Books, 1998.

———. *Cultivating a Landscape of Peace; Iroquois-European Encounters in Seventeenth-Century America.* Ithaca, NY: Cornell University Press, 1993.

Dowd, Gregory Evans. A *Spirited Resistance: The North American Indian Struggle for Unity,* 1745–1815. Baltimore, MD: Johns Hopkins University Press, 1992.

Edmunds, R. David. *The Shawnee Prophet.* Lincoln, NE: University of Nebraska Press, 1983.

Klackhohn, Clyde. *Navaho Witchcraft.* Cambridge, MA: Harvard University Press, 1944.

Shimony, Annemarie. "Iroquois Witchcraft at Six Nations," In *Systems of North American Witchcraft and Sorcery,* ed. Deward E. Walker Jr. Moscow, ID: University of Idaho Press, 1970.

Sunmons, William S. "Cultural Bias in the New England Puritans' Perception of Indians." *William and Mary Quarterly,* 3d ser. 38 (January 1981): 56–72.

White, Richard, *The Middle Ground: Indians, Empires, and Republics in the Great Lakes Region,* 1650–1815. Cambridge, UK: Cambridge University Press, 1991.

MATTHEW DENNIS is Professor of History at the University of Oregon and author of *Cultivating a Landscape of Peace: Iroquois-European Encounters in Seventeenth-Century America* (Cornell University Press, 1993), *Red, White, and Blue Letter Days; an American Calendar* (Cornell University Press, 2002), and co-editor with William Pencak and Simon P. Newman of *Riot and Revelry in Early America* (Pennsylvania State University Press, 2002). He is currently at work on *Seneca Possessed: Witchcraft, Gender, and Colonialism on the Frontier of the Early American Republic.*

From *OAH Magazine of History,* July 2003, pp. 21–23, 27. Copyright © 2003 by Organization of American Historians. Reprinted by permission via the Copyright Clearance Center.

Slavery in the North

SHANE WHITE

In late eighteenth-century New England, a small settlement of free blacks managed to establish itself at Parting Ways, near the fork in the road that ran from Plymouth to Plympton. Before the Revolution, the residents of this community—Cato Howe, Prince Goodwin, Plato Turner, and Quamany—had been slaves in a society in which black people were a tiny minority of the population. During the Revolution, they fought in the Continental Army. On both grounds, we would expect them to be well acculturated to white society. Yet evidence from an archaeological dig at Parting Ways hints at a more complex picture. Although the houses these men built were of much the same material as others in New England, their design was different. It utilized an African or African American 12-foot floor pattern, rather than the 16-foot pattern typical of Anglo-American dwellings. Furthermore, the four houses were clustered together at the intersection of the four tracts of land rather than in the center of each block, an arrangement that quite possibly reflected the more communal patterns of Africa.[1] There are indications, then, that, after living a good proportion of their lives as slaves within white New England society, these black men, upon gaining their freedom and greater control of their lives, drew on their African past to build a settlement that, in important ways, was at variance with those of their Yankee neighbors.

The example of Parting Ways points to the varied and eclectic nature of the evidence that historians investigating the lives of black people in the seventeenth and eighteenth centuries may need to examine. Such evidence is often hard won and ambiguous, allusive rather than definitive. Interdisciplinary analysis and imagination are required to tease out its full significance. Those who work with these sources must look with envious eyes at the cornucopia of evidence available to historians of the antebellum period—particularly the numerous autobiographies written by former slaves in the nineteenth century and the interviews of former slaves compiled by the federal Works Project Administration in the twentieth century. They quickly become aware that the difficulty of attempts to recover the lives of colonial slaves and free blacks increases exponentially when, as was the case in New England and most of the North, blacks were often a very small, minority of the population. Yet for all that, the importance of historians' findings about African American life in the North has become increasingly apparent over the last decade or so. Thousands of Africans and African Americans lived and died as slaves in the North, and the fact that they did so under rather different conditions from those prevalent in Virginia or South Carolina has helped to reveal more about the nature of slavery and slave life elsewhere in America.[2] As the evidence from Parting Ways suggests, the extent of African influence on black culture was dependent on much more than the ratio of black to white people.

Among the factors shaping black life in the North was slavery's peculiar geography. Although slaves constituted only two to three percent of New England's population during the eighteenth century, these blacks were not scattered randomly; they were concentrated around the coastal urban centers, along the rivers and estuaries, especially in the Narragansett region of Rhode Island. In the mid-Atlantic colonies, the slave population was larger but followed much the same pattern of distribution. Most slaves lived in New York City and its hinterland on Long Island and in New Jersey, along the Hudson River Valley, or in and around Philadelphia.

In these areas, slaveowning was commonplace and slaveholders were a diverse group ranging from gentlemen and merchants to farmers, shopkeepers, widows, and a good number of artisans. Northern slavery was characterized by small holdings, with most slave masters owning no more than one or two slaves. Historians have discovered a high turnover among the owners of slaves, suggesting that, in the North, slaves were a relatively flexible form of labor. Owning a slave or two in New York or Philadelphia was less a commitment to a way of life than a response to immediate labor needs. Northern slavery was also disproportionately urban, a fact that was most apparent in colonial New York City, where, on the eve of the Revolution, one Scottish visitor commented that "it rather hurts an Europian eye to see so many negro slaves upon the streets".[3]

Unlike the plantation South, most northern slaves lived and worked alongside their owners, usually sleeping in the kitchens or garrets of their masters' houses. Earlier generations of historians argued that the small-scale and personal nature of northern slavery lessened the brutality of the system, an assertion based on the dubious assumption that close physical contact promoted understanding and that the "family nature" of the institution prevented or at least inhibited violence. A moment's reflection on the sharp increases in divorce and murder rates associated with contemporary family gatherings on Thanksgiving or Christmas should quickly disabuse one of this notion. Nor should it be forgotten that two of the largest instances of slave resistance in mainland North America—the 1712 revolt and the 1741 conspiracy—occurred not in the plantation South, but in New York City. Indeed, the mildness of northern slavery is less impressive than the ease with which the everyday negotiations, part and parcel of slavery in this region, erupted into violence. The very variety of conditions under which slaves worked prompted all manner of discontents as they compared their lot with that of compatriots living down the road. It often took little for these resentments to surface, as they did, for example, in a little known case that occurred in colonial Massachusetts.

In the late 1740s, in Charlestown, Massachusetts, John Codman—characterized as "a thrifty saddler, seacaptain, and merchant"—was the owner of several slaves. The use of words such as "thrifty" to describe a slaveowner never augured well for the lives of his or her slaves and there was considerable tension between the flinty New England master and his human property, particularly a slave named Mark. Mark was extremely keen to be sold to a new master and go to Boston. It was revealed later on that, in 1749, he had persuaded his fellow slave, Phillis, to burn down Codman's workhouse on the assumption that the ensuing financial pressure would force Codman to sell Phillis and himself. But Mark had understimated Codman's tenacity. For at least some of the next few years, Mark did manage to convince his owner to let him live in Boston, but even during this time he discussed the possibility of poisoning Codman with Phillis and another slave, Phebe. In 1755, Codman brought Mark home from Boston, a decision that would cost him his life. The resentful Mark now embarked on an extensive campaign to convince his fellow slaves to poison their owner. A literate man who had read the Bible in its entirety, Mark told the others that "it was no Sin to kill him if they did not lay violent Hands on him So as to shed Blood." According to Phillis, Mark also emphasized time and time again that slaves on a neighboring estate had poisoned their owner and "were never found out, but had got good masters, & so might we." We shall never know what tipped the balance, whether Mark was a particularly persuasive conspirator or Codman a particularly insufferable master. What is clear is that it took remarkably little time for the other plotters to agree that their owner had to go.

The conspirators obtained poisons from the slaves of various owners of apothecary stores from as far afield as North Boston, and, over the following days, did their best to garnish his food and drink with them. They tried potter's lead in Codman's pudding, but he merely "complain'd it was gritty." What killed him in the end was arsenic, which, incredibly enough, the conspirators administered at least seven times, mostly in his chocolate drink.

Officials ruled Codman's death a murder, and the law moved into action quickly and brutally. Phebe testified against her fellow conspirators and was probably transported to the West Indies. Mark and Phillis were convicted and executed. On a Thursday afternoon towards the end of September 1755, Mark was hanged and Phillis burned at the stake, little more than ten yards distant from the gallows. For almost two decades, Mark's body was left hanging on the gibbet. In 1758, a surgeon on his way to join the expedition against Ticonderoga noted in his journal that the "skin was but very little broken, although he had hung there near three or four years." Paul Revere, in describing a minor incident on his famous ride, recounted that it had occurred after he had passed Charlestown Neck and "was nearly opposite where Mark was hung in chains".[4] The bleaching bones of this recalcitrant slave, twisting slowly in the breeze, had become a part of local knowledge, as much a part of the remembered fabric of the New England landscape as were the clapboard houses that fronted Charlestown's main street.

The slaveholder's murder and the slave's execution reveal much about the dynamics of slavery in the North. Mark's desire to go to Boston was never explained by any of the participants in the trial, but the chances are that it had something to do with the attractions of living in a city among his fellow blacks and the promise of family life. The latter was particularly important, as northern slavery subverted the slaves' desire for a secure domestic life. The combination of the small holdings and the high turnover of owners meant that the chances of the same master owning a married couple were small. Even if a couple managed to cohabit for a time, they would most likely be split up before long. Young slave men and women must have found it enormously difficult to find, meet, and court a sexual partner. It would take decades after slavery ended in this region before African American family life achieved any semblance of stability and even then it would be bedeviled by poverty.

Following the same imperatives that had motivated Mark, other northern slaves, whenever possible, made their way to New York, Philadelphia, or New Haven. Hardly surprisingly, most of the efforts of historians have been expended on charting the contours of African American culture in these urban centers. I must confess, however, to being fascinated with the plight of another group of northern slaves: those banished to the edges of European settlement. These slaves come into clearer focus at the end of the eighteenth century, when decennial federal censuses provide a clear view of individual households. Western New York provides a good example. In 1800, the area to the north and west of Albany contained 47,640 white households and, of these, 1,372, or about one in thirty-five, owned on average two slaves each. Ontario County in 1800 was one of the most obscure spots in America, but even so, 36 out of the 2,566 white households in the county owned slaves. One can only guess what life must have been like for the two slaves living in Sparta, and the two in Palmyra, or the one slave living in Phelps, or the solitary slave in the hopelessly inappropriately named Jerusalem. Just as perplexing are the occasional owners of substantial numbers of slaves living in the middle of nowhere. For example, in 1810 Robert Rose of Fayette, Seneca County, owned 37 slaves and William Helm of Bath, Steuben County, possessed 31 slaves. According to the 1810 census it was still the case that about one in fifty (1,906 out of 91,914) white households in frontier New York State owned slaves.[5]

Although most northern slaves were not as far removed from the sight and sound of fellow African Americans as those in the far reaches of New York State, it is still the case that their small numbers and the way they were dispersed were key factors in the development of the most distinctive feature of northern slave culture. In the middle third of the eighteenth century, northern slaves created two great African American festivals, Negro Election Day in New England and Pinkster in New York and New Jersey. These years saw a transformation of African American culture in the northern colonies, brought about by an increasing reliance on slave labor, and more importantly by the new practice of importing slaves directly from Africa rather than from the West Indies. Initially, slaves merely participated in the activities organized by their masters. But gradually they took these festivals over, infusing them with new life and meanings, so that what had begun as white practices, relics of a European past, had come to be recognized as African American events by the end of the century. These festivals helped break up the work year for northern slaves and, most importantly, they provided a rare and valued opportunity for African Americans to socialize.

Election Day and Pinkster occurred sporadically in the eighteenth century throughout New England, New York, and New Jersey, and usually lasted for one or two days in May or June, although Pinkster could occupy a week. The rituals varied considerably from place to place and over time, but typically a slave—usually designated a king or governor and usually African-born—was in charge of the proceedings and slaves from the surrounding area gathered to drink, eat, gamble, listen to music, and dance. Generally, all slaves attending attired themselves in their best clothes, but, inevitably, most attention was focused on the candidates for office and on the black kings and governors, who often borrowed items of clothing, and even swords and horses, from their owners in order to create a spectacular visual display.

Negro Election Day and Pinkster were shaped by the specifics of northern slave society. In the plantation South where there were many more slaves, African Americans did not create any festivals until well into the nineteenth century. At these fetes, which seem to have begun only in the 1820s, the action was firmly centered on the slaveowners and took place under the very shadow of the plantation house. In the North, they occurred on marginal land on the edge of cities and towns and to a remarkable extent the slaves were left to their own devices. Although we only know about these events from white observers, the African American kings and governors were clearly in control and the spotlight firmly focused on the slaves. Negro Election Day and Pinkster were syncretic performances, imaginative fusions of the diverse elements that the slaves saw all around them into something new. To be sure, they were infused with memories of Africa, evidenced in the music and dance that were at the crux of these festivals, as well as in the frequency with which African-born slaves assumed the positions of governor or king. For me, though, the achievement of these festivals lies less in this than in the creative ways in which the slaves adapted that African culture to their circumstances in the New World. Consider the example of King Charles, who presided over Pinkster in Albany at the end of the eighteenth century and who was perhaps the most fascinating of all northern slaves. On what had originally been a Dutch holiday in America, this African-born slave wearing a British brigadier's scarlet broadcloth jacket, Native American buckskins, and a French three-cornered cocked hat, ruled over a motley crew of slaves, free blacks, and whites.[6] There have been few better examples of the multicultural possibilities of life in eighteenth-century America.

For northern slaves, life was hard, unforgiving, and often soul-destroying, but for all of that there was much more to their existence than mere oppression. Negro Election Day and Pinkster were the apogee of a northern slave culture that, although fashioned out of adversity, displayed the creative responses of black people to those conditions. Throughout much of African American history, black cultural production has focused primarily on performance, on the development and expression of distinctive African American aesthetic principles at some remove from those prized by the dominant culture, and there are few better examples of this than these slave festivals. Slaves came to them to drink, to gamble, to dance, to talk, and to mingle among their own people. But permeating such gatherings was a sense of exhilaration at being, if only for a few brief hours, free. White onlookers, in control of their own lives, looked disdainfully at what they saw as puerile sociability, but, in a society in which rural slaves were scattered and average slaveholdings were minuscule, these face-to-face interactions between African Americans performed a crucial function. Whether they were elected king, or decided to drink themselves insensible while telling stories about their owners, or gambled away their meager savings at "paw-paw," or just danced for hours with other young black men and women to a pulsing African beat, did not really matter. What was important about Election Day and Pinkster was that, for a while at least, slaves were in control of their lives, able to transcend the confines of a normally relentless and humdrum existence.

In my experience, it is important when teaching (and for that matter, writing) about slavery in the United States to include the North simply to show that the terms "slavery" and "South" were not coterminous, to emphasize that there were scores of thousands of African Americans living in the North well before the Great Migration. Northern slavery and the culture forged by northern slaves were different from what was created in the Chesapeake, or in the Carolina Low Country, but those differences are not nearly enough to let white northerners off the hook: in the end, white New Yorkers and Philadelphians were just as implicated in the institution of slavery as white Virginians and Carolinians. It is important to remember that slavery was part and parcel of the fabric of eighteenth-century American life in both the North and South; indeed, it was not until well into the nineteenth century that there was anything peculiar at all about the so-called "peculiar institution."

Notes

1. James Deetz, *In Small Things Forgotten: The Archaeology of Early American Life,* (Garden City, NY: Anchor Books, 1977), 138–54.

2. Exemplary in this regard (and many others) is Ira Berlin, *Many Thousands Gone: The First Two Centuries of Slavery in North America,* (Cambridge, MA: The Belknap Press of Harvard University Press, 1998).

3. As quoted in Shane White, *Somewhat More Independent: The End of Slavery in New York City, 1770-1810,* (Athens, GA: University of Georgia Press, 1991), 3.

4. All details of this case are taken from Abner Cheney Goodell Jr., *The Trial and Execution, For Petit Treason, of Mark and Phillis, Slaves of Capt. John Codman,* (Cambridge, MA: John Wilson and Son, 1883).

5. Census details come from Shane White, "Slavery in New York State in the Early Republic," *Australasian Journal of American Studies* 14 (December 1995): 1–29.

6. Details about Pinkster and Negro Election Day are drawn from Shane White, "It Was a Proud Day": African Americans, Festivals, and parades in the North, 1741–1834," *Journal of American History* 81 (June 1994): 13–51.

SHANE WHITE is currently chair of the Department of History at the University of Sydney. He writes about African American culture and has published articles on that subject in the *Journal of American History, American Quarterly, Journal of American Folklore,* and *Past and Present. Stories of Freedom in Black New York* (2002) is his most recent work. White also coauthored *Stylin': African American Expressive Culture From its Beginnings to the Zoot Suit* (1998) with Graham White (unrelated) and both men are currently finishing *The Sounds of Slavery,* a book accompanied by an audio CD.

Were American Indians the Victims of Genocide?

GUENTER LEWY

On September 21, the National Museum of the American Indian will open its doors. In an interview early this year, the museum's founding director, W. Richard West, declared that the new institution would not shy away from such difficult subjects as the effort to eradicate American-Indian culture in the 19th and 20th centuries. It is a safe bet that someone will also, inevitably, raise the issue of genocide.

The story of the encounter between European settlers and America's native population does not make for pleasant reading. Among early accounts, perhaps the most famous is Helen Hunt Jackson's *A Century of Dishonor* (1888), a doleful recitation of forced removals, killings, and callous disregard. Jackson's book, which clearly captured some essential elements of what happened, also set a pattern of exaggeration and one-sided indictment that has persisted to this day.

Thus, according to Ward Churchill, a professor of ethnic studies at the University of Colorado, the reduction of the North American Indian population from an estimated 12 million in 1500 to barely 237,000 in 1900 represents a "vast genocide . . . , the most sustained on record." By the end of the 19th century, writes David E. Stannard, a historian at the University of Hawaii, native Americans had undergone the "worst human holocaust the world had ever witnessed, roaring across two continents non-stop for four centuries and consuming the lives of countless tens of millions of people." In the judgment of Lenore A. Stiffarm and Phil Lane, Jr., "there can be no more monumental example of sustained genocide—certainly none involving a 'race' of people as broad and complex as this—anywhere in the annals of human history."

The sweeping charge of genocide against the Indians became especially popular during the Vietnam war, when historians opposed to that conflict began drawing parallels between our actions in Southeast Asia and earlier examples of a supposedly ingrained American viciousness toward non-white peoples. The historian Richard Drinnon, referring to the troops under the command of the Indian scout Kit Carson, called them "forerunners of the Burning Fifth Marines" who set fire to Vietnamese villages, while in *The American Indian: The First Victim* (1972), Jay David urged contemporary readers to recall how America's civilization had originated in "theft and murder" and "efforts toward . . . genocide."

Further accusations of genocide marked the run-up to the 1992 quincentenary of the landing of Columbus. The National Council of Churches adopted a resolution branding this event "an invasion" that resulted in the "slavery and genocide of native people." In a widely read book, *The Conquest of Paradise* (1990), Kirkpatrick Sale charged the English and their American successors with pursuing a policy of extermination that had continued unabated for four centuries. Later works have followed suit. In the 1999 *Encyclopedia of Genocide,* edited by the scholar Israel Charny, an article by Ward Churchill argues that extermination was the "express objective" of the U.S. government. To the Cambodia expert Ben Kiernan, similarly, genocide is the "only appropriate way" to describe how white settlers treated the Indians. And so forth.

That American Indians suffered horribly is indisputable. But whether their suffering amounted to a "holocaust," or to genocide, is another matter.

It is a firmly established fact that a mere 250,000 native Americans were still alive in the territory of the United States at the end of the 19th century. Still in scholarly contention, however, is the number of Indians alive at the time of first contact with Europeans. Some students of the subject speak of an inflated "numbers game"; others charge that the size of the aboriginal population has been deliberately minimized in order to make the decline seem less severe than it was.

The disparity in estimates is enormous. In 1928, the ethnologist James Mooney proposed a total count of 1,152,950 Indians in all tribal areas north of Mexico at the time of the European arrival. By 1987, in *American Indian Holocaust and Survival,* Russell Thornton was giving a figure of well over 5 million, nearly five times as high as Mooney's, while Lenore Stiffarm and Phil Lane, Jr. suggested a total of 12 million. That figure rested in turn on the work of the anthropologist Henry Dobyns, who in 1983 had estimated the aboriginal population of North America as a whole at 18 million and of the present territory of the United States at about 10 million.

From one perspective, these differences, however startling, may seem beside the point: there is ample evidence, after all, that the arrival of the white man triggered a drastic reduction in the number of native Americans. Nevertheless, even if the higher figures are credited, they alone do not prove the occurrence of genocide.

To address this issue properly we must begin with the most important *reason* for the Indians' catastrophic decline—namely, the spread of highly contagious diseases to which they had no immunity. This phenomenon is known by scholars as a "virgin-soil epidemic"; in North America, it was the norm.

The most lethal of the pathogens introduced by the Europeans was smallpox, which sometimes incapacitated so many adults at once that deaths from hunger and starvation ran as high as deaths from disease; in several cases, entire tribes were rendered extinct. Other killers included measles, influenza, whooping cough, diphtheria, typhus, bubonic plague, cholera, and scarlet fever. Although syphilis was apparently native to parts of the Western hemisphere, it, too, was probably introduced into North America by Europeans.

About all this there is no essential disagreement. The most hideous enemy of native Americans was not the white man and his weaponry, concludes Alfred Crosby, "but the invisible killers which those men brought in their blood and breath." It is thought that between 75 to 90 percent of all Indian deaths resulted from these killers.

To some, however, this is enough in itself to warrant the term genocide. David Stannard, for instance, states that just as Jews who died of disease and starvation in the ghettos are counted among the victims of the Holocaust, Indians who died of introduced diseases "were as much the victims of the Euro-American genocidal war as were those burned or stabbed or hacked or shot to death, or devoured by hungry dogs." As an example of actual genocidal conditions, Stannard points to Franciscan missions in California as "furnaces of death."

But tight away we are in highly debatable territory. It is true that the cramped quarters of the missions, with their poor ventilation and bad sanitation, encouraged the spread of disease. But it is demonstrably untrue that, like the Nazis, the missionaries were unconcerned with the welfare of their native converts. No matter how difficult the conditions under which the Indians labored—obligatory work, often inadequate food and medical care, corporal punishment—their experience bore no comparison with the fate of the Jews in the ghettos. The missionaries had a poor understanding of the causes of the diseases that afflicted their charges, and medically there was little they could do for them. By contrast, the Nazis knew exactly what was happening in the ghettos, and quite deliberately deprived the inmates of both food and medicine; unlike in Stannard's "furnaces of death," the deaths that occurred there were *meant* to occur.

The larger picture also does not conform to Stannard's idea of disease as an expression of "genocidal war." True, the forced relocations of Indian tribes were often accompanied by great hardship and harsh treatment; the removal of the Cherokee from their homelands to territories west of the Mississippi in 1838 took the lives of thousands and has entered history as the Trail of Tears. But the largest loss of life occurred well before this time, and sometimes after only minimal contact with European traders. True, too, some colonists later welcomed the high mortality among Indians, seeing it as a sign of divine providence;

that, however, does not alter the basic fact that Europeans did not come to the New World in order to infect the natives with deadly diseases.

Or did they? Ward Churchill, taking the argument a step further than Stannard, asserts that there was nothing unwitting or unintentional about the way the great bulk of North America's native population disappeared: "it was precisely malice, not nature, that did the deed." In brief, the Europeans were engaged in biological warfare.

Unfortunately for this thesis, we know of but a single instance of such warfare, and the documentary evidence is inconclusive. In 1763, a particularly serious uprising threatened the British garrisons west of the Allegheny mountains. Worried about his limited resources, and disgusted by what he saw as the Indians' treacherous and savage modes of warfare, Sir Jeffrey Amherst, commander-in-chief of British forces in North America, wrote as follows to Colonel Henry Bouquet at Fort Pitt: "You will do well to try to inoculate the Indians [with smallpox] by means of blankets, as well as to try every other method, that can serve to extirpate this execrable race."

Bouquet clearly approved of Amherst's suggestion, but whether he himself carried it out is uncertain. On or around June 24, two traders at Fort Pitt did give blankets and a handkerchief from the forts quarantined hospital to two visiting Delaware Indians, and one of the traders noted in his journal: "I hope it will have the desired effect." Smallpox was already present among the tribes of Ohio; at some point after this episode, there was another outbreak in which hundreds died.

A second, even less substantiated instance of alleged biological warfare concerns an incident that occurred on June 20, 1837. On that day, Churchill writes, the U.S. Army began to dispense " 'trade blankets' to Mandans and other Indians gathered at Fort Clark on the Missouri River in present-day North Dakota." He continues:

> Far from being trade goods, the blankets had been taken from a military infirmary in St. Louis quarantined for smallpox, and brought upriver aboard the steamboat St. Peter's. When the first Indians showed symptoms of the disease on July 14, the post surgeon advised those camped near the post to scatter and seek "sanctuary" in the villages of healthy relatives.

In this way the disease was spread, the Mandans were "virtually exterminated," and other tribes suffered similarly devastating losses. Citing a figure of "100,000 or more fatalities" caused by the U.S. Army in the 1836–40 smallpox pandemic (elsewhere he speaks of a toll "several times that number"), Churchill refers the reader to Thornton's *American Indian Holocaust and Survival*.

Supporting Churchill here are Stiffarm and Lane, who write that "the distribution of smallpox-infected blankets by the U.S. Army to Mandans at Fort Clark ... was the causative factor in the pandemic of 1836–40." In evidence, they cite the journal of a contemporary at Fort Clark, Francis A. Chardon.

But Chardon's journal manifestly does not suggest that the U.S. Army distributed infected blankets, instead blaming the epidemic on the inadvertent spread of disease by a ship's passenger. And as for the "100,000 fatalities," not only does Thornton fail to allege such obviously absurd numbers, but he too points to infected passengers on the steamboat *St. Peter's* as the cause. Another scholar, drawing on newly discovered source material, has also refuted the idea of a conspiracy to harm the Indians.

Similarly at odds with any such idea is the effort of the United States government at this time to vaccinate the native population. Smallpox vaccination, a procedure developed by the English country doctor Edward Jenner in 1796, was first ordered in 1801 by President Jefferson; the program continued in force for three decades, though its implementation was slowed both by the resistance of the Indians, who suspected a trick, and by lack of interest on the part of some officials. Still, as Thornton writes: "Vaccination of American Indians did eventually succeed in reducing mortality from smallpox."

To sum up, European settlers came to the New World for a variety of reasons, but the thought of infecting the Indians with deadly pathogens was not one of them. As for the charge that the U.S. government should itself be held responsible for the demographic disaster that overtook the American-Indian population, it is unsupported by evidence or legitimate argument. The United States did not wage biological warfare against the Indians; neither can the large number of deaths as a result of disease be considered the result of a genocidal design.

Still, even if up to 90 percent of the reduction in Indian population was the result of disease, that leaves a sizable death toll caused by mistreatment and violence. Should some or all of these deaths be considered instances of genocide?

We may examine representative incidents by following the geographic route of European settlement, beginning in the New England colonies. There, at first, the Puritans did not regard the Indians they encountered as natural enemies, but rather as potential friends and converts. But their Christianizing efforts showed little success, and their experience with the natives gradually yielded a more hostile view. The Pequot tribe in particular, with its reputation for cruelty and ruthlessness, was feared not only by the colonists but by most other Indians in New England. In the warfare that eventually ensued, caused in part by intertribal rivalries, the Narragansett Indians became actively engaged on the Puritan side.

Hostilities opened in late 1636 after the murder of several colonists. When the Pequots refused to comply with the demands of the Massachusetts Bay Colony for the surrender of the guilty and other forms of indemnification, a punitive expedition was led against them by John Endecott, the first resident governor of the colony; although it ended inconclusively, the Pequots retaliated by attacking any settler they could find. Fort Saybrook on the Connecticut River was besieged, and members of the garrison who ventured outside were ambushed and killed. One captured trader, tied to a stake in sight of the fort, was tortured for three days, expiring after his captors flayed his skin with the help of hot timbers and cut off his fingers and toes. Another prisoner was roasted alive.

The torture of prisoners was indeed routine practice for most Indian tribes, and was deeply ingrained in Indian culture. Valuing bravery above all things, the Indians had little sympathy for those who surrendered or were captured. Prisoners, unable to withstand the rigor of wilderness travel were usually killed on the spot. Among those—Indian or European—taken back to the village, some would be adopted to replace slain warriors, the rest subjected to a ritual of torture designed to humiliate them and exact atonement for the tribe's losses. Afterward the Indians often consumed the body or parts of it in a ceremonial meal, and proudly displayed scalps and fingers as trophies of victory.

Despite the colonists' own resort to torture in order to extract confessions, the cruelty of these practices strengthened the belief that the natives were savages who deserved no quarter. This revulsion accounts at least in part for the ferocity of the battle of Fort Mystic in May 1637, when a force commanded by John Mason and assisted by militiamen from Saybrook surprised about half of the Pequot tribe encamped near the Mystic River.

The intention of the colonists had been to kill the warriors "with their Swords," as Mason put it, to plunder the village, and to capture the women and children. But the plan did not work out. About 150 Pequot warriors had arrived in the fort the night before, and when the surprise attack began they emerged from their tents to fight. Fearing the Indians' numerical strength, the English attackers set fire to the fortified village and retreated outside the palisades. There they formed a circle and shot down anyone seeking to escape; a second cordon of Narragansett Indians cut down the few who managed to get through the English line. When the battle was over, the Pequots had suffered several hundred dead, perhaps as many as 300 of these being women and children. Twenty Narragansett warriors also fell.

A number of recent historians have charged the Puritans with genocide: that is, with having carried out a premeditated plan to exterminate the Pequots. The evidence belies this. The use of fire as a weapon of war was not unusual for either Europeans or Indians, and every contemporary account stresses that the burning of the fort was an act of self-protection, not part of a preplanned massacre. In later stages of the Pequot war, moreover, the colonists spared women, children, and the elderly, further contradicting the idea of genocidal intention.

A second famous example from the colonial period is King Philip's War (1675–76). This conflict, proportionately the costliest of all American wars, took the life of one in every sixteen men of military age in the colonies; large numbers of women and children also perished or were carried into captivity. Fifty-two of New England's 90 towns were attacked, seventeen were razed to the ground, and 25 were pillaged. Casualties among the Indians were even higher, with many of those captured being executed or sold into slavery abroad.

The war was also merciless, on both sides. At its outset, a colonial council in Boston had declared "that none be Killed or Wounded that are Willing to surrender themselves into Custody." But these rules were soon abandoned on the grounds that the Indians themselves, failing to adhere either to the laws of war or to the law of nature, would "skulk" behind trees, rocks, and bushes rather than appear openly to do "civilized" battle. Similarly creating a desire for retribution were the cruelties perpetrated by Indians when ambushing English troops or overrunning strongholds housing women and children. Before long, both colonists and Indians were dismembering corpses and displaying body parts and heads on poles. (Nevertheless, Indians could not be killed with impunity. In the summer of 1676, four men were tried in Boston for the brutal murder of three squaws and three Indian children; all were found guilty and two were executed.)

The hatred kindled by King Philip's War became even more pronounced in 1689 when strong Indian tribes allied themselves with the French against the British. In 1694, the General Court of Massachusetts ordered all friendly Indians confined to a small area. A bounty was then offered for the killing or capture of hostile Indians, and scalps were accepted as proof of a kill. In 1704, this was amended in the direction of "Christian practice" by means of a scale of rewards graduated by age and sex; bounty was proscribed in the case of children under the age often, subsequently raised to twelve (sixteen in Connecticut, fifteen in New Jersey). Here, too, genocidal intent was far from evident; the practices were justified on grounds of self-preservation and revenge, and in reprisal for the extensive scalping carried out by Indians.

We turn now to the American frontier. In Pennsylvania, where the white population had doubled between 1740 and 1760, the pressure on Indian lands increased formidably; in 1754, encouraged by French agents, Indian warriors struck, starting a long and bloody conflict known as the French and Indian War or the Seven Years' War.

By 1763, according to one estimate, about 2,000 whites had been killed or vanished into captivity. Stories of real, exaggerated, and imaginary atrocities spread by word of mouth, in narratives of imprisonment, and by means of provincial newspapers. Some British officers gave orders that captured Indians be given no quarter, and even after the end of formal hostilities, feelings continued to run so high that murderers of Indians, like the infamous Paxton Boys, were applauded rather than arrested.

As the United States expanded westward, such conflicts multiplied. So far had things progressed by 1784 that, according to one British traveler, "white Americans have the most rancorous antipathy to the whole race of Indians; and nothing is more common than to hear them talk of extirpating them totally from the face of the earth, men, women, and children."

Settlers on the expanding frontier treated the Indians with contempt, often robbing and killing them at will. In 1782, a militia pursuing an Indian war party that had slain a woman and a child massacred more than 90 peaceful Moravian Delawares. Although federal and state officials tried to bring such killers to justice, their efforts, writes the historian Francis Prucha, "were no match for the singular Indian-hating mentality of the frontiersmen, upon whom depended conviction in the local courts."

But that, too, is only part of the story. The view that the Indian problem could be solved by force alone came under vigorous challenge from a number of federal commissioners who from 1832 on headed the Bureau of Indian Affairs and supervised the network of agents and subagents in the field. Many Americans on the eastern seaboard, too, openly criticized the rough ways of the frontier. Pity for the vanishing Indian, together with a sense of remorse, led to a revival of the 18th-century concept of the noble savage. America's native inhabitants were romanticized in historiography, art, and literature, notably by James Fenimore Cooper in his *Leatherstocking Tales* and Henry Wadsworth Longfellow in his long poem, *The Song of Hiawatha.*

On the western frontier itself, such views were of course dismissed as rank sentimentality; the perceived nobility of the savages, observed cynics, was directly proportional to one's geographic distance from them. Instead, settlers vigorously complained that the regular army was failing to meet the Indian threat more aggressively. A large-scale uprising of the Sioux in Minnesota in 1862, in which Indian war parties killed, raped, and pillaged all over the countryside, left in its wake a climate of fear and anger that spread over the entire West.

Colorado was especially tense. Cheyenne and Arapahoe Indians, who had legitimate grievances against the encroaching white settlers, also fought for the sheer joy of combat, the desire for booty, and the prestige that accrued from success. The overland route to the East was particularly vulnerable: at one point in 1864, Denver was cut off from all supplies, and there were several butcheries of entire families at outlying ranches. In one gruesome case, all of the victims were scalped, the throats of the two children were cut, and the mother's body was ripped open and her entrails pulled over her face.

Writing in September 1864, the Reverend William Crawford reported on the attitude of the white population of Colorado: "There is but one sentiment in regard to the final disposition which shall be made of the Indians: 'Let them be exterminated—men, women, and children together.' " Of course, he added, "I do not myself share in such views." The *Rocky Mountain News,* which at first had distinguished between friendly and hostile Indians, likewise began to advocate extermination of this "dissolute, vagabondish, brutal, and ungrateful race."

With the regular army off fighting the Civil War in the South, the western settlers depended for their protection on volunteer regiments, many lamentably deficient in discipline. It was a local force of such volunteers that committed the massacre of Sand Creek, Colorado on November 29, 1864. Formed in August, the regiment was made up of miners down on their luck, cowpokes tired of ranching, and others itching for battle. Its commander, the Reverend John Milton Chivington, a politician and ardent Indian-hater, had urged war without mercy, even against children. "Nits make lice," he was fond of saying. The ensuing orgy of violence in the course of a surprise attack on a large Indian encampment left between 70 and 250 Indians dead, the majority women and children. The regiment suffered eight killed and 40 wounded.

News of the Sand Creek massacre sparked an outcry in the East and led to several congressional inquiries. Although some of the investigators appear to have been biased against Chivington, there was no disputing that he had issued orders not to give quarter, or that his soldiers had engaged in massive scalping and other mutilations.

The sorry tale continues in California. The area that in 1850 became admitted to the Union as the 31st state had once held an Indian population estimated at anywhere between 150,000 and 250,000. By the end of the 19th century, the number had dropped to 15,000. As elsewhere, disease was the single most important factor, although the state also witnessed an unusually large number of deliberate killings.

The discovery of gold in 1848 brought about a fundamental change in Indian-white relations. Whereas formerly Mexican ranchers had both exploited the Indians and provided them with a minimum of protection, the new immigrants, mostly young single males, exhibited animosity from the start, trespassing on Indian lands and often freely killing any who were in their way. An American officer wrote to his sister in 1860: "There never was a viler sort of men in the world than is congregated about these mines."

What was true of miners was often true as well of newly arrived farmers. By the early 1850's, whites in California outnumbered Indians by about two to one, and the lot of the natives, gradually forced into the least fertile parts of the territory, began to deteriorate rapidly. Many succumbed to starvation; others, desperate for food, went on the attack, stealing and killing livestock. Indian women who prostituted themselves to feed their families contributed to the demographic decline by removing themselves from the reproductive cycle. As a solution to the growing problem, the federal government sought to confine the Indians to reservations, but this was opposed both by the Indians themselves and by white ranchers fearing the loss of labor. Meanwhile, clashes multiplied.

One of the most violent, between white settlers and Yuki Indians in the Round Valley of Mendocino County, lasted for several years and was waged with great ferocity. Although Governor John B. Weller cautioned against an indiscriminate campaign— "[Y]our operations against the Indians," he wrote to the commander of a volunteer force in 1859, "must be confined strictly to those who are known to have been engaged in killing the stock and destroying the property of our citizens . . . and the women and children under all circumstances must be spared"—his words had little effect. By 1864 the number of Yukis had declined from about 5,000 to 300.

The Humboldt Bay region, just northwest of the Round Valley, was the scene of still more collisions. Here too Indians stole and killed cattle, and militia companies retaliated. A secret league, formed in the town of Eureka, perpetrated a particularly hideous massacre in February 1860, surprising Indians sleeping in their houses and killing about sixty, mostly by hatchet. During the same morning hours, whites attacked two other Indian rancherias, with the same deadly results. In all, nearly 300 Indians were killed on one day, at least half of them women and children.

Once again there was outrage and remorse. "The white settlers," wrote a historian only 20 years later, "had received great provocation. . . . But nothing they had suffered, no depredations the savages had committed, could justify the cruel slaughter of innocent women and children." This had also been the opinion of a majority of the people of Eureka, where a grand jury condemned the massacre, while in cities like San Francisco all such killings repeatedly drew strong criticism. But atrocities continued: by the 1870's, as one historian has summarized the situation in California, "only remnants of the aboriginal populations were still alive, and those who had survived the maelstrom of the preceding quarter-century were dislocated, demoralized, and impoverished."

Lastly we come to the wars on the Great Plains. Following the end of the Civil War, large waves of white migrants, arriving simultaneously from East and West, squeezed the Plains Indians between them. In response, the Indians attacked vulnerable white outposts; their "acts of devilish cruelty," reported one officer on the scene, had "no parallel in savage warfare." The trails west were in similar peril: in December 1866, an army detachment of 80 men was lured into an ambush on the Bozeman Trail, and all of the soldiers were killed.

To force the natives into submission, Generals Sherman and Sheridan, who for two decades after the Civil War commanded the Indian-fighting army units on the Plains, applied the same strategy they had used so successfully in their marches across Georgia and in the Shenandoah Valley. Unable to defeat the Indians on the open prairie, they pursued them to their winter camps, where numbing cold and heavy snows limited their mobility. There they destroyed the lodges and stores of food, a tactic that inevitably resulted in the deaths of women and children.

Genocide? These actions were almost certainly in conformity with the laws of war accepted at "the time. The principles of limited war and of noncombatant immunity had been codified in Francis Lieber's *General Order No. 100,* issued for the Union Army on April 24, 1863. But the villages of warring Indians who refused to surrender were considered legitimate military objectives. In any event, there was never any order to exterminate the Plains Indians, despite heated pronouncements on the subject by the outraged Sherman and despite Sheridan's famous quip that "the only good Indians I ever saw were dead." Although Sheridan did not mean that all Indians should be shot on sight, but rather that none of the warring Indians on the Plains could be trusted, his words, as the historian James Axtell rightly suggests, did "more to harm straight thinking about Indian-white relations than any number of Sand Creeks or Wounded Knees."

As for that last-named encounter, it took place on December 29, 1890 on the Pine Ridge Reservation in South Dakota. By this time, the 7th Regiment of U.S. Cavalry had compiled a reputation for aggressiveness, particularly in the wake of its surprise assault in 1868 on a Cheyenne village on the Washita River in Kansas, where about 100 Indians were killed by General George Custer's men.

Still, the battle of Washita, although one-sided, had not been a massacre: wounded warriors were given first aid, and 53 women and children who had hidden in their lodges survived the assault and were taken prisoner. Nor were the Cheyennes unarmed innocents; as their chief Black Kettle acknowledged, they had been conducting regular raids into Kansas that he was powerless to stop.

The encounter at Wounded Knee, 22 years later, must be seen in the context of the Ghost' Dance religion, a messianic movement that since 1889 had caused great excitement among Indians in the area and that was interpreted by whites as a general call to war. While an encampment of Sioux was being searched for arms, a few young men created an incident; the soldiers, furious at what they considered an act of Indian treachery, fought back furiously as guns surrounding the encampment opened fire with deadly effect. The Army's casualties were 25 killed and 39 wounded, mostly as a result of friendly fire. More than 300 Indians died.

Wounded Knee has been called "perhaps the best-known genocide of North American Indians." But, as Robert Utley has concluded in a careful analysis, it is better described as a regrettable, tragic accident of war," a bloodbath that neither side intended. In a situation where women and children were mixed with men, it was inevitable that some of the former would be killed. But several groups of women and children were in fact allowed out of the encampment, and wounded Indian warriors, too, were spared and taken to a hospital. There may have been a few deliberate killings of noncombatants, but on the whole, as a court of inquiry ordered by President Harrison established, the officers and soldiers of the unit made supreme efforts to avoid killing women and children.

On January 15, 1891, the last Sioux warriors surrendered. Apart from isolated clashes, America's Indian wars had ended.

The genocide Convention was approved by the General Assembly of the United Nations on December 9, 1948 and came into force on January 12, 1951; after a long delay, it was ratified by the United States in 1986. Since genocide is now a technical term in international criminal law, the definition established by the convention has assumed prima-facie authority, and it is with this definition that we should begin in assessing the applicability of the concept of genocide to the events we have been considering.

According to Article II of the convention, the crime of genocide consists of a series of acts "committed *with intent to destroy, in whole or in part,* a national, ethnical, racial, or religious group *as such*" (emphases added). Practically all legal scholars accept the centrality of this clause. During the deliberations over the convention, some argued for a clear specification of the reasons, or motives, for the destruction of a group. In the end, instead of a list of such motives, the issue was resolved by adding the words "as such"—i.e., the motive or reason for the destruction must be the ending of the group as a national, ethnic, racial, or religious entity. Evidence of such a motive, as one legal scholar put it, "will constitute an integral part of the proof of a genocidal plan, and therefore of genocidal intent."

The crucial role played by intentionality in the Genocide Convention means that under its terms the huge number of Indian deaths from epidemics cannot be considered genocide. The lethal diseases were introduced inadvertently, and the Europeans cannot be blamed for their ignorance of what medical science would discover only centuries later. Similarly, military engagements that led to the death of noncombatants, like the battle of the Washita, cannot be seen as genocidal acts, for the loss of innocent life was not intended and the soldiers did not aim at the destruction of the Indians as a defined group. By contrast, some of the massacres in California, where both the perpetrators and their supporters openly acknowledged a desire to destroy the Indians as an ethnic entity, might indeed be regarded under the terms of the convention as exhibiting genocidal intent.

Even as it outlaws the destruction of a group "in whole or in part," the convention does not address the question of what percentage of a group must be affected in order to qualify as genocide. As a benchmark, the prosecutor of the International Criminal Tribunal for the Former Yugoslavia has suggested "a reasonably significant number, relative to the total of the group as a whole," adding that the actual or attempted destruction should also relate to "the factual opportunity of the accused to destroy a group in a specific geographic area within the sphere of his control, and not in relation to the entire population of the group in a wider geographic sense." If this principle were adopted, an atrocity like the Sand Creek massacre, limited to one group in a specific single locality, might also be considered an act of genocide.

Of course, it is far from easy to apply a legal concept developed in the middle of the 20th century to events taking place many decades if not hundreds of years earlier. Our knowledge of many of these occurrences is incomplete. Moreover, the malefactors, long since dead, cannot be tried in a court of law, where it would be possible to establish crucial factual details and to clarify relevant legal principles.

Applying today's standards to events of the past raises still other questions, legal and moral alike. While history has no statute of limitations, our legal system rejects the idea of retroactivity (*ex post facto* laws). Morally, even if we accept the idea of universal principles transcending particular cultures and periods, we must exercise caution in condemning, say, the conduct of war during America's colonial period, which for the most part conformed to then-prevailing notions of right and wrong. To understand all is hardly to forgive all, but historical judgment, as the scholar Gordon Leff has correctly stressed, "must always be contextual: it is no more reprehensible for an age to have lacked our values than to have lacked forks."

The real task, then, is to ascertain the context of a specific situation and the options it presented. Given circumstances, and the moral standards of the day, did the people on whose conduct we are sitting in judgment have a choice to act differently? Such an approach would lead us to greater indulgence toward the Puritans of New England, who fought for their survival, than toward the miners and volunteer militias of California who often slaughtered Indian men, women, and children for no other reason than to satisfy their appetite for gold and land. The former, in addition, battled their Indian adversaries in an age that had little concern for humane standards of warfare, while the latter committed their atrocities in the face of vehement denunciation not only by self-styled humanitarians in the faraway East but by many of their fellow citizens in California.

Finally, even if some episodes can be considered genocidal—that is, tending toward genocide—they certainly do not justify condemning an entire society. Guilt is personal, and for good reason the Genocide Convention provides that only "persons" can be charged with the crime, probably even ruling out legal proceedings against governments. No less significant is that a massacre like Sand Creek was undertaken by a local volunteer militia and was not the expression of official U.S. policy. No regular U.S. Army unit was ever implicated in a similar atrocity. In the majority of actions, concludes Robert Utley, "the Army shot noncombatants incidentally and accidentally, not purposefully." As for the larger society, even if some elements in the white population, mainly in the West, at times advocated extermination, no official of the U.S. government ever seriously proposed it. Genocide was never American policy, nor was it the result of policy.

The violent collision between whites and America's native population was probably unavoidable. Between 1600 and 1850, a dramatic surge in population led to massive waves of emigration from Europe, and many of the millions who arrived in the New World gradually pushed westward into America's seemingly unlimited space. No doubt, the 19th-century idea of America's "manifest destiny" was in part a rationalization for acquisitiveness, but the resulting dispossession of the Indians was as unstoppable as other great population movements of the past. The U.S. government could not have prevented the westward movement even if it had wanted to.

In the end, the sad fate of America's Indians represents not a crime but a tragedy, involving an irreconcilable collision of cultures and values. Despite the efforts of well-meaning people in both camps, there existed no good solution to this clash. The Indians were not prepared to give up the nomadic life of the hunter for the sedentary life of the farmer. The new Americans, convinced of their cultural and racial superiority, were unwilling to grant the original inhabitants of the continent the vast preserve of land required by the Indians' way of life. The consequence was a conflict in which there were few heroes, but which was far from a simple tale of hapless victims and merciless aggressors. To fling the charge of genocide at an entire society serves neither the interests of the Indians nor those of history.

GUENTER LEWY, who for many years taught political science at the University of Massachusetts, has been a contributor to COMMENTARY since 1964. His books include *The Catholic Church & Nazi Germany, Religion & Revolution, America in Vietnam,* and *The Cause that Failed: Communism in American Political Life.*

UNIT 2

Revolutionary America

Unit selections

11. **Dirty Little Secret,** Simon Schama
12. **Midnight Riders,** Charles J. Caes
13. **God and the Founders,** John Meacham
14. **The Rocky Road to Revolution,** John Ferling
15. **A Day to Remember: July 4, 1776,** Charles Philips
16. **Washington Takes Charge,** Joseph J. Ellis
17. **Winter of Discontent,** Norman Gelb
18. **Evacuation Day,** Erik Peter Axelson
19. **The Necessity of Refusing My Signature,** Mark Bernstein

Key Points to Consider

- Most slaves and former slaves fought on the side of the colonists during the Revolutionary War. Why did others side with the British? What incentives were there for them to do so?

- Discuss the differences between those colonists who wished to pry concessions from the British but who still wanted to remain in the empire, and those who sought nothing less than independence. How and why did the latter group prevail?

- What purposes was the Declaration of Independence meant to serve? Who were the audiences to which it was addressed?

- What were George Washington's strengths and weaknesses as a general? What was his symbolic importance?

- Why was it so important to some that there be a Bill of Rights attached to the Constitution? What arguments did those who opposed such a bill offer?

Student Web Site

www.mhcls.com/online

Internet References

Further information regarding these Web sites may be found in this book's preface or online.

The Early America Review
http://www.earlyamerica.com/review/

House of Representatives
http://www.house.gov

National Center for Policy Analysis
http://www.public-policy.org/web.public-policy.org/index.php

Supreme Court/Legal Information Institute
http://supct.law.cornell.edu/supct/index.html

U.S. Senate
http://www.senate.gov

The White House
http://www.whitehouse.gov/

The World of Benjamin Franklin
http://www.fi.edu/franklin/

We live in an age of instant communication. Our call to complain about a credit card may be answered by someone in India. Television satellites permit the simultaneous viewing of events all over the world. Imagine what it was like in the 18th Century when it took weeks for a message to be delivered from London to one of the colonies, and weeks more to receive a reply. Under such circumstances the British understandably gave wide latitude to royal governors who were on the scene and who knew more about local conditions than could the bureaucrats at home. The fact that the American colonies were but part of the British world empire also discouraged attempts to micromanage their affairs.

According to economic theory at the time, an empire could be likened to an organism with each part functioning in such a way as to benefit the whole. The ideal role of a colony, aside from helping to defend the empire when the need arose, was to serve as a protected market for the mother country's manufactured goods and as a provider of raw material for its mills and factories. Because imperial rivalries often led to war, particular emphasis was placed on achieving self-sufficiency. An imperial power did not wish to be dependent on another empire for materials, especially those of strategic value such as shipbuilding materials that might be cut off if the two came into conflict.

With regard to the American colonies, those in the South most nearly fit the imperial model. Southern colonies produced goods such as cotton and tobacco that could not be grown in Great Britain, and Southerners were disinclined to become involved in activities that would compete with British manufactures. The New England and the middle colonies were another matter. Individuals in both areas often chafed at imperial restrictions that prevented them from purchasing products more cheaply from other countries or from engaging in manufacturing their own. What served to temper discontent among these colonists was the knowledge that they depended on the British army and navy against threats by other powers, most notably the French.

During the middle decades of the 1700s, London permitted the colonists to exercise a great deal of control over their own internal affairs so long as they played their designated economic role within the empire. This attitude, which came to be known as "benign neglect," meant that colonies for all practical purposes became nearly autonomous. The passage of time and the great distances involved combined to make British rule more of an abstraction than a day-to-day relationship. Most colonists never visited the mother country, and they might go months or years without seeing any overt signs of British authority. They came to regard this as the normal order of things.

This casual relationship was altered in 1763 when what the colonists called the French and Indian War came to an end after seven years of fighting. The peace brought two results that had

National Archives and Records Administration (public)

enormous consequences. First, British acquisition of French possessions in North America meant that the military threat to the colonists had ended. Second, the war had been enormously costly to the British people who were suffering under staggering tax burdens. The government in London, taking the understandable view that the colonists ought to pay their fair share of the costs, began levying a variety of new taxes and enforcing shipping regulations that had previously been ignored.

The new British crackdown represented to the colonists and unwarranted assault on the rights and privileges they had long enjoyed. Disputes over economic matters escalated into larger concerns about rights and freedoms in other areas. Many colonists who regarded themselves as loyal subjects of the crown at first looked upon the situation as a sort of family quarrel that could be smoothed out provided there was good will on both sides. When clashes escalated instead, more and more people who now regarded themselves as "Americans" began calling for independence form the motherland. The British, of course, had no intention of handing over portions of their hard-won empire to the upstarts. War became inevitable.

"Dirty Little Secret" analyzes the relatively unknown fact that many slaves looked upon the British more as liberators than as oppressors. This article analyzes the revolution through the eyes of slaves and explains why they fought for the crown. "God and the Founders" discusses a dispute that arose at the meeting of the First Continental Congress over whether it should be opened with a prayer. The issue was resolved in such as way as to acknowledge religion without permitting it to become divisive.

Even after the early battles of the Revolutionary War, many colonists sought a negotiated settlement with Great Britain rather than to embark on the uncertain quest for independence. "The Rocky Road to Revolution" analyzes this debate, and shows how those who wanted to break with the mother country triumphed. "A Day to Remember: July 4, 1776" tells how the Declaration of Independence emerged in its final form from the Second Continental Congress.

There is little question that George Washington was the dominating figure in the American Revolution. His first command was to preside over the battle of Boston in 1775. He failed to defeat the British there, but achieved his goals six years later at the battle of Yorktown. "Washington Takes Charge" provides an assessment of Washington's strengths and weaknesses. The British occupied New York City from 1776 to November 23, 1783. The latter date became known as "Evacuation Day" to New Yorkers. "Evacuation Day" analyzes the important role the city played during the revolutionary period.

A debate arose during the Constitutional Convention over whether the document should contain a Bill of Rights. Some argued that these rights were embodied in the Constitution itself and that it was unnecessary to spell them out separately. Others, such as the prominent Virginian George Mason, believed these rights must be made specific. "The Necessity of Refusing My Signature" analyzes this dispute and Mason's role in it.

Dirty Little Secret

To see the Revolutionary War through the eyes of slaves is to better understand why so many of them fought for the crown.

SIMON SCHAMA

Ten years after the surrender of George III's army to General Washington at Yorktown, a man known as British Freedom was hanging on in North America. Along with a few hundred other souls, he was scratching a living from the stingy soil around Preston, a few miles northeast of Halifax, Nova Scotia. Like most of the Preston people, British Freedom was black and had come from a warmer place. Now he was a hardscrabbler stuck in a wind-whipped corner of the world between the blue spruce forest and the sea. But he was luckier than most.

British Freedom had title to 40 acres, and another one and a half of what the lawyers' clerks in Halifax were pleased to call a "town lot." It didn't look like much of a town, though, just a dirt clearing with rough cabins at the center and a few chickens strutting around and maybe a mud-caked hog or two. Some of the people who had managed to get a team of oxen to clear the land of bald gray rocks grew patches of beans and corn and cabbages, which they carted to market in Halifax along with building lumber. But even those who prospered—by Preston standards—took themselves off every so often into the wilderness to shoot some birch partridge, or tried their luck on the saltwater ponds south of the village.

What were they doing there? Not just surviving. British Freedom and the rest of the villagers were clinging to more than a scrap of Nova Scotia; they were clinging to a promise. Some of them even had that promise printed and signed by officers of the British Army on behalf of the king himself, that the bearer so-and-so was at liberty to go wherever he or she pleased and take up whatever occupation he or she chose. That meant something for people who had been slaves. And the king's word was surely a bond. In return for their loyal service in the late American war, they were to be granted two gifts of unimaginably precious worth: their freedom and their acres.

It was, they told themselves, no more than their due. They had done perilous, dirty, exhausting work. They had been spies amid the Americans; guides through the Georgia swamps; pilots taking ships over treacherous sandbars; sappers on the ramparts of Charleston as French cannonballs took off the limbs of the men beside them. They had dug trenches; buried bodies blistered with the pox; powdered the officers' wigs and, marching smartly drummed the regiments in and out of disaster. The women had cooked and laundered and nursed the sick; dabbed at the holes on soldiers' bodies; and tried to keep their children from harm. Some of them had fought. There had been black dragoons in South Carolina; waterborne gangs of black partisans for the king on the Hudson River; bands of black guerrillas who would descend on Patriot farms in New Jersey and take whatever they could, even white American prisoners.

So they were owed. They had been given their liberty, and some of them got land. But the soil was thin and strewn with boulders, and the blacks had no way, most of them, to clear and work it unless they hired themselves or their families out to the white Loyalists. That meant more cooking and laundering; more waiting on tables and shaving pink chins; more hammering rocks for roads and bridges. And still they were in debt, so grievously that some complained their liberty was no true liberty at all but just another kind of slavery in all but name.

But names counted. British Freedom's name said something important: that he was no longer negotiable property. For all its bleak hardships, Preston was not a Georgia plantation. Other Prestonians—Decimus Murphy, Caesar Smith—had evidently kept their slave names as they had made the passage to liberty. But British Freedom must have been born, or bought, as someone else. He may have shaken off that name, like his leg irons, on one of the 81 sailings out of New York in 1783, which had taken 30,000 Loyalists, black and white, to Nova Scotia, for no one called British Freedom is listed in the Book of Negroes, which recorded those who, as free men and women, were at liberty to go where they wished. It is also possible that British Freedom could have found his way to Nova Scotia in one of the earlier Loyalist evacuations—from Boston in 1776 or from Charleston in 1782. In the frightening months between the end of the war and the departure of the British fleets, as American planters were attempting to locate the whereabouts of escaped slaves, many of them changed their names to avoid identification. British Freedom may just have gone one step further in giving himself an alias that was also a patriotic boast.

Whichever route he had taken, and whatever trials he was enduring, British Freedom's choice of name proclaims something startling: a belief that it was the British monarchy rather than the new American republic that was more likely to deliver Africans from slavery. Although Thomas Jefferson, in the Declaration of Independence, had blamed "the Christian King" George III for the institution of slavery in America, blacks like British Freedom did not see the king that way at all. On the contrary, he was their enemy's enemy and thus their friend, emancipator and guardian.

Tens of thousands of African-Americans clung to the sentimental notion of a British freedom even when they knew that the English were far from being saints in respect to slavery. Until 1800, when its courts decisively ruled the institution illegal, there were slaves, as well as free blacks, in Nova Scotia, and there were hundreds of thousands more in the British Caribbean. Nonetheless, in 1829 one of the first militant African-American emancipationists, David Walker, wrote from Boston in his Appeal to the Coloured Citizens of the World that the "English" were "the best friends the coloured people have upon earth. Though they have oppressed us a little and have colonies now in the West Indies which oppress us sorely—Yet notwithstanding [the English] have done one hundred times more for the melioration of our condition, than all the other nations of the earth put together." White Americans, on the other hand, with their posturing religiosity and their hollow cant of freedom, he consigned to the lowest reaches of hypocritical infamy.

Whether the British deserved this reputation as the most racially broadminded among nations and empires is, to say the least, debatable. But during the Revolutionary War there is no question that tens of thousands of Africans, enslaved in the American South, did look to Britain as their deliverer, to the point where they were ready to risk life and limb to reach the lines of the royal army. To give this astounding fact its due means being obliged to tell the story of Anglo-American conflict, both during the Revolution and after, in a freshly complicated way.

To be sure, there were also many blacks who gave the Patriots the benefit of the doubt when they listened and read of their war as a war for liberty. If there was a British Freedom, there was also a Dick Freedom—and a Jeffery Liberty—fighting in a Connecticut regiment on the American side. Blacks fought and died for the American cause at Concord, Bunker Hill, Rhode Island and finally at Yorktown (where they were put in the front line-whether as a tribute to their courage or as expendable sacrifices is not clear). At the Battle of Monmouth in New Jersey, black troops on both sides fought each other. But until the British aggressively recruited slaves in 1775 and 1776, state assemblies, even in the North, as well as the multistate Continental Congress, flinched from their enlistment. In February 1776 Congress instructed Washington that, while free Negroes might be retained, no more should be enlisted. Slaves, of course, were to be excluded from the Continental Army set up by Congress.

By contrast, the proclamation of John Murray; Lord Dunmore, the last Colonial governor of Virginia, from HMS William on November 7, 1775, unequivocally promised outright liberty to all slaves escaping from Rebel plantations, reaching British lines and serving in some capacity with the army. The promise was made from military rather than humanitarian motives, and for every British Freedom who lived to see it kept, there were many more who would be unconscionably betrayed. Yet from opportunist tactics, some good might still arise. Dunmore's words, sanctioned by the British government and reiterated by Generals William Howe and Henry Clinton (who extended the definition of those entitled to liberty to black women and children), took wing in the world of the slaves, and they themselves took off, in their tens of thousands, shortly after.

Seeing the Revolutionary War through the eyes of enslaved blacks turns its meaning upside down. In Georgia, the Carolinas and much of Virginia, the vaunted war for liberty was, from the spring of 1775 to the late summer of 1776, a war for the perpetuation of servitude. The contortions of logic were so perverse, yet so habitual, that George Washington could describe Dunmore as "that arch traitor to the rights of humanity" for promising to free slaves and indentured servants.

Henry Melchior Muhlenberg, a Pennsylvania Lutheran pastor, knew what he was talking about when he wrote that the black population "secretly wished the British army might win, for then all Negro slaves will gain their freedom. It is said that this sentiment is universal among all the Negroes in America." And every so often truth broke through the armor of Patriot casuistry. In December 1775, Lund Washington wrote to his cousin George of both blacks and indentured servants, who were departing from the Washington properties at speed, that "there is not a man of them but would leave us if they believ'd they could make there [sic] escape . . . Liberty is sweet."

The founding fathers were themselves candid about the extent of the disappearance of their slaves, not least because so many of them experienced serious personal losses. Thomas Jefferson, who had seen his own attempt to incorporate a paragraph attacking slavery in the Declaration of Independence stricken out by Congress, lost 30 of his own during the few weeks in the spring of 1781, when Lord Cornwallis' troops were not far from his home, Monticello. He believed—and the judgment of most modern historians concurs—that at least 30,000 slaves had escaped from Virginia plantations in attempts to reach the British lines. The same went for the rest of the South.

The story of this mass flight, aptly characterized by historian Gary Nash as the Revolutionary War's "dirty little secret," is shocking in the best sense, in that it forces an honest and overdue rethinking of the war as involving, at its core, a third party. This third party of African-Americans, moreover, accounted for 20 percent of the entire population of 2.5 million Colonists, rising in Virginia to as much as 40 percent. When it came to the blacks caught up in their struggle, neither side, British nor American, behaved very well. But in the end, as British Freedom and multitudes like him appreciated, it was the royal, rather than the republican, road that seemed to offer a surer chance of liberty. Although the history that unfolded from the entanglement between black desperation and British paternalism would often prove to be bitterly tragic, it was, nonetheless, a formative moment in the history of African-American freedom.

It was among the Loyalist Africans that some of the earliest free Baptist and Methodist churches were created in and near Shelburne, Nova Scotia; there too that the first whites to be converted by a black preacher were baptized in those red rivers by the charismatic minister David George. The first schools expressly for free black children were opened in the Loyalist diaspora of Nova Scotia, where they were taught by black teachers like Catherine Abernathy in Preston and Stephen Blucke in Birchtown. In Sierra Leone, where more than a thousand of the "Nova Scotians" ended up after journeying back across the Atlantic, this time as persons not property, the American blacks experienced for the first time (and all too ephemerally) a meaningful degree of local law and self-government. It was another first when an elected black constable, the ex-slave Simon Proof, administered a flogging to a white sailor found guilty of dereliction of duty.

The history of black loyalism, however, is much more than a catalog of "firsts." The story also gives the lie to the stereotype of the Africans as passive, credulous pawns of American or British strategy. Whether they opted for the Patriot or for the Loyalist side, many of the blacks, illiterate or not, knew exactly what they were doing, even if they could never have anticipated the magnitude of the perils, misfortunes and deceits that would result from their decision. Often, their choice was determined by a judgment of whether, sooner or later, a free America would be forced to honor the Declaration of Independence's principle that the birthright of all men was liberty and equality; or whether (in the South especially), with the spectacle of runaways being hunted down and sent to labor in lead mines or saltpeter works, fine sounding promises were likely to be indefinitely deferred. It was not a good sign when enlistment incentives offered to white recruits in Georgia and South Carolina included a bounty of a free slave at the end of the war.

Throughout 1773 and 1774 the tempo of reported runaways gathered ominous momentum from New York to Georgia. Escapes were now imagined to be the prelude to a concerted rising. In New York concern about illicit "assemblies" of Negroes was so serious that instructions were issued to apprehend any blacks appearing in any sort of numbers after dark. To the jumpier Americans it did not bear contemplating what might happen should the slaves, especially in the Southern plantation Colonies, take it into their head that the vaunted liberties of Old England somehow applied to them. In the Virginia Gazette, one of many advertisements offering rewards for the recapture of runaways mentioned a Gabriel Jones and his wife, said to be on their way to the coast to board a ship for England, "where they imagine they will be free (a Notion now prevalent among the Negroes greatly to the vexation and prejudice of their Masters)."

Now where could slaves get such absurd ideas? Another advertisement supplies the answer. One Bacchus, it seems, in Augusta County, Georgia, ran away, leading his master to believe that he too might head for a port, there "to board a vessel for Great Britain from the knowledge he has of the late determination of the Somerset case."

What was this? Did slaves read law reports? How could it be that a judgment rendered in June 1772 by Lord. Chief Justice Mansfield in the court of the King's Bench in the case of a runaway African, James Somerset, recaptured by his master, could light a fire in the plantations?

Mansfield had set Somerset free, but had taken pains not to make a general ruling on the legality of slavery in England. However, the "Negro frolicks" in London celebrating the court decision had swept legal niceties aside. Across the Atlantic word spread, and spread quickly, that slavery had been outlawed in Britain. In 1774 a pamphlet written under the name "Freeman," published in Philadelphia, told American slaves that they could have liberty merely by "setting foot on that happy Territory where slavery is forbidden to perch." Before the Patriots knew it, the birds had already begun to fly the coop.

SIMON SCHAMA is university professor of art history and history at Columbia.

Midnight Riders

Following a convoluted series of events, Paul Revere and William Dawes were sent to alert Lexington and Concord that the British were coming. But it was a virtually forgotten third rider who would complete their mission.

CHARLES J. CAES

In the days leading up to April 15, 1775, Dr. Joseph Warren had been receiving reports of unusual movements within the British army as well as increased activity aboard the king's ships in Boston Harbor. On that Sunday, Warren, now nearly in complete charge of the radical groups increasingly protesting British rule, including the action-oriented Sons of Liberty, decided that the reported movements were suspicious enough to be brought to the attention of John Hancock and John Adams in Lexington. The man Warren called on to give that warning was none other than Paul Revere, one of the leaders of the Sons.

Revere was a popular and often recruited messenger: He was swift, intelligent and dependable. An engraver and silversmith by profession, Revere longed for a military commission but found he could best serve the colonies as a courier, printer and gunpowder manufacturer. He would eventually get his chance to command troops, but that opportunity would not present itself until the war was 3 years old.

For now, Revere was satisfied to work with the Sons of Liberty, the group of freedom fighters who had banded together a decade earlier in response to British taxation. Since 1765, the Sons had been threatening and harassing British officials, ostracizing or punishing supporters of the king, and coercing merchants to stop buying goods from the mother country. Samuel Adams, who was looking for every opportunity to break with England, and other leaders of the revolutionary element were gaining impressive ground, though the true extent of their popular support remained unsure. Colonials were an independent lot.

Revere made haste to Lexington, trying to attract as little attention as possible. He knew that the British commander, General Thomas Gage, had at least one spy among the Sons and that this spy and other Gage men always kept an eye on his movements. Nevertheless, Revere made the 15-mile journey without incident. He duly reported at his destination, "Boats belonging to the transports were all launched and carried under the Sterns of Men of War." He may also have reported that, the day before, British troops in Boston had been taken off regular duties and might be preparing to march the 18 miles to Concord, where they could seize or destroy the arms and ammunition in the town's well-known arsenal.

"I returned at night through Charlestown," Revere recalled in a 1798 account given to Dr. Jeremy Belknap, founder of the Massachusetts Historical Society. "There I agreed with a Colonel [William] Conant, and some other gentleman, that if the British went out by water, we would shew two lanthorns in the Old North Church steeple; and if by land, one, as a signal; for we were apprehensive it would be difficult to cross the Charles River, or get over Boston neck."

Dr. Warren probably realized that he would soon have to ask Revere to carry another message from him, and it might be one that would forever change the course of Colonial history. Warren was well aware the conflict between England and its colonies might soon come to blows. He knew that the majority of colonists still saw themselves as citizens of England, and although they might support the protests against the crown, simply sought the same political and economic rights as full British subjects rather than a complete break with the motherland. Warren also realized that some of the more outspoken Colonial leaders sought full independence. What he didn't know was whether or not the independent citizens-at-large would give their support to the Sons of Liberty and other Patriots who might decide to take up arms against the British.

Relations between England and the colonies had been deteriorating rapidly following an event that had occurred some 16 months before. On the evening of December 16, 1773, about 60 men disguised as Mohawk braves had raided three ships in Boston Harbor. Two thousand others from Boston and neighboring towns watched as the raiders went into the ships' holds, carried out more than 300 chests of tea, and for the next three or four hours tossed the tea overboard and destroyed the chests. Their well-rehearsed mission was carried out with the discipline of highly trained operatives, and, except for the splashing water, there was hardly a whisper or even much noise resulting from their numbers and hard work. When most of the cargo of tea had been destroyed, the "Mohawks" lined up on the wharf, dusted themselves off, and filed away. They left silently, leaving behind no one hurt and no property damage but the tea.

Of this event John Adams, who would one day become president, wrote in his diary, using the chaotic capitalization of the time: "The people should never rise without doing something to be remembered—something notable and striking. The Destruction of the Tea is so bold, so daring, so firm, intrepid and inflexible, and it must have so important Consequences, and so lasting, that I can't but consider it as an Epocha in History."

Not everyone, however, shared Adams' view, and Revere and most of the Boston Patriots were surprised to learn that their Tea Party, as it came to be called, was condemned not only by the Tories—those loyal to the British crown—but also by some of the more radical members of the Patriots' cause. In fact, even Ben Franklin chided them publicly, calling what they had done "an act of violent injustice." He insisted Boston should be required to make the necessary restitution.

The reasons for the decision to target tea for a defiant display of resentment had been many. In May 1773, the British Parliament had passed the Tea Act, intended to bolster the privately owned and financially troubled East India Company. The act provided that tea could be shipped to the colonies only in East India vessels, was to be stored in company warehouses to be built in the colonies, and could be sold directly to retailers only by East India agents. It also adjusted import duties to allow East India to undercut the prices of Colonial merchants and smugglers who had offered strong competition. In essence, the East India Company was granted a monopoly on the tea trade to the colonies.

Colonists were angered because Parliament had again passed legislation that meddled in Colonial affairs without giving voice, vote or legal recourse to those most affected. In addition, the legislated monopoly immediately threatened to put legitimate Colonial tea merchants out of business and to undersell the smugglers. (By the time of the Boston Tea Party, some estimates suggest that 90 percent of the tea consumed in the colonies was smuggled in, and many noted patriots, including John Hancock, found that trade both adventurous and highly profitable.)

In late 1773, with three British tea-laden vessels, *Dartmouth, Eleanor* and *Beaver,* waiting to be offloaded in Boston Harbor, Patriot spokesmen attempted to negotiate with Royal Governor of Massachusetts Thomas Hutchinson and the East India Company's agents—two of whom were Hutchinson's sons—to have the tea sent back to England. When those negotiations failed, a general boycott of English tea was called for and it was decided that the raid on the three ships was the best way to express how serious the matter was to the colonists.

When news of the Tea Party reached England, King George III declared that the Colonials had finally gone too far and petitioned Parliament to design measures for a suitable response. The result was a series of acts specifically designed to punish Massachusetts. Among other provisions, the English closed the port of Boston until the tea was paid for, made illegal any town meeting except those authorized by the governor or necessary for the regular election of officers, and allowed public buildings so designated to be used to house the military. Called the "Intolerable Acts" by the colonists, they were intrinsically punitive measures, and the other colonies feared that if the British were to get away with punishing Massachusetts in this way, a precedent would be set for dealing with all the colonies.

The result was demonstrations in all major cities. The protests and demands of the colonists increased, and before long mere protests became outcries for the colonies to unite. These events led to a proposal in the Massachusetts House of Representatives that a Congress be convened in Philadelphia that year to respond to British demands. The First Continental Congress went into session on September 3 and continued to October 26. Representatives from all the colonies except Georgia attended.

Each colony was given one vote, and it became quite clear that when the votes were counted, they would reflect a Congress well resolved to fight the British Acts. As it turned out, the Congress declared the Intolerable Acts had no constitutional foundation and recommended that Massachusetts should form an independent government and withhold payment of any taxes until the Acts were repealed. It also established the Continental Association to promote boycotts of British goods and recommended that each colony establish an armed militia.

The Tea Act, the Tea Party, the Intolerable Acts and the First Continental Congress had created a political tide that could not be avoided. Dr. Warren probably realized that there was no way of sailing against it, and all he could do was command as best he could while being driven by its force. That General Gage had increased his Boston garrison to about 10,000 men was a sign to the Patriot leadership that the British were ready to move against the colony.

If Gage had his way, he would have had 20,000 men in the garrison, but Parliament winced at this request, thinking there was hardly any real threat of a rebellion. After all, they believed, Gage's true threat was simply a small number of disorganized radicals egged on by Colonial money, with profit as motive. It was preposterous to think that the entire Massachusetts colony would ever consider taking up arms against the motherland.

Parliament made one thing very clear to Gage: He had to crush the Sons of Liberty and other radical groups once and for all, and soon. By the time of Revere's April 15 dispatch to Adams and Hancock, Gage already had in his possession direct orders from British Secretary of State Lord Dartmouth to act with force.

Gage was not enthusiastic about his orders. Like most soldiers of rank and experience, he knew no one could ever be sure just how a battle might turn out. Besides, in this case, it would be friend against friend in many instances: Mutual respect had developed between British officials and soldiers and the colonists with whom they had entered congenial social and business relationships. Gage had hoped that a show of force on his part would make the Colonials realize that armed resistance was of no avail and was therefore disappointed when Parliament would not allow him more troops. Nevertheless, if he were to fight, he would do so with all skill and determination, and with all the force he could command.

Organizing his best troops for what he advertised as a training exercise, Gage prepared them for a search-and-destroy mission to Concord. At the same time he would also attempt to find, and capture or kill, Hancock and Adams. To command the forces against Concord, he selected Colonel Francis Smith. Second-in-command was Major John Pitcairn, whose surname is best recognized outside of England for its attachment to the Pacific island named for his son Robert.

Expecting only token opposition, Gage gave no specific orders on how to handle armed resistance. He only advised his commanders to move swiftly on the evening of April 18, 1775, for he knew the citizens of Concord were relocating their munitions. To stop them, he planned to move light infantry and grenadiers by long-boat across Boston's Back Bay, and then march them to Concord. Meanwhile, he put patrols on the roads from both Boston and Charlestown with orders to lay hold of anyone attempting to warn Concord. The plan would have been seamless except that there were not enough boats to keep the schedule. Ferrying could not be completed until after midnight.

Early in the evening of the 18th, as soon as Dr. Warren was aware that Gage's men were marching to Boston Common, he called for two messengers to carry word to Lexington and Concord. The warning had to get out, and two messengers on different pathways increased the odds of success.

Warren called for the first, William Dawes Jr., a tanner and neighbor who lived on Ann Street no more than 300 yards from Warren, and Dawes responded instantly. He either arrived with his uncle Josiah Waters or met him at Warren's house. Once there, Dawes received instructions to take a very specific route to deliver messages at Roxbury, Cambridge, Menotomy (now Arlington), Lexington and Concord. But his journey would not end there. From Concord, he was to proceed to Waltham, where he would instruct the militia to prepare an ambush. Once this mission was complete, Dawes was to return to Menotomy for additional instructions from Warren.

Dawes wasted no time in riding off, but proceeded slowly at first since his uncle was following on foot at a distance to see that Dawes got past the British checkpoints at Boston Neck. Uncle Josiah reported the successful passage to Dr. Warren as his nephew rode on to Roxbury. There, Dawes reported to Patriot General William Heath and instructed him to meet Warren and the Committee of Safety in Menotomy, explaining that from there Heath and Warren would proceed on to Lexington, where Heath would assume command of the militia.

The second rider called was Revere, who would be given a shorter route. Why Warren waited until 10 P.M. to summon him is hard to discern. In any event, by the time Revere appeared, Dawes had already been to Roxbury and was on his way to Cambridge. Warren was in an anxious mood when Revere arrived and implored him to leave immediately for Lexington to report on the latest news about British troop movements.

Revere was quickly on his way. He assumed he had been given the same instructions as Dawes, but later realized their missions were not exactly the same. He no doubt also realized that his own high profile often worked against him, and that Warren, well aware of this, was using him as backup.

Popular literature leaves the impression of a quick dash to his horse and a gallop to Lexington. The start of Revere's journey was actually far less theatrical. "I left Dr. Warren, called upon a friend, and desired him to make the signals," Revere recalled. The friend was Robert Newman, and the signal was to be that of the two lanterns. "I then went home took my boots and surtout [a tight-fitting coat], and went to the north part of town, where I kept a boat; two friends rowed me across the river . . . " and past a man-of-war. When they arrived on the Charlestown side, he hurried into town, where he met Colonel William Conant and some others. Revere learned they were already advised of the British strategy thanks to the double-lantern signal from Newman. Reporting all he knew about Gage's movements and possible intentions, Revere borrowed a horse, possibly named Brown Beauty, and raced off toward Lexington. At one point around Charlestown Neck, he was chased by two British officers, but some talented riding and a soft-bottomed pond that trapped one of the Britons allowed Revere to escape capture.

By this time, Dawes had already been to Cambridge to warn that British troops were on their way over water to Concord from Charlestown, but that the majority of the force was traveling by land with heavier battle equipment. In order to further thwart the British, the townspeople tore up most of the planks from the Great Bridge and left them stacked at the Cambridge end.

Revere went on to Medford and then Menotomy. "In Medford," he recorded, "I awaked the Captain of the minutemen; and after that, I alarmed almost every house, till I got to Lexington. I found Messrs. Hancock and Adams at the Rev. Mr. Clark's. I told them of my errand, and inquired of Mr. Dawes."

Revere was afraid that Dawes might have been captured by the British, perhaps by the same two officers who had chased him. In fact, Dawes was in Menotomy warning the Committee of Safety that they might be taken prisoner if found. Dawes, however, did indeed come close to capture but avoided it by entering into conversation and riding along with some British soldiers. He finally arrived in Lexington to warn Hancock and Adams about a half-hour after Revere.

After allowing themselves time to refresh, Revere and Dawes set off to warn Concord and tell its militia to move its arsenals to safer places. Along the way, they heard a rider approaching, and at first both were apprehensive, for little that night could be predictable. But the rider was alone and friendly enough.

He was 24-year-old Dr. Samuel Prescott, who had just spent the evening with a young lady with whom he was evidently quite smitten. Prescott's personality, mannerisms, voice and knowledge of the Sons of Liberty—in which he claimed membership—won the trust of Dawes and Revere. While Prescott was not another of Warren's official messengers, when he learned of the mission Revere and Dawes were on, he was eager to play his role in warning the people of Concord.

"I likewise mentioned, that we had better alarm all the inhabitants till we got to Concord," Revere noted in his account for the Massachusetts Historical Society. "The young doctor much approved of it, and said, he would stop with either of us, for the people between [there] and Concord knew him. And would give the more credit to what we said."

The three horsemen continued on their journey, Revere riding perhaps a 100 yards ahead of Dawes and Prescott, probably to scout or draw out trouble in time for the others to get away. As it turned out, the strategy paid off. They were riding right into a British patrol commanded by Major Edward Mitchell.

Revere called out a warning to Dawes and Prescott. Dawes immediately turned his horse and started for Lexington. Prescott galloped toward Revere, instinctively intent on facing whatever challenge was at hand, but by the time he reached Revere, the British were too well positioned, their guns or swords drawn for the kill. Prescott knew the terrain, however; he wheeled his horse about suddenly and, riding pell-mell, jumped a stone wall and raced off toward Concord. Two British horsemen sped after him.

An expert horseman, the young doctor fearlessly guided his horse through the forest, leading his pursuers toward a swamp too threatening for the British to enter. They feared being led into a trap or finding themselves and their mounts sinking deep into mud and water. Prescott, on the other hand, knowing the terrain, guided his horse swiftly through the mud and water or around it.

Prescott pushed through a thicket, on the other side of which he knew was the home of a fellow minuteman. After quietly riding around to the rear of the house, he began banging on the kitchen door until he had awakened every one. When Sergeant Samuel Hartwell, of the Lincoln Minute Men, recognized Prescott, he came to the window and asked why he was there. The young physician explained that the British were on the march and told Hartwell to alert his fellow militiamen. He then turned his mount toward his hometown, and, as he raced away, the sergeant prepared himself to spread the word on the road back toward Lexington.

Mitchell's men captured Revere, but Mitchell, worried that he and his men were in harm's way or insufficiently prepared to take advantage of an opportunity, was extremely angry that the other two riders had escaped. He had Revere brought to him and quickly put a gun to Revere's head. "I'm about to ask you some questions," he warned. "If I do not get the true answers, I will blow your brains out."

Revere made up a story that Mitchell was in greater danger than he, claiming he had already warned the entire colony about what Gage was planning, and that hundreds of men were between Mitchell and Boston. Most important, Revere pointed out, Mitchell could expect no reinforcements; the troops he was expecting from across the river had run aground.

Mitchell could not decide if Revere was lying, but thought it best to retreat to Lexington. On their way, Mitchell heard a shot, then a volley of shots. He feared that it might be the result of a skirmish and that, perhaps, Revere was telling the truth after all. In fact, the shots had been fired by members of the local militia testing their firearms.

Unsure of the reason for the gunfire, Mitchell decided his best course of action was to cut across Lexington Common with maximum speed. Movement, he decided, would be safer and swifter without prisoners, so he reluctantly released Revere and others he was holding.

Although Revere's horse had been given to one of Mitchell's men, Revere knew the area well and took little time running through a cemetery and across pastures to reach the Hancock-Clarke House. There he found both Hancock and Adams eagerly awaiting the latest news while debating whether to stay and fight or head for safety.

Since they were the brains behind the revolt, their capture would be costly to the cause as well as devastating to morale.

Hancock wanted to join the militia and stand against the British; Adams argued that they were better off retreating to Philadelphia. Hancock eventually agreed that Adams' judgment was, perhaps, the better, and the leaders asked Revere to see to their safe escort for part of their journey to Philadelphia. They were pleased when he agreed.

While Revere and another man were moving a chest of papers from a tavern room for Hancock, Captain John Parker, a veteran of the French and Indian War, was mustering about 80 minutemen onto Lexington Green. As they assembled, Colonel Pitcairn marched a column of light infantry up the road toward Parker. It was shortly after 5 A.M., and there was enough light for Revere and his friend to see what poor Parker was up against. Revere, a veteran soldier, must have wondered if the minutemen had any chance at all.

When the minutemen realized the British were fearless, determined and well-armed, they considered that this might be their very last day on earth, so they began to back away. Parker ordered them to stand fast. The minutemen on Lexington Green watched the determined and well-armed British troops march toward them, counted their far superior number, and heard Pitcairn call out for Parker and his men to lay down their arms and disperse. Parker's instinct told him the odds were against him, and he responded by ordering his men to put down their weapons and leave the scene.

As they began to do so, a shot rang out, followed by more. The British answered with a volley and charged with bayonets drawn. When it was over, eight minute-men lay dead, another 10 wounded. The war for independence had begun.

Because Revere had been captured by Mitchell, he was never able to complete in its entirety the mission for which he was recruited. Dawes was instrumental in bringing the necessary warnings to Roxbury, Cambridge, Menotomy and Lexington (though here, after Revere), but after his escape from Mitchell and his men, Dawes was unable to race on to Concord. In fact, records are unclear on just where he finally wound up on the morning of the 19th. However, thanks to the swashbuckling young Dr. Prescott, Warren's message did reach Concord in time for its arsenal to be moved to safer ground. By the time the British marched on Concord, they found only a small number of arms and supplies.

Boston born and bred, Paul Revere remains the most historically popular of the three riders. He fought in the French and Indian War and was, to name a few of his talents and skills, a silversmith, an engraver, a printer and even a dentist before the revolution. After the revolution, he served as a lieutenant colonel of artillery, designed the first seal for the united colonies, and managed to stay employed in lucrative ventures.

After the famous ride, Dawes fought in the war and possibly at Bunker Hill. Afterward, he and his brother-in-law, John Coolidge, opened a general store in Worcester, Mass. From 1786 to 1787, he saw duty as a clerk in the Ancient and Honorable Artillery Company of Massachusetts. Life after the war was not particularly easy for William, for he had aged parents to take care of as well as his own family, and his meager finances provided only a minimum amount of security. About 1790, he began raising cash by selling properties he owned in Boston (his birthplace) and Worcester. Widowed and remarried, he died in Marlboro.

Samuel Prescott, who remains mostly a mystery to historians, received little recognition for his famous ride. Up until the time of the revolution, he was a practicing physician, having served his apprenticeship under the tutelage of his father, Abel Prescott, a successful doctor. Even less is known about his life after the war began, except that he was a surgeon in the Ticonderoga campaign, and later served aboard a privateer. Two stories have emerged about his death. One says that he was captured at Ticonderoga, there to die in prison. Another tells that he was captured at sea and died in British custody at Halifax. There is no record of his having married.

Prescott's courage, daredevil riding and strong voice did more than bring timely warning to his friends and neighbors in Concord. His rousing of other Sons of Liberty along the way increased the network of "expresses" who rapidly and thoroughly spread the message in outlying areas that the British were on their way. As the records show, only Prescott finished the midnight ride to Concord; not Dawes, not Revere.

From *American History*, December 2004, pp. 34–41. Copyright © 2004 by Primedia Enterprises. Reprinted by permission.

God and the Founders

Battles over faith and freedom may seem never-ending, but a new book, 'American Gospel,' argues that history illuminates how religion can shape the nation without dividing it.

Jon Meacham

America's first fight was over faith. As the Founding Fathers gathered for the inaugural session of the Continental Congress on Tuesday, September 6, 1774, at Carpenters' Hall in Philadelphia, Thomas Cushing, a lawyer from Boston, moved that the delegates begin with a prayer. Both John Jay of New York and John Rutledge, a rich lawyer-planter from South Carolina, objected. Their reasoning, John Adams wrote his wife, Abigail, was that "because we were so divided in religious sentiments"—the Congress included Episcopalians, Congregationalists, Presbyterians, and others—"we could not join in the same act of worship." The objection had the power to set a secular tone in public life at the outset of the American political experience.

Things could have gone either way. Samuel Adams of Boston spoke up. "Mr. S. Adams arose and said he was no bigot, and could hear a prayer from a gentleman of piety and virtue who was at the same time a friend to his country," wrote John Adams. "He was a stranger in Philadelphia, but had heard that Mr. Duche (Dushay they pronounce it) deserved that character, and therefore he moved that Mr. Duche, an Episcopal clergyman, might be desired to read prayers to the Congress tomorrow morning." Then, in a declarative nine-word sentence, John Adams recorded the birth of what Benjamin Franklin called America's public religion: "The motion was seconded and passed in the affirmative."

The next morning the Reverend Duche appeared, dressed in clerical garb. As it happened, the psalm assigned to be read that day by Episcopalians was the 35th. The delegates had heard rumors—later proved to be unfounded—that the British were storming Boston; everything seemed to be hanging in the balance. In the hall, with the Continental Army under attack from the world's mightiest empire, the priest read from the psalm: " 'Plead my cause, O Lord, with them that strive with me: fight against them that fight against me.' "

Fight against them that fight against me: John Adams was at once stunned and moved. "I never saw a greater effect upon an audience," he told Abigail. "It seemed as if Heaven had ordained that Psalm to be read on that morning." Adams long tingled from the moment—the close quarters of the room, the mental vision in every delegate's head of the patriots supposedly facing fire to the north, and, with Duche's words, the summoning of divine blessing and guidance on what they believed to be the cause of freedom.

As it was in the beginning, so it has been since: an American acknowledgment of God in the public sphere, with men of good will struggling to be reverent yet tolerant and ecumenical. That the Founding Fathers debated whether to open the American saga with prayer is wonderfully fitting, for their conflicts are our conflicts, their dilemmas our dilemmas. Largely faithful, they knew religious wars had long been a destructive force in the lives of nations, and they had no wish to repeat the mistakes of the world they were rebelling against. And yet they bowed their heads.

More than two centuries on, as millions of Americans observe Passover and commemorate Easter next week, the role of faith in public life is a subject of particularly pitched debate. From stem cells and science to the Supreme Court, from foreign policy and the 2008 presidential campaign to evangelical "Justice Sundays," the question of God and politics generates much heat but little light. Some Americans think the country has strayed too far from God; others fear that religious zealots (from the White House to the school board) are waging holy war on American liberty; and many, if not most, seem to believe that we are a nation hopelessly divided between believers and secularists.

History suggests, though, that there is hope, for we have been fighting these battles from our earliest days and yet the American experiment endures.

However dominant in terms of numbers, Christianity is only a thread in the American tapestry—it is not the whole tapestry. The God who is spoken of and called on and prayed to in the public sphere is an essential character in the American drama, but He is not specifically God the Father or the God of Abraham. The right's contention that we are a "Christian nation" that has fallen from pure origins and can achieve redemption by some kind of return to Christian values is based on wishful thinking, not convincing historical argument. Writing to the Hebrew Congregation in Newport, Rhode Island, in 1790, George Washington assured his Jewish countrymen that the American government "gives to bigotry no sanction." In a treaty with the Muslim nation of Tripoli initiated by Washington, completed by John Adams, and ratified by the Senate in 1797, we declared "the Government of the United States is not, in any sense, founded on the Christian religion. . . ." The Founders also knew the nation would grow ever more diverse; in Virginia, Thomas Jefferson's bill for religious freedom was "meant to comprehend, within the mantle of its protection, the Jew and the Gentile, the Christian and the Mahometan, the Hindoo and infidel of every denomination." And thank God—or, if you choose, thank the Founders—that it did indeed.

In Jefferson's words, 'The God who gave us life gave us liberty'—including the liberty to believe or not to believe.

Understanding the past may help us move forward. When the subject is faith in the public square, secularists reflexively point to the Jeffersonian "wall of separation between church and state" as though the conversation should end there; many conservative Christians defend their forays into the political arena by citing the Founders, as though Washington, Adams, Jefferson, and Franklin were cheerful Christian soldiers. Yet to claim that religion has only recently become a political force in the United States is uninformed and unhistorical; in practice, the "wall" of separation is not a very tall one. Equally wrongheaded is the tendency of conservative believers to portray the Founding Fathers as apostles in knee britches.

The great good news about America—the American gospel, if you will—is that religion shapes the life of the nation without strangling it. Driven by a sense of providence and an acute appreciation of the fallibility of humankind, the Founders made a nation in which faith should not be singled out for special help or particular harm. The balance between the promise of the Declaration of Independence, with its evocation of divine origins and destiny, and the practicalities of the Constitution, with its checks on extremism, remains the most brilliant of American successes.

The Founding Fathers and presidents down the ages have believed in a God who brought forth the heavens and the earth, and who gave humankind the liberty to believe in Him or not, to love Him or not, to obey Him or not. God had created man with free will, for love coerced is no love at all, only submission. That is why the religious should be on the front lines of defending freedom of religion.

Our finest hours—the Revolutionary War, abolition, the expansion of the rights of women, hot and cold wars against terror and tyranny, Martin Luther King Jr.'s battle against Jim Crow—can partly be traced to religious ideas about liberty, justice, and charity. Yet theology and scripture have also been used to justify our worst hours—from enslaving people based on the color of their skin to treating women as second-class citizens.

Still, Jefferson's Declaration of independence grounded America's most fundamental human rights in the divine, as the gift of "Nature's God." The most unconventional of believers, Jefferson was no conservative Christian; he once went through the Gospels with a razor to excise the parts he found implausible. ("I am of a sect by myself, as far as I know," he remarked.) And yet he believed that "the God who gave us life gave us liberty at the same time," and to Jefferson, the "Creator" invested the individual with rights no human power could ever take away. The Founders, however, resolutely refused to evoke sectarian—specifically Christian—imagery: the God of the Declaration is largely the God of Deism, an Enlightenment-era vision of the divine in which the Lord is a Creator figure who works in the world through providence. The Founding Fathers rejected an attempt to rewrite the Preamble of the Constitution to say the nation was dependent on God, and from the Lincoln administration forward presidents and Congresses refused to support a "Christian Amendment" that would have acknowledged Jesus to be the "Ruler among the nations."

At the same time, the early American leaders were not absolute secularists. They wanted God in American public life, but in a way that was unifying, not divisive. They were politicians and philosophers, sages and warriors, churchmen and doubters. While Jefferson edited the Gospels, Franklin rendered the Lord's Prayer into the 18th-century vernacular, but his piety had its limits: he recalled falling asleep in a Quaker meeting house on his first day in Philadelphia. All were devoted to liberty, but most kept slaves. All were devoted to virtue, but many led complex—the religious would say sinful—private lives.

The Founders understood that theocracy was tyranny, but they did not feel they could—or should—try to banish religion from public life altogether. Washington improvised "So help me, God" at the conclusion of the first presidential oath and kissed the Bible on which he had sworn it. Abraham Lincoln issued the Emancipation Proclamation, he privately told his cabinet, because he had struck a deal with "my Maker" that he would free the slaves if the Union forces triumphed at Antietam. The only public statement Franklin D. Roosevelt made on D-Day 1944 was to read a prayer he had written drawing on the 1928 Episcopal Book of Common Prayer. John Kennedy said that "on earth, God's work must truly be our own," and Ronald Reagan was not afraid to say that he saw the world as a struggle between light and dark, calling the Soviet empire "the focus of evil in the modern world." George W. Bush credits Billy Graham with saving him from a life of drift and drink, and once said that Christ was his favorite philosopher.

Sectarian language, however, can be risky. In a sermon preached on the day George Washington left Philadelphia to take command of the Continental Army, an Episcopal priest said: "Religion and liberty must flourish or fall together in America. We pray that both may be perpetual." The battle to preserve faith and freedom has been a long one, and rages still: keeping religion and politics in proper balance requires eternal vigilance.

Our best chance of summoning what Lincoln called "the better angels of our nature" may lie in recovering the true sense and spirit of the Founding era and its leaders, for they emerged from a time of trial with a moral creed which, while imperfect, averted the worst experiences of other nations. In that history lies our hope.

From *American Gospel* by John Meacham (Random House, 2006). Copyright © 2006 by John Meacham. Reprinted by permission.

The Rocky Road to Revolution

While most members of Congress sought a negotiated settlement with England, independence advocates bided their time.

JOHN FERLING

We hold these truths to be self-evident, that all men are created equal, that they are endowed by their Creator with certain unalienable Rights, that among these are Life, Liberty and the pursuit of Happiness—That to secure these rights, Governments are instituted among Men, deriving their just powers from the consent of the governed . . .

Laboring at his desk in the midst of a Philadelphia heat wave in June 1776, Thomas Jefferson hastened to complete a pressing assignment. A Congressional committee, recognizing his "happy talent for composition," had given the 33-year-old Jefferson responsibility for drafting a declaration of independence, a document that Congress needed almost immediately. Jefferson, one of Virginia's seven delegates to the Second Continental Congress, worked in his two-room apartment on the second floor of a tradesman's house at Market and Seventh streets, a heavily trafficked corner. He rose before sunrise to write and, after the day's long Congressional session, he returned to his lodging to take up his pen again at night. Toward the end of his life, Jefferson would say that his purpose had been to "place before mankind the common sense of the subject." Congress, he recalled, required an "expression of the American mind."

Jefferson well knew that America was at a defining moment in its history. Independence would sever ties with a long colonial past and propel the 13 states—and the new American nation to which they would belong—into an extremely uncertain future. Jefferson also knew that Congress wanted the declaration completed by July 1, less than three weeks after he was given the assignment.

No one appreciated better than he the irony in the sudden desire for haste. Jefferson had been prepared to declare independence perhaps as much as a year earlier, from the moment that war against the mother country erupted on April 19, 1775. Yet Congress had refused. In the 14 months since American blood had been shed at Lexington and Concord, American soldiers had also died at Bunker Hill, in the siege of Boston, and during an ill-fated invasion of Canada. In addition, the Royal Navy had bombarded and burned American towns, and the colonists' commerce had been nearly shut down by a British blockade. Still, Congress had not declared independence.

But not even Jefferson, passionate advocate of independence that he was, fully grasped the importance of the document he was preparing. Nor did his colleague, John Adams of Massachusetts, who had masterminded the arduous struggle within Congress to declare independence. Focused single-mindedly on that contentious undertaking, Adams regarded the actual statement itself as a mere formality—he would call it "a theatrical show"—a necessary instrument of propaganda. Jefferson, for his part, said little about his accomplishment. Not long after his work was completed, he would depart Philadelphia to return to his responsibilities in the Virginia legislature. Still, he was more than mildly vexed that Congress had made revisions—or "mutilations," as he put it—to the language of his original draft. Historians now agree that Congress' alterations and excisions enhanced the Declaration's power. Jefferson's magisterial opening passage, and indeed, much of his original language, actually survived intact.

Today, the passage of time has dulled our memory of the extent to which many Americans, including a majority in the Continental Congress, were, for a very long period, reluctant to break ties completely and irrevocably with Britain. The creation of the document we have come to regard as the seminal expression of revolutionary ardor was by no means inevitable. More than two-and-a-quarter centuries after the Declaration was signed, this eloquent assertion of individual rights, reinstalled last September in a state-of-the-art glass encasement at the National Archives in Washington, D.C., can be assessed in all of its complexity—as the product of the protracted political debate that preceded its formulation.

By the summer of 1776, the patience of many congressmen had been sorely tried by bitter wrangling over the question of whether or not to declare independence. Many of the legislators thought it nonsensical to fight a war for any purpose other than independence, yet others disagreed. For month after bloody month Congress had sat on its hands, prompting John Adams to exclaim early in 1776 that America was caught "between Hawk and Buzzard," fighting a war it could not win unless it declared independence from Britain, thereby prompting England's enemies, most prominently France, to aid in the struggle.

America's war with the mother country had commenced when a British army of nearly 900 men, acting on orders from London, had marched from Boston to Concord, intending to destroy a colonial arsenal and, if possible, capture ringleaders John Hancock and Samuel Adams. The Second Continental Congress, which assembled in Philadelphia just three weeks later, had barely been gaveled to order when John Rutledge of South Carolina, a 35-year-old lawyer from Charleston, raised the critical question: "Do We aim at independancy? or do We only ask for a Restoration of Rights & putting of Us on Our old footing [as subjects of the crown]?" It would take Congress 14 months to answer that question.

Congress quickly divided into two factions. One felt that the British actions at Lexington and Concord in April required nothing less than a clean break from the motherland; they believed colonists would always be second-class citizens in the British Empire. This faction would have declared independence in May or June 1775. But a second faction, which comprised a substantial majority in Congress, yearned to be reconciled with Britain. These delegates believed in waging war only to compel London to accept America's terms—Rutledge's "old footing"—to return to the way things were before Parliament tried to tax Americans and claim unlimited jurisdiction over them.

Opposition to Parliament had been growing since it enacted the first American tax, the Stamp Act of 1765. At the First Continental Congress, which met in Philadelphia in September 1774, some delegates wanted to force repeal of it and other repressive measures through a trade embargo. A more conservative faction had pushed for a compromise to provide American representation in Parliament. In the end, Congress adopted the trade boycott, and war had come. "Nothing," wrote John Adams, "but Fortitude, Vigour, and Perseverance can save Us."

Most who had attended the First Continental Congress now sat in the Second, where they were joined by several fresh faces. For instance, Hancock, who had escaped capture at Lexington thanks to Paul Revere's timely warning, was now a member of the Massachusetts delegation. Sixty-nine-year-old Benjamin Franklin, who had just returned to Philadelphia after a decade in London, had been named a delegate from Pennsylvania. Gone were those from the First Continental Congress who refused to countenance a war against Britain, prompting Richard Henry Lee of Virginia to observe that a "perfect unanimity" existed in the Second Continental Congress, at least on the war issue.

John Adams concurred that a "military Spirit" that was "truly amazing" had seized the land. Militiamen were "as thick as Bees," he said, marching and drilling everywhere, including in the steamy streets outside the Pennsylvania State House where Congress met. His cousin, Samuel Adams, believed an equally militant spirit gripped Congress and that every member was committed to "the Defence and Support of American Liberty." The Adams cousins soon discovered, however, that while all in Congress supported the war, sentiment for severing ties with Britain was strong only in New England and Virginia. Reconciliationists prevailed everywhere else.

John Adams counseled patience. "We must Suffer People to take their own Way," he asserted in June 1775, even though that path might not be the "Speedyest and Surest." He understood that to push too hard for independence was to risk driving conservative Americans back into Britain's arms. Thus, for most of 1775, the pro-independence faction never spoke openly of a break with Britain. Adams likened America to that of "a large Fleet sailing under Convoy. The fleetest Sailors must wait for the dullest and slowest." For the foreseeable future, he lamented, "Progress must be slow."

But Adams was confident that those who favored reconciliation would be driven inexorably toward independence. In time, he believed, they would discover that London would never give in to America's demands. Furthermore, he expected that war would transform the colonists' deep-seated love for Britain into enmity, necessitating a final break.

Reconciliationists were strongest in the Middle Atlantic colonies (New York, New Jersey, Pennsylvania, Maryland and Delaware) and in South Carolina, all of which had long since been drawn into the economic web of the Atlantic world. Before the war, the products of the backcountry—furs, hides and lumber—as well as grain, had moved through New York and Philadelphia to markets in the Caribbean and England. Charleston exported indigo and rice. In return, English-manufactured goods entered the colonies through these ports. Business had flourished during most of the 18th century; in recent years Philadelphia's merchants had routinely enjoyed annual profits of more than 10 percent.

The great merchants in Philadelphia and New York, who constituted a powerful political force, had other compelling reasons for remaining within the empire. Many relied upon credit supplied by English bankers. The protection afforded to transatlantic trade by the Royal Navy minimized insurance and other overhead costs. Independence, Philadelphia merchant Thomas Clifford asserted in 1775, would "assuredly prove unprofitable." The "advantages of security and stability," said another, "lie with . . . remaining in the empire."

And there was fear of the unknown. Some in Congress spoke of a break with Britain as a "leap in the dark," while others likened it to being cast adrift on "an Unknown Ocean." To be sure, many things *could* miscarry should America try to go it alone. After all, its army was composed of untried soldiers led, for the most part, by inexperienced officers. It possessed neither a navy nor allies and lacked the funds to wage a lengthy conflict. The most immediate danger was that the fledgling nation might lose a war for independence. Such a defeat could unleash a series of dire consequences that, the reconciliationists believed, might be avoided only if the colonies, even in the midst of war, were to negotiate a settlement *before* breaking absolutely with Britain. The reconciliationists held that it was still possible to reach a middle ground; this view seemed, to men such as John Adams, a naive delusion. Finally, the anti-independence faction argued, losing the war might well result in retaliation, including the loss of liberties the colonists had long enjoyed.

Even victory could have drawbacks. Many felt independence could be won only with foreign assistance, which raised the specter of American dependence on a European superpower, most likely autocratic and Roman Catholic France. But Adams believed that fear of anarchy accounted for most conservative opposition to independence. More than anything, said Adams, it rendered "Independency . . . an Hobgoblin, of so frightfull Mein" to the reconciliationists.

Pennsylvania's John Dickinson soon emerged as the leader of those who sought rapprochement with Britain. Dickinson, who was 43 in 1775, had been raised on plantations in Maryland and Delaware. One of the few supporters of the war to have actually lived in England, where he had gone to study law, in London, he had not been impressed by what he found there. The English, he concluded, were intemperate and immoral; their political system was hopelessly corrupt and run by diabolical mediocrities. Returning to Philadelphia to practice law in 1757, he was soon drawn to politics.

Tall and thin, Dickinson was urbane, articulate and somewhat prickly. A patrician accustomed to having his way, he could be quick-tempered with those who opposed him. He had once brawled with a political adversary and challenged him to a duel. Early in the Second Continental Congress, following an incendiary speech by Adams, Dickinson pursued him into the State House yard and, in a venomous outburst, as recounted by Adams, demanded: "What is the reason, Mr. Adams, that you New Englandmen oppose our Measures of Reconciliation. . . . Look Ye," he threatened, "If you don't concur with Us, in our pacific System, I, and a Number of Us, will break off from you . . . and We will carry on the Opposition by ourselves in our own Way." Adams was infuriated by Dickinson's invective: the two never spoke again.

Dickinson had a distinguished record. In 1765 he had served in the Stamp Act Congress convened to protest that measure. Two years later, he published his cogent and illuminating *Letters from a Farmer in Pennsylvania*, America's most popular political tract before 1776, which assumed that Parliament, though possessed of the right to regulate trade, lacked authority to tax the colonists. That was the very stand taken by 1774's First Continental Congress, and a constitutional settlement along those lines—not independence—was what the reconciliationists hoped to achieve through war. Dickinson charged that London had launched an "inexpressibly cruel War." Its "Sword is opening our Veins," he said, compelling Americans to fight for their freedom.

But he also warned that a war for independence would be interminable. British prime minister Lord Frederick North had pledged an implacable fight to maintain "every Advantage" that Britain derived from its control of the colonies. Before any war for independence ended, Dickinson prophesied, Americans would have "tasted deeply of that bitter Cup called the Fortunes of War." Not only would they have to "wade thro Seas of Blood," but in due course, hostilities would bring on mas-

sive unemployment within the maritime trades, heinous cruelties along the frontier, slave insurrections in the South and the relentless spread of disease from armies to civilians. And even in the unlikely event independence was achieved, Dickinson argued, yet another catastrophe might well lie in store: France and Spain would destroy the infant United States. In contrast, a war for reconciliation would be short-lived. Confronted with "a bloody & tedious Contest attended with Injury to their Trade," Lord North's government would collapse. Its successor would be compelled to accept Congress' terms: American "Dependence & Subordination" on the Crown, but with it a recognition from London that Parliament's only power over the colonies was the regulation of American trade.

Given Dickinson's position as a longtime foe of Parliamentary taxation, it was only to be expected that he would emerge as a leader in Congress. Adams' rise, however, was a different story. When he became leader of the independence forces—what one contemporary observer, Dr. Benjamin Rush, described as the "first man in the House"—many were caught by surprise. Before his election to Congress in 1774, Adams was largely inexperienced in public life. He had served only one term in the Massachusetts assembly and had not even headed the Massachusetts delegation at the First Congress—cousin Sam had assumed that responsibility.

Forty years old in 1775, John Adams had grown up on a small farm just south of Boston, where his father moonlighted as a shoemaker to earn the money to send his oldest son to Harvard. Like Dickinson, Adams had practiced law, and also like him, had advanced rapidly. Within a dozen years of opening his law office, Adams maintained the heaviest caseload of any attorney in Boston. Unlike Dickinson, Adams was initially wary of the American protest against British policies, believing that the ministry had simply erred in its actions and might be expected to mend its ways. He had been converted to open support of the popular cause only in 1773.

Adams came to keenly desire a leadership role, but feared that his physical limitations—he was portly and balding—and irascible manner would frustrate his ambitions. Furthermore, he was no jovial backslapper. Gruff and argumentative, he was maladroit when it came to talking about what he regarded as the favorite topics of men: dogs, horses and women. Nevertheless, those who penetrated his churlish exterior discovered a good-natured, self-effacing and exceptionally bright individual. And he possessed the skills needed to be an effective legislator. He was tireless, a skilled debater, an incisive, if not flamboyant, orator and a trenchant thinker. He quickly won a reputation as the Congressional authority on diplomacy and political theory. His colleagues found him to be unfailingly well prepared, prudent, honest and trustworthy—in short, just the man to follow in this high-stakes endeavor.

The first issue to truly divide the Second Continental Congress arose early on. In May 1775, as it considered the creation of the Continental Army, Dickinson insisted on petitioning the king with what he characterized as a "Measure of Peace." Adams privately branded it a "Measure of

Imbecility" and raged that some delegates, at least those from the mercantile colonies of New York and Pennsylvania, were "selfish and avaricious." For those congressman, he charged, "a ship [was] dearer than" the lives of Continental soldiers. In October 1774, the First Continental Congress had petitioned the monarch; Adams feared that to do so again was to risk appearing weak. Franklin concurred. "It is a true old saying," he remarked, "that *make yourselves sheep and the wolves will eat you.*"

Nevertheless, the independence faction wanted no confrontation with Dickinson's at this crucial juncture of the war, and the Olive Branch Petition, as the peace measure was known, was approved, though only after a contentious debate over its wording. Richard Penn, a former governor of Pennsylvania, carried it to England. Franklin advised a London friend, a director of the Bank of England, that this was Britain's last hope for preventing "a total Separation" by the colonies. To another friend in England he wrote: "If you flatter yourselves with beating us into submission, you know neither the [American] people nor the country."

At about the same time, Congress created a committee to draft a "Declaration of the Causes and Necessity of Taking Up Arms." Among others, it appointed Jefferson, who had only recently joined the Virginia delegation, and Dickinson to the committee. Jefferson, who enjoyed a reputation as a facile writer, was asked to draft the document. With views similar to Adams', he produced a paper that reiterated the charges of British tyranny and harshly cataloged the ministry's "avowed course of murder and devastation." Dickinson was appalled. He feared that such a provocative statement would make a measured response to the Olive Branch Petition impossible. He demanded, and obtained, an opportunity to tone down Jefferson's draft. Dickinson's softer proclamation stipulated that "we mean not to dissolve that Union" with Britain. It was adopted in July 1775.

The reconciliationists held sway through the summer of 1775, but as hostilities unfolded and Congress was required to prosecute the war, their hold gradually weakened. By the end of 1775, Congress had issued a Continental currency, drawn up regulations applying to all militia, created a Continental post office and taken control of Indian relations. Feeling "a little of the Seafaring Inclination," as Adams put it, Congress also established an American navy and two battalions of marines. It regulated American trade, assumed responsibility for the enforcement of the embargo of British commerce, attempted to resolve intercolonial territorial disputes and even acted as the national judiciary, hearing appeals from state courts in cases that involved the seizure of British ships.

Congress additionally began to conduct foreign policy. It created a Secret Committee to contract for arms imports and a Committee of Secret Correspondence to establish contact with "our friends" throughout the world. In March 1776, Congress dispatched one of its own, Silas Deane of Connecticut, to Versailles to pursue talks with the French government. In fact, if not in name, the Second Continental Congress had become the government of an autonomous union of American provinces.

Back in November 1775, word had arrived that George III had branded the colonists rebels and traitors and had contemptuously refused to accept the Olive Branch Petition. Two months later, the full text of the king's speech to Parliament reached Philadelphia. In it the monarch unsparingly assailed those colonists who supported hostilities, charging that they were part of a "wicked" and "desperate conspiracy." In addition, he revealed his intention to obtain foreign mercenaries to help suppress the rebellion. Hancock, by now president of Congress, wryly remarked that the Crown's actions "don't look like a Reconciliation." John Adams gleefully noted that Dickinson "sinks . . . in the public opinion."

Indeed, evidence was mounting that the mood of the country was changing. Already, by the summer of 1775, when Congress began authorizing the colonies to create their own governments, supplanting those chartered by the Crown, it had taken its most radical step since the creation of the army. Dickinson and his principal ally, James Wilson of Pennsylvania, fought back. In January 1776 they proposed that Congress adopt yet another "humble & dutiful Petition" disclaiming independence to the king. This time Congress refused. Some members, such as Samuel Adams, had begun to see the reconciliationists as "Tools of a Tyrant."

Yet Congress still remained unwilling to declare independence. Had a vote been taken in early January 1776, the measure would likely have failed. On the 17th of that month, however, word reached Philadelphia of a devastating military setback, the young army's first. The news was instrumental in propelling Congress on its final journey toward independence.

As Washington's army besieged British regulars in Boston during the summer of 1775, Congress had authorized an invasion of lightly defended Canada in order to defeat British forces there. It was a troubled campaign from the start, and on December 31 disaster struck. An attack on Quebec was repulsed; 500 men, half of America's invading army, were lost: 100 were killed or wounded and another 400 taken prisoner. So much for any expectation of a short-lived war. Overnight, many in Congress came to believe that no victory would ever be possible without foreign assistance; all understood that no aid from any outside power would be forthcoming so long as America fought for the "purpose of repairing the breach [with Britain]," as Thomas Paine had observed in his incendiary pamphlet *Common Sense,* published in January 1776.

Soon after the debacle at Quebec, John Adams observed that there now existed "no Prospect, no Probability, no Possibility" of reconciliation. Late in February came still more stunning news. Congress learned that Parliament had enacted the American Prohibitory Act, shutting down all trade with the colonies and permitting seizure of colonial vessels. John Adams called the law "a Gift" to the pro-independence party. Virginia's Richard Henry Lee concurred, saying that it severed the last ties with the mother country. It was "curious," he stated, that Congress yet hesitated to declare independence when London had already "put the two Countries asunder."

As spring foliage burst forth in Philadelphia in 1776, ever larger numbers of Americans were coming round to independence. The "Sighing after Independence" in Massachusetts,

© Getty Images/Hisham F. Ibrahim

said James Warren, speaker of the colony's House of Representatives, had become nearly "Universal." By mid-May every Southern colony had authorized its delegates to vote for breaking off ties with Britain.

Within Congress, emotions ran high. "I cannot conceive what good Reason can be assignd against [independence]," Samuel Adams railed in mid-April. He exclaimed that the "Salvation of the Country depends on its being done speedily. I am anxious to have it done." John Adams maintained that had independence been declared months earlier, America's armies would already possess French arms. Elbridge Gerry, a Massachusetts delegate, complained that "timid Minds are terrified at the Word Independency," while Franklin deplored those who clutched at the "vain Hope of Reconciliation." As for General Washington, he said he believed that Congress had "long, & ardently sought for reconciliation upon honourable terms," only to be rebuffed at every turn. He had long been of the opinion that "all Connexions with a State So unjust" should be broken.

Still, the reconciliationists held out, encouraged by a passage in the Prohibitory Act that authorized the monarch to appoint commissioners to grant pardons and to receive the grievances of colonists. Dickinson and his followers viewed the appointees as peace commissioners and held out hope that they were being sent to resolve differences. Many in Congress refused to budge until they learned just what the envoys had to offer. John Adams disdainfully predicted that this was "a Bubble" and a misbegotten "Messiah that will never come." Samuel Adams said that he was "disgusted" both with the "King & his Junto," who spoke of peace while making "the most destructive Plans," and with the reconciliationists who were willing to be "Slaves" to "a Nation so lost to all Sense of Liberty and Virtue."

In May, as American newspapers published the text of Britain's treaties with several German principalities, authorizing the hiring of mercenaries, outrage toward the Crown skyrocketed. Many were now convinced, as Richard Henry Lee said, that the action proved Britain was bent "upon the absolute conquest and subduction of N. America." Nearly simultaneously, word arrived of yet more calamities in Canada. Congress had dispatched reinforcements following the failed attack in December, but smallpox and desertions soon thinned their ranks. With the arrival of British reinforcements in May, the American army commenced a long, slow retreat that lasted until mid-June. Now, said Lee, it "is not choice then but necessity that calls for Independence, as the only means by which a foreign Alliance can be obtained."

One final matter helped the slowest sailors in Congress catch up with the swiftest. Month after month had passed with no sign of the so-called peace commissioners. Then, in the spring, it was learned that, although some commissioners had been named, they had been ordered not to treat with Congress. That proved a final blow; all but the most ardent reconciliationists were persuaded that the king's envoys were coming for the sole purpose of dividing American opinion and derailing the war effort.

With the tide so turned, in mid-May, Congress declared that "every kind of authority under the . . . Crown should be totally suppressed" and instructed each colony to adopt a new government suitable for providing for the "happiness and safety of their constituents and . . . America in general." John Adams, who called this the "last Step," believed this was tantamount to a declaration of independence. Even Maryland's Thomas Stone, a foe of separation, disconsolately allowed that the "Dye is cast. The fatal Stab is given to any future Connection between this Country & Britain." Only a formal declaration of independence remained, and that could not now be long in coming.

On June 7, three weeks after Congress urged changes in the provincial governments, Lee introduced a motion for independence: "*Resolved,* That these United Colonies are, and of right ought to be, free and independent States, that they are absolved from all allegiance to the British Crown, and that all political connection between them and the State of Great Britain is, and ought to be, totally dissolved."

Congress rancorously debated Lee's motion for two days. Several reconciliationists from the Middle-Atlantic colonies made their final stand, even threatening to "secede from the Union" if Congress declared independence. But their threats and recriminations no longer frightened the majority, including Oliver Wolcott of Connecticut, who recognized that America was in the "Midst of a great Revolution . . . leading to the lasting Independancy of these Colonies." On June 11, Congress created a five-member committee to prepare a statement on independence. Adams, Franklin, Jefferson, Roger Sherman of Connecticut and Robert Livingston of New York were given until July 1 to complete their work. Once again it was to Jefferson that a panel turned, this time for the fateful task of drafting the declaration.

Jefferson and his colleagues beat the deadline by two days, submitting on June 28 a document that explained and defended independence. By July 1, the final consideration of Lee's motion to declare independence was taken up. That day's session, John Adams told a friend in a letter written early that morning, would see "the greatest Debate of all." With the outcome no longer in doubt, he said that he prayed for "the new born Republic" about to be created.

When debate began midmorning on that hot, steamy Monday, Dickinson was first on his feet to make one last speech against independence. Speaking emotionally for perhaps as much as two hours in the stifling heat of the closed room (windows were kept shut to keep spies from listening in), Dickinson reviewed the familiar arguments: America could not win the war; at best, it could fight Britain to a stalemate, and deadlocked wars often ended in partition treaties in which territory is divided among the belligerents; therefore, after all the killing, some colonies would remain part of the British Empire, while others would pass under the control of France or Spain.

It was John Adams—soon to be christened "the Atlas of Independence" by New Jersey's Richard Stockton—who rose to answer Dickinson. Striving to conceal his contempt for his adversary, Adams spoke extemporaneously in subdued tones. Once again, he reviewed the benefits of independence. Although his speech was not transcribed, he surely invoked the ideas he had expressed and the phrases he had used on many another occasion. Breaking ties with Britain, he argued, would ensure freedom from England's imperial domination; escape from the menace of British corruption; and the opportunity to create a republic based on equality of representation.

Others then took the floor. The speeches stretched past the customary 4 o'clock adjournment and into the evening. The business was "an idle Mispence of Time," Adams remarked sourly, as "nothing was Said, but what had been repeated and hackneyed in that Room an hundred Times for Six Months past." After the Congress reconvened the next morning, July 2, the delegates cast their momentous votes. Twelve states—the colonies would become states with the vote—voted for independence. Not one voted against the break with Britain. New York's delegation, which had not yet been authorized by the New York legislature to separate from the mother country, did not vote. (Dickinson and Robert Morris did not attend, and Pennsylvania cast its vote for independence by a three-to-two margin.)

Adams predicted that July 2 would ever after "be solemnized with Pomp and Parade, with Shews, Games, Sports, Guns, Bells,

Bonfires and Illuminations from one End of this Continent to the other." He was wrong, of course, for July 4, the date that Congress approved the formal Declaration of Independence, would become the commemorative day. But Adams had made one prediction that would prove tellingly correct. With the Union intact after a 15-month battle for independence, and with the step finally taken that could secure foreign assistance in America's desperate war, Adams declared he could "see the Rays of ravishing Light and Glory" that would accompany military victory.

HISTORIAN JOHN FERLING is the author of *A Leap in the Dark: The Struggle to Create the American Republic.*

A Day to Remember: July 4, 1776

CHARLES PHILLIPS

O n Independence Day every year, millions of Americans turn out for myriad parades, public and backyard barbecues, concerts of patriotically stirring music and spectacular pyrotechnic displays, and they do so to celebrate the day on which we declared our independence from Great Britain.

But America did not declare its independence on July 4, 1776. That happened two days earlier, when the second Continental Congress approved a resolution stating that "these United Colonies are, and of a right ought to be, free and independent States." The resolution itself had first been introduced back on June 7, when Virginia's Richard Henry Lee rose in the sweltering heat of the Congress' Philadelphia meeting house to propose an action many delegates had been anticipating- and not a few dreading-since the opening shots of the American Revolution at Lexington and Concord.

Lee asked for a newly declared independent government, one that could form alliances and draw up a plan for confederation of the separate Colonies. The need for some such move had become increasingly clear during the last year, especially to George Washington, if for no other reason than as a rallying cry for his troops. The Virginia soldier chosen by Congress to general its Continental Army languished in New York, short of supplies, short of men and short of morale while facing the threat of a massive British offensive.

But many in Congress, some sent with express instructions against independence, were leery of Lee's proposal despite the growing sentiment for independence stirred up by such rebel rousers as Boston's Samuel Adams and the recent émigré Thomas Paine. Paine's political pamphlet, Common Sense, openly attacked King George III and quickly became a bestseller in the Colonies; Paine donated the proceeds to the Continental Congress. Lee was so closely associated with Adams that critics charged Lee with representing Massachusetts better than he did Virginia. On the night before Lee offered up his resolution, Adams boasted to friends that Lee's resolution would decide the most important issue Americans ever had faced.

Little wonder that the more conservative delegates, men such as Pennsylvania's John Dickinson and South Carolina's Edward Rutledge, balked. Treat with France? Surely. Draw up articles of confederation? Fine. But why declare independence? The Colonies, they argued, were not even sure they could achieve it. To declare their intent now would serve merely to warn the British, and hence forearm them. Dickinson wanted to postpone the discussion-forever if he could-and he managed to muster support for three weeks of delay. At the same time, Lee's faction won approval to appoint committees to spend the three weeks preparing drafts on each point of the resolution.

Sam Adams was named to the committee writing articles of confederation. His cousin, John Adams, a great talker, headed the committee drawing up a treaty with France. John Adams also was appointed to help draft a declaration of independence along with the inevitable choice, the celebrated author and internationally renowned philosopher Benjamin Franklin. Congress also assigned New York conservative Robert Livingston and Connecticut Yankee Roger Sherman to the committee but fell to arguing over a fifth member.

Southern delegates wanted one of their own to achieve balance. But many in Congress disfavored the two obvious candidates, considering Lee too radical and his fellow Virginian Benjamin Harrison too conservative. There was another Virginian, however, a 32-year-old lanky, red-haired newcomer named Thomas Jefferson, who had a reputation for learning in both literature and science. Though he seemed to shrink from public speaking, the Adamses liked him, and John pushed so effectively for Jefferson to join the committee that, when the votes were counted, he tallied more than anyone else.

Franklin's health was clearly failing, and he wouldn't be able to draft the declaration. Adams was busy with what he probably considered at the time the more important work of Grafting an alliance with France (though he would live to regret such an opinion). Neither Livingston nor Sherman evidently had the desire nor, most probably, the talent to pen the kind of document needed. To Jefferson, then, with his reputation as a fine writer, fell the task of drafting a resolution whose language, edited and approved by the committee, would be acceptable to all the delegates.

Jefferson worried about his sick wife, Martha, back home and longed to be in Virginia working on the colony's new constitution, then under debate in Williamsburg. Nevertheless, he set to work and quickly produced what, given the time constraints, was a remarkable document. A justification to the world of the action being taken by Britain's American Colonies assembled in Congress, the declaration was part bill of indictment and part philosophical assertion, the latter an incisive summary of Whig political thought.

With the document's key sentiments much inspired, say some, by such Scottish Enlightenment figures as Francis Hutcheson, and its thinking much influenced, say many, by John Locke's Two Treatises of Government, the declaration summarized common notions expressed everywhere in the Colonies in those days. Many such notions could be found in numerous local proclamations. Especially relevant, because it was on Jefferson's mind, was the language of the new Virginia constitution with its elaborate Bill of Rights penned by his cohort, George Mason. Indeed, Jefferson's assignment was to capture the sense of the current rebellion in the 13 Colonies and distill its essence into a single document.

In this, as everyone recognized, he greatly succeeded, though he did not do it alone. Despite what Jefferson himself later wrote, and John Adams, too, when age and the glory of the Revolution led them both to embroider their accounts, the committee reviewed Jefferson's work, and then he ran it past both senior members, Adams and Franklin. He incorporated suggested changes before writing a clean copy. Still, Jefferson personally was quite proud of the draft he laid before Congress on June 28, 1776.

On the first day of July, with Jefferson's manuscript at the ready, the delegates once more took up Richard Henry Lee's resolution to openly declare independence. Lee was off in Virginia, where Jefferson wished to be, so he was not there to see John Dickinson's last protest seemingly cow the Congress, before an eloquent rebuttal by a determined John Adams carried the motion. Congress on July 2 without dissent voted that the American Colonies were from that day forward free and independent states.

That evening an exultant John Adams wrote home to his wife that July 2, 1776, would "be celebrated by succeeding generations as the great anniversary festival." It was his day of triumph, as well he knew, and he imagined it "commemorated as the day of deliverance by acts of devotion to God Almighty. It ought to be solemnized with pomp and parade, with shows, games, sports, guns, bells, bonfires and illuminations from one end of the continent to the other, from this time forward forever more."

Congress immediately turned to consider Jefferson's document. It would have to serve as a sort of early version of a press release—an explanation that could be disseminated at home and around the globe by broadside and to be read aloud at gatherings. Its statements had to inspire the troops and garner public support for the action Congress had just taken. Not surprisingly, Congress paid close attention to the document's language.

The delegates took the time to spruce it up a little and edit out what they found objectionable. In general the Congress was fine with the vague sentiments of the early paragraphs that have since become the cornerstone of American democracy: "We hold these truths to be self-evident: that all men are created equal, that they are endowed by their Creator with certain unalienable rights; that among these are life, liberty, and the pursuit of happiness; that to secure these rights, governments are instituted among men, deriving their just powers from the consent of the governed" and so on.

What the delegates were more interested in, however, and what they saw as the meat of the document, were the more concrete declarations. For years, they had based their resistance to England on the belief they were not fighting a divinely chosen king, but his ministers and parliament. But during the previous 14 months the Crown had waged war on them, and King George had declared the Colonials in rebellion, that is, outside his protection. Common Sense had gotten them used to thinking of the king as that "royal brute" and this document was supposed to explain why he should be so considered. Thus Jefferson had produced a catalog of George III's tyrannies as its heart and soul.

Congress at length struck out some sentimental language in which Jefferson tried to paint the British people as brothers indifferent to American suffering and a paragraph where he ran on about the glories the two people might otherwise have realized together. But more substantive changes were especially telling. Among George's crimes, Jefferson had listed the slave trade, contending that the king had "waged a cruel war against human nature" by assaulting a "distant people" and carrying them into slavery in "another hemisphere." This was too much for Jefferson's fellow slaveholders in the South, especially South Carolina, and certain Yankee traders who had made fortunes from what Jefferson called the "execrable commerce." Together, representatives of these Southern and Yankee interests deleted the section.

For the rest, the delegates also changed a word here and there, usually improving some of the hasty writing. They worked the language of Lee's resolution into the conclusion and added a reference to the Almighty, which Jefferson would have been happier without. "And," the document now concluded, "for support of this Declaration, with a firm reliance on the protection of divine Providence, we mutually pledge to each other our lives, our fortunes, and our sacred honor."

None of this sat well with the young author. He made a copy of the declaration as he submitted it and the "mutilated" version Congress approved, and sent both to his friends and colleagues, including Richard Henry Lee, who agreed the original was superior, though most historians since have concluded otherwise.

In any case, after more than two days of sometimes-heated debate, on July 4, 1776, the Continental Congress approved the revised document that explained its declaration of independence of July 2. The approval was not immediately unanimous, since the New York delegates had to await instructions from home and did not assent until July 9. At the time of approval, Congress ordered the document "authenticated and printed," and that copies "be sent to several assemblies, conventions and committees, or councils of safety, and to the several commanding officers of the continental troops; that it be proclaimed in each of the United States, and at the head of the army." If any delegates officially signed the approved document on the glorious Fourth, they were President John Hancock and Secretary Charles Thomson.

Within days the printed document was circulated across the land. The declaration was read aloud in the yard of the Philadelphia State House to much loud cheering. When New York formally accepted the declaration, the state celebrated by releasing its debtors from prison; Baltimoreans burned George III in effigy; the citizens of Savannah, Ga., gave him an official funeral.

The carefully engrossed copy we see reproduced everywhere today, with its large handwritten calligraphy, was not ordered prepared until July 19, and it was not ready for signing until August 2. Delegates probably dropped in throughout the summer to add their names to the bottom of the document. In any event, since the proceedings were secret and the signers all in danger of their lives, the names were not broadcast.

Even before the engrossed copy was ready, and long before it was signed by all, the legends were growing—how Hancock signed the parchment so boldly that John Bull could read his name without spectacles. How Hancock remarked to Benjamin Franklin: "We must be unanimous. There must be no pulling in different ways. We must all hang together." And how Franklin replied, "Yes, we must indeed all hang together, or most assuredly we shall hang separately."

Almost from the start, confusion blurred the distinctions between the July 2 act of declaring independence, the July 4 approval of the document explaining that declaration, and the actual signing of the Declaration. That confusion might best be represented by John Trumbull's famous 1819 painting, which now hangs in the Capitol Rotunda and appears on the back of the $2 bill. Thought by most Americans to represent the signing of the Declaration of Independence, it was intended by Trumbull "to preserve the resemblance of the men who were the authors of this memorable act," not to portray a specific day or moment in our history.

The Fourth of July was not as widely celebrated during the heat of the Revolutionary War or during the period of confederation as it was afterward. It became much more popular as a national holiday in the wake of the War of 1812 and with the passing of the Revolutionary generation.

And then four score and seven years after that July 4, 1776, President Abraham Lincoln used the lofty ideas and flowing words of the Declaration as the basis for his famous Gettysburg Address to sanctify the country's sacrifices in the Civil War and, in so doing, he redefined the nation as a land of equality for all. Ever since, those early paragraphs of the Declaration, with their beautifully phrased abstractions and sentiments, have served virtually to define the American faith in secular democracy. His well-chosen remarks and our July 4 Independence Day celebrations, like Trumbull's painting, honor not a single event but, rather, the democratic process, the ideas proposed back then and the men who directly made them possible.

CHARLES PHILLIPS is the author and co-author of numerous works of history and biography. These include *What Every American Should Know About American History, The Macmillan Dictionary of Military Biography; Cops, Crooks, and Criminologists; What Everyone Should Know About the Twentieth Century, Tyrants, Dictators, and Despots;* and *The Wages of History.* Phillips has edited several multivolume historical reference works, including the *Encyclopedia of the American West, the Encyclopedia of War* and *the Encyclopedia of Historical Treaties.*

From *American History,* August 2006, pp. 15–16. Copyright © 2006 by Weider History Group. Reprinted by permission.

Washington Takes Charge

Confronting the British in Boston in 1775, Gen. George Washington honed the personal qualities that would carry the day in war and sustain the new nation in peace.

Is any American more venerated than George Washington? Or more conspicuous? From our currency to our public places and schools to the names of so many of our citizens, the nation's first president is woven inextricably into America's cultural fabric. And more than two centuries after his death, the historical thirst for more Washingtonia by historians remains undiminished: the University of Virginia is compiling every available scrap of paper sent to or by Washington into what is expected to fill some 90 volumes. But while we may have committed to memory Henry "Light-Horse Harry" Lee's eulogy of Washington as "first in war, first in peace and first in the hearts of his countrymen," today he remains more monument than man.

A new biography of Washington by historian Joseph Ellis helps turn marble back to flesh. By focusing tightly on Washington's character in His Excellency, published in November by Alfred A. Knopf, Ellis seeks to recover what he calls "the more vital, more combustible and more dynamic aspects of his personality." Washington, Ellis says, was "not a nice guy" but a force: the "most ambitious, determined and potent personality of his age." What sets him apart from his peers is his "capacity of judgment. He makes the big decisions correctly." In the excerpt that follows, Washington's first engagement as commander in chief of the Continental Army—the siege of Boston from June 1775 to March 1776—foreshadows the strength of character and other traits that would carry him to victory over the British and into the presidency.

JOSEPH J. ELLIS

Although there was no way George Washington could have known it at the time, when Philadelphia's Continental Congress appointed him military commander in June 1775, he was about to oversee the longest declared war in American history. He was 43 years old when he rode out of his Mount Vernon estate in May 1775. He was 51 and the most famous man in the world when he arrived back home on Christmas Eve 1783, following the American victory over Great Britain. The cause that he headed had not only smashed two British armies and destroyed the first British Empire, it had also set in motion a political movement committed to principles that were destined to topple the monarchical and aristocratic dynasties of the Old World.

The American Revolution was the central event in Washington's life, the crucible for his development as a mature man, a prominent statesman and a national hero. And while zealous students of the Civil War might contest the claim, the movement that Washington found himself heading was also the most consequential event in American history, the crucible within which the political personality of the United States took shape. In effect, the character of the man and the character of the nation congealed and grew together during those eight fateful years. Washington was not clairvoyant about history's next destination. But he did realize from the start that, wherever history was headed, he and America were going there together.

The siege of Boston from June 1775 to March 1776 marked Washington's debut as commander in chief. Here, for the first time, he encountered the logistical challenges he would face during the ensuing years of the war. He met many of the men who would comprise his general staff for the duration. And here he demonstrated both the strategic instincts and the leadership skills that would sustain him, and sometimes lead him astray, until the glorious end.

The story of the siege can be told in one sentence: Washington's makeshift army kept more than 10,000 British troops bottled up in the city for more than nine months, at which point the British sailed away to Halifax. Less a battle than a marathon staring match, the conflict exposed the anomalous political circumstance created by the Continental Congress, which was prepared to initiate war a full year before it was ready to declare American independence. Although Washington subsequently claimed that he knew by the early fall of 1775 that King George III was determined to pursue a military rather than political solution to the imperial crisis, he went along with the prevalent fiction that the British garrison in

Boston contained "Ministerial Troops," meaning that they did not represent the king's wishes so much as those of evil and misguided ministers. And although Washington eventually expressed his frustration with the moderate faction in the Continental Congress, who were "still feeding themselves upon the dainty food of reconciliation," as he put it in a letter to his brother John Augustine, he also recognized that the radical faction, led by John Adams, needed to exhaust all the diplomatic alternatives and patiently wait for public opinion outside New England to mobilize around the novel notion of American independence.

Events of enduring significance had occurred before Washington assumed command of 16,000 colonial militia on July 3, 1775, in Cambridge. On June 17, about 2,200 British troops made three frontal assaults on New England militia units entrenched on Breed's Hill. Later misnamed the Battle of Bunker Hill, the fight was a tactical victory for the British, but at the frightful cost of more than 1,000 casualties, nearly half the attacking force. When word of the battle reached London, several British officers observed caustically that a few more such victories and the entire British Army would be annihilated. On the American side, Bunker Hill was regarded as a great moral triumph that reinforced the lesson of Lexington and Concord: that militia volunteers fighting for a cause they freely embraced could defeat disciplined British mercenaries.

Two seductive illusions were converging here. The first was the perennial belief harbored by both sides at the start of most wars that the conflict would be short. The second, which became the central myth of American military history, was that militia volunteers fighting for principle made better soldiers than trained professionals. Washington was not completely immune to the first illusion, though his version of a quick American victory depended on the willingness of the British commander, Gen. William Howe, to commit his force in a decisive battle outside Boston, in a repeat of the Bunker Hill scenario, which would then prompt the king's ministers to propose acceptable terms for peace. Neither Howe nor the British ministry was prepared to cooperate along these lines, and since the only acceptable peace terms on the American side—independence of Parliament's authority—were at this stage nonnegotiable on the British side, even Washington's narrow hope had no realistic prospects.

Washington was thoroughly immune to the second illusion about the innate superiority of militia. Based on his earlier experience as commander of the Virginia Regiment, reinforced by what he witnessed on a day-to-day basis at his Cambridge encampment, he was convinced that an army of short-term volunteers, no matter how dedicated to the cause, could not win the war. "To expect then the same service from Raw, and undisciplined Recruits as from Veteran Soldiers," he explained in a February 1776 letter to John Hancock, "is to expect what never did, and perhaps never will happen." His convictions on this score only deepened and hardened over the years, but from the start he believed that militia were only peripheral supplements to the hard core, which needed to be a professional army of disciplined troops who, like him, signed on for the duration. His model, in effect, was the British Army. This, of course, was richly ironic, since opposition to a standing army had been

a major source of colonial protest during the prewar years. To those who insisted that a militia was more compatible with revolutionary principles, Washington was brutally frank: those principles can only flourish, he insisted, if we win the war, and that can only happen with an army of regulars.

Another significant development occurred on his way to Cambridge, an event less conspicuous than the Battle of Bunker Hill but with even more far-reaching implications. Both the New York and the Massachusetts legislatures wrote congratulatory letters addressed to "His Excellency," which soon became his official designation for the remainder of the war. To be sure, "His Excellency" is not quite the same as "His Majesty," but throughout the summer and fall of 1775, even as delegates to the Continental Congress struggled to sustain the fiction that George III remained a friend to American liberty, poets and balladeers were already replacing the British George with an American version of the same name.

This new semi-royal status fit in the grooves of Washington's own personality and proved an enduring asset as important politically as his wife Martha Custis' huge dowry had been economically. The man who was obsessed with control was now the designated sovereign of the American Revolution. The man who could not bear to have his motives or personal integrity questioned was assured that he enjoyed more trust than any American alive. The British would change commanding generals four times; Washington was forever. Certain deficiencies in his character—aloofness, a formality that virtually precluded intimacy—were now regarded as essential byproducts of his special status, indeed expressions of his inherent dignity. And the man who had bristled at the presumptive condescension of British officers and officials during his service in the French and Indian War was now in charge of the military instrument designed to obliterate all vestiges of British power in North America.

On the other hand, the political and even psychological ramifications of his public role did require some personal adjustments. In August 1775 he made several critical comments about the lack of discipline in the New England militia units under his command and described New Englanders in general as "an exceedingly dirty & nasty people." As a mere Virginia planter such expressions of regional prejudice would have been unexceptional. But as the symbolic spokesman for what were still being called "the United Colonies," the comments created political firestorms in the Massachusetts Legislature and the Continental Congress. When Joseph Reed, a Philadelphia lawyer who served briefly as Washington's most trusted aide-de-camp, apprised him of the hostile reaction, Washington expressed his regrets for the indiscretion: "I will endeavor at a reformation, as I can assure you my dear Reed that I wish to walk in such a Line as will give most general Satisfaction."

Even within what he called "my family," Washington needed to remain circumspect, because his family included staff and aides-de-camp. We know that Billy Lee, his mulatto servant, accompanied him on foot or on horseback at all times, brushed his hair and tied it in a queue every morning, but no record of their conversations has survived. We know that Martha joined him at Cambridge in January 1776, as she would at winter quarters during all subsequent campaigns, but their correspondence, which almost surely contained the fullest expression of personal opinion Washington allowed himself, for that very reason was destroyed after he died. The bulk of his correspondence during the war years, so vast in volume and officious in tone that modern-day readers risk mental paralysis, was written by his aides-de-camp. It is therefore the expression of an official, composite personality, usually speaking a platitudinous version of revolutionary rhetoric. For example, here are the General Orders for February 27, 1776, when Washington was contemplating a surprise attack on the British defenses: "It is a noble Cause we are engaged in, it is the Cause of virtue and mankind, every temporal advantage and comfort to us, and our posterity, depends upon the Vigour of our exertions; in short, Freedom or Slavery must be the result of our conduct, there can therefore be no greater Inducement to men to behave well." The inflated rhetoric concluded with the more candid warning that anyone attempting to retreat or desert *will be instantly shot down.*"

Aware of his own limited formal education, Washington selected college graduates who were "Pen-men" as aides. His most trusted lieutenants—Joseph Reed was the first, followed by Alexander Hamilton and John Laurens later in the war—became surrogate sons who enjoyed direct access to the general in after-dinner sessions, when Washington liked to encourage conversation as he ate nuts and drank a glass of Madeira. Part extended family and part court, these favored aides traded influence for total loyalty. "It is absolutely necessary therefore, for me to have persons that can think for me," Washington explained, "as well as execute Orders." The price for what he called his "unbounded confidence" was their equally unbounded service to his reputation. It was understood as a matter of honor that they would write no revealing memoirs after the war, and none of them did.

His other "family" was the cast of senior officers that assembled around him during the siege of Boston. Of the 28 generals who served under Washington in the war, almost half were present at Cambridge in 1775-76. Four of them—Charles Lee, Horatio Gates, Nathanael Greene and Henry Knox—provide the outline of the prevalent patterns that would shape his treatment of high-ranking subordinates.

Lee and Gates were both former officers in the British Army with greater professional experience than Washington. Lee was a colorful eccentric. The Mohawks had named him Boiling Water for his fiery temperament, which at Cambridge took the form of threats to place all deserters on a hill as targets within musket-shot of British pickets. Lee presumed a greater familiarity with Washington than other generals, addressing him as "My Dear General" rather than "His Excellency." Lee also questioned Washington's preferred strategy of engaging British regulars on their own terms in a European-style war, favoring guerrilla tactics and a greater reliance on militia. Gates was called Granny Gates because of his age (he was 50) and the wire-rimmed spectacles dangling from his nose. He cultivated a greater familiarity with his troops than Washington thought appropriate and, like Lee, favored a greater reliance on militia. Gates thought that Washington's plan for an assault on the British garrison in Boston was pure madness and, given his

experience, felt free to speak out for a more defensive strategy. Both men ended up colliding with Washington later in the war and becoming early exhibits of the primal principle of revolutionary-era politics: cross Washington and you risk ruination.

Greene and Knox were both inexperienced amateurs drawn to military service by their zeal for American independence. Greene was a Rhode Island Quaker who was cast out of the Society of Friends because of his support for the war. He volunteered to serve in a local militia company, the Kentish Guards, at the rank of private, but ascended to brigadier general within a year on the basis of his obvious intelligence and disciplined dedication. By the end of the war, especially during the Carolina campaigns, he demonstrated strategic and tactical brilliance; he was Washington's choice as successor if the great man went down in battle. Knox was also a gifted amateur, a Boston bookseller well read in engineering whom Washington plucked from the ranks to head an artillery regiment. Knox demonstrated his resourcefulness in December 1775 by transporting the British cannon captured at Ticonderoga over the ice and snow on 40 sleds driven by 80 yoke of oxen to Cambridge. Like Greene, he worshiped the ground Washington walked on. Both men were subsequently showered with glory, Knox living on to become Washington's secretary of war in the 1790s.

The pattern is reasonably clear. Washington recruited military talent wherever he could find it, and he had a knack for discovering ability in unlikely places and then allowing it to ride the same historical wave he was riding into the American pantheon. But he was extremely protective of his own authority. While he did not encourage sycophants, if dissenters ever broached their criticism out-of-doors, as both Lee and Gates ended up doing, he was usually unforgiving. One could make a plausible case, as several scholars have done, that Washington's insistence on personal loyalty was rooted in insecurity. But the more compelling explanation is that he understood instinctively how power worked, and that his own quasi-monarchical status was indispensable to galvanize an extremely precarious cause.

From the very start, however, he made a point of insisting that his expansive mandate was dependent upon, and subordinate to, the will of the American citizenry as represented in the Continental Congress. His letters to John Hancock, the first president of the Congress, always took the form of requests rather than demands. And he established the same posture of official deference toward the New England governors and provincial governments that supplied troops for his army. Washington did not use the term "civilian control," but he was scrupulous about acknowledging that his own authority derived from the elected representatives in the Congress. If there were two institutions that embodied the emerging nation—the Continental Army and the Continental Congress—he insisted that the former was subordinate to the latter.

A delegation from the Continental Congress that included Benjamin Franklin met with Washington and his staff in Cambridge in October 1775 to approve troop requests for an army of 20,372 men. But strictly speaking, the Continental Army did not exist until the start of the new year; until then, Washington was commanding a collection of provincial militia units whose enlistments ran out in December 1775. The endorsement of Washington's troop requests by the Continental Congress was deceptively encouraging, since compliance depended upon approval by the respective state governments, which insisted that all recruits be volunteers and serve limited terms of no more than one year. But in reality, the vaunted principles of state sovereignty, volunteerism and limited enlistments produced a military turnstile that bedeviled Washington throughout the war. Instead of a hard core of experienced veterans, the Continental Army became a constantly fluctuating stream of amateurs, coming and going like tourists.

In this first year of the war, when the revolutionary fires burned their brightest, Washington presumed that he would enjoy a surplus of recruits. In October 1775 a council of war voted unanimously "to reject all slaves & by a great Majority to reject Negroes altogether." The following month Washington ordered that "Neither Negroes, Boys unable to bear arms, nor old men unfit to endure the fatigues of the campaign, are to be enlisted." But within a few months, as it became clear that there would not be enough new recruits to fill the ranks, he was forced to change his mind: "It has been represented to me," he wrote Hancock, "that the free negroes who have Served in this Army, are very much dissatisfied at being discarded—and it is to be apprehended that they may Seek employ in the ministerial Army—I have presumed to depart from the Resolution respecting them, & have given licence for them being enlisted; if this is disapproved of by Congress, I will put a stop to it." In this backhanded fashion Washington established the precedent for a racially integrated Continental Army, except for a few isolated incidents the only occasion in American military history when blacks and whites served alongside one another in the same unit until the Korean War.

The siege of Boston also afforded the first extended glimpse at Washington's cast of mind as a military strategist. His motives for supporting American independence were always more elemental than refined. Essentially, he saw the conflict as a struggle for power in which the colonists, if victorious, destroyed British presumptions of superiority and won control over half a continent for themselves. While it would be somewhat excessive to say that his central military goal was an equally elemental urge to smash the British Army in one decisive battle, there was a tendency to regard each engagement as a personal challenge to his own honor and reputation. At Cambridge, once it became clear that General Howe was unwilling to come out from behind his Boston redoubts and face him in open battle, it took the form of several risky offensive schemes to dislodge the British regulars. On three occasions, in September 1775, then again in January and February 1776, Washington proposed frontal assaults against the British defenses, arguing that "a Stroke, well aim'd at this critical juncture, might put a final end to the War." (In one of the plans, he envisioned a night attack across the ice with advanced units wearing ice skates.) His staff rejected each proposal on the grounds that the Continental Army lacked both the size and the discipline to conduct such an attack with sufficient prospects for success. Eventually, Washington accepted a more limited tactical scheme to occupy Dorchester Heights, which placed Howe's garrison within range of American artillery, thereby forcing Howe's decision to evacuate or see his army slowly destroyed. But throughout the siege Washington kept looking for a more direct and conclusive battle, suggesting that he himself was ready for a major engagement even if his army was not.

His most aggressive proposal, which *was* adopted, called for a separate campaign against Quebec. Once it was clear that Howe did not intend to oblige him by coming out of Boston, Washington decided to detach 1,200 troops from Cambridge and send them up the Kennebec River into Canada under the command of a young colonel named Benedict Arnold. Washington's thinking reflected his memories of the French and Indian War, in which Canadian forts had been the strategic keys to victory, as well as his belief that the stakes in the current war included the entire eastern half of North America. As he put it to Arnold, "I need not mention to you the great importance of this place & the consequent possession of all Canada in the Scale of American affairs—to whomsoever It belongs, in there [sic] favour probably, will the Balance turn."

However conventional his thinking about Quebec's strategic significance, Washington's commitment to a Canadian campaign was recklessly bold. Arnold's force had to traverse 350 miles of the most difficult terrain in New England during the outset of the winter snows. Within a month the troops were eating their horses, dogs and moccasins, dying by the scores from exposure and disease. After a truly heroic effort, Arnold and his troop linked up with a force commanded by Gen. Richard Montgomery as planned and made a desperate night assault on Quebec in a blinding snowstorm on December 31, 1775. The result was a catastrophic defeat, both Arnold and Montgomery falling in the first minutes of the battle. (Arnold suffered a serious leg wound but survived, while Montgomery had his face shot off and died on the spot.) If Canada was the key, the British now held it more firmly than before. The Quebec debacle was a decisive blow, but not the kind Washington had intended.

Finally, the Cambridge chapter revealed another Washington trait that has not received sufficient attention in the existent scholarship because it is only indirectly connected to military strategy. Historians have long known that more than two-thirds of the American casualties in the war were the result of disease. But only recently—and this is rather remarkable—have they recognized that the American Revolution occurred within a virulent smallpox epidemic of continental scope that claimed about 100,000 lives. Washington first encountered the epidemic outside Boston, where he learned that between 10 and 30 funerals were occurring each day because of the disease. British troops, though hardly impervious to the smallpox virus, tended to possess greater immunity because they came from English, Scottish and Irish regions, where the disease had existed for generations, allowing resistance to build up within families over time. Many soldiers in the Continental Army, on the other hand, tended to come from previously unexposed farms and villages, so they were extremely vulnerable. At any point in time, between one-fourth and one-fifth of Washington's army at Cambridge was unfit for duty, the majority down with smallpox.

Washington, of course, was immune to smallpox because of his exposure to it as a youth on a trip to Barbados (his one and only foreign excursion) in 1751. (Subsequent admirers claimed that he was immune to everything.) Equally important, he understood the ravaging implications of a smallpox epidemic within the congested conditions of his encampment, and he quarantined the patients in a hospital at Roxbury. When the British began their evacuation of Boston in March 1776, he ordered that only troops with pockmarked faces be allowed into the city. And although many educated Americans opposed inoculation, believing that it actually spread the disease, Washington strongly supported it. It would take two years before inoculation became mandatory for all troops serving in the Continental Army, but the policy began to be implemented in the first year of the war. When historians debate Washington's most consequential decisions as commander in chief, they almost always argue about specific battles. A compelling case can be made that his swift response to the smallpox epidemic and to a policy of inoculation was the most important strategic decision of his military career.

After lingering in Boston Harbor for over a week, the British fleet sailed away on March 17, 1776. The American press reported the retreat as a crushing blow to the British Army. The Continental Congress ordered a gold medallion cast in Washington's honor. Harvard College awarded him an honorary degree. And John Hancock predicted that he had earned "a conspicuous Place in the Temple of Fame, which Shall inform Posterity, that under your Directions, an undisciplined Band of Husbandmen, in the Course of a few Months became Soldiers," defeating "an Army of Veterans, commanded by the most experienced Generals."

As uplifting as this appraisal may have been, subsequent events would soon show that it was overly optimistic. Washington was not, by any standard, a military genius. He lost more battles than he won; indeed, he lost more battles than any victorious general in modern history. Moreover, his defeats were frequently a function of his own overconfident personality, especially during the early stages of the war, when he escaped to fight another day only because the British generals opposing him seemed choked with the kind of caution that, given his resources, Washington should have adopted as his own strategy.

But in addition to being fortunate in his adversaries, Washington was blessed with the personal qualities that counted most in a protracted war. He was composed, indefatigable and able to learn from his mistakes. He was convinced that he was on the side of destiny—or, in more arrogant moments, sure that destiny was on his side. Even his critics acknowledged that he could not be bribed, corrupted or compromised. Based on his bravery during several battles, he apparently believed he could not be killed. Despite all his mistakes, events seemed to align themselves with his own instincts. He began the war in July 1775 at the siege of Boston determined to deliver a decisive blow against more disciplined and battle-tested British regulars. He would end it in October 1781 at the siege of Yorktown doing precisely that.

JOSEPH J. ELLIS is a history professor at Mount Holyoke College.

Winter of Discontent

Even as he endured the hardships of Valley Forge, George Washington faced another challenge: critics who questioned his fitness to lead.

NORMAN GELB

George Washington's troops could easily be followed as they trudged through the wintry expanse of southeastern Pennsylvania in late December 1777. The soldiers, many of them ragged and shoeless, left bloody footprints in the snow, marking the grueling progress of this army of the American Revolution toward winter quarters at Valley Forge.

There was no shelter for the men when they reached the exposed, hilly landscape of that misnamed redoubt, actually a plateau Washington chose largely for its defensibility. (A nearby hollow had once been the site of a smithy hence the designation.) Tents provided their only barrier against frost and wind. Their commander in chief insisted that he, too, would shelter in a tent until his troops were able to cut down trees and construct log huts for themselves.

Washington despaired for the fate of his army. "The whole of them," said his comrade in arms, Gen. John Sullivan, were "without watch coats, one half without blankets, and more than one third without shoes . . . many of them without jackets . . . and not a few without shirts." None had enough to eat: some had gone hungry for days. Exhausted and ill, men were deserting in great numbers, heading home to their families and farms. It was a dark moment for the Revolution and for Washington. From his makeshift headquarters, he wrote to warn Congress: "unless some great and capital change suddenly takes place . . . this army must inevitably... starve, dissolve or disperse."

At that instant, stays Revolutionary era historian Edmund Morgan, Washington was indeed "giving Congress the facts of life: you can't fight a war without an army. He was operating at a big disadvantage; the state militias offered larger bounties than Congress did for serving in the Continental army."

Yet even as Washington attempted to keep his army from disintegrating, he found himself challenged on another front. Prominent figures in the independence movement—most notably, some members of Congress—had begun to question his very fitness to command. Over the course of the next several months—until mid-March—Washington would be plagued by a small but vocal contingent calling for his ouster. They engineered a very real distraction at a moment of grave crisis.

More than two years before, on June 15, 1775, Congress had unanimously chosen the tall, 43-year-old Virginia plantation owner and gentleman farmer "to command all the continental forces, raised or to be raised, for the defense of American liberty." During the French and Indian War two decades earlier, he had proved himself a courageous and levelheaded officer, serving under British command and as a colonel in the Virginia militia.

Washington had immediately justified the confidence placed in him by bringing order to the hodgepodge of militia contingents he led in what was becoming America's war of national liberation. From disarray and muddle, he created an American army and, in March 1776, orchestrated its first significant achievement, besieging the British and causing them to withdraw from Boston, the principal redcoat base in America at the time. "This was the moment," says historian John Ferling, author of the definitive Washington biography *The First of Men,* "that George Washington first captured the imagination of the American people."

But after Boston, his army suffered a series of serious reverses, including defeat at Brooklyn Heights on August 27, 1776, and the loss of New York. "At this point," says Ferling, "Washington was on the run. He nearly got trapped two or three times. During this period the British, under the command of General Howe, could have defeated him."

Washington's daring strikes against the enemy at Trenton on December 26 and Princeton on January 3, 1777, in New Jersey, boosted morale, but otherwise had little lasting military importance. Then came Brandywine Creek, in Pennsylvania. On September 11, 1777, where Washington failed to stop the British from advancing on Philadelphia, the capital of the Revolution. Members of Congress, who faced execution if taken prisoner, fled the city. This fiasco was followed by the Battle of Germantown, Pennsylvania, on October 4, where the Continental army snatched defeat from the jaws of victory through blunders in the field. Washington's four-pronged attack for taking the city proved too complex for inexperienced troops to carry out. As his soldiers maneuvered in a dense fog, they accidentally fired on one another. Given this turn of events, few in Congress observed the progress of the war without growing anxiety.

In the small Pennsylvania market town of York, about 100 miles west of Philadelphia, where Congress reconvened, there was talk that the commander in chief was indecisive and overly dependent on the advice of his senior subordinates. Congressman Thomas Burke of North Carolina decried what he called the "want of abilities in our superior officers and want of order and discipline in our army." Pennsylvania's new attorney general, Jonathan Dickinson Sergeant, a former congressman, charged that Washington was responsible for "such blunders as might have disgraced a soldier of three months' standing." In a moment of despair, John Adams, although ever fearful that a tyrant might emerge to fill the gap left by the discarded British king, pleaded in his diary while en route from Philadelphia to York, "Oh, Heaven! grant Us one great Soul! . . . One leading Mind would extricate the best Cause, from that Ruin which seems to await it."

Suddenly, it seemed, that desperate prayer had been answered: a patriot paladin appeared on the scene. Less than nine weeks before Washington's troops retreated to Valley Forge—the main column arrived there on December 19—the Continental army had scored a decisive victory. On October 17, at Saratoga in eastern New York, American forces, under the command of Gen. Horatio Gates, inflicted the first major defeat of the war on the redcoats, their German mercenary auxiliaries and Indian allies. For Gates, the 49-year-old English-born son of a duke's housekeeper, it was a moment of both tactical and symbolic triumph. The dashing John Burgoyne, campaigning down from Canada to split the states and crush the Revolution, was ignominiously forced to surrender himself and his army to the gruff, battle-hardened American, himself a former British officer. "One cannot underestimate the importance of Saratoga," says Ferling. "It is this victory that induces France to come into the war."

Gates' success greatly lifted American spirits. But his victory also drew attention to the fact that Washington, his superior officer, could claim no equivalent battle honors. Within Congress, criticism of Washington's performance escalated. Perhaps, some legislators suggested, the victor at Saratoga would make a better commander in chief than the general who had not prevented the British from taking Philadelphia.

Massachusetts Congressman James Lovell was scarcely alone in his view, as he wrote Gates, "The army will be totally lost unless you . . . , collect the virtuous band who wish to fight under your banner." Dr. Benjamin Rush, a signer of the Declaration of Independence, contrasted Gates, "exulting in the success of schemes planned with wisdom and executed with vigor and bravery," with Washington, "outgeneralled and twice beaten."

Most of the delegates at York, however, along with the majority of the Continental army's officers and its ordinary soldiers, continued to esteem their commander in chief. They were well aware that it was Washington who had kept the army from dissolving, despite the paucity of resources provided by either the strapped and deeply shaken Congress or the newly independent states. When it was suggested to hulking Gen. Daniel Morgan, whose corps of riflemen had played a decisive role at Saratoga, that a handful of senior officers intended to resign unless Washington was removed, he unhesitatingly responded, "Under no other man than Washington as Commander-in-Chief would I ever serve."

Dr. Benjamin Rush, a signer of the Declaration of Independence, referred to Washington as "outgeneralled and twice beaten."

Washington knew well that he was blamed, in certain quarters, for the poor performance of his army. But he was fitted with far more pressing matters. He had troops to feed, clothe, prepare for battle—and, most important, inspire: he understood that he must rally his remaining troops—about 11,000 all told at Valley Forge—and dissuade them from deserting. The commander of the Continental army was, according to Philander D. Chase, editor of *The Papers of George Washington* at the University, of Virginia, "astute enough to take a longer view of things. He understood that criticism, fair or unfair, real or apprehended, was part of the price that he had to pay to remain an effective leader and to achieve the aims of the Revolution."

In addition, Washington was engaged in planning offensive campaigns against a powerful, well-supplied foe. "The British were indeed formidable," says Ferling. "They had defeated the French in the French and Indian War; they also had the best navy in the world."

To add to Washington's concerns, for months he had contended with an assortment of European military officers, most of them French, who had converged on America to volunteer their services. They were recruited in Paris by Silas Deane, America's first official diplomat.

Some of the officers Deane commissioned may have shared the principles that had sparked the American Revolution. But most had signed on to further their own military careers, hoping to leapfrog into higher ranks back in Europe. Washington welcomed some of those volunteers, who would prove of great value to the American cause. Notable among them were the Marquis de Lafayette, the 19-year-old French nobleman who became one of Washington's most trusted aides; Friedrich von Steuben, the German soldier who would transform Washington's ragged army into a disciplined fighting force at Valley Forge; and Tadeusz Kosciuszko, the Polish military engineer who contributed greatly to the American victory at Saratoga.

But some foreign officers who laid claim to senior command in the Continental army were a nuisance or worse—none more so than Col. Thomas Conway. He would figure prominently among Washington's detractors, whom history would come to designate the Conway Cabal. A French officer of Irish origin, the 42-year-old Conway, high browed, thin lipped and supercilious, made it plain that he had come to America "to increase my fortune and that of my family." He was a seasoned soldier who joined the French Army at the age of 14. Gen. John Sullivan, under whom he served in the ill-fated Battle of Germantown, believed "his knowledge of military matters in general far exceeds any officer we have."

Congress quickly awarded Conway the rank of brigadier general; his military background and charisma earned him many an admirer in York. When he threatened to return to France unless promoted to major general, more than a few congressmen, convinced that Washington needed experienced commanders, took up Conway's cause.

At first, Washington, too, had been impressed by Conway's credentials. Over time, however, he had come to believe that the French officer's "importance in this Army, exists more in his imagination than in reality." What troubled him most was Congress's readiness to promote Conway over the heads of Washington's own loyal brigadiers. Many of his officers, he warned, would refuse to serve under Conway and would simply go home. "I have been a slave to the service," Washington informed Virginia Congressman Richard Henry Lee on October 17, 1777. "But it will be impossible for me to be of any further service if such insuperable obstacles are thrown in my way."

While some in Congress would have welcomed Washington's resignation in favor of Gates, the prospect of sowing confusion in the ranks, or even of causing an already demoralized army to disband, was alarming. The Continental army embodied the Revolution.

At this juncture, during the fall of 1777, Washington prevailed and Congress failed to act on Conway's promotion. But Congress also, at this moment, reorganized its Board of War. That Congressional committee, charged with overseeing the struggle for independence, was in fact composed of members who possessed little understanding of military matters. Until then, the board had intervened only minimally when it came to the army. Now the committee would include senior officers; Washington, the commander in chief, was not consulted about whom they would be.

It was rumored that Conway might be among them. From the moment of his arrival in America in the spring of 1777, Conway had found that the organization of the Continental army clashed with his European understanding of how military units should be commanded, trained and deployed. He did not hesitate in expressing his deprecating views. After Congress, acting on the basis of Washington's firm intercession, had failed to support his promotion to major general, Conway stepped up his campaign to defame the commander in chief. He informed General Gates that he wished to serve under him because "the more I see of [Washington's] army the less I think it fit for general action."

Recognizing the delicacy of the situation, Congress did not name Conway to the board. But it did appoint Thomas Mifflin, the army's former quartermaster general. Once Washington's friend, Mifflin had differed sharply on strategy and was now among the general's most acerbic critics. He jealously asserted that the commander's "favourites . . . had an undue influence on him" and told Gates that Conway's criticism of Washington contained "just sentiments."

But the most significant appointment to the board turned out to be none other than the hero of Saratoga himself: it was a decision bound to create problems. Ever since his victory only a matter of weeks earlier, Gates had behaved disdainfully toward Washington, his superior officer. He even failed to formally notify the commander in chief of the triumph at Saratoga. Instead, Gates reported directly to Congress, a gesture that implied he claimed equal status with Washington. He had been slow to respond to Washington's request that some of Gates' troops, no longer essential for much-reduced northern operations, be released to the south, where they were desperately needed. Now Gates emerged as the leader of the board that would superintend the operations of Washington and his ragtag army.

Conway informed General Gates that "the more I see of Washington's army the less I think it fit for general action."

Although Washington surely must have been offended by this high-handed treatment, he refused to engage in a squabble over the appointments. Whatever his complaints about Congress's shortcomings in providing supplies and pay for his men, he recognized the legislature's authority over the military wing of the Revolution.

Substantial changes, too, in the character of the Congress that had ringingly declared American independence more than a year earlier, on July 4, 1776, intensified the divisiveness. Many of the original founding fathers had already left the legislature or were soon to depart. Thomas Jefferson had returned to Virginia to assist its transition from a royal colony to an independent state. Benjamin Franklin was in Paris seeking French assistance for America in the war. John Adams was preparing to join him there. Twenty-one-year-old Lt. Col. Alexander Hamilton, Washington's aide-de-camp, angrily demanded, "The great men who composed our first council; are they dead, have they deserted the cause, or what has become of them?"

Among the new delegates, few were as gifted, or would prove as memorable, as their predecessors. Much time was wasted in futile bickering. Henry Laurens of South Carolina, president of Congress during much of its York exile, grumbled, "Some sensible things have been said [here], and as much nonsense as ever I heard in so short a space." Charles Carroll of Maryland complained, "We murder time, and chat it away in idle impertinent talk."

Meanwhile, detractors in Congress were becoming increasingly critical of Washington. After visiting York, Lafayette returned to Valley Forge and declared himself outraged by "stupid men who without knowing a single word about war, undertake to judge you."

The move to replace the commander in chief with Gates—or even, it was muttered, with Conway—came to a head early in 1778 after the Continental army had arrived at the glacial hell of Valley Forge. One of every four soldiers who wintered in that place would die there. Even hardened veterans, among them Albigence Waldo of Connecticut, an army surgeon who had served since 1775, were appalled by what they saw: "There comes a soldier," Waldo wrote, "his bare feet are seen thro' his worn-out shoes, his legs nearly naked from the tattered remains of an only pair of stockings, his Breeches not sufficient to cover his nakedness. . . . He crys . . . I am Sick, my feet lame, my legs are sore, my body covered with this tormenting Itch."

Reluctantly, Washington sent troops to seize food from nearby farmers. Already weighed down with dire anxieties, he suffered another blow. On December 13, he learned Congress had reversed itself and decided to appoint Conway to the Board of War, as inspector general of the army. What was more, Congress elevated Conway to the rank of major general—the promotion previously denied because of Washington's objections.

Conway wasted no time in presenting himself at army headquarters, where, predictably, he was received with cold formality. Washington informed Conway that the newly conferred rank—a promotion the commander in chief dryly referred to as "extraordinary"—would offend many senior officers; he then asked to see specific instructions Conway had received from the Board of War. When Conway failed to produce such a communique, Washington had him shown out.

Upon his departure from Valley Forge, Conway sent Washington a letter barbed with sarcasm and self-justification, complaining their meeting had been a reception "as I never met with before with any general during the course of thirty years in a very respectable [French] Army."

His patience exhausted, Washington decided to confront the Conway issue. He passed the new inspector general's comments on to Congress, along with a bitter rebuttal of each accusation. Washington denied that he had received Conway with anything less than "proper respect to his official character" as an appointee of Congress. Nevertheless, he concluded, "My feelings will not permit me to make professions of friendship to a man I deem my enemy."

All the while, despite reports from friends that members of Congress were maneuvering to install Gates in his place, Washington had not sought to clash with the victor of Saratoga. He refused to believe that the new president of the Board of War was conspiring against him. "Being honest himself," Joseph Reed, Washington's former military secretary wrote, "he will not readily suspect the virtue of others." However, recognition of the challenge to his position became unavoidable.

Washington's trusted friend Dr. James Craik, a senior army medical officer, wrote to inform him that although "they dare not appear openly as your enemies . . . the new Board of War is composed of such leading men as will throw such obstacles and difficulties in your way as to force you to resign." Without consulting Washington, Gates' board secured Congressional approval of a campaign to pursue the English into Canada (the plans were later aborted). Patrick Henry, the governor of Virginia, forwarded to Washington a disturbing anonymous letter warning that "unless a Moses or a Joshua are raised up in our behalf, we must perish before we reach the promised land."

Increasingly exasperated by such taunts, Washington told a friend he would be happy to resign his command. "There is not an Officer in the Service of the United States," he declared, "that would return to the sweets of domestic life with more heart felt joy than I should." But he would do so, he added, only if the will of the people ordained it: he feared destabilizing consequences if he stepped down.

"My Enemies take an ungenerous advantage of me," Washington wrote. "I cannot combat their insinuations."

The unkindest cut, however, came from those who suggested he had concealed the appalling condition of his army in order to deflect criticism of his command. "My Enemies take an ungenerous advantage of me," Washington protested to Henry Laurens. "They know I cannot combat their insinuations, however injurious, without disclosing secrets it is of the utmost moment to conceal." Had they known its state, the redcoats, a mere 18 miles away in Philadelphia, might well have launched an attack.

While Washington hoped that the British commander, Lord William Howe, remained ignorant of the extent of the patriot army's vulnerability as it bivouacked on frozen ground, members of Congress began arriving at Valley Forge to survey conditions for themselves. A shocked John Harvie of Virginia told Washington, "My dear General, if you had given some explanation, all these rumors [denigrating Washington] would have been silenced a long time ago."

Within Congress, a growing recognition of Washington's extraordinary leadership at Valley Forge—not only was he preventing the Continental army from dissolving, he was somehow inspiring his men under the cruelest of conditions—made a profound impression. Joseph Jones, a congressman from Virginia and a long-standing friend to Washington, wrote to offer his support: "The same equal and disinterested conduct, the same labor and attention, which you have manifested in the public service from the first of the contest, will shield and protect you from the shafts of envy and malevolence."

Still, Washington decided the time had come to take up the festering matter of a letter that Conway had written to Gates that autumn, which referred to a "weak general" who might prove the ruin of America.

He had learned of the letter when one of Gates' own aides had disclosed its contents to an officer loyal to Washington. When Gates discovered that the letter had been leaked to Washington, he wrote to him, demanding the identity of the "wretch" who had "stealingly copied" his private correspondence. Bent on dramatizing his challenge to the commander in chief's integrity, Gates sent a copy of this letter to Congress.

It would prove an enormous blunder. Washington was, quite rightly, able to take the high ground when he replied to the slander. Why, he inquired of Congress, would anyone want to add needlessly to the burdens on the beleaguered legislature, pestering it with details of a personal disagreement? He pointed out that he had learned of the malicious Conway letter to Gates through an indiscretion by one of Gates' own aides. Washington added that he had not previously gone public with the matter because he was "desirous . . . of concealing every matter that could give the smallest interruption to the tranquility of this army." In the end, the episode caused the hero of Saratoga, and Conway along with him, to appear small-minded and vindictive.

But what conclusively undermined Washington's critics was the recognition that, whatever his shortcomings, Washington remained the individual who most represented the cause of liberty in the minds of the American people and its army. Mercy Otis Warren reported to her husband, Continental Navy Board member James Warren, that "The toast among the soldiers" is "Washington or no Army." Thomas Paine, the conscience mad primary propagandist of the Revolution, expressed the fervent hope that he could "shame [Washington's critics]" or at least "convince them of their error."

Congressman Jones accurately foretold that whatever the conspirators had intended, "it will redound to their own disgrace." Men who had spoken belittlingly of the commander in chief would later deny they had ever held him in anything but the highest regard. Gates soon tried to effect a reconciliation with Washington, but his attempt was rebuffed. Congress later removed him from the Board of War and assigned him to a succession of field commands. His reputation as a military hero would soon come to grief in South Carolina where, at the Battle of Camden on August 16, 1780, his troops were routed by the British. During a hasty retreat, Gates' undisguised anxiety for his own personal safety made him an object of ridicule among his men. "The general's frantic dash from the scene," says historian John Ferling, "proved his ruination."

Mifflin also suffered a measure of disgrace. Charged with having contributed to the troops' hardships at Valley Forge through mismanagement of funds as quartermaster general, he was forced to resign from the Board of War. He denied conspiring against Washington, insisting he had always "dearly loved and greatly admired" him.

As for Conway, who was scarcely the most significant figure in the Conway Cabal—despite the name by which it became known—Congress acted with crushing decisiveness. Still denied a senior command in the army, he offered his resignation April 1778 and was surprised when it was accepted. Before returning to France, he wrote Washington "You are in my eyes the great and the good man. May you long enjoy the love, veneration and esteem of these States, whose liberties you have asserted by your virtues." In that, at least, his wish would be realized.

Historians disagree over the significance of the attacks on Washington. In his monumental biography of Washington, Douglas S. Freeman stated that "the imperative reason for defeating [the cabal] was to keep the Army and the country united in the hard battle for freedom." But Ferling tends to minimize its importance. "I don't really think the cabal existed as an organized conspiracy," he says. "It existed more in Washington's mind than in reality." Certainly, Washington was convinced that a "malignant faction" had conspired to remove him. So, too, was Patrick Henry, who, along with others, feared for the patriot cause if such efforts had succeeded.

Whatever the strength of those who considered Washington a liability, it is impossible to calculate the consequences for the Continental army, the American Revolution and the embryonic United States of America had their sentiments found greater resonance in Congress—and forced or provoked the man who would later be called the Father of the Country to resign his command.

NORMAN GELB, author of numerous histories, is currently working on a study of military leadership in the American Revolution.

Evacuation Day
New York City's Forgotten Past

ERIK PETER AXELSON

For New Yorkers, November 25 is a date of special significance that long rivaled the Fourth of July in engendering patriotic celebrations. New York City has the distinction of being the American city held by a foreign country for the longest time. From the summer of 1776 to the fall of 1783 the British occupied the city. After the British forces were finally defeated on the battlefield by the upstart nation, New York City would become their last enclave on American soil.

New York was a growing urban center of about 20,000 crowded onto the southern tip of Manhattan Island when the rebellious Colonies declared their independence from England in 1776. The city was promptly occupied in the wake of a series of American defeats and retreats in the summer and fall of 1776. The landing of British troops and Hessian mercenaries in Brooklyn on August 22, 1776, and the American loss at the Battle of Long Island, led to the retreat of General George Washington's Continental Army across the East River to Manhattan. Subsequent battles in mid-September at Kips Bay and Harlem Heights pushed the Patriot forces into the northern third of the island. British reinforcements made the American position untenable, and in November came the surrender of Fort Washington, the highest natural point on the island. The complete evacuation of American troops from Manhattan soon followed as Washington retreated farther north to Westchester County, N.Y., and later across the Hudson River into New Jersey, with much of his army intact to fight another day.

By the time the British had control of the city, it bore scant resemblance to the bustling port of prior decades. What had been the second largest city in America, between Philadelphia and Boston in size, was now a shell of its former self. Several thousand pro-American residents had departed with the Continental Army, their homes and farms now occupied by British and Hessian troops or confiscated by their Loyalist neighbors. On September 21, 1776, a devastating fire of unknown origin had destroyed more than a quarter of the city, including Trinity Church and other public buildings. Ironically, Washington had requested permission from the Continental Congress to torch the city as he retreated to prevent the British from successfully occupying it, but Congress had forbidden it. "In speaking of New York," Washington later wrote to his cousin, Lund Washington, "I had forgot to mention that Providence—or some good, honest Fellow,

has done more for us than we are disposed to do for ourselves, as near One fourth of the City is supposed consumed . . . however enough of it remains to answer their purposes."

New York would remain the seat of British administration in the Colonies for the remaining seven years of the war. A succession of British commanders—Sir William Howe, Sir Henry Clinton and Sir Guy Carleton—ruled the city and nearby Long Island as virtual military dictators, with the collaboration of leading native Tories such as James Rivington, William Smith and Oliver DeLancey. Thousands of American prisoners of war were confined in New York in a prison on the Common and in the city's makeshift jails as well as on pestilential prison ships that were moored across the East River in Wallabout Bay.

In his 1948 *Father Knickerbocker Rebels*, historian Thomas J. Wertenbaker recounted the hard life in occupied New York:

> By the end of the first half-year of British occupation, life in New York City had assumed the pattern it was to follow for the remainder of the war. The dearness of food, the inadequate supply of fuel, the eager desire to have news from the front, the return of the sick and wounded, the uneasiness over the international situation, the absence of civil government, the growing importance of privateering, the squalor of the group shanties and tents known as canvas town amid the blackened ruins left by the fire, the well-to-do families now forced to live on charity—all these things were to mark Tory New York.

American and British commanders alike had considered New York the strategic key to the continent, particularly if British forces in the city were to march north up the Hudson Valley to meet a British army moving south from Canada, as was planned. Such a convergence would divide New England from Pennsylvania and the Southern states and vastly complicate Patriot communication, troop deployments and the war for independence itself. However, such a strategic pincer movement failed to materialize. While Sir John Burgoyne and Colonel Barry St. Leger advanced from Canada into northern New York, Sir Henry Clinton failed to move quickly enough north from the city. The advance from Canada was halted in the summer and fall of 1777—St. Leger and his Iroquois allies were defeated at Oriskany in the Mohawk Valley, and Burgoyne surrendered his remaining army of 5,700 at Saratoga. The British defeat at Saratoga was a historic turning point that convinced France to join the Americans as an ally, and later led Spain and the Netherlands to declare war on Britain, further stretching British resources.

French intervention brought needed supplies and funds to the American cause but, most important, it brought a significant naval force into the conflict in North America. While fleets of French warships menaced New York Harbor at least twice during the British occupation, Washington elected to avoid the danger of direct assault on the city, leaving it in British hands.

French intervention ultimately proved decisive in defeating British forces in battle. Washington combined his army with one commanded by French General comte de Rochambeau and transferred them south by land and sea to join an army led by the Marquis de Lafayette that had succeeded in bottling up Lord Charles Cornwallis' forces near Yorktown, Va. Two French fleets maintained naval superiority in Chesapeake Bay, landed siege artillery for Lafayette and prevented the British army from evacuating by sea. The final battle at Yorktown in October 1781 found the British outnumbered by the combined American and French troops. Cornwallis surrendered his army on October 19, as an American band played "The World Turned Upside Down."

While armed hostilities in North America essentially ended in 1781, it took more than two years for British troops to relinquish New York City. Many British leaders initially viewed Yorktown as just a setback, and made plans for additional offensive military operations. Indeed, six weeks after Yorktown, King George III had defiantly declared to Parliament, "[B]y the valour of my fleets and armies, and by the vigourous, animated and united exertion of the faculties and resources of my people, I shall be able to restore the blessings of a safe and honourable peace to all my Dominions."

Clinton and Cornwallis returned to Britain, and command of British forces passed to Carleton, who had looked askance at the policies that had driven the Colonies to war. In March 1782, the House of Commons voted to discontinue the war, and a few days later the pro-war government of Prime Minister Frederick North fell, to be replaced by one determined to negotiate a peace with independence for the Colonies.

Loyalists in New York were devastated by the turn of events. In a letter to Clinton, Beverly Robinson, one of New York's leading Loyalists, wrote, "And, oh my dear Sir, what dreadful and distressing tidings does [a British ship] bring us—the independence of America given up by the King without any conditions whatever, the Loyalists of America to depend upon the mercy of their enemies for the restoration of their possessions, which we are assured they will never grant, the greatest part of the states that have been confiscated by them are already sold."

Benjamin Franklin's Loyalist son, William, the last royal governor of New Jersey, sailed for London to make the case for protecting the American Tories to the new government and to King George. Though sympathetic, the king and prime minister were now most interested in concluding negotiations and liquidating the American war.

Washington's army had fortified positions north and west of Manhattan to be prepared to forcibly evict the British from the city. Carleton's troops withdrew closer to the city and adopted a static defensive posture to minimize conflicts with the Americans. British forces evacuated their garrisons from the two other remaining large cities they controlled—Savannah in July 1782 and Charleston in January 1783. New York was then the last major British outpost in the American Colonies.

Peace negotiations in Paris between American and British representatives resulted in preliminary articles concluding peace on November 30, 1782. A draft treaty of peace between Britain, the United States, France and Spain was signed in January 1783. The following month, King George proclaimed a "Cessation of Arms," news of which reached New York in late March. The royal proclamation was read to the residents in front of City Hall on April 8, 1783, and caused much consternation among the Loyalist residents. "When the reading was concluded, no one huzza'd or showed any mark of joy or approbation," the London Chronicle later reported. "[N]othing but groans and hisses prevailed, attended by bitter reproaches and curses upon the king for having deserted them in the midst of their calamities."

At the same time, all the prisoners of war held by the British in the city and environs, and aboard ships in the East River were released. (It is estimated that more than 10,000 American prisoners had died in confinement on the prison ships.) The return of former residents who had left their homes and property in 1776 led to altercations with Loyalists. In spite of provisions in the preliminary peace articles to protect Tory residents and their property, previous laws passed by New York state's new Patriot legislature provided for confiscation of Loyalist property and, in certain cases, execution for Americans who had defected to the British during the war. Much Patriot ire was reserved for Tories who had formed the Associated Loyalists, paramilitary organizations in support of the British.

Most of the Loyalists accepted British offers to relocate them to other parts of the empire. Ships sailed from New York, carrying Tory families and their goods to such outposts as the Bahamas, islands in the Caribbean and, especially, to Canada. The vast majority of Loyalist refugees settled in Nova Scotia and Newfoundland. Among these were more than 1,000 former black slaves who had gained their freedom by fighting on the British side. Ultimately, nearly 30,000 Loyalists departed out of New York before the British evacuation in November 1783. Some Tories remained, determined to make a go of it in the new republic. One was the printer James Rivington, who opportunistically dropped the word Royal from the title of his newspaper, now named Rivington's New-York Gazette.

The status of newly freed slaves, including those who chose to remain in New York, had come up in a conference between Carleton and Washington. The two opposing commanders met, along with New York Governor George Clinton (no relation to the British commander Henry Clinton) and British Admiral Robert Digby, at Tappan, N.Y., in May 1783 to prepare for repatriation of New York to the Americas. In response to Washington's request to return stolen property—including slaves—to the Americans, Carleton asserted an obligation of honor to protect the freed slaves. A proposal that the British would pay American slave owners was ultimately accepted. (Although many feed blacks gravitated to the city during the ensuing decades and the number of slaves had dwindled by then, slavery was not abolished in New York until 1827.)

A final peace agreement, the Treaty of Paris, was signed on September 3, 1783. As word of the treaty reached New York, more American citizens began to return to the city, and thousands of Loyalists continued to leave on British transports. Carleton had refrained from fixing a precise date for completing evacuation of British forces because of the large number of Loyalist residents still waiting to leave the city. But finally, on November 19, the British commander proposed to Washington to evacuate outlying areas on November 21, with evacuation of Brooklyn and the city itself to begin at noon on November 25.

As British troops left garrisons on Long Island and northern Manhattan, American forces moved in to replace them. Among the most important was at McGowan's Pass, located in the northwest corner of present-day Central Park. General Washington and Governor Clinton rode into Harlem on November 21 and established a headquarters in a tavern, located at present-day West 126th Street and Frederick Douglass Boulevard, to await the final British withdrawal. Meanwhile, groups of Americans who had returned to the city formed committees to receive Washington and Clinton, preparing uniform cockades and garlands as badges of distinction for the happy day.

November 25, 1783, was cold and clear. Eager patriots crowded the city streets to await Washington's triumphal return. Many city residents festooned their homes and businesses with American flags, some of which were torn down by unrepentant Tories still in the city. British soldiers, set to leave Fort George at the foot of Broadway at State Street at 1 P.M., sabotaged and greased the flagpole to make it more difficult for the Americans to raise Old Glory. Undeterred, inventive soldiers and sailors jury-rigged a new halyard to raise the American flag at the fort for the first time since September 15, 1776.

Meanwhile, General Washington continued on his eight-mile-long procession from Harlem. As he and his party rode down its length, they could not fail to note the decrepit condition of this strategic island—virtually denuded of trees that had been used for fires, abandoned farms and destroyed houses, and few if any cattle or other farm animals. In addition, many wells reportedly had dried up during the occupation. From the prosperous port city of 21,683 residents before the Revolutionary War, New York had declined to a barely functioning settlement of about 12,000 people.

After entering the city proper along The Bowery at Chatham Square, General Washington and his party continued on and passed the burned-out skeleton of Trinity Church. But the deprived condition of the city and its environs could not dim the joy the Patriot residents felt at their deliverance. Major Benjamin Tallmadge, in the advance party, described Washington's return to the city along with 800 troops accompanying him: General Knox, at the head of a select corps of American troops, entered the city as the rear of the British troops embarked; soon after which the Commander-in-chief, accompanied by Governor Clinton and their respective suites, made their public entry into the city on horseback, followed by the Lieut.-governor and members of the Council. The officers of the army, eight abreast, and citizens on horseback, eight abreast, accompanied by the Speaker of the Assembly, and citizens on foot, eight abreast, followed after the Commander-in-chief and Gov. Clinton. So perfect was the order of march, that entire tranquility prevailed, and nothing occurred to mar the general republican principles over the military despotism which had so long pervaded the now happy city.

Another observer wrote: "On all corners one saw the flag of thirteen stripes flying, cannon salutes were fired, and all the bells rang. The shores were crowded with people who threw their hats in the air, screaming and boisterous with joy." As the flag-bedecked city celebrated, several remaining British ships weighed anchor on the high tide and set out for the Atlantic. That night General Washington was the guest of honor at a banquet given by Governor Clinton at Fraunces Tavern, which still stands at the corner of present-day Broad and Pearl Streets. Future Mayor Stephen Allen wrote, "This was a happy day for the real friends of America and it was celebrated accordingly by young and old, particularly by those who had left the city at the commencement of the troubles and had now returned for the first time from an exile of eight long years."

Washington remained in the city for about 10 days, attending celebratory banquets nearly every night, and tending to army business during the day. On December 4 he met with his officers at Fraunces Tavern, where they exchanged toasts and bid each other an emotional farewell. General Washington waited to leave the city until British commander Carleton and his last forces departed Staten Island by ship that afternoon. Washington appointed General Henry Knox as commander of southern New York, and then walked to the Whitehall Slip and boarded a barge for the voyage across the harbor to New Jersey to begin his long farewell procession to his home at Mount Vernon in Virginia. On the way he stopped at Annapolis, Md., where the U.S. Congress was meeting, to formally resign his commission as commander in chief. Washington would finally arrive at Mount Vernon on Christmas Eve 1783.

New York, of course, revived and prospered following Evacuation Day. Civil government returned to the city, led by ardent Patriots such as Isaac Sears, Marinus Willett and Richard Varick; a fractious Common Council met alongside the state government in the Old City Hall, now the site of Federal Hall at Broad and Wall streets. Reprisals against the remaining Tories in the city flared up, along with a campaign to limit the influence of such Tory institutions as the Anglican Trinity Parish. Despite the hard feelings engendered by the war, many New Yorkers pushed for reconciliation and rebuilding. New leaders, such as Alexander Hamilton, became vital to the city's resurgence, helping to found banks and other institutions and to clear the way for resumed trade.

By the spring of 1784, the first American merchant ship had set sail from New York's harbor to Asia, and resurging trade began to be the engine for the city's revival. A rising artisan class in New York opposed Governor Clinton's protectionist trade policies and became the nucleus of Hamilton's Federalist Party. Contested elections for the state assembly and other offices spread political power among several factions, the beginning of vibrant self-government. The city's population rebounded and grew from 12,000 in 1783 to more then 60,000 by century's end.

Historian Barnet Schecter, in his 2002 The Battle for New York, summed up the changes wrought by war: "The social and political consensus that evolved in post war New York left the city's major institutions in the hands of a moderate and conservative ruling class, as Hamilton believed they should be . . . . Nevertheless, during the course of the Revolution and its immediate aftermath, the manor lords and the merchant princes had lost many of their traditional privileges and had seen a broader electorate organize itself and use its influence."

Vestiges of British rule were quickly discarded. Streets with names that hearkened back to the city's colonial status were replaced with more appropriate republican names—Crown Street became Liberty Street, Queen Street became Pearl Street, and King Street was renamed Pine Street, though Hanover Street and Square escaped renaming and still-existent King's College was rechartered as Columbia College (later Columbia University). Fort George was dismantled and those stones from its walls and fortification reused as landfill to create the Battery just to the south.

New York prospered in the following decades for many of the same reasons that the original Dutch an English colony had thrived—a magnificent port unmatched for world trade, easy water access to the agricultural hinterland, a concentration of artisans and early venture capitalists that facilitated manufacturing, a skilled and educated workforce, and tremendous cultural diversity. New York was the seat of government under the Articles of Confederation from 1784 to 1789, and was instrumental in the process of ratifying the U.S. Constitution in 1788. The city served as the first seat of the new national government in 1789–90. George Washington took the oath as the nation's first president under the Constitution at Federal Hall in New York on April 30, 1789.

Though it later ceded its position as political capital to Philadelphia and then to the new city of Washington, D.C., New York City soon became the nation's financial capital. The successors to financial institutions established in the 1780s and 1790s still do business today, including Chase Manhattan, founded by Aaron Burr, and the Bank of New York, founded by Alexander Hamilton. The opening of the Erie Canal in 1825 increased the importance of the port, and during the 19th century, millions of immigrants would flood into New York through its harbor. In short order, New York became the most populous city in the new nation. The Empire City became the clothier to America, the largest center of manufacturing in the country, the center of newspapers and publishing, and the home of hundreds of large corporations.

For generations after Evacuation Day of 1783, New Yorkers annually celebrated the British decampment and General Washington's procession into the city. Parades, fireworks, pageants and other festivities marked succeeding anniversaries of the British evacuation. But as the city grew and time passed, Evacuation Day began to lose some of its luster. British writer Thomas Hamilton attended the festivities on Evacuation Day 1830 and found them a tad dispirited:

> In truth, I had calculated on a site [sic] altogether different. I expected to see a vast multitude animated by one pervading feeling of generous enthusiasm; to hear the air rent by the triumphant shouts of tens of thousands of freemen hailing, the bloodless dawn of liberty in a mighty member of the brotherhood of nations. As it was, I witnessed nothing so sublime. Throughout the day there was not the smallest demonstration of enthusiasm on the part of the vast concourse of spectators. There was no cheering, no excitement, no general expression of feeling of any sort . . . the moral of the display, if I may so speak, was utterly overlooked.

During the same period, the British actress Fanny Kemble was struck by the lack of spit and polish as she observed an Evacuation Day parade from her hotel window: "The militia are not dressed to match, hats are askew, and weapons are carried every which way . . . as these worthies on horse-back came down the street, some trotting, some galloping, some ambling."

Though its spirit may have been panned by British visitors, the celebration in 1830 was still a big deal for New Yorkers. Events that day also celebrated the 1830 popular revolt in France that had brought the "citizen-king" Louis-Phillippe to power, echoing America's republican traditions. Evacuation Day that year was centered on the new and urbane Washington Square, which had been developed as a militia parade ground in 1827. More than 50,000 participants took part in events that were presided over by a former president, James Monroe, and a former mayor, Philip Hone.

As the Revolutionary War veterans died off, Evacuation Day continued to lose some of its zeal. Diarist George Templeton Strong wrote in 1842 that its "glories have departed and nobody thinks of it now." In the course of the next few decades, the growing popularity of Thanksgiving, which was revived during the Civil War and occurred at roughly the same time of the year, came to overshadow Evacuation Day remembrances.

The centennial celebration of Evacuation Day in 1883 offered an opportunity for renewed meaning and resonance. The iconic bronze statue of George Washington overlooking the steps of the Subtreasury Building, now Federal Hall, was unveiled during the festivities on that day. Governor Grover Cleveland presided over the events, which had been organized by the New York chapter of the Sons of Revolution, and included a parade of 20,000 celebrants viewed by 500,000 spectators. A naval procession of 300 ships steamed up the Hudson and East rivers; one superb vantage point was from the just-dedicated Brooklyn Bridge. Historian Clifton Hood, a professor of history at Hobart and William Smith Colleges, dates the decline of widespread celebration of Evacuation day from this period. In his view, the holiday was captured by the Sons of the Revolution and other patriotic groups, completing "the tradition's journey into the unusable past by privatizing the holiday." Evacuation Day largely passed into memory during World War I, as the United States was allied with Great Britain against the Central Powers, and it was considered unseemly to revisit the depredations of the British occupation.

In New York City, the 200th anniversary of Evacuation Day in 1983 was marked by nothing more than an exhibit at Fraunces Tavern Museum of prints, letters, photographs and artifacts from previous celebrations, failing to engender a renewal of annual celebrations. Today the only memorial to the evacuation is an equestrian statue of George Washington at the southern end of New York City's Union Square Park. While Massachusetts also cele-brates an Evacuation Day to mark the withdrawal of British forces from Boston in March 1776, that holiday is now celebrated on St. Patrick's Day, and few celebrants are aware of its non-Hibernian significance. Moreover, Boston's celebration marks a British withdrawal that occurred less than a year into Revolutionary War.

No other city in the United States has been occupied by a foreign army for so long and under such deprivations as had New York. Evacuation Day may have receded in the consciousness of a city and nation so much changed in the course of more than two centuries—where the former occupiers have for a century been America's closest friend and ally. However, its significance as a true ending point for the American Revolution and beginning of a new era remains.

The Necessity of Refusing My Signature

Although the mastermind of liberty, when it came to the Constitution, George Mason just said no.

MARK BERNSTEIN

"Let us never lose sight of this fundamental maxim—that all power was originally lodged in, and consequently is derived from, the people. We should wear it as a breastplate, and buckle it on as our armour." Thus spoke Virginian George Mason of his guiding principles on the eve of revolution, a truth that ultimately would drive him to refuse to sign the Constitution and in the process fall from grace among many of the nation's founders. Although vindication would come through the first 10 amendments to the Constitution, withholding his signature from that historic document cost Mason more than his friendship with his neighbor George Washington—it also dimmed his standing within the consensus version of American history that places the Constitution and its signers on all but hallowed ground. That, of course, may not have greatly troubled Mason, whose "indifference for distinction," as fellow Virginian Edmund Randolph once wrote, was well known. Mason himself once said somewhat grandly that he "would not forfeit the approbation of my own mind for the approbation of any man, or all the men upon earth."

George Mason was commonly at pains to avoid political gatherings. Early in his public life, in 1760, he declined reelection to Virginia's House of Burgesses. In 1790, near the end of his life, he refused appointment to the U.S. Senate. In between, Mason rarely stirred from Gunston Hall, his estate just six miles south of George Washington's far better known Mount Vernon. Indeed, only once did Mason journey outside his native state—that was in May 1787, when he traveled to Philadelphia to help draft the Constitution of the United States.

Mason's credentials for that task were of the first order. In 1776 he was chief author both of the Virginia Declaration of Rights—the archetype for written bills of citizens' rights—and of that state's constitution—the first written constitution in modern history. His personal influence was considerable: He was political mentor to the younger Washington, whom he befriended when the latter was a teenager, and of James Madison, who wrote that Mason had "the greatest talents for debate of any man" he knew.

At the Philadelphia convention, Mason spoke often—indeed, his 136 recorded speeches were the fifth most of anyone attending. His was a key voice for popular government, for a restrained executive and for the hard-won compromise that resolved the conflict between the larger and smaller states. Masons most consequential act, however, came when the Constitution's drafting was complete. Ignoring Benjamin Franklin's impassioned plea to the convention for unanimity, Mason refused to sign the document.

Mason's refusal to sign the new Constitution was grounded chiefly in what it lacked: a bill of rights such as he had drafted for Virginia. And his refusal set in motion the events that shortly before his death led to the adoption of the first 10 amendments, so inextricably linked with the Constitution that they are commonly viewed as a part of the nation's founding covenant.

George Mason was the essential Virginian of the Revolutionary era. He was, first, an exceedingly rich man. Unlike Washington, he did not marry money; unlike Jefferson, he did not squander it. He inherited land, and expanded his holdings to 5,000 acres at Gunston, and eventually 75,000 more elsewhere. With wealth, he believed, came responsibility. Mason served as a town trustee of Alexandria, Va., and as a vestryman of the local Anglican church—the small tasks of governance by which colonists learned the craft of democracy.

Mason's life mirrors the stirrings of Colonial resistance to British authority. When tension over Britain's right to tax the Colonies first arose in 1765, Mason wrote to a relative in England, "There are not five men of sense in America who would accept of independence if it was offered." Still, he drew a line: "We will not submit to have our money taken from out of our pockets without our consent. . . . We owe our Mother Country the duty of subjects; we will not pay her the submission of slaves."

As tensions mounted, Mason in 1774 wrote the Fairfax Resolves, which asserted Colonial rights and urged a boycott of British goods until those rights were recognized. Mason's tones were hardly those of a supplicant. He began: "Virginia can not be considered as a conquered Country; and if it was, that the present Inhabitants are the Descendants not of the Conquered, but of the Conquerors." Virginians owed England nothing but allegiance, as the colony "was not settled at the national Expense of England, but at the private Expense of the Adventurers, our Ancestors," who carried with them to America all legal rights.

George Washington presented the Resolves to the Colonial legislature in Williamsburg. Mason remained at Gunston Hall. He avoided political gatherings in part because, with the tragic early death of his wife, he was sole parent to nine children. He did so, as well, because he suffered recurring gout, which made the bumpy carriage travel quite painful. But, most, he avoided such events because of his low opinion of those who gathered at them.

In 1776, appointed to the committee that was to frame Virginia's new government, Mason wrote to Richard Henry Lee that the committee "is, according to custom, over-charged with useless members." He anticipated that "a thousand ridiculous and impractical proposals" would come forth. Still, if Mason were to be present, then he was going to take charge. Taking the lead, Mason produced the Virginia Declaration of Rights and the state's first constitution. Virginian Edmund Randolph noted that while many ideas had been put forward, the plan "proposed by George Mason swallowed up all the rest."

Mason's statement of rights formed the basis for those soon adopted by Pennsylvania, Maryland, North Carolina and Delaware and affirmed that all power derives from the people. It guaranteed trial by jury, carried the first-ever protections for a free press and affirmed religious toleration, among other concepts that are familiar to modern ears.

Mason's Declaration itself opens with familiar words, as they were soon felicitously rephrased by his fellow Virginian, Thomas Jefferson: "That all Men are born equally free and independent, and have certain inherent natural Rights, of which they can not by any Compact, deprive or divest their Posterity; among which are the Enjoyment of Life and Liberty, with the Means of acquiring and possessing Property, and pursuing and obtaining Happiness and Safety."

Independence secured, Mason served with the state's wartime government; later, he took part briefly and unhappily in the new legislature. More generally, he withdrew to Gunston Hall, cultivated his cherry trees and collected his thoughts. In 1785, when Mason was chosen to represent Virginia at a convention in Annapolis, Md., to consider questions of trade between the new states, he declined to attend. However, when that convention called for a national gathering to rethink government more generally, Mason agreed to serve.

At age 62, Mason departed for Philadelphia in May 1787 well aware of the gravity of the undertaking. Mason wrote his son, "The expectations and hopes of all the Union center on this Convention." He did not think it would be easy to craft a national government of needed power without that power encroaching on the individual states. Success, he wrote, would require coolness, liberality and candor—traits, he added with characteristic asperity, that were "very rare commodities, by the bye."

Today, the Articles of Confederation that the convention was called to revise are viewed as having been wholly inadequate. At the time, however, they did not bear so sharp a judgment. As Jefferson wrote, "With all the imperfections of our present government, it is without comparison the best existing or that ever existed." Still, government revenues were uncertain at best; the veto power each state wielded made concerted action difficult.

The U.S. Constitution is now among the world's oldest governing documents. The gathering of statesmen at Philadelphia offers an arresting scene: the austere, validating presence of George Washington in the chair; the aging Benjamin Franklin carried to and fro between sessions; the immensely wealthy Gouverneur Morris, punctuating his sentences with thumps of his wooden leg. But whatever the view from the present, at the time, the convention addressed concerns then pressing: how to reconcile conflicting political philosophies, central authority with states rights, large states with small and competing economic interests.

Mason was the last of the Virginia delegation to arrive, reaching Philadelphia on May 17. Meanwhile, James Madison politicked for what came to be called the Virginia Plan, which served as a framework for discussion. While Jefferson may have been willing to praise the Articles, Madison intended to bury them. Madison's plan called for legislative, executive and judicial branches. The public would elect the lower house, based on proportional representation, which would itself elect an upper house. These, in turn, would choose the president and the federal judiciary.

It was a plan for a republic, though hardly a full democracy; the public's only direct political role was to vote for the lower house. Even this was too democratic for many. Eldridge Gerry of Massachusetts, Roger Sherman of Connecticut and others urged that representatives be selected by state legislatures. The people were not trustworthy; as Gerry put it, they "do not want virtue, but are the dupes of pretended patriots."

Notably, during deliberations, all voting was done by state; no individual votes were recorded. The influence of an individual delegate, including George Mason, can be discerned from the judgment of historians who wrote of the event.

With Gerry and others arguing for greater aristocracy, the case for the public was made, in the words of historian Charles Mee, by that "patrician country gentleman," George Mason. A government selected by a broad base, Mason said, would heed "the rights of every class of people." Mason appealed to the self-interest of the largely affluent assembly. He had "often wondered at" the apparent indifference of the wealthy to the rights of the common; whatever one's current position, he noted, time and chance would "distribute their posterity throughout the lowest classes of society." The only way to protect the rights of one's descendants was to protect the rights of all. Mason, not Gerry, spoke to the gathering's strongest sentiment; Madison put forth the question, and direct election of the lower house was approved.

The question that would most divide the convention was how to reconcile the interests of large and small states. Virginia had 16 times the population of Delaware. A plan that gave Virginia 16 times the representation in a lower house, which would in turn choose the upper house and chief executive, would reduce Delaware to irrelevance. A second question attached itself: With proportional representation, how were slaves to be counted?

One proposal was to count all free citizens and three-fifths of "all other persons," a euphemism for slaves.

Here, Masons position was striking. He was one of the largest slaveholders in Virginia—indeed, Gunston Hall, in the arresting but accurate phrase of historian Roger Wilkins, was a "private penal colony." And the "three-fifths rule" would increase the political strength of Southern states such as Mason's Virginia. Nonetheless, Mason wanted no sanction of slavery in the Constitution. The institution of slavery, he later told delegates, "brings the judgment of Heaven upon a country. As nations can not be rewarded or punished in the next world, they must be in this." If the convention adopted the three-fifths rule, he threatened, he would quit Philadelphia. The rule was adopted. Mason remained, however.

The three-fifths rule helped ensure Southern support for Madison's plan when it was countered by a rival "New Jersey Plan"—backed largely by those who sought to amend the existing Articles, not junk them. One such delegate questioned the convention's authority to replace the Articles. Mason—never in doubt of his own authority—replied that in crisis public men must rise to their responsibilities. On June 19, Madison's plan was approved by a 7-3 vote.

While Madison's framework was endorsed, the question of how to apportion power between large and small states remained. Deadlock ensued. Washington wrote, "I almost despair of seeing a favorable issue to the proceedings of our Convention." Mason agreed. Resolution of the question "is at present very doubtful," he wrote. Of this moment, Gouverneur Morris later commented, "The fate of America was suspended by a hair."

Mason served on the committee that was established to break the impasse. He backed the proposal worded by Benjamin Franklin that called for equal state representation in the upper house. Madison was strongly opposed. A union of only the larger states, he argued, would in time draw in the lesser; their opposition could be safely ignored. Mason wanted the issue resolved then and there. It was, he told the assembly, at least as inconvenient for him to remain in Philadelphia as for any one present; however, he "would bury his bones in this city rather than expose his country to the consequences of a dissolution of the Convention without anything being done." Put to a vote on July 16, Franklin's proposal passed by the narrowest of margins, 5-4, with the remaining states split or absent.

With adoption of this "Great Compromise," delegates moved to other matters. Mason advocated strongly on four points, losing, as it happens, as often as he won.

One matter, addressed late in the convention, was an issue little remembered today: On what standing should new states be admitted? As proposed, the existing Congress would decide how many representatives would be given to each new state, 10 of which might be created in the West. Morris, for one, feared their rise. The Constitution should fix predominance on the settled East, whose "busy haunts of men" were "the proper school of political talents," he said. The rude West was unfit "to furnish men equally enlightened," Morris continued.

Mason now argued equality for the states. If Congress determined representation, then the natural propensity of those with power to protect it would keep them from fully enfranchising the newcomers. New states, he argued, "will have the same pride and passions which we have, and will either not unite with or will speedily revolt from the Union, if they are not in all respects placed on an equal footing with their brethren." His argument carried.

Mason's influence is clear in shaping the presidency—or, more particularly, in limiting its power by the threat of impeachment, and by the legislature's power to overturn a veto.

On impeachment, Mason argued: "Shall any man be above justice? Above all shall that man be above it who can commit the most extensive injustice?" As drafted, impeachment was limited to treason and bribery. Mason thought that that definition was too narrow. "Attempts to subvert the Constitution may not be treason," he noted, suggesting that "maladministration" be added to the fist. Madison objected to this as vague, and Mason substituted words that stand as among the Constitution's more ambiguous phrases: "high crimes and misdemeanors."

On limiting veto power, Mason argued that unless the executive could be overruled, "We are not indeed constituting a British Government, but a more dangerous monarchy, an elective one." A veto was appropriate to "suspend offensive laws" while objections to them could be considered, but such laws would stand if they were re-passed "by a larger majority than that which first enacted them." Mason suggested a two-thirds vote to override. Morris proposed three-fourths. The difference, he noted, was only two additional votes in the Senate and perhaps five in the House. Mason responded that no great mastery of arithmetic "was necessary to understand that three-fourths was more than two-thirds." Mason's standard was accepted.

Economics as well as politics figured in debate. The middle states—with Mason sharing this view—wanted a two-thirds legislative majority required to pass navigation acts; otherwise, they feared, a simple majority of Northern shipping states might act to hamstring their trade. Looking to their own interests, the Northern states preferred majority rule. Georgia and South Carolina, too, had a trade interest, and they wanted the slave trade continued. In effect, a deal was put forward. New England would support a continued trade in slaves at least until 1808. In exchange, Georgia and South Carolina would support majority rule on navigation acts.

On the convention floor, the unlikely combination of Mason and Morris denounced the plan. Slavery, Morris argued, was "the curse of heaven on the states where it prevailed." Mason was no less condemnatory, claiming that slavery was a national, not a state, issue. The prospect of slave rebellion fomented by a foreign foe placed the entire nation at risk. It was also a bar to development. "Slavery discourages arts and manufactures," Mason said. "The poor despise labor when performed by slaves. They prevent the immigration of whites who really enrich and strengthen a country." Finally, slavery was an assault on character. "Every master of slaves," said Mason—a category that, not incidentally, included himself—"is born a petty tyrant."

Connecticut's Oliver Ellsworth rather pointedly responded that, not ever having owned a slave, he could not vouch for the effect of slavery on the owners. If slavery was as bad as Mason suggested, why not ban it entirely? With perhaps feigned optimism, Ellsworth added: "As population increases poor laborers will be so plentiful as to render slaves useless. Slavery in time will not be a speck in our country." John Rutledge of South Carolina was more direct. There was no moral issue. "The true question at present," he said, "is whether the Southern states shall or shall not be parties to the Union." No slave trade, no support for ratification. The compromise carried by a vote of 7-4.

By September 14, the draft Constitution was complete. Three delegates, however, saw work that remained. Edmund Randolph of Virginia urged that a second convention be held once states had considered the document. Mason, supported by Eldridge Gerry, rose to seek inclusion of a bill of rights—he could, he added, present a draft in several hours.

Roger Sherman argued that no bill of rights was needed. The government of limited powers they were creating had no authority to invade the rights proclaimed by the various states. Mason countered that a bill of rights "would give great quiet to the people." Both Randolph's call for a second convention and Masons for a bill of rights were rejected. Mason, as author of the first state bill of rights and the model of others, may have imagined his offer as the high point of his work at the convention. Politically, he was defeated; he may also have felt insulted.

On September 17, Mason, Randolph and Gerry attended the signing ceremony, but declined to sign. Mason soon thereafter wrote Jefferson, then in Paris, "Upon the most mature Consideration I was capable of, and from motives of sincere patriotism, I was under the necessity of refusing my signature." Reviewing the Constitution, Jefferson expressed his own misgivings about the lack of a bill of rights. Perhaps, he soon wrote, the nine states that were needed to ratify the pact could do so, but the remaining four, by withholding approval, might force inclusion of a statement of rights.

The subsequent campaign to ratify the Constitution was without precedent. People were self-consciously considering a wholly new system of government. The broad argument for the Constitution, wrote historian Max Farrand, was that it was a straight-forward document proposing needed remedies; to the extent it failed, provision existed to amend it. Its advocates included the remarkable trio of James Madison, Alexander Hamilton and John Jay, who published their arguments as the Federalist Papers.

The opposition also counted figures of note. In Mason's Virginia, opponents included Patrick Henry; a young James Monroe; John Tyler and Benjamin Harrison—each the father of a future president; and Richard Henry Lee, who argued that to create a bad government out of fear of anarchy "is really saying that we must kill ourselves, for fear of dying."

Back at Gunston Hall, Mason wrote out 16 objections to the Constitution. His principal one was that the Constitution had no bill of rights and would supersede state constitutions that did. He had others—the sanction of the slave trade; the fear that Virginia would be subject to navigation acts ruinous to its trade; and the concern that the "necessary and proper" clause included in the powers of Congress was a loophole through which endless imposition on the public would spill.

Interesting from a historical perspective, Mason feared the proposed Senate. Since its members would be selected by state legislatures for terms of six years, he believed it was a body inherently divorced from the public. Its special powers—to impeach and to approve treaties and judges—would, he believed, bring it into close consort with the president. In time, Mason feared, a sort of junta would develop. "This government will set out a moderate aristocracy," he wrote. "[I]t is at present impossible to foresee whether it will, in its operation, produce a monarchy, or a corrupt, tyrannical aristocracy; it will most probably vibrate some years between the two, and then terminate in the one or the other."

Mason's Objections, published and distributed throughout the Colonies, focused the thinking of the Anti-Federalists—those opposing ratification. A key concern was that, absent a bill of rights, the Constitution would leave the citizenship unprotected against the centralized authority that was being created. The issue was hard fought. In February 1788, Federalists in Massachusetts outmaneuvered Anti-Federalists to secure a 187-168 margin for ratification.

Mason's position came at personal cost. One Federalist pamphleteer attributed opposition to the Constitution to "the madness of Mason, and the enmity of the Lee faction to General Washington." For his part, Washington considered their long association at an end, referring to Mason as "my quondam friend." When Mason spoke as a candidate to the state ratifying convention, one heckler called out, "Mr. Mason, you are an old man, and the public notices that you are losing your faculties." Mason, never one to curry favor, responded, "Sir, the public will never notice when you lose yours."

When Virginia's delegates assembled at Richmond, two factors aided ratification. The first was the expectation that, if the system of government were approved, Virginia's George Washington would be the first president. The second was that Edmund Randolph, who had declined to sign in Philadelphia, had switched sides, on the understanding that James Madison would seek a bill of rights from the First Congress. Mason was unmoved by the promises of Madison or the defection of Randolph, whom he termed a Benedict Arnold. George Mason and Patrick Henry argued that ratification would quickly follow if a bill of rights was adopted first. Henry placed before delegates a formal motion to defer action until such a document was presented to all states. The motion failed narrowly, 88-80. The Virginia Convention then voted to ratify the Constitution. Two days later, however, the convention's Committee on Amendments approved a draft bill of rights for Madison to advocate in the First Congress. Mason served on that committee and its work closely paralleled his 1776 Declaration.

In the end, the outcome was rather like that which Jefferson had wished from Paris—the new government was established, but opposition proved sufficiently strong to force inclusion of a bill of rights. As historian Wilkins wrote, the opposition to ratification led by Mason "was strong enough, finally, to force Madison to promise the amendments would be offered during the First Congress." Those amendments, passed by Congress, were quickly ratified. By December 5, 1791, the requisite number of states gave their approval and the Bill of

Rights that Mason had so long advocated was added to the Constitution.

Mason, in declining health, imagined no further public role for himself. "I have no reason to expect my interest will have much weight in the new government," he wrote to an associate, "having, as you know, warmly opposed it." He did, at least, retain the warm approval of Jefferson, who wrote to Mason,

"Certainly whenever I pass your road I shall do myself the pleasure of turning into it."

Jefferson did so the final week of September 1792. He stayed at Gunston Hall, querying his host on the Constitutional Convention and other matters. Jefferson then headed to Philadelphia to take up his duties as America's first secretary of state. Mason died a week later.

UNIT 3

National Consolidation and Expansion

Unit Selections

Key Points to Consider

- Discuss the opposing visions of Alexander Hamilton and Thomas Jefferson as the new government got underway. Who tended to win out during the Washington administration?

- Why can the Louisiana Purchase be considered a "revolution?" Discuss the ramifications of this acquisition at the time and for the future course of United States history.

- Compare and contrast the status of white women and black slaves during the early Republic. White women obviously had certain advantages, but what were the similarities?

- Manufacturing during the nation's early years moved from the home, to the shop, to the factory. How did this transition affect the status and treatment of workers?

- How did Andrew Jackson remove the Cherokee Indians from Georgia, and why? Why was the Indians' migration referred to as the "Trail of Tears?"

- What did the phrase "Manifest Destiny" mean to people at the time? How could Americans insist that their desire to expand was fundamentally different from European imperialism?

Student Web Site

www.mhcls.com/online

Internet References

Further information regarding these Web sites may be found in this book's preface or online.

Consortium for Political and Social Research
http://www.icpsr.umich.edu

Department of State
http://www.state.gov

Mystic Seaport
http://amistad.mysticseaport.org/

Social Influence Web site
http://www.workingpsychology.com/intro.html

University of Virginia Library
http://www.lib.virginia.edu/exhibits/lewis_clark/

Women in America
http://xroads.virginia.edu/ ~HYPER/DETOC/FEM/

Women of the West
http://www.wowmuseum.org/

The individuals who wrote the American Constitution could only provide a general structure under which the government would work. Those involved in actually making the system function had to venture into uncharted territory. There were no blueprints as to exactly which body had what powers, or what their relationships with one another would be. And, if disputes arose, which individual or group would act as arbiter? Officials during the first few years after 1789 were conscious that practically everything they did would be regarded as setting precedents for the future. Even such apparently trivial matters as the proper form of addressing the president caused debate. From hindsight of more than 200 years, it is difficult to appreciate how tentative they had to be in establishing this newborn government.

The most fundamental difference over the Constitution arose over whether it should be interpreted strictly or loosely. That is, should governmental powers be limited to those expressly granted in the document, or were there "implied" powers that could be exercised as long as they were not expressly prohibited? Many of the disputes were argued on principles, but the truth is that most individuals were trying to promote programs that would benefit the interests they represented.

George Washington, as first president, was a towering figure who provided a stabilizing presence during the seemingly endless squabbles. He believed that he served the entire nation, and that there was no need for political parties (he disdainfully referred to them as "factions"), which he regarded as divisive. Despite his disapproval, nascent political parties did begin to develop fairly early on in his first administration. "Remembering Martha" argues that knowing more about Martha Washington provides insights about George.

Washington's first Secretary of the Treasury, Alexander Hamilton, almost invariably favored those measures that would benefit the commercial and manufacturing interests of the Northeast. Secretary of State Thomas Jefferson and his ally James Madison just as often spoke for the rural and agricultural interests of the West and the South. These two groups frequently clashed over what the Constitution did or did not permit, what sources of revenue should be tapped to pay for government, and a host of other issues. The fact that Washington most often sided with Hamilton's views made him a partisan despite his wish to remain above the fray. "The Best of Enemies" analyzes the Hamilton-Jefferson struggle.

The United States already was a large country by 1803, stretching from the Atlantic Ocean to the Mississippi River. Some said it was too large. Propertied Easterners complained that the western migration lowered property values and raised wages, and they feared population shifts would weaken their section's influence in government. Others thought that the great distances involved might cause the system to fly apart, given the primitive means of communication and transportation at the time. When

Library of Congress, Prints and Photographs Division [LC-USZ62-52623]

Thomas Jefferson had the unexpected opportunity to double the nation's size by purchasing the huge Louisiana Territory, as discussed in "The Revolution of 1803," he altered the course of American history.

What we call the War of 1812 did not go well for the United States at first. Indeed, by 1814 the nation was on the verge of collapse. The British planned an attack on New Orleans, which if successful, would have split the country in two. "Saving New Orleans" discusses the role played by pirate Jean Laffite in defense of the city. The British had tried to bribe Laffite into joining them. Instead he revealed their plans to General Andrew Jackson and volunteered his own forces to fight the invasion.

Two articles analyze the conditions under which dispossessed Americans had to live during these years. "Women in the Early Republic" argues that although a great deal of attention has been paid to the history of women in recent years, the period 1790 to 1830 has been neglected. This essay helps explain why. Similarly, author Gary B. Nash in "African Americans in the Early Republic" points out a number of neglected areas in the study of

Black History. Among these are the rise of free Black communities and early efforts to achieve abolition.

Manufacturing in the early years moved from the home to small shops, which in turn gave way to factories employing relatively large numbers of people. At first some owners of these factories attempted to retain customs and relationships characteristic of the earlier period. In time these efforts were abandoned and workers were treated impersonally as just another cost of production. "Liberty Is Exploitation" describes this process.

Much has been written about the "Underground Railway" and its part in spiriting runaway slaves to freedom. In 1833 a Detroit judge ruled that a young Black couple who had escaped must be returned to their owners. His decision touched off a number of riots in Detroit. When both husband and wife escaped again, this time to Canada, demands were made that they be extradited back to the United States. These demands were refused, thereby serving notice that Canada would be a refuge for slaves seeking their freedom.

Accounts of settling the west also have changed over the years. Once presented in the relatively simplistic terms of "taming the wilderness," the westward movement was far more complicated than the story of hardy pioneers overcoming obstacles. "Andrew Jackson Versus the Cherokee Nation" tells of the forcible removal of the Cherokees from Georgia to west of the Mississippi. The trek had such awful consequences that it became known as "the trail of tears." The phrase "Manifest Destiny" became popular during the 1840s. Advocates believed that the United States was destined to dominate Mexico and the Caribbean. "Storm over Mexico" examines this phenomenon, with particular reference to one of its most ardent advocates, a woman named Jane McManus. She was a dynamo who was a political journalist, a land speculator and a pioneer settler in Texas.

Personality Profile

Remembering Martha

Robert P. Watson

He is more myth than man. As elementary school students, we learned about his exploits during the Revolutionary War and remember him appropriately as the "Father of the Nation." Yet, despite his status as an enduring symbol of America, details of George Washington, the man, remain unknown to many of the very same individuals who celebrate him. However, recent efforts by Washington scholars have improved the situation. The year 1999 marked the two-hundredth anniversary of the death of our first president, and historians and Washington scholars used the occasion to undertake a year-long celebration of the hero of Valley Forge.

Part of the commemoration was an effort to reinvigorate his slightly tarnished image. After years of being ranked solidly in the second spot behind Abe Lincoln, recent polls of historians have seen the general slip from second to third and even fourth place in the presidential rankings (1). Scholars (not to mention the public) today cast a much more critical eye on slaveholders, and Washington owned many slaves. In fact, after reaching a high mark in 1964, the number of visitors to Mount Vernon, Washington's plantation home and burial site, declined steadily in subsequent years (2). The alarmed caretakers of Mount Vernon, responding with focus group sessions to determine public opinion of Washington, uncovered a distant, aloof figure. Dusting him off and reintroducing him to the American public, the year-long Washington festivities in 1999 included museum shows featuring such Washington memorabilia as his sword and locks of his hair, a re-enactment of his death and funeral at Mount Vernon, and a $9 million renovation of the 555-foot-tall Washington Monument. However, noticeably absent from the ceremonies was any serious consideration of Martha Washington. This is unfortunate because neglecting the life of Martha Washington undermines our ability to truly know her husband. Indeed, a closer inspection reveals Martha's fingerprints all over George Washington's public life, so much so that it is not unreasonable to suggest that, without Martha, George never would have become president. Hindsight favors the historian, and the lesson learned in 1999 might be that the best way to reconsider George is to consider Martha as well.

A "Worthy Partner" for Washington

Martha's influence on George's life and career began with their marriage on 6 January 1759. When the two married, George was a military officer of modest fame but considerable ambition who longed for a career as a top officer in the British army and a life as a wealthy gentleman planter. Martha was an heiress to a booming plantation business and was perhaps the wealthiest woman in Virginia.

As a teen Martha married Daniel Parke Custis, who was twenty years her senior and son of one of the colony's leading families. However, tragedy struck after seven years of marriage when Martha's husband died unexpectedly. It was then, shortly after the death of Custis, that George Washington began courting the then Martha Dandridge Custis, an older, twenty-six year old widow with two infant children, John Parke and Martha Parke Custis, and 17,500 choice acres of land. It could be said that George married "up" the social ladder. Moreover, their union provided the young military officer with his life dream: instant membership in the upper echelons of Virginia's tidewater society. It also furnished him with the requisite social and political connections necessary to embark on a public career. But Martha provided more than wealth and status. As the oldest of eight children, she had already developed impressive domestic skills by the time she was a young woman. Having been raised in and around prominent families, she possessed social grace.

George and Martha's relationship was solid and productive, although childless. They held similar values and a shared appreciation for disciplined order, virtue, and the merits of a good reputation. Where their personalities differed, they ended up complementing each other. For instance, Martha was warmer and more relaxed than George, and her social graces and refinement balanced his aloofness and temper. Not surprisingly, George and Martha became partners in their prosperous plantation home, their busy social life, and George's public career.

Lady Washington: Helpmate and Framer of the First Ladyship

During the Revolutionary War Martha displayed a sense of duty and courage that was not lost on the colonial militia, her husband, or the country. Each winter she made the difficult trip to join George at his headquarters, staying at camp until the spring and enduring the hardships of camp life. While in camp Martha tended to sick and injured soldiers and assisted her husband with his official correspondence. From reading Martha's letters of this period, it is clear that George confided in her about the status of the war (3). Her presence in camp created a sense of home and normalcy for the suffering troops and, perhaps more importantly, had a calming and positive effect on her husband. Although it is not well known, the general was prone to spells of self-doubt and melancholy stemming from the pressures of the war. To lift spirits in camp, Martha hosted George's officers for dinner.

It is no coincidence that "Lady Washington" was beloved by the troops or that Martha became a symbol of the Revolution. Martha Washington raised consciousness about the war by wearing clothing made in the colonies, leading drives to collect clothing and materials for the war effort, and lending her considerable fame to championing the revolutionary cause. And she did all this with indifference to her personal safety, an amused humility to the fuss made over her, and a strength of character reserved for heroes from the pages of military history.

Martha's influence continued in the years after the war when many questions remained concerning the new nation and its inaugural president. Amidst this whirlwind of expectation and uncertainty, the Washingtons went to the new, temporary capital in New York. If little was known about the specific duties of the president, even less was known about the role of the first lady. Although apprehensive, Martha quickly asserted herself as the nation's social hostess, presiding over public receptions and greeting curious visitors on her first full day in the capital. She continued to create precedents for the new office by hosting regular Friday socials that were well attended and successful. Her confidence, poise, and good nature won her many supporters.

One of the greatest challenges she faced was in setting the tone for the office through her socials and the formal affairs of state. On one hand, the public desired a simple, common approach befitting the new spirit of popular democracy. On the other hand, there was pressure to provide a sense of dignity and formality to the office in a style appropriate to the courts of Europe. Somehow Martha managed to balance these competing interests with a minimum of criticism.

She literally developed the role of president's spouse, and her actions set a precedent for all first ladies who followed. Martha was also a constant source of support for her husband during his two terms in office. She cared for him through bouts of severe illness and was politically astute enough to invite each member of Congress to dine with the president during legislative sessions.

The (Extra)Ordinary "Mother of the Nation"

Martha's service both during the war and throughout her husband's long public career, becomes all the more impressive when one considers that she did not enjoy public life and served only out of a sense of duty to her country and husband. Still, her service was marked by dignity and selflessness. Martha was an intensely private person with a grandmotherly manner and simple tastes. This reveals another paradox in the life of Martha Washington: she was an extraordinarily ordinary person, a self-described "old-fashioned Virginia house-keeper" who appears almost naively unaffected by the monumental events of her lifetime (4). For instance, when rumors surfaced of a British plan to kidnap the wife of General Washington during the Revolutionary War, she casually dismissed it. When she was greeted by huge crowds shouting "Long live Lady Washington!" and thirteen-cannon salutes during her trip from Mount Vernon to the new capital to meet her husband, she could not understand the need for such fanfare. And during the inaugural presidency she often remarked that she found all the pomp and pageantry surrounding state functions to be little more than "empty ceremonies."

Martha longed for a normal, private life that continually eluded her, as the events of the late eighteenth century precluded a quiet family setting for the wife of the age's foremost public figure. But she was incredibly resilient. As a young woman, Martha had overcome the loss of her father, first husband, and two infant children all within a three year period. The young widow with two surviving children was then thrust into managing one of the largest businesses in the colony of Virginia. Under her stewardship it continued to prosper. The Revolutionary War and two presidential terms also took her away from home. Even after George's death in 1799, the quiet of private life was not to be found; she spent the final two years of her life greeting the constant stream of well-wishers visiting the home of their fallen hero.

Lady Washington was an intriguing person in her own right, simultaneously appearing to be extraordinary and ordinary. For instance, extraordinary Martha was the general's source of strength during the war's most critical hours, the gifted hostess who impressed guests of the first president, and the most beloved woman of her time. Ordinary Martha was a grandmother who, as the old saying goes, spoiled her grandson rotten, was so insecure about her grammar that she often had her husband pen her letters, and during her husband's presidency even counted the days until she could return to a quiet home life. Martha was clearly a complex individual, yet appears to be much easier to understand than her image-conscious, overly formal husband. Martha and her life experiences are more familiar and "real" to most people than those of George, and therein she offers a means of empathizing with the unknowable, mythical first president. She provides a window for analyzing the "Father of the Country."

Legacy

Martha Washington's resilience and many sacrifices in the name of public service alone make her worthy of our admiration. But it is also clear that to know George Washington one must consider Martha. When George Washington assumed command of the Continental Army, they had already been husband and wife for sixteen years, and their marriage was beginning its third decade when George took the presidential oath of office. They were partners throughout their forty year marriage, and she was a vital part of his success. This is her legacy and a key part of understanding George Washington, the man.

Martha lived on another two years past her husband, passing away on 22 May 1802 from "severe fever." Her obituary accurately described the wife of George Washington as a "worthy partner." After the renewed interest in the study of George brought on by the historic anniversary of his death in 1999, it is time to rethink Martha's life and honor her rightful place in history.

Notes

1. There have been many polls ranking the presidents such as the Arthur Schlesinger polls ["The U.S. Presidents," *Life* 65 (1948) and "Our Presidents: A Rating by 75 Scholars," *New York Times Magazine*, 29 July 1962]; Gary Maranell and Richard Dodder, "Political Orientation and Evaluation of Presidential Prestige," *Social Science Quarterly* 51 (September 1970); Robert E. DiClerico, *The American President* (Englewood Cliffs, NJ: Prentice Hall, 1979); the Chicago Tribune Poll, *U.S. News and World Report*, 25 January 1982. Most of these well known polls ranked Washington second. However, beginning in the 1980s polls such as Robert K. Murray's, which appeared in the *Journal of American History* in December 1983 placed Washington in the #3 spot with Franklin D. Roosevelt moving to #2. The comprehensive Siena Research Institute Poll in 1994 listed Washington fourth, falling behind both Franklin and Teddy Roosevelt.

2. Mount Vernon Ladies Association, Mount Vernon, VA.

3. A collection of Martha Washington's letters appears in Joseph E. Fields, *"Worthy Partner:" The Papers of Martha Washington* (Westport, CT: Greenwood Press, 1994). Nearly all of the letters exchanged between George and Martha are lost, however, after Martha destroyed the letters upon the death of her husband.

4. Martha's remaining letters exchanged with friends and family reveal humility and what seems to be boredom and a lack of interest in the presidency. In addition to calling herself an "old-fashioned Virginia house-keeper," Martha, in a letter written on 22 October 1789 to her friend Fanny Bassett, describes her life as wife of the president, saying "I live a very dull life here" and "I am more like a state prisoner than anything else." Fields, "Worthy Partner," 1994.

ROBERT P. WATSON, PhD is an associate professor of political science at the University of Hawaii, Hilo, and author of, most recently, *The Presidents' Wives: Reassessing the Office of the First Lady* (1999) and *First Ladies of the United States: A Biographical Dictionary* (forthcoming). He is currently working on a biography of Martha Washington, which will be part of the *Presidential Wives* series (Nova Social Science Books), for which he is also serving as series editor.

The Best of Enemies

Jefferson was visionary and crafty. In Hamilton, he met his match. How the rivalry lives on.

RON CHERNOW

On March 21, 1790, Thomas Jefferson belatedly arrived in New York City to assume his duties as the first Secretary of State after a five-year ministerial stint in Paris. Tall and lanky, with a freckled complexion and auburn hair, Jefferson, 46, was taken aback by the adulation being heaped upon the new Treasury Secretary, Alexander Hamilton, who had streaked to prominence in his absence. Few people knew that Jefferson had authored the Declaration of Independence, which had yet to become holy writ for Americans. Instead, the Virginian was eclipsed by the 35-year-old wunderkind from the Caribbean, who was a lowly artillery captain in New York when Jefferson composed the famous document. Despite his murky background as an illegitimate orphan, the self-invented Hamilton was trim and elegant, carried himself with an erect military bearing and had a mind that worked with dazzling speed. At first, Hamilton and Jefferson socialized on easy terms, with little inkling that they were destined to become mortal foes. But their clash inside George Washington's first Cabinet proved so fierce that it would spawn the two-party system in America. It also produced two divergent visions of the country's future that divide Americans to the present day.

For Hamilton, the first Treasury Secretary, the supreme threat to liberty arose from insufficient government power. To avert that, he advocated a vigorous central government marked by a strong President, an independent judiciary and a liberal reading of the Constitution. As the first Secretary of State, Jefferson believed that liberty was jeopardized by concentrated federal power, which he tried to restrict through a narrow construction of the Constitution. He favored states' rights, a central role for Congress and a comparatively weak judiciary.

At first glance, Hamilton might seem the more formidable figure in that classic matchup. He took office with an ardent faith in the new national government. He had attended the Constitutional Convention, penned the bulk of the Federalist papers to secure passage of the new charter and spearheaded ratification efforts in New York State. He therefore set to work at Treasury with more unrestrained gusto than Jefferson—who had monitored the Constitutional Convention from his post in Paris—did at State. Jefferson's enthusiasm for the new political

order was tepid at best, and when Washington crafted the first government in 1789, Jefferson didn't grasp the levers of power with quite the same glee as Hamilton, who had no ideological inhibitions about shoring up federal power.

Hamilton—brilliant, brash and charming—had the self-reliant reflexes of someone who had always had to live by his wits. His overwhelming intelligence petrified Jefferson and his followers. As an orator, Hamilton could speak extemporaneously for hours on end. As a writer, he could crank out 5,000- or 10,000-word memos overnight. Jefferson never underrated his foe's copious talents. At one point, a worried Jefferson confided to his comrade James Madison that Hamilton was a one-man army, "a host within himself."

Despite Jefferson's policy battles, there was a playful side to his politics. On New Year's Day 1802, supporters in Cheshire, Mass., sent him, as a gift, a mammoth cheese that measured more than 4 ft. in diameter and 17 in. in height and weighed 1,235 lbs. President Jefferson took the pungent present in good humor. Reportedly, he stood in the White House doorway, arms outstretched, waiting for the cheese's delivery. The smelly gift was served to guests for at least a year, perhaps more.

Whether in person or on paper, Hamilton served up his opinions promiscuously. He had a true zest for debate and never left anyone guessing where he stood. Jefferson, more than a decade older, had the quiet, courtly manner of a Virginia planter. He was emphatic in his views—Hamilton labeled him "an atheist in religion and a *fanatic in politics*"—but shrank from open conflict. Jefferson, a diffident speaker, mumbled his way through his rare speeches in a soft, almost inaudible voice and reserved his most scathing strictures for private correspondence.

The epic battle between these two Olympian figures began not long after Jefferson came to New York City to assume his State Department duties in March 1790. By then Hamilton was in the thick of a contentious campaign to retire massive debt inherited from the Revolution. America had suspended principal and interest payments on its obligations, which had traded as low as 15¢ on the dollar. In an audacious scheme to restore public credit, Hamilton planned to pay off that debt at face value, causing the securities to soar from depressed levels. Jefferson and Madison thought the original holders of those securities—many of them war veterans—should profit from that appreciation even if they had already sold their paper to traders at depressed prices. Hamilton thought it would be impractical to track them down. With an eye on future U.S. capital markets, he wanted to enshrine the cardinal principle that current owners of securities incurred all profits and losses, even if that meant windfall gains for rapacious speculators who had only recently bought the securities.

That skirmish over Hamilton's public credit plan was part of a broader tussle over the U.S.'s economic future. Jefferson was fond of summoning up idyllic scenes of an agrarian America peopled by sturdy yeoman farmers. That poetic vision neglected the underlying reality of large slave plantations in the South. Jefferson was a fine populist on paper but not in everyday life, and his defense of Virginia interests was inextricably bound up with slavery. Hamilton—derided as a pseudo aristocrat, an elitist, a crypto-monarchist—was a passionate abolitionist with a far more expansive economic vision. He conceded that agriculture would persist for decades as an essential component of the economy. But at the same time he wanted to foster the rudiments of a modern economy—trade, commerce, banks, stock exchanges, factories and corporations—to enlarge economic opportunity. Hamilton dreamed of a meritocracy, not an aristocracy, while Jefferson retained the landed gentry's disdain for the vulgar realities of trade, commerce and finance. And he was determined to undermine Hamilton's juggernaut.

Because we celebrate Jefferson for his sonorous words in the Declaration of Independence—Hamilton never matched Jefferson's gift for writing ringing passages that were at once poetic and inspirational—we sometimes overlook Jefferson's consummate skills as a practicing politician. A master of subtle, artful indirection, he was able to marshal his forces without divulging his generalship. After Hamilton persuaded President Washington to create the Bank of the United States, the country's first central bank, Jefferson was aghast at what he construed as a breach of the Constitution and a perilous expansion of federal power. Along with Madison, he recruited the poet Philip Freneau to launch an opposition paper called the *National Gazette*. To subsidize the paper covertly, he hired Freneau as a State Department translator. Hamilton was shocked by such flagrant disloyalty from a member of Washington's Cabinet, especially when Freneau began to mount withering assaults on Hamilton and even Washington. Never one to suffer in silence, Hamilton retaliated in a blizzard of newspaper articles published under Roman pseudonyms. The backbiting between Hamilton and Jefferson grew so acrimonious that Washington had to exhort both men to desist.

Instead, the feud worsened. In early 1793, a Virginia Congressman named William Branch Giles began to harry Hamilton with resolutions ordering him to produce, on short deadlines, stupendous amounts of Treasury data. With prodigious bursts of energy, Hamilton complied with those inhuman demands, foiling his opponents. Jefferson then committed an unthinkable act. He secretly drafted a series of anti-Hamilton resolutions for Giles, including one that read, "Resolved, That the Secretary of the Treasury has been guilty of maladministration in the duties of his office and should, in the opinion of Congress, be removed from his office by the President of the United States." The resolution was voted down, and the effort to oust Hamilton stalled. Jefferson left the Cabinet in defeat later that year.

Throughout the 1790s, the Hamilton-Jefferson feud continued to fester in both domestic and foreign affairs. Jefferson thought Hamilton was "bewitched" by the British model of governance, while Hamilton considered Jefferson a credulous apologist for the gory excesses of the French Revolution. Descended from French Huguenots on his mother's side, Hamilton was fluent in French and had served as Washington's liaison with the Marquis de Lafayette and other French aristocrats who had rallied to the Continental Army. The French Revolution immediately struck him as a bloody affair, governed by rigid, Utopian thinking. On Oct. 6, 1789, he wrote a remarkable letter to Lafayette, explaining his "foreboding of ill" about the future course of events in Paris. He cited the "vehement character" of the French people and the "reveries" of their "philosophic politicians," who wished to transform human nature. Hamilton believed that Jefferson while in Paris "drank deeply of the French philosophy in religion, in science, in politics." Indeed, more than a decade passed before Jefferson fully realized that the French Revolution wasn't a worthy sequel to the American one so much as a grotesque travesty.

According to the new book *Jefferson's Second Revolution*, by Susan Dunn, for more than a week in early July 1800, Federalist newspapers gleefully carried the (false) story that Jefferson had died. "I am much indebted to my enemies," Jefferson said, "for proving, by their recitals of my death, that I have friends."

If Jefferson and Hamilton define opposite ends of the political spectrum in U.S. history and seem to exist in perpetual conflict, the two men shared certain traits, feeding a mutual cynicism. Each scorned the other as excessively ambitious. In his secret diary, or *Anas*, Jefferson recorded a story of Hamilton praising Julius Caesar as the greatest man in history. (The tale sounds dubious, as Hamilton invariably used Caesar as shorthand for "an evil tyrant.") Hamilton repaid the favor. In one essay he likened Jefferson to "Caesar *coyly refusing* the proffered diadem" and rejecting the trappings, but "tenaciously grasping the substance of imperial domination."

Similarly, both men hid a potent hedonism behind an intellectual facade. For all their outward differences, the two politicians stumbled into the two great sex scandals of the early Republic. In 1797 a journalist named James T. Callender exposed that Hamilton, while Treasury Secretary and a married man with four children, had entered into a yearlong affair with grifter Maria Reynolds, who was 23 when it began. In a 95-page pamphlet, Hamilton confessed to the affair at what many regarded as inordinate length. He wished to show that the money he had paid to Reynolds' husband James had been for the favor of her company and not for illicit speculation in Treasury securities, as the Jeffersonians had alleged. Forever after, the Jeffersonians tagged Hamilton as "the amorous Treasury Secretary" and mocked his pretensions to superior morality.

By an extraordinary coincidence, during Jefferson's first term as President, Callender also exposed Jefferson's relationship with Sally Hemings. Callender claimed that "Dusky Sally," a.k.a. the "African Venus," was the President's slave concubine, who had borne him five children. "There is not an individual in the neighborhood of Charlottesville who does not believe the story," Callender wrote, "and not a few who know it." Jefferson never confirmed or denied Callender's story. But the likely truth of the Hemings affair was dramatically bolstered by DNA tests published in 1998, which indicated that a Jefferson male had sired at least one of Hemings' children.

The crowning irony of the stormy relations between Hamilton and Jefferson is that Hamilton helped install his longtime foe as President in 1801. Under constitutional rules then in force, the candidate with the majority of electoral votes became President; the runner-up became Vice President. That created an anomalous situation in which Jefferson, his party's presumed presidential nominee, tied with Aaron Burr, its presumed vice presidential nominee. It took 36 rounds of voting in the House

Hamilton

Favored a strong Federal Government

Pushed for an economy in which trade, finance and manufacturing supplemented agriculture

Feared closer relations with France and was an Anglophile

Wanted the U.S. to have a professional federal army

Jefferson

Argued strongly for states' rights

Admired farming and the simple, rural life and hoped America would remain an agrarian nation

Favored warm, fraternal relations with France and was an Anglophobe

Thought the country should rely on state militias

to decide the election in Jefferson's favor. Faced with the prospect of Burr as President, a man he considered unscrupulous, Hamilton not only opted for Jefferson as the lesser of two evils but also was forced into his most measured assessment of the man. Hamilton said he had long suspected that as President, Jefferson would develop a keen taste for the federal power he had deplored in opposition. He recalled that a decade earlier, in Washington's Cabinet, Jefferson had seemed like a man who knew he was destined to inherit an estate—in this case, the presidency—and didn't wish to deplete it. In fact, Jefferson, the strict constructionist, freely exercised the most sweeping powers as President. Nothing in the Constitution, for instance, permitted the Louisiana Purchase. Hamilton noted that with rueful mirth.

CHERNOW is the author of *The House of Morgan, Titan* and the recent best-selling biography *Alexander Hamilton*.

Cliffhanger

Presidential candidates Thomas Jefferson and Aaron Burr were deadlocked in the House of Representatives with no majority for either. For seven days, as they maneuvered and schemed, the fate of the young republic hung in the ballots.

JOHN FERLING

On the afternoon of September 23, 1800, Vice President Thomas Jefferson, from his Monticello home, wrote a letter to Benjamin Rush, the noted Philadelphia physician. One matter dominated Jefferson's thoughts: that year's presidential contest. Indeed, December 3, Election Day—the date on which the Electoral College would meet to vote—was only 71 days away.

Jefferson was one of four presidential candidates. As he composed his letter to Rush, Jefferson paused from time to time to gather his thoughts, all the while gazing absently through an adjacent window at the shimmering heat and the foliage, now a lusterless pale green after a long, dry summer. Though he hated leaving his hilltop plantation and believed, as he told Rush, that gaining the presidency would make him "a constant butt for every shaft of calumny which malice & falsehood could form," he nevertheless sought the office "with sincere zeal."

He had been troubled by much that had occurred in incumbent John Adams' presidency and was convinced that radicals within Adams' Federalist Party were waging war against what he called the "spirit of 1776"—goals the American people had hoped to attain through the Revolution. He had earlier characterized Federalist rule as a "reign of witches," insisting that the party was "adverse to liberty" and "calculated to undermine and demolish the republic." If the Federalists prevailed, he believed, they would destroy the states and create a national government every bit as oppressive as that which Great Britain had tried to impose on the colonists before 1776.

The "revolution . . . of 1776," Jefferson would later say, had determined the "form" of America's government; he believed the election of 1800 would decide its "principles." "I have sworn upon the altar of God eternal hostility against every form of tyranny over the mind of Man," he wrote.

Jefferson was not alone in believing that the election of 1800 was crucial. On the other side, Federalist Alexander Hamilton, who had been George Washington's secretary of treasury, believed that it was a contest to save the new nation from "the

fangs of Jefferson." Hamilton agreed with a Federalist newspaper essay that argued defeat meant "happiness, constitution and laws [faced] endless and irretrievable ruin." Federalists and Republicans appeared to agree on one thing only: that the victor in 1800 would set America's course for generations to come, perhaps forever.

Only a quarter of a century after the signing of the Declaration of Independence, the first election of the new 19th century was carried out in an era of intensely emotional partisanship among a people deeply divided over the scope of the government's authority. But it was the French Revolution that had imposed a truly hyperbolic quality upon the partisan strife.

That revolution, which had begun in 1789 and did not run its course until 1815, deeply divided Americans. Conservatives, horrified by its violence and social leveling, applauded Great Britain's efforts to stop it. The most conservative Americans, largely Federalists, appeared bent on an alliance with London that would restore the ties between America and Britain that had been severed in 1776. Jeffersonian Republicans, on the other hand, insisted that these radical conservatives wanted to turn back the clock to reinstitute much of the British colonial template. (Today's Republican Party traces its origins not to Jefferson and his allies but to the party formed in 1854–1855, which carried Lincoln to the presidency in 1860.)

A few weeks before Adams' inauguration in 1796, France, engaged in an all-consuming struggle with England for world domination, had decreed that it would not permit America to trade with Great Britain. The French Navy soon swept American ships from the seas, idling port-city workers and plunging the economy toward depression. When Adams sought to negotiate a settlement, Paris spurned his envoys.

Adams, in fact, hoped to avoid war, but found himself riding a whirlwind. The most extreme Federalists, known as Ultras, capitalized on the passions unleashed in this crisis and scored great victories in the off-year elections of 1798, taking charge of both the party and Congress. They created a provisional army and pressured Adams into putting Hamilton in charge. They passed heavy taxes to pay for the army and, with Federalist sympathizers in the press braying that "traitors must be silent," enacted the Alien and Sedition Acts, which provided jail terms and exorbitant fines for anyone who uttered or published "any false, scandalous, and malicious" statement against the United States government or its officials. While Federalists defended the Sedition Act as a necessity in the midst of a grave national crisis, Jefferson and his followers saw it as a means of silencing Republicans—and a violation of the Bill of Rights. The Sedition Act, Jefferson contended, proved there was no step, "however atrocious," the Ultras would not take.

All along, Jefferson had felt that Federalist extremists might overreach. By early 1799, Adams himself had arrived at the same conclusion. He, too, came to suspect that Hamilton and the Ultras wanted to precipitate a crisis with France. Their motivation perhaps had been to get Adams to secure an alliance with Great Britain and accept the Ultras' program in Congress. But avowing that there "is no more prospect of seeing a French Army here, than there is in Heaven," Adams refused to go along with the scheme and sent peace envoys to Paris. (Indeed, a treaty would be signed at the end of September 1800.)

It was in this bitterly partisan atmosphere that the election of 1800 was conducted. In those days, the Constitution stipulated that each of the 138 members of the Electoral College cast two votes for president, which allowed electors to cast one vote for a favorite son and a second for a candidate who actually stood a chance of winning. The Constitution also stipulated that if the candidates tied, or none received a majority of electoral votes, the House of Representatives "shall chuse by Ballot one of them for President." Unlike today, each party nominated two candidates for the presidency.

Federalist congressmen had caucused that spring and, without indicating a preference, designated Adams and South Carolina's Charles Cotesworth Pinckney as the party's choices. Adams desperately wanted to be re-elected. He was eager to see the French crisis through to a satisfactory resolution and, at age 65, believed that a defeat would mean he would be sent home to Quincy, Massachusetts, to die in obscurity. Pinckney, born into Southern aristocracy and raised in England, had been the last of the four nominees to come around in favor of American independence. Once committed, however, he served valiantly, seeing action at Brandywine, Germantown and Charleston. Following the war, he sat in the Constitutional Convention; both Washington and Adams had sent him to France on diplomatic missions.

In addition to Jefferson, Republicans chose Aaron Burr as their candidate, but designated Jefferson as the party's first choice. Jefferson had held public office intermittently since 1767, serving Virginia in its legislature and as a wartime governor, sitting in Congress, crossing to Paris in 1784 for a five-year stint that included a posting as the American minister to France, and acting as secretary of state under Washington. His second place finish in the election of 1796 had made him vice president, as was the custom until 1804. Burr, at age 44 the youngest of the candidates, had abandoned his legal studies in 1775 to enlist in the Continental Army; he had experienced the horrors of America's failed invasion of Canada and the miseries of Valley Forge. After the war he practiced law and represented New York in the U.S. Senate. In 1800, he was serving as a member of the New York legislature.

In those days, the Constitution left the manner of selecting presidential electors to the states. In 11 of the 16 states, state legislatures picked the electors; therefore, the party that controlled the state assembly garnered all that state's electoral votes. In the other five states, electors were chosen by "qualified" voters (white, male property owners in some states, white male taxpayers in others). Some states used a winner-take-all system: voters cast their ballots for the entire slate of Federalist electors or for the Republican slate. Other states split electors among districts.

Presidential candidates did not kiss babies, ride in parades or shake hands. Nor did they even make stump speeches. The candidates tried to remain above the fray, leaving campaigning to surrogates, particularly elected officials from within their parties. Adams and Jefferson each returned home when Congress adjourned in May, and neither left their home states until they returned to the new capital of Washington in November.

But for all its differences, much about the campaign of 1800 was recognizably modern. Politicians carefully weighed which procedures were most likely to advance their party's interests. Virginia, for instance, had permitted electors to be elected from districts in three previous presidential contests, but after Federalists carried 8 of 19 congressional districts in the elections of 1798, Republicans, who controlled the state assembly, switched to the winner-take-all format, virtually guaranteeing they would get every one of Virginia's 21 electoral votes in 1800. The ploy was perfectly legal, and Federalists in Massachusetts, fearing an upsurge in Republican strength, scuttled district elections—which the state had used previously—to select electors by the legislature, which they controlled.

Though the contest was played out largely in the print media, the unsparing personal attacks on the character and temperament of the nominees resembled the studied incivility to which today's candidates are accustomed on television. Adams was portrayed as a monarchist who had turned his back on republicanism; he was called senile, a poor judge of character, vain, jealous and driven by an "ungovernable temper." Pinckney was labeled a mediocrity, a man of "limited talents" who was "illy suited to the exalted station" of the presidency. Jefferson was accused of cowardice. Not only, said his critics, had he lived in luxury at Monticello while others sacrificed during the War of Independence, but he had fled like a jack rabbit when British soldiers raided Charlottesville in 1781. And he had failed egregiously as Virginia's governor, demonstrating that his "nerves are too weak to bear anxiety and difficulties." Federalists further insisted Jefferson had been transformed into a dangerous radical during his residence in France and was a "howling atheist." For his part, Burr was depicted as without principles, a man who would do anything to get his hands on power.

Also like today, the election of 1800 seemed to last forever. "Electioneering is already begun," the first lady, Abigail Adams, noted 13 months before the Electoral College was to meet. What made it such a protracted affair was that state legislatures were elected throughout the year; as these assemblies more often than not chose presidential electors, the state contests to determine them became part of the national campaign. In 1800 the greatest surprise among these contests occurred in New York, a large, crucial state that had given all 12 of its electoral votes to Adams in 1796, allowing him to eke out a three-vote victory over Jefferson.

The battle for supremacy in the New York legislature had hinged on the outcome in New York City. Thanks largely to lopsided wins in two working-class wards where many voters owned no property, the Republicans secured all 24 of New York's electoral votes for Jefferson and Burr. For Abigail Adams, that was enough to seal Adams' fate. John Dawson, a Republican congressman from Virginia, declared: "The Republic is safe . . . . The [Federalist] party are in rage & despair."

But Adams himself refused to give up hope. After all, New England, which accounted for nearly half the electoral votes needed for a majority, was solidly in his camp, and he felt certain he would win some votes elsewhere. Adams believed that if he could get South Carolina's eight votes, he would be virtually certain to garner the same number of electoral votes that had put him over the top four years earlier. And, at first, both parties were thought to have a shot at carrying the state.

When South Carolina's legislature was elected in mid-October, the final tally revealed that the assembly was about evenly divided between Federalists and Republicans—though unaffiliated representatives, all pro-Jefferson, would determine the outcome. Now Adams' hopes were fading fast. Upon hearing the news that Jefferson was assured of South Carolina's eight votes, Abigail Adams remarked to her son Thomas that the "consequence to us personally is that we retire from public life." All that remained to be determined was whether the assembly would instruct the electors to cast their second vote for Burr or Pinckney.

The various presidential electors met in their respective state capitals to vote on December 3. By law, their ballots were not to be opened and counted until February 11, but the outcome could hardly be kept secret for ten weeks. Sure enough, just nine days after the vote, Washington, D.C.'s *National Intelligencer* newspaper broke the news that neither Adams nor Pinckney had received a single South Carolina vote and, in the voting at large, Jefferson and Burr had each received 73 electoral votes. Adams had gotten 65, Pinckney 64. The House of Representatives would have to make the final decision between the two Republicans.

Adams thus became the first presidential candidate to fall victim to the notorious clause in the Constitution that counted each slave as three-fifths of one individual in calculating population used to allocate both House seats and electoral votes. Had slaves, who had no vote, not been so counted, Adams would have edged Jefferson by a vote of 63 to 61. In addition, the Federalists fell victim to the public's perception that the Republicans stood for democracy and egalitarianism, while the Federalists were seen as imperious and authoritarian.

In the House, each state would cast a single vote. If each of the 16 states voted—that is, if none abstained—9 states would elect the president. Republicans controlled eight delegations—New York, New Jersey, Pennsylvania, Virginia, North Carolina, Georgia, Kentucky and Tennessee. The Federalists held six: New Hampshire, Massachusetts, Rhode Island, Connecticut, Delaware and South Carolina. And two delegations—Maryland and Vermont—were deadlocked.

Though Jefferson and Burr had tied in the Electoral College, public opinion appeared to side with Jefferson. Not only had he been the choice of his party's nominating caucus, but he had served longer at the national level than Burr, and in a more exalted capacity. But if neither man was selected by noon on March 4, when Adams' term ended, the country would be without a chief executive until the newly elected Congress convened in December, nine months later. In the interim, the current, Federalist-dominated Congress would be in control.

Faced with such a prospect, Jefferson wrote to Burr in December. His missive was cryptic, but in it he appeared to suggest that if Burr accepted the vice presidency, he would be given greater responsibilities than previous vice presidents. Burr's response to Jefferson was reassuring. He pledged to "disclaim all competition" and spoke of "your administration."

Meanwhile, the Federalists caucused to discuss their options. Some favored tying up the proceedings in order to hold on to power for several more months. Some wanted to try to invalidate, on technical grounds, enough electoral votes to make Adams the winner. Some urged the party to throw its support to Burr, believing that, as a native of mercantile New York City, he would be more friendly than Jefferson to the Federalist economic program. Not a few insisted that the party should support Jefferson, as he was clearly the popular choice. Others, including Hamilton, who had long opposed Burr in the rough and tumble of New York City politics, thought Jefferson more trustworthy than Burr. Hamilton argued that Burr was "without Scruple," an "unprincipled . . . voluptuary" who would plunder the country. But Hamilton also urged the party to stall, in the hope of inducing Jefferson to make a deal. Hamilton proposed that in return for the Federalist votes that would make him president, Jefferson should promise to preserve the Federalist fiscal system (a properly funded national debt and the Bank), American neutrality and a strong navy, and to agree to "keeping in office all our Foederal Friends" below the cabinet level. Even Adams joined the fray, telling Jefferson that the presidency would be his "in an instant" should he accept Hamilton's terms. Jefferson declined, insisting that he "should never go into the office of President . . . with my hands tied by any conditions which should hinder me from pursuing the measures" he thought best.

In the end, the Federalists decided to back Burr. Hearing of their decision, Jefferson told Adams that any attempt "to defeat the Presidential election" would "produce resistance by force, and incalculable consequences."

Burr, who had seemed to disavow a fight for the highest office, now let it be known that he would accept the presidency if elected by the House. In Philadelphia, he met with several

Republican congressmen, allegedly telling them that he intended to fight for it.

Burr had to know that he was playing a dangerous game and risking political suicide by challenging Jefferson, his party's reigning power. The safest course would have been to acquiesce to the vice presidency. He was yet a young man, and given Jefferson's penchant for retiring to Monticello—he had done so in 1776, 1781 and 1793—there was a good chance that Burr would be his party's standard-bearer as early as 1804. But Burr also knew there was no guarantee he would live to see future elections. His mother and father had died at ages 27 and 42, respectively.

Burr's was not the only intrigue. Given the high stakes, every conceivable pressure was applied to change votes. Those in the deadlocked delegations were courted daily, but no one was lobbied more aggressively than James Bayard, Delaware's lone congressman, who held in his hands the sole determination of how his state would vote. Thirty-two years old in 1800, Bayard had practiced law in Wilmington before winning election to the House as a Federalist four years earlier. Bayard despised Virginia's Republican planters, including Jefferson, whom he saw as hypocrites who owned hundreds of slaves and lived "like feudal barons" as they played the role of "high priests of liberty." He announced he was supporting Burr.

The city of Washington awoke to a crippling snowstorm Wednesday, February 11, the day the House was to begin voting. Nevertheless, only one of the 105 House members did not make it in to Congress, and his absence would not change his delegation's tally. Voting began the moment the House was gaveled into session. When the roll call was complete, Jefferson had carried eight states, Burr six, and two deadlocked states had cast uncommitted ballots; Jefferson still needed one more vote for a majority. A second vote was held, with a similar tally, then a third. When at 3 A.M. the exhausted congressmen finally called it a day, 19 roll calls had been taken, all with the same inconclusive result.

By Saturday evening, three days later, the House had cast 33 ballots. The deadlock seemed unbreakable.

For weeks, warnings had circulated of drastic consequences if Republicans were denied the presidency. Now that danger seemed palpable. A shaken President Adams was certain the two sides had come to the "precipice" of disaster and that "a civil war was expected." There was talk that Virginia would secede if Jefferson were not elected. Some Republicans declared they would convene another constitutional convention to restructure the federal government so that it reflected the "democratic spirit of America." It was rumored that a mob had stormed the arsenal in Philadelphia and was preparing to march on Washington to drive the defeated Federalists from power. Jefferson said he could not restrain those of his supporters who threatened "a dissolution" of the Union. He told Adams that many Republicans were prepared to use force to prevent the Federalists' "legislative usurpation" of the executive branch.

In all likelihood, it was these threats that ultimately broke the deadlock. The shift occurred sometime after Saturday's final ballot; it was Delaware's Bayard who blinked. That night, he sought out a Republican close to Jefferson, almost certainly John Nicholas, a member of Virginia's House delegation. Were Delaware to abstain, Bayard pointed out, only 15 states would ballot. With eight states already in his column, Jefferson would have a majority and the elusive victory at last. But in return, Bayard asked, would Jefferson accept the terms that the Federalists had earlier proffered? Nicholas responded, according to Bayard's later recollections, that these conditions were "very reasonable" and that he could vouch for Jefferson's acceptance.

The Federalists caucused behind doors on Sunday afternoon, February 15. When Bayard's decision to abstain was announced, it touched off a firestorm. Cries of "Traitor! Traitor!" rang down on him. Bayard himself later wrote that the "clamor was prodigious, the reproaches vehement," and that many old colleagues were "furious" with him. Two matters in particular roiled his comrades. Some were angry that Bayard had broken ranks before it was known what kind of deal, if any, Burr might have been willing to cut. Others were upset that nothing had been heard from Jefferson himself. During a second Federalist caucus that afternoon, Bayard agreed to take no action until Burr's answer was known. In addition, the caucus directed Bayard to seek absolute assurances that Jefferson would go along with the deal.

Early the next morning, Monday, February 16, according to Bayard's later testimony, Jefferson made it known through a third party that the terms demanded by the Federalists "corresponded with his views and intentions, and that we might confide in him accordingly." The bargain was struck, at least to Bayard's satisfaction. Unless Burr offered even better terms, Jefferson would be the third president of the United States.

At some point that Monday afternoon, Burr's letters arrived. What exactly he said or did not say in them—they likely were destroyed soon after they reached Washington and their contents remain a mystery—disappointed his Federalist proponents. Bayard, in a letter written that Monday, told a friend that "Burr has acted a miserable paultry part. The election was in his power." But Burr, at least according to Bayard's interpretation, and for reasons that remain unknown to history, had refused to reach an accommodation with the Federalists. That same Monday evening a dejected Theodore Sedgwick, Speaker of the House and a passionate Jefferson hater, notified friends at home: "the gigg is up."

The following day, February 17, the House gathered at noon to cast its 36th, and, as it turned out, final, vote. Bayard was true to his word: Delaware abstained, ending seven days of contention and the long electoral battle.

Bayard ultimately offered many reasons for his change of heart. On one occasion he claimed that he and the five other Federalists who had held the power to determine the election in their hands—four from Maryland and one from Vermont—had agreed to "give our votes to Mr. Jefferson" if it became clear that Burr could not win. Bayard also later insisted that he had acted from what he called "imperious necessity" to prevent a civil war or disunion. Still later he claimed to have been swayed by the public's preference for Jefferson.

Had Jefferson in fact cut a deal to secure the presidency? Ever afterward, he insisted that such allegations were "absolutely false." The historical evidence, however, suggests otherwise. Not only did many political insiders assert that Jefferson had indeed agreed to a bargain, but Bayard, in a letter dated February 17, the very day of the climactic House vote—as well as five years later, while testifying under oath in a libel suit—insisted that Jefferson had most certainly agreed to accept the Federalists' terms. In another letter written at the time, Bayard assured a Federalist officeholder, who feared losing his position in a Republican administration: "I have taken good care of you . . . . You are safe."

Even Jefferson's actions as president lend credence to the allegations. Despite having fought against the Hamiltonian economic system for nearly a decade, he acquiesced to it once in office, leaving the Bank of the United States in place and tolerating continued borrowing by the federal government. Nor did he remove most Federalist officeholders.

The mystery is not why Jefferson would deny making such an accord, but why he changed his mind after vowing never to bend. He must have concluded that he had no choice if he wished to become president by peaceful means. To permit the balloting to continue was to hazard seeing the presidency slip from his hands. Jefferson not only must have doubted the constancy of some of his supporters, but he knew that a majority of the Federalists favored Burr and were making the New Yorker the same offer they were dangling before him.

Burr's behavior is more enigmatic. He had decided to make a play for the presidency, only apparently to refuse the very terms that would have guaranteed it to him. The reasons for his action have been lost in a confounding tangle of furtive transactions and deliberately destroyed evidence. It may have been that the Federalists demanded more of him than they did of Jefferson. Or Burr may have found it unpalatable to strike a bargain with ancient enemies, including the man he would kill in a duel three years later. Burr may also have been unwilling to embrace Federalist principles that he had opposed throughout his political career.

The final mystery of the election of 1800 is whether Jefferson and his backers would have sanctioned violence had he been denied the presidency. Soon after taking office, Jefferson claimed that "there was no idea of [using] force." His remark proves little, yet during the ongoing battle in the House, he alternately spoke of acceding to the Federalists' misconduct in the hope that their behavior would ruin them, or of calling a second Constitutional Convention. He probably would have chosen one, or both, of these courses before risking bloodshed and the end of the Union.

In the days that followed the House battle, Jefferson wrote letters to several surviving signers of the Declaration of Independence to explain what he believed his election had meant. It guaranteed the triumph of the American Revolution, he said, ensuring the realization of the new "chapter in the history of man" that had been promised by Thomas Paine in 1776. In the years that followed, his thoughts often returned to the election's significance. In 1819, at age 76, he would characterize it as the "revolution of 1800," and he rejoiced to a friend in Virginia, Spencer Roane, that it had been effected peacefully "by the rational and peaceful instruments of reform, the suffrage of the people."

Historian **JOHN FERLING** is the author of *Adams vs. Jefferson: The Tumultuous Election of 1800* (Oxford University Press).

The Revolution of 1803

The Louisiana Purchase of 1803 was "the event which more than any other, after the foundation of the Government and always excepting its preservation, determined the character of our national life." So said President Theodore Roosevelt on the 100th anniversary of this momentous acquisition. As we celebrate the 200th anniversary, it's clear that the extraordinary real estate deal also shaped America's perception of its role in the world.

PETER S. ONUF

If there was one thing the United States did not seem to need in 1803, it was more land. The federal government had plenty to sell settlers in the new state of Ohio and throughout the Old Northwest (stretching from the Ohio and Mississippi rivers to the Great Lakes), as did New York, Pennsylvania, and other states. New Englanders were already complaining that the westward exodus was driving up wages and depressing real estate prices in the East.

The United States then consisted of 16 states: the original 13, strung along the Atlantic seaboard, and three recent additions on the frontier: Vermont, which had declared its independence from New York during the Revolution, was finally recognized and admitted in 1791, and Kentucky and Tennessee, carved out of the western reaches of Virginia and North Carolina in 1792 and 1796, respectively, extended the union of states as far as the Mississippi River. The entire area east of the Mississippi had been nominally secured to the United States by the Peace of Paris in 1783, though vast regions remained under the control of Indian nations and subject to the influence of various European imperial powers.

Many skeptical commentators believed that the United States was already too big and that the bonds of union would weaken and snap if new settlements spread too far and too fast. "No paper engagements" could secure the connection of East and West, Massachusetts congressman Rufus King wrote in 1786, and separatist movements and disunionist plots kept such concerns alive in subsequent years. Expansionists had a penchant for naturalistic language: At best, the "surge" or "tide" of white settlement might be channeled, but it was ultimately irresistible.

Though President Thomas Jefferson and the American negotiators who secured the Louisiana Purchase in 1803 had not even dreamed of acquiring such a vast territory, stretching from the Mississippi to the Rockies, the expansion of the United States has the retrospective feel of inevitability,

however much some modern Americans may bemoan the patriotic passions and imperialistic excesses of "Manifest Destiny" and its "legacies of conquest." Indeed, it's almost impossible for us to imagine any other outcome now, or to recapture the decidedly mixed feelings of Americans about their country's expansion at the start of the 19th century.

Jefferson and his contemporaries understood that they were at a crossroads, and that the American experiment in republican self-government and the fragile federal union on which it depended could easily fail. They understood that the United States was a second-rate power, without the "energy" or military means to project—or possibly even to defend—its vital interests in a world almost constantly at war. And they understood all too well that the loyalties of their countrymen—and, if they were honest with themselves, their own loyalties—were volatile and unpredictable.

There were good reasons for such doubts about American allegiances. Facing an uncertain future, patriotic (and not so patriotic) Americans had only the dimmest sense of who or what should command their loyalty. The Union had nearly collapsed on more than one occasion, most recently during the presidential succession crisis of 1800-01, which saw a tie in the Electoral College and 36 contentious ballots in the House of Representatives before Jefferson was elevated to the presidency. During the tumultuous 1790s, rampant partisan political strife between Federalists and Jefferson's Republicans roiled the nation, and before that, under the Articles of Confederation (1781–89), the central government ground to a virtual halt and the Union almost withered away before the new constitution saved it. Of course, everyone professed to be a patriot, dedicated to preserving American independence. But what did that mean? Federalists such as Alexander Hamilton preached fealty to a powerful, consolidated central government capable of doing the people's will (as they loosely construed it); Republican oppositionists championed a strictly construed federal constitution that left power in the hands of the people's (or peoples') state governments. Each side accused the other of being subject to the corrupt influence of a foreign power: counterrevolutionary England in the case of Federalist "aristocrats" and "monocrats"; revolutionary France for Republican "Jacobins."

In Jefferson's mind, and in the minds of his many followers, the new Republican dispensation initiated by his ascension to power in "the Revolution of 1800" provided a hopeful answer to all these doubts and anxieties. Jefferson's First Inaugural Address, which the soft-spoken, 57-year-old president delivered to Congress in a nearly inaudible whisper in March 1801, seemed to his followers to herald a new epoch in American affairs. "We are all republicans, we are all federalists," he insisted in the speech. "Let us, then, unite with one heart and one mind." The president's inspiring vision of the nation's future augured, as he told the English radical Joseph Priestley, then a refugee in republican Pennsylvania, something "new under the sun."

While Jefferson's conciliatory language in the inaugural address famously helped mend the partisan breach—and, not coincidentally, helped cast Hamilton and his High Federalist minions far beyond the republican pale—it also anticipated the issues that would come to the fore during the period leading up to the Louisiana Purchase.

First, the new president addressed the issue of the nation's size. Could an expanding union of free republican states survive without jeopardizing the liberties won at such great cost by the revolutionary generation? Jefferson reassured the rising, post-revolutionary generation that it too had sufficient virtue and patriotism to make the republican experiment work and to pass on its beneficent legacy. "Entertaining a due sense of our equal right to the use of our own faculties" and "enlightened by a benign religion, professed, indeed, and practiced in various forms, yet all of them inculcating honesty, truth, temperance, gratitude, and the love of man; acknowledging and adoring an over-ruling Providence, which by all its dispensations proves that it delights in the happiness of man here and his greater happiness hereafter," Americans were bound to be "a happy and a prosperous people."

Jefferson congratulated his fellow Americans on "possessing a chosen country, with room enough for our descendants to the thousandth and thousandth generation," a vast domain that was "separated by nature and a wide ocean from the exterminating havoc of one quarter of the globe." Jefferson's vision of nationhood was inscribed on the American landscape: "An overruling Providence, which by all its dispensations proves that it delights in the happiness of man here and his greater happiness hereafter" provided this fortunate people with land enough to survive and prosper forever. But Jefferson knew that he was not offering an accurate description of the nation's current condition. Given the frenzied pace of westward settlement, it would take only a generation or two—not a thousand—to fill out the new nation's existing limits, which were still marked in the west by the Mississippi. Nor was the United States as happily insulated from Europe's "exterminating havoc" as the new president suggested. The Spanish remained in control of New Orleans, the key to the great river system that controlled the continent's heartland, and the British remained a powerful presence to the north.

Jefferson's vision of the future was, in fact, the mirror opposite of America's present situation at the onset of the 19th century. The nation was encircled by enemies and deeply divided by partisan and sectional differences. The domain the president envisioned was boundless, continent-wide, a virgin land waiting to be taken up by virtuous, liberty-loving American farmers. In this providential perspective, Indian nations and European empires simply disappeared from view, and the acquisition of new territory and the expansion of the Union seemed preordained. It would take an unimaginable miracle, acquisition of the entire Louisiana territory, to begin to consummate Jefferson's inaugural promise.

Jefferson's expansionist vision also violated the accepted axioms of contemporary political science. In his *Spirit of the Laws* (1748), the great French philosopher Montesquieu taught that the republican form of government could survive only in small states, where a virtuous and vigilant citizenry could effectively monitor the exercise of power. A large state, by contrast, could be sustained only if power were concentrated in a more energetic central government; republicanism in an expanding state would give way to more "despotic," aristocratic, and monarchical regimes. This "law" of political science was commonly understood in mechanical terms: Centrifugal forces, pulling a state apart, gained momentum as territory expanded, and they could be checked only by the "energy" of strong government.

James Madison had grappled with the problem in his famous *Federalist* 10, in which he argued that an "extended republic" would "take in a greater variety of parties and interests," making it "less probable that a majority of the whole will have a common motive to invade the rights of other citizens." Modern pluralists have embraced this argument, but it was not particularly persuasive to Madison's generation—or even to Madison himself a decade later. During the struggle over ratification of the Constitution, Antifederalists effectively invoked Montesquieu's dictum against Federalist "consolidationism," and in the 1790s, Jeffersonian defenders of states' rights offered the same arguments against Hamiltonian High Federalism. And Jefferson's "Revolution of 1800," vindicating the claims of (relatively) small state-republics against an overly energetic central government, seemed to confirm Montesquieu's wisdom. Montesquieu's notion was also the basis for the popular interpretation of what had caused the rise of British tyranny in the colonies before the American Revolution.

At the same time, however, Montesquieu's logic posed a problem for Jefferson. How could he imagine a continental republic in 1801 and negotiate a land cession that doubled the country's size in 1803? To put the problem somewhat differently, how could Jefferson—who had, after all, drafted the controversial Kentucky Resolutions of 1798, which threatened state nullification of federal authority—overcome his own disunionist tendencies?

Jefferson's response in his inaugural was to call on his fellow Americans to "pursue our own federal and republican principles, our attachment to union and representative government," with "courage and confidence." In other words, a sacred regard for states' rights ("federal principles") was essential to the preservation and strength of a "union" that depended on the "attachment" of a people determined to secure its liberties ("republican principles"). This conception of states as republics would have been familiar and appealing to many Americans, but Jefferson's vision of the United States as a *powerful* nation, spreading across the continent, was breathtaking in its boldness. How could he promise Americans that they could have it both ways, that they could be secure in their liberties yet have a federal government with enough "energy" to preserve itself? How could he believe that the American government, which had only recently endured a near-fatal succession crisis and which had a pathetically small army and navy, was "the strongest Government on earth"?

Jefferson responded to these questions resoundingly by invoking—or perhaps more accurately, inventing—an American people or nation, united in devotion to common principles, and coming together over the course of succeeding generations to constitute one great family. Thus, the unity the president imagined was prospective. Divided as they might now be, Americans would soon come to realize that they were destined to be a great nation, freed from "the throes and convulsions of the ancient world" and willing to sacrifice everything in defense of their country. In Jefferson's vision of progressive continental development, the defensive vigilance of virtuous republicans, who were always ready to resist the encroachments of power from any and every source, would be transformed into a patriotic devotion to the transcendent community of an inclusive and expanding nation, "the world's best hope." "At the call of the law," Jefferson predicted, "every man . . . would fly to the standard of the law, and would meet invasions of the public order as his own personal concern."

Jefferson thus invoked an idealized vision of the American Revolution, in which patriotic citizen-soldiers rallied against British tyranny, as a model for future mobilizations against internal as well as external threats. (It was an extraordinary—and extraordinarily influential—exercise in revisionist history. More dispassionate observers, including those who, unlike Jefferson, actually had some military experience, were not inclined to give the militias much, if any, credit for winning the war.)

Jefferson's conception of the American nation imaginatively countered the centrifugal forces, the tendency toward anarchy and disunion, that republicanism authorized and unleashed. Devotion to the Union would reverse this tendency and draw Americans together, even as their private pursuits of happiness drew them to the far frontiers of their continental domain. It was a paradoxical, mystifying formulation. What seemed to be weakness—the absence of a strong central government—was, in fact, strength. Expansion did not attenuate social and political ties; rather, it secured a powerful, effective, and affective union. The imagined obliteration of all possible obstacles to the enactment of this great national story—the removal of Indians and foreigners—was the greatest mystification of all, for it disguised how the power of the federal state was to be deployed to clear the way for "nature's nation."

In retrospect, the peaceful acquisition of the Louisiana Territory, at the bargain-basement price of $15 million, seemed to conform to the expansionist scenario in Jefferson's First Inaugural Address. The United States bought land from France, just as individuals bought land from federal and state land offices, demonstrating good intentions (to be fruitful and multiply, to cultivate the earth) and their respect for property rights and the rule of law. Yet the progress of settlement was inexorable, a "natural" force, as the French wisely recognized in ceding their claims.

The threat of armed conflict was, nonetheless, never far below the surface. When the chilling news reached America in 1802 that Spain had retroceded Louisiana to France, under pressure from Napoleon Bonaparte, some Federalists agitated for a preemptive strike against New Orleans before Napoleon could land troops there and begin to carry out his plan for a reinvigorated French empire in the Western Hemisphere. As if to provide a taste of the future, Spanish authorities in New Orleans revoked the right of American traders to store goods in the city for export, thereby sending ripples of alarm and economic distress through farms and plantations of the Mississippi valley. Americans might like to think, with Jefferson, that the West was a vast land reserve for their future generations, but nature would issue a different decree if the French gained control of the Mississippi River system.

As Senator William Wells of Delaware warned the Senate in February 1803, if Napoleon were ensconced in New Orleans, "the whole of your Southern States" would be at his mercy; the French ruler would not hesitate to foment rebellion among the slaves, that "inveterate enemy in the very bosom of those States." A North Carolina congressman expected the French emperor to do even worse: "The tomahawk of the savage and the knife of the negro would confederate in the league, and there would be no interval of peace." Such a confederation—a powerful, unholy alliance of Europeans, Indians, and slaves—was the nightmarish antithesis of the Americans' own weak union. The French might even use their influence in Congress to revive the vicious party struggles that had crippled the national government during the 1790s.

Jefferson had no idea how to respond to the looming threat, beyond sending his friend and protégé James Monroe to join U.S. Minister to France Robert R. Livingston in a desperate bid to negotiate a way out of the crisis. At most, they hoped that Napoleon would sell New Orleans and the Floridas to the United States, perhaps with a view to preempting an Anglo-American alliance. Jefferson dropped a broad hint to Livingston (undoubtedly for Napoleon's edification) that if France ever took "possession of N. Orleans . . . we must marry ourselves to the British fleet and nation." For the Anglophobe Jefferson this must have been a horrible thought, even if it was a bluff. But then, happily for Jefferson—and crucially for his historical reputation—fortune intervened.

Napoleon's intentions for the New World hinged on control of Saint-Domingue (now Haiti), but a slave revolt there, led by the brilliant Toussaint L'Ouverture, complicated the emperor's plans. With a strong assist from yellow fever and other devastating diseases, the rebels fought a French expeditionary force of more than 20,000 to a standstill. Thwarted in his western design and facing the imminent resumption of war in Europe, Napoleon decided to cut his losses. In April 1803, his representative offered the entire Louisiana Territory to a surprised Livingston. By the end of the month, the negotiators had arrived at a price. For $15 million, the United States would acquire 828,000 square miles of North America, stretching from the Mississippi River to the Rocky Mountains and from the Gulf of Mexico to the Canadian border. Over time 13 states would be carved from the new lands.

When the news reached America in July, it proved a great deal more than anyone had been contemplating but was met with general jubilation. There was widespread agreement that national security depended on gaining control of the region around New Orleans; and Spanish Florida, occupying the critical area south of Georgia and the territory that the state had finally ceded to Congress in 1802, was high on southern planters' wish list of territorial acquisitions. But it was hard to imagine any immediate use for the trans-Mississippi region, notwithstanding Jefferson's inspiring rhetoric, and there was some grumbling that the negotiators had spent more than Congress had authorized. A few public figures, mostly New England Federalists, even opposed the transaction on political and constitutional grounds.

The Lewis and Clark expedition, authorized before the Purchase was completed, testifies to Americans' utter ignorance of the West in 1803. The two explorers were sent, in effect, to feel around in the dark. Perhaps, Jefferson mused, the trans-Mississippi region could be used as a kind of toxic waste dump, a place to send emancipated slaves beyond harm's way. Or, a more portentous thought, Indian nations might be relocated west of the river—an idea President Andrew Jackson later put into effect with his infamous removal policy.

What gripped most commentators as they celebrated the news of the Purchase in 1803 was simply that the Union had survived another awful crisis. They tended to see the new lands as a buffer. "The wilderness itself," Representative Joseph Nicholson of Maryland exclaimed, "will now present an almost insurmountable barrier to any nation that inclined to disturb us in that quarter." And another congressman exulted that America was now "insulated from the rest of the world."

David Ramsay, the South Carolina historian and devout Republican, offered the most full-blown paean to the future of the "chosen country" as Jefferson had envisioned it. Echoing Jefferson's First Inaugural, he asked, "What is to hinder our extension on the same liberal principles of equal rights till we have increased to twenty-seven, thirty-seven, or any other number of states that will conveniently embrace, in one happy union, the whole country from the Atlantic to the Pacific ocean, and from the lakes of Canada to the Gulf of Mexico?" In his Second Inaugural, in 1805, Jefferson himself would ask, "Who can limit the extent to which the federative principle may operate effectively?" Gone were his doubts about the uses to which the new lands could be put. "Is it not better that the opposite bank of the Mississippi should be settled by our own brethren and children, than by strangers of another family?"

Jefferson's vision of the American future has ever since provided the mythic master narrative of American history. In the western domains that Jefferson imagined as a kind of blank slate on which succeeding generations would inscribe the image of American nationhood, it would be all too easy to overlook other peoples and other possibilities. It would be all too easy as well to overlook the critical role of the state in the progress of settlement and development. When Americans looked back on events, they would confuse effects with causes: War and diplomacy eliminated rival empires and dispossessed native peoples; an activist federal state played a critical role in pacifying a "lawless" frontier by privatizing public lands and promoting economic development. In the mythic history of Jefferson's West, an irresistible westward tide of settlement appears to be its own cause, the manifest destiny of nature's nation.

Yet if the reality of power remains submerged in Jefferson's thought, it's not at any great depth. The very idea of the nation implies enormous force, the power of a people enacting the will of "an overruling Providence." In Jefferson's Declaration of Independence, Americans claimed "the separate & equal station to which the laws of nature and of nature's God entitle them." The first law of nature, the great natural law proclaimed by writers of the day, was self-preservation, and the defining moment in American history was the great mobilization of American power to secure independence in the Revolution. President Jefferson's vision of westward expansion projected that glorious struggle into the future and across the continent. It was a kind of permanent revolution, reenacting the nation's beginnings in the multiplication of new, self-governing republican states.

Born in war, Jefferson's conception of an expanding union of free states constituted a peace plan for the New World. But until it was insulated from Europe's "exterminating havoc," the new nation would remain vulnerable, unable to realize its historic destiny. By eliminating the clear and present danger of a powerful French presence at the mouth of the Mississippi, the Louisiana Purchase guaranteed the survival of the Union—for the time being, at least. By opening the West to white American settlers, it all but guaranteed that subsequent generations would see their own history in Jefferson's vision of their future, a mythic, nation-making vision yoking individual liberty and national power and promising a future of peace and security in a dangerous world. Two hundred years later, that vision remains compelling to many Americans.

PETER S. ONUF is a professor of history at the University of Virginia. His most recent book is *Jefferson's Empire: The Language of American Nationhood* (2001). Copyright © 2003 by Peter Onuf.

From *Wilson Quarterly,* Winter 2003, pp. 22–29. Copyright © 2003 by Peter S. Onuf. Reprinted by permission of the author.

Saving New Orleans

In a new book, *Patriotic Fire,* the author of *Forrest Gump* paints an uncommonly vivid picture of an overlooked chapter in American history—and its unlikely hero.

WINSTON GROOM

By Autumn 1814, the United States of America, barely 30 years old, was on the verge of dissolving. The treasury was empty, most public buildings in Washington, including the Capitol, the White House (then known as the President's House) and the Library of Congress, had been burned by a victorious and vengeful British Army, in one of the most dramatic incursions of the War of 1812. Festering tensions—arising out of Britain's interference with neutral America's lucrative maritime commerce—had erupted into hostilities in June of 1812. American seaports from the Atlantic to the Gulf of Mexico were blockaded by the British Navy, and the economy was in ruins. The U.S. Army was stymied and stalemated; the Navy, such as it was, had fared little better.

Then, as leaves began to fall, a mighty British armada appeared off the Louisiana coast with the stated purpose of capturing New Orleans, America's gateway to the great Mississippi River Basin. The misfortune would have split the United States in two. New Orleans was as nearly defenseless as a city could be in those days, with only two understrength Regular Army regiments totaling about 1,100 soldiers and a handful of untrained militia to throw against nearly 20,000 veterans of the British Army and Navy, who were descending upon it as swiftly and surely as a hurricane.

Orders from the secretary of war went out to the legendary Indian fighter Gen. Andrew Jackson, then in nearby Mobile, Alabama. He should go immediately to New Orleans and take charge.

Central to the British Design for the capture of Louisiana, which had been admitted to the Union in 1812, was an extraordinary scheme devised by Col. Edward Nicholls to enlist the services of the "pirates of Barataria"—so named for the waters surrounding their barrier island redoubt—who were for the most part not pirates at all but privateers, operating under letters of marque from foreign countries. Under the agreed concessions of maritime law, these official letters, or commissions, allowed privateers to prey on the merchant shipping of any nation at war with the issuing country without—in the event they were captured—being subject to hanging as pirates.

In the Gulf of Mexico, a large gathering of these ruthless men had set up operations on Grand Terre Island, Louisiana, which lies about 40 miles south of New Orleans as the crow flies. The leader of this band was a tall, handsome, magnetic Frenchman named Jean Laffite, who, using his blacksmith shop in New Orleans as a front, came to run a phenomenal smuggling business for the grateful citizens of New Orleans, rich and poor alike, who had been harmed for years by an American embargo on international trade—a measure intended to deprive Europe of raw materials—and by a British blockade designed to stifle American commerce.

It was to the Baratarians that Colonel Nicholls dispatched his emissaries from HMS *Sophie* to see if they could be enlisted into the British effort against New Orleans. On the morning of September 3, 1814, the *Sophie* dropped anchor off Grand Terre. Through spyglasses the British observed hundreds of sleepy-eyed, ill-dressed men gathering on a sandy beach. Presently a small boat was launched from the beach, rowed by four men with a fifth man in the bow. From the *Sophie,* a longboat was likewise launched, carrying its captain, Nicholas Lockyer, and a Captain McWilliams of the Royal Marines. The boats met in the channel, and Lockyer, in his best schoolboy French, asked to be taken to Monsieur Laffite; the response from the man at the prow of the small boat was that Laffite could be found ashore. Once on the beach, the two British officers were led through the suspicious crowd by the man in the bow, along a shaded path, and up the steps of a substantial home with a large wraparound gallery. At that point he genially informed them, "Messieurs, I am Laffite."

Jean Laffite remains among the most enigmatic figures in the American historical experience, right up there with Davy Crockett, Daniel Boone, Kit Carson, Wyatt Earp and Wild Bill Hickok. The youngest of eight children, Laffite was born in Port-au-Prince in the French colony of San Domingo (now Haiti) around 1782. His father had been a skilled leather-worker in Spain, France and Morocco before he opened a prosperous leather shop on the island. Jean's mother died "before I could remember her," he said, and he was raised by his maternal grandmother.

His older brothers, Pierre and Alexandre, would figure prominently in his life. After a rigorous education beginning at age 6, Jean and Pierre, two and a half years his elder, were sent away for advanced schooling on the neighboring islands of St. Croix and Martinique and then to a military academy on St. Kitts.

Alexandre—11 years Jean's senior—returned occasionally from his adventures as a privateer attacking Spanish ships in the Caribbean and regaled his younger brothers with stories of his exploits. They were so captivated by his tales that nothing would do but for them to follow him to sea.

When Jean and Pierre arrived in Louisiana from Haiti in 1807, they came as privateersmen—a barely respectable and an unquestionably dangerous business. Laffite, then in his mid-20s, was described as dark-haired, about six feet tall, with "dark piercing eyes," a furious vertical crease in his brow and a comportment something like a powerful cat. He was also said to be intelligent, convivial and a gambling and drinking man.

Joseph Sauvinet, a Frenchman who had become one of the principal businessmen of New Orleans, quickly recognized the value of a resourceful man such as Laffite. Sauvinet set up Jean and his brothers in the smuggling business, with instructions on how to avoid U.S. Customs by offloading their goods downriver below a bend called English Turn, from where the cargo could be transported to Sauvinet's warehouses for resale in New Orleans.

Laffite and his men chose as their base of operations the remote Barataria Bay. It must have seemed a paradise, a place of breathtaking natural beauty and serenity. In addition, Grand Terre was elevated enough to provide protection from all but the worst hurricanes.

Under Jean's stewardship, the privateers captured more than 100 vessels and their cargoes, the most valuable of which were slaves taken in the waters around Havana, which had become the center of the slave trade in the Western Hemisphere.

With the exception of Laffite, who still attired himself as a gentleman, the rest of the Baratarians—there would be probably more than 1,000 of them—dressed like swashbuckling pirates: red-and-black striped blouses, pantaloons, tall boots, and colorful bandannas tied around their heads. Many wore gold earrings, and all carried cutlasses, knives and pistols.

As business grew, the Baratarians became increasingly outrageous. They posted fliers in broad daylight on buildings throughout New Orleans, announcing their booty auctions, held in the swamp halfway between Grand Terre and New Orleans. These were attended by the city's most prominent men, who bought up everything from slaves to pig iron, as well as dresses and jewelry for their wives.

Meanwhile, Laffite began to squirrel away large stores of arms, gunpowder, flints and cannonballs at secret locations. These munitions would prove critically important when the Battle of New Orleans broke out.

The British delegation that came to enlist Laffite in the attack on New Orleans handed over a packet of documents signed by Capt. W. H. Percy, the British senior naval commander in the Gulf of Mexico. Percy threatened to send a fleet to destroy the Baratarians and their stronghold because of their privateering activities against Spanish and British shipping. But if the Baratarians would join with the British, he said they would receive "lands within His Majesty's colonies in America" and the opportunity to become British subjects with a full pardon for any previous crimes.

A personal note from Colonel Nicholls to Laffite also requested the use of all the boats and ships of the Baratarians and the enlistment of Baratarian gunners and fighters in the invasion of Louisiana. The privateers' assistance, Nicholls informed Laffite, was crucial. Once New Orleans was secured, the British planned to move the army upriver and "act in concert" with British forces in Canada, as Laffite later recalled, "to shove the Americans into the Atlantic Ocean." The British officers indicated that His Majesty's forces also intended to set free all the slaves they could find and enlist their help in subduing the Americans.

The two Englishmen next offered Laffite their *piéce de résistance:* a bribe of 30,000 British pounds (more than $2 million today) if he would convince his followers to join with the British. Playing for time against the threatened British assault on his stronghold, Laffite told the two envoys he needed two weeks to compose his men and put his personal affairs in order. After that, Laffite promised the Englishmen, he and his men would be "entirely at your disposal."

As he watched the British sail away, Laffite must have considered taking the bribe. He must have also considered the British promise to free his brother Pierre, who had been charged with piracy and was locked in a New Orleans jail facing the hangman's noose. On the other hand, Jean, though a Frenchman by birth, apparently considered himself something of a patriot where America was concerned. After all, the country had been good to him. He had amassed a fortune (though in blatant contravention of its laws) by smuggling on its shores. He promptly sat down with pen and paper and proceeded to double-cross his newfound British friends.

Laffite's letter to the U.S. authorities amounted to a declaration of patriotism. Addressing himself to his powerful friend Jean Blanque, a member of the Louisiana legislature, Laffite revealed the entire British scheme: a huge fleet containing an entire army was at the moment gathering for an attack on the city.

If Laffite thought that the New Orleans authorities were now going to forgive him for smuggling, however, he was mistaken. Blanque delivered Laffite's communiqué to Louisiana governor William C.C. Claiborne, who convened the legislature's recently organized Committee of Public Safety. Most committee members insisted that the letters must be forgeries and that Laffite was a lowdown pirate simply trying to get his brother out of jail. But Gen. Jacques Villeré, head of the Louisiana militia, declared that the Baratarians had adopted the United States as their country and that they could be trusted. In any event, Cmdre. Daniel

Patterson and Col. Robert Ross announced they were going ahead with their expedition to oust Laffite from Grand Terre.

The pirate Jean Laffite, who called himself "a stray sheep wishing to come back into the fold," offered his services "in defense of the country."

Laffite, who had been anxiously on the lookout for the return of his messenger, was both surprised and delighted to see in the messenger's pirogue none other than his brother Pierre, who had magically "escaped" from jail. (The magic probably had something to do with bribery). Laffite's spies in New Orleans also returned with the unpleasant news that Patterson's flotilla and army were assembling at New Orleans to put him out of business. This prompted Laffite to write another letter, this time to Claiborne himself, in which Laffite candidly admitted his sin of smuggling but offered his services and those of the Baratarians "in defense of the country," asking in return a pardon for himself, Pierre, and any other of his men who were indicted or about to be. "I am a stray sheep," he wrote, "wishing to come back into the fold."

When Andrew Jackson saw Laffite's offer to bring his Baratarians to the defense of New Orleans in exchange for a pardon, Jackson denounced the Baratarians as "hellish Banditti."

Laffite, for his part, was well aware that his time limit to join the British invasion had expired and that several of His Majesty's warships now lay off Barataria Bay. Now the Americans, too, were organizing a force against him. Accordingly, he ordered most of the Baratarians to sail from Grand Terre with whatever of value they could carry, including munitions. He put his brother Alexandre, a.k.a. Dominique You, in charge of the island with about 500 men, instructing him to fight the British if they attacked and, if that proved unsuccessful, to burn all the warehouses and ships at anchor. Laffite then fled with Pierre, who had become ill, to a friend's plantation northwest of the city.

The American attack on Barataria came the next day, September 16, 1814. Jean's instructions to his men had been to not resist the Americans. As the ships, headed by the schooner-of-war *Carolina,* neared, word rang out that they were American. The Baratarians began to scramble for any means of escape—pirogues, rowboats, gigs—and headed into the trackless marshes.

"I perceived the pirates were abandoning their vessels and were flying in all directions," said Patterson. "I sent in pursuit of them." Most got away, but about 80, including Dominique, were captured and thrown into a lice-infested New Orleans jail known as the calaboose. The Americans burned the Baratarians' buildings—40 in all—and sent the captured goods up to New Orleans to be cataloged and filed for themselves as claims in the prize court. It was quite a haul for Patterson and Ross—estimated at more than $600,000 at the time—and that was the end of Barataria, though not of the Baratarians.

On November 22, Jackson finally responded to calls from New Orleans by saddling up with his staff and journeying overland from Mobile, personally scouting possible landing sites for a British invasion. By that time the general had become wracked with dysentery. When he arrived in New Orleans nine days later, gaunt and pallid, he could barely stand, but he was cheered by grateful crowds.

To some his appearance might not have inspired confidence: his clothes and boots were filthy from more than a week on the trail, his face was prematurely wrinkled for his 47 years, and his great head of hair had gone gray. But later that day, when he appeared on the balcony of his headquarters on Royal Street, there was something in his voice and his icy blue eyes that convinced most in the crowd that the city's salvation had arrived. Jackson "declared that he had come to protect the city, that he would drive the British into the sea, or perish in the effort."

Soon, events began to overtake New Orleans. On December 12, the British invasion force arrived offshore. Laffite, for his part, was still *persona non grata* in the city and, with an arrest warrant hanging over him, remained in hiding.

Just before 11 A.M. on December 14, the battle began on Lake Borgne, about 40 miles from the city. British sailors and marines quickly boarded American gunboats positioned there. The British suffered 17 killed and 77 wounded and captured five American gunboats with all their armaments and several boatloads of prisoners. Ten Americans had been killed and 35 wounded.

Jackson was once again faced with the question of what to do about Laffite and his Baratarians, many now scattered in hiding throughout the swamps. After a series of complex negotiations involving the Louisiana legislature and a federal judge, Laffite was escorted to Jackson's Royal Street headquarters. To his surprise, Jackson beheld not a desperado in pirate garb but a man with the manners and mien of a gentleman.

Nor did it hurt Laffite's case that Jackson, who already had commandeered many of Laffite's cannons, had found that New Orleans could offer very little in the way of ammunition and gunpowder. Laffite still had munitions in abundance, squirreled away in the swamps. Again he offered them to Jackson, as well as the services of his trained cannoneers and swamp guides. Jackson concluded that Laffite and his men might well prove useful to the cause.

The Baratarians, accordingly, were organized into two artillery detachments, one under Dominique You and the other under the Laffites' cousin, Renato Beluche. Laffite himself was given an unofficial post as aide-de-camp to Jackson, who instructed him to supervise the defenses leading into the city from Barataria Bay.

On December 23, Jackson was shocked to learn that a British force had massed at a sugar plantation south of New Orleans. In a bold move, American soldiers attacked the British at night, slaughtering them with musket fire, tomahawks and knives. Their assault left the field strewn with British casualties—and slowed their advance.

Jackson moved his forces back a mile and began his defenses. All Christmas Eve and Christmas Day, Jackson's men labored to build and strengthen his soon-to-be-famous parapet. While walking the lines of the main fortification with his friend Edward Livingston, a prominent Louisiana lawyer, Laffite saw something that might have caused a shiver of fear to flow over him. At the far left end of the line, where it entered the cypress swamp, the rampart abruptly ended. Everywhere else, Laffite told Livingston, the army could fight from behind a rampart, but here the British were afforded an opportunity to get behind the American position—which was precisely what the British intended to do. Jackson immediately agreed with this assessment and ordered the rampart extended and manned so far back into the swamp that no one could get around it. Laffite's advice might well have been the best Jackson received during the entire battle.

The fortification took an incredible effort, and when it was at last finished two weeks later, it was more than half a mile long, behind which lay a berm seven or eight feet high, bristling with eight batteries of artillery placed at intervals. In front of it, the men had dug out a ten-foot-wide moat.

On the morning of December 27, when the sun had risen enough to present a field of fire, the British battery opened on the *Carolina*, positioned in the Mississippi downriver of Jackson, at point-blank range. The warship blew up in a fantastic roar of smoke and flame. Another American vessel, the *Louisiana*, was able to avoid a similar fate by having her sailors pull her upriver. They anchored her right across from Jackson's ditch, his first line of defense.

Jackson decided to meet the British attack head-on. This was no easy decision, considering that his people were outnumbered in both infantry and artillery. But Jackson trusted his two Tennessee commanders, John Coffee and William Carroll, and had faith in the courage and loyalty of their men, with whom he had fought the Creek War. Likewise, he had come to trust the Creole fighters of Louisiana under their French-speaking officers.

Lastly, Jackson, who now looked upon Laffite's Baratarians as a godsend, ordered Dominique You and his cut-throat artillerists to come at once to the barricade. The Baratarians responded resolutely, with squat Dominique You, smiling his perpetual grin and smoking a cigar, leading the way. They arrived ready for a fight about dawn on December 28.

When the British Army came into view, it must have been both a magnificent and a disturbing sight. With drummer boys beating out an unnerving cadence, there soon appeared thousands of redcoats in two columns, 80 men abreast. They pressed forward until mid-afternoon, with American rifle fire—especially from the Tennesseans' long rifles—and the artillery taking their toll. Finally, the British commander, Gen. Sir Edward Pakenham, had seen enough; he called off the assault and took his army out of range of the American guns.

Much of the effective American artillery fire probably was the work of Laffite's Baratarian gunners. Laffite himself, some accounts say, had supervised the installation of two of the largest and most powerful guns in the line, the 24-pounders, which Jackson had ordered dragged down from New Orleans a day or so earlier. If so, Laffite had thus deliberately placed himself in a perilous position; had he been captured by the British, he would surely have been hanged for his double cross, if not on piracy charges. One gun was commanded by Dominique You and the other by Renato Beluche.

Then came New Year's Day, 1815. At 10 A.M., the British artillery began blasting away. Singled out for particular attention was the Macarty plantation house, Jackson's headquarters, wrecked by more than 100 cannonballs during the first ten minutes. Miraculously, neither Jackson nor any of his staff was injured. Covered with plaster dust, they rushed out to form up the army for battle.

According to the German merchant Vincent Nolte, the main British battery, situated near a road that ran through the center of sugar cane fields, "directed its fire against the battery of the pirates Dominique You and Beluche." Once, as Dominique was examining the enemy through a spyglass, "a cannon shot wounded his arm; he caused it to be bound up, saying, 'I will pay them for that!' . . . He then gave the order to fire a 24-pounder, and the ball knocked an English gun carriage to pieces and killed six or seven men." Not long afterward, a British shot hit one of Dominique's guns and knocked it off its carriage. While it was being repaired, someone asked about his wound. "Only some scratch, by gar," he growled, as he ordered his other cannon loaded with chain shot that "crippled the largest British gun and killed or wounded six men."

By noon, two-thirds of the British guns had been put out of action. General Pakenham had just learned that a 2,000-man brigade of British reinforcements had arrived in the Mississippi Sound. It would take a few days to transfer them to his army; after that, Pakenham determined to go all out at the Americans, now a force of about 5,000. For the British, the matter of supplies was becoming desperate. Their army of 8,000 to 10,000 men had been on the Mississippi for nine days and had devoured their provisions, in addition to ransacking the surrounding plantations for food.

With New Orleans just a few miles in the rear, Jackson had no such problem, and Laffite's supply of munitions seemed endless. Still, Jackson was fearful. He was outnumbered; his position on the Rodriguez Canal was just about the only thing standing between the British and New Orleans. On January 7, he spent most of the afternoon in the heavily damaged Macarty house, observing the British encampment. "They will attack at daybreak," he predicted.

On Sunday morning, January 8, the final battle began. Despite heavy fire from the Americans, the British came on relentlessly. Then, on Jackson's left, the British 95th Regiment waded across the ditch in front of Jackson's line and, since no fascines or scaling ladders had yet arrived, began desperately trying to carve steps into the rampart with their bayonets. Meanwhile, against orders, the leading companies of the British 44th stopped and began to shoot at the Americans, but when they were answered by a ruinous volley from Carroll's Tennesseans and Gen. John Adair's Kentuckians, they ran away, setting into motion a chain of events that would soon shudder through the entire British Army. "In less time than one can write it," the British quartermaster E. N. Borroughs would recall, "the 44th Foot was swept from the face of the earth. Within five minutes the regiment seemed to vanish from sight."

At one point Jackson ordered his artillery batteries to cease firing and let the clouds of smoke blow away; in order to fix the British troops clearly for more of the same. In Battery No. 3, he observed Capt. Dominique You standing to his guns, his broad Gallic face beaming like a harvest moon, his eyes burning and swelling from the powder smoke. Jackson declared, "If I were ordered to storm the gates of hell, with Captain Dominique as my lieutenant, I would have no misgivings of the result."

In only 25 minutes, the British Army had lost all three of its active field generals, seven colonels and 75 other officers—that is, practically its whole officer corps. General Pakenham was dead, cut down by American rifle fire. By now the entire British Army was in irredeemable disarray. A soldier from Kentucky wrote, "When the smoke had cleared and we could obtain a fair view of the field, it looked at first glance like a sea of blood. It was not blood itself, but the red coats in which the British soldiers were dressed. The field was entirely covered in prostrate bodies."

Even Jackson was flabbergasted by the sight. "I never had so grand and awful an idea of the resurrection as on that day," he later wrote, as scores of redcoats rose up like dim purgatorial souls with their hands in the air and began walking toward the American lines. "After the smoke of the battle had cleared off somewhat, I saw in the distance more than five hundred Britons emerging from the heaps of their dead comrades, all over the plain, rising up, and . . . coming forward and surrendering as prisoners of war to our soldiers." These men, Jackson concluded, had fallen at the first fire and then hidden themselves behind the bodies of their slain brethren. By midmorning, most of the firing had ceased.

Laffite, who was returning from an inspection of his stores of powder and flints deep in the swamp, got to the grisly field just as the battle ended, but he did not know who had won. "I was almost out of breath, running through the bushes and mud. My hands were bruised, my clothing torn, my feet soaked. I could not believe the result of the battle," he said.

On the morning of January 21, the victorious troops marched in formation the six miles from the battlefield to New Orleans. Two days later, Jackson's army was drawn up on three sides of the city's parade ground. The Tennesseans and Kentuckians were there, too, as were Laffite's red-shirted Baratarian buccaneers. Bands played, church bells pealed and a celebratory cannonade roared from the banks of the levee.

Laffite felt a particular gratitude "at seeing my two elder brothers and some of my officers lined up in the parade . . . whom the public admired and praised with elegies and honor for their valor as expert cannoneers."

On February 6, President Madison sent out a proclamation pardoning Laffite and all the other Baratarians who had fought with the Army. Laffite assumed this also freed him to recover the property that had been confiscated by Commodore Patterson and Colonel Ross following their September raid on Grand Terre. Patterson and Ross disagreed; they had the property now and were backed up by the Army and the Navy. Laffite's lawyers flied suit, but Ross and Patterson began to auction off the property anyway; including 15 armed privateering ships. Laffite persuaded his old partners—who remained among the wealthiest and most influential citizens of New Orleans—to surreptitiously repurchase them for him, which they did. Laffite resumed preying on Spanish shipping under letters of marque from Cartagena.

In 1816, with some 500 of his men, he relocated to Galveston, 300 miles to the west. The Galveston enterprise quickly became profitable, and by 1818, Laffite had made arrangements to sell his captured goods to various merchants in the interior, as far away as St. Louis, Missouri. It wasn't long before the authorities in Washington got wind of his doings; President James Monroe sent a message to the effect that Laffite and his crews must depart Galveston or face eviction by U.S. troops.

Then, in late September 1818, a hurricane roared through Galveston Island, drowning a number of Laffite's men and wiping out most of the settlement's houses and buildings. Laffite set about rebuilding, managing to keep the authorities at bay for another two years. Finally, in 1821, he abandoned the Galveston redoubt and for all intents disappeared.

What became of him after Galveston has been the subject of much contradictory speculation. He was reportedly killed in a sea battle, drowned in a hurricane, hanged by the Spanish, succumbed to disease in Mexico, and murdered by his own crew.

If you believe his own journal—scholars disagree about its authenticity—Laffite had departed Galveston for St. Louis. There, he found God, married a woman named Emma Mortimere, fathered a son and settled down to the life of a landlubber.

According to the disputed memoir, at some point a chagrined Laffite, now turning portly, grew a beard and changed his name to John Lafflin. During his later years, he settled in Alton, Illinois, across the river from St. Louis, where he began writing a journal of his life. He lived there until his death in 1854 at the age of about 70.

He wrote in the memoir that he never got over the shabby treatment he felt he had received from the federal government and from the city he had risked his life and treasure to defend. And he mused bitterly over what might have happened if, instead of siding with the Americans, he had taken the British bribe. Answering his own hypothetical, he concluded that the Americans would have lost the battle, as well as Louisiana—and that there would have been no president of the United States named Andrew Jackson. The very name of Jackson, wrote Laffite, "would have tumbled into oblivion."

WINSTON GROOM is the author of numerous histories, including *1942: The Year That Tried Men's Souls, Shrouds of Glory* and *A Storm in Flanders,* as well as the novel *Forrest Gump.*

Women in the Early Republic

PATRICIA CLINE COHEN

The field of U.S. women's history in the early republic presents unusual opportunities and challenges for scholars and teachers. The four decades that separate 1790 from 1830 have until recently remained a relatively underworked segment of the field, being bracketed at either end by the revolutionary and the Jacksonian eras, two periods far more event-laden and therefore, frankly, easier to teach. A glance at general U.S. history survey textbooks for the high school and college markets confirms this: chapters on the Revolution introduce daughters of liberty and republican mothers and then typically drop women as a topic until the 1830s when the cult of domesticity, the Lowell mill girls, and female reformers and abolitionists take their turns briefly on the center stage. The traditional history of the intervening years of the early republic has long been framed by a narrative of political and economic events—the rise of the party system, contested elections, embargoes and the War of 1812, courts and banking, the Missouri Compromise, canals and steamboats. These events, of so masculine a cast, appeared to leave little room for attention to women.

But it was not merely an unrelentingly masculine narrative that squeezed out the women. In part, this hiatus developed because of the initial conceptualization of the field of women's history. Back in the early 1970s, an emerging generation of scholars in pursuit of women's past was naturally drawn to the mid nineteenth century, a period marked by women's social activism and the first women's rights movement. Here there were female public figures with life stories to be told, along with organizations, conventions, strikes, manifestos, and agendas to be explained. Historians were also able to recover patterns in the lives of ordinary white women, because the spread of female literacy generated abundant manuscript and printed sources. The books, periodicals, and newspapers of the period offered evidence both of real women's lives and of an all-encompassing, sentimentalized, often cloying ideology of women's proper sphere (variously called the cult of true womanhood or the cult of domesticity, terms pioneered by historians Barbara Welter and Aileen Kraditor in the 1960s). Private letters and diaries allowed more immediate access to the world of women and permitted reconstruction of daily domestic life, female friendships, and what was termed "women's culture," seen as distinctly different from the realm of men.

The revolutionary years also beckoned to early scholars, because the research questions were so compelling. How did this democratic revolution, stirred by high-minded pronouncements about the equality of all men and the civic virtue of citizens, make any difference to the place of women in the polity? Two signal books of 1980, Mary Beth Norton's *Liberty's Daughters* and Linda Kerber's *Women of the Republic,* led the way in showing the gradual politicization of women and the impact of revolutionary ideology on thinking about gender. Both books left off in the 1790s on a cautiously rising note, showing that some women were indeed beginning to claim a special female contribution to the healthy workings of the republic. Kerber coined the apt phrase "republican motherhood" to capture a sentiment promoted and widely endorsed in the 1790s: the idea that women best served the republic by becoming educated, virtuous mothers able to train their sons to be the thinking, rational citizens required by a government founded on the consent of the governed. In a bold stroke, republican motherhood incalculably advanced the cause of women's education and led to the founding of many female academies, even as it perpetuated the notion that women's most salient connection to the state was channeled through maternal duties. In short, the legacy of the revolution was mixed, one of potentialities that remained to be realized.

In contrast, the years after the 1790s and up to the Age of Jackson have been much less attended to. Let me venture to guess that most college courses in women's history skip right over it. With few timeline-worthy events to point to, and few famous women to anchor a lecture, the years understandably get short shrift, especially in a course that has to cover a lot of ground in ten or fourteen weeks. Yet the historical processes inaugurated during those early years clearly are crucial for explaining the newly evolving gender system of the later nineteenth century. I became convinced of this back in the 1980s, when I encountered the intense puzzlement of my students at the midpoint of my course. Lectures and readings would take them up through the Revolution, capped by the midterm exam; then the following week would open with the antebellum decades, leaving them to ask in bewilderment: what happened to those potentially powerful ideas about women's advancement through education? How could the stifling glorification of domesticity replace the sturdy version of woman's sphere exemplified by Abigail Adams and Mercy Otis Warren?

Texts produced for this specialized market perpetuate the problem, for they also bound over the chasm between republican motherhood and the cult of domesticity. Nancy Woloch's standard survey, *Women and the American Experience,* moves from a pair of chapters on the eighteenth century to a second pair on the early nineteenth, where the dates 1800–1860 appear in the chapter title but the content is framed by the inauguration of *Godey's Ladies Book,* founded in 1828. Sara Evans's *Born for Liberty* makes the same leap, moving from the end of the Revolution to a new chapter that starts with the 1820s. In a similar fashion, the classroom readings book edited by Mary Beth Norton and Ruth M. Alexander, *Major Problems in American Women's History,* contains no articles centrally concerned with the 1800–1830 period. And only in the very latest edition of the Linda Kerber and Jane DeHart reader, *Women's America,* has an early-nineteenth-century essay just been added, a study of sexual coercion by Sharon Bloch.

Yet during those decades, the stage was being set for the more dramatic changes in women's lives so apparent by the mid nineteenth century. The engines of change were mostly processes, rarely attributable to individual persons or discrete events, which only makes it harder to distill them for textbook presentation or locate them on a timeline. For example, the novel argument for female education first broached in the 1790s eventually led to the founding of many hundreds of public and private schools admitting girls, with inaugural dates dotted throughout the next four decades. As a result, by the 1830s literacy for white females was at an all-time high. In the field of law, important but incremental changes in some dozen states' statute codes and in legal practice slowly built up during the early national period; by the 1830s new patterns were evident in areas like divorce and tort actions for seduction. Such a transition reveals new ways of thinking about women, sexuality, and autonomy, but the piecemeal nature of the legal process thwarts easy generalization. Likewise, a slow accumulation of alterations in men's employment patterns and the gradual incursion of a wage-based economy slowly but powerfully exerted pressure on the social definitions of women's non-waged work; but it is hard to put a finger on the moment in time when those definitions actually changed. Finally, perhaps most difficult of all to explain or even to get a handle on at the level of the individual (because of thin documentation), there occurred a slow but impressive and unmistakable decline in the birth rate in the years from 1800 to 1820, kicking off a century-long descent of momentous proportions both for women's history and for all of American history.

Taken together, these trends in education, law, work, and fertility indicate that the years of the early republic set in motion large-scale forces with profound consequences for women. As subterranean social processes, they can be challenging to teach, especially to first time history students. A discussion of some pathways by which scholars have been mapping out this shadowy territory can suggest approaches for integrating the topic into the classroom.

Some scholars concentrate on women and politics, pushing beyond the 1790s' conception of republican motherhood to larger questions of the meaning of female citizenship. Linda Kerber remains at the center of this enterprise with two recent books: *Toward an Intellectual History of Women* and *No Constitutional Right to be Ladies.* In the latter book, Kerber takes up the interesting question of the obligations of citizenship (rather than the privileges, such as voting), and she locates

an 1805 lawsuit that wonderfully reveals contested notions of female citizenship in this transitional phase between republican motherhood and the cult of domesticity. The case involved the property rights of heirs of a loyalist wife who had fled America with her husband during the Revolutionary War. Was the wife a political traitor in her own right who therefore deserved to lose her dower property, confiscated by the state, or was she a mere feme covert, a legal nonperson obliged to accompany her husband? The judicial outcome was a clear victory for the common law of domestic relations: a wife could not presume to exercise political choice independent of her husband. One of the lawyers on the winning side elaborated: "If he commanded it [fleeing the country], she was bound to obey him, by a law paramount to all other laws—the law of God." The remarkable point, however, is that lawyers on the losing side were able even to frame and sustain the contrary argument—that women were political actors—up to the state supreme court.

Another teachable episode that reveals a sense of the possibilities for women opened by the Revolution—and then decidedly shut during the early republic—was the experience of suffrage in New Jersey. Between 1775 and 1807, the state constitution permitted all persons worth over fifty pounds to vote. Free blacks and single women were technically enfranchised under this provision, but not married women, who could have no independent claim to ownership of fifty pounds. Historians long regarded the provision as a fluke, a mistake by state law framers so certain of white male prerogative that they simply forgot to specify the sex and race of voters. But a recent article by Judith Apter Klinghoffer and Lois Elkis argues that it was intentional, demonstrates that some women claimed the vote, and then explains its demise in the changing political climate of the early 1800s.

Rosemarie Zagarri is at work on a book on women and politics in the 1790s, and a foretaste of her research appears in a 1998 article, "The Rights of Man and Woman in Post-Revolutionary America." A particularly accessible and highly readable book for entry-level college students is Zagarri's brief biography of a remarkable woman of the late eighteenth century, *A Woman's Dilemma: Mercy Otis Warren and the American Revolution.* The book carries Warren into her final two decades in the new republic, and in the process it illuminates the cooling receptivity of the country to talented public women. Sheila Skemp has published a concise version of the life of Judith Sargent Murray in the Bedford Books series, examining the intellectual career of the most advanced American thinker on the question of women's common humanity with men. Murray's writings, signed with the pseudonyms "Constantia" and "The Gleaner," generated considerable interest and debate in the 1790s, but a series of personal affronts and hurtful criticism caused her to withdraw from print after 1798. By the time she died in 1820, her protofeminism was nearly forgotten. Taken together, Kerber, Zagarri, and Skemp show us a remarkable array of public expressions of women's claim to near equality with men that pepper the 1790s and then disappear. One question near the top of the research agenda is to explain what restrained and subdued those ideas in the first two decades of the nineteenth century.

The history of women and religion in the early republic shows a similar pattern of eighteenth-century opportunity followed by declension. By 1800 women made up the majority of Protestant congregants, while the church hierarchy remained exclusively male. Recent work by Susan Juster finds that in some New England Baptist congregations, remarkably egalitarian practices took hold during the mid eighteenth century, only to be deliberately scaled back by the 1810s. And Catherine Brekus has brought to light over a hundred women preachers and exhorters active in the years 1740–1845, whose lives signify a startling infringement of the traditional prohibition against female public speaking and the exercise of religious authority.

One such woman, Jemina Wilkinson of Rhode Island, transformed herself into a genderless religious leader called The Universal Friend. The Friend eschewed gendered pronouns, adopted ambiguous but mostly male-style clothes, and led a group of some 250 followers into a settlement called New Jerusalem in upstate New York in the 1790s. Such unusual assertions of female leadership came in for serious criticism. Religious periodicals in the early 1800s printed frequent reminders of the biblical prohibition, "Let your women learn to keep silence in the churches." Brekus finds that not a few of the female preachers she so painstakingly resurrected were literally erased from the official records of their churches. The religious history of the early republic's Second Great Awakening encapsulates two contradictory tendencies: a rising value on women's special piety and enthusiastic participation, coupled with an ever-louder chorus of admonitions about women's God-ordained subordination to men.

One way to approach the puzzle of the early nineteenth century is to try to decipher the thoughts, feelings, and ambitions of women themselves, through a close analysis of letters and diaries. Female literacy advanced early enough in New England for Nancy Cott to undertake an extensive study of hundreds of diaries and letter collections, forming the backbone of *The Bonds of Womanhood.* Cott sorted her material into the thematic subjects of work, domesticity, education, religion, and sisterhood. One surprising finding was that many of the central ideas about women's natural piety and submissive nature—later codified by the prescriptive cult of domesticity of the 1830s—can be delineated in young girls' diaries of the century's opening decades. Glorification of domesticity as expressed by women's literary periodicals and advice books thus cannot be written off as a plot to subdue and infantilize young women who might otherwise be unruly, impertinent, or dangerously confident; in some sense, it had its origins among the young women themselves well before the 1830s.

Another study that engages in close analysis of a woman's diary is Laurel Thatcher Ulrich's superb study of a Maine midwife, *A Midwife's Tale.* Ulrich explores the mental world and daily life of a taciturn but observant, dedicated woman and meticulously reconstructs Martha Ballard's medical practice and social networks, showing along the way the gendered household economy of the Maine frontier and the courtship and sexual practices of the day.

Young women in Ballard's town in the 1790s participated in the waning years of a somewhat looser system of sexual regulation; to be pregnant and then marry—the reverse of the usual order—was not that uncommon around New England in the eighteenth century. Thirty-eight percent of the first births that Ballard delivered, in her career total of 814 deliveries, were to mothers who conceived before they were married. But in the early republic, prenuptial pregnancies began to plummet, and loss of virginity in women began to carry a terrible stigma. How such a sea change in courtship customs was inaugurated and enforced is one of the open and fascinating questions of the period of women's history. A partial look at the story in one town, Augusta, Maine—the same town Martha Ballard inhabited—is carried forward in my own book about a servant girl in Augusta, Helen Jewett, whose fall from virtue in the 1820s earned her the scorn of her employers and other townsfolk and directly set her on the path to a spectacular career in prostitution.

Ulrich's careful delineation of male and female work in Ballard's town shows us a social world where women's domestic labor intersected with men's and earned respect and value as a significant contribution to the household economy. Jeanne Boydston carries that story forward to the 1830s in *Home and Work.* Boydston presents a model analysis of how incremental changes in the nature of men's work slowly altered the value and sentiment attached to women's domestic labor. Boydston coined the phrase "the pastoralization of housework" to refer to the process by which housework lost its association with productive labor (in contrast to men's waged labor and market relations) and instead became sentimentalized as service provided as a feminine gift. Her book shows how behavior unchanged over time could mean very different things in separate eras. The housewife of 1780 and of 1820 faced much the same set of daily tasks, but the cultural meaning attached to housework had shifted and thereby rendered it invisible as work.

Finally, family law in the early republic remained mostly unchanged, with one important exception. Politicians in state after state framed new legal codes in light of republican theory and sentiment, but significantly failed to consider rewriting the rules on "Baron and Feme," as it was called, the ancient terms "lord and wife" indicating just how much reliance was placed on old legal customs that established wives as full dependents under husbands. The legal doctrine of feme covert, for example, remained in place as it had existed in English common law.

The one departure from English precedent was a significant one: state after state provided means for divorce. Norma Basch, in *Framing American Divorce,* locates the provision of divorce in the mix of Revolution-inspired legal change. Just as Americans had dissolved the bonds of empire with Britain in the Revolution, now the new states provided a way to dissolve the bonds of matrimony. Divorce was of course based on the finding of fault with one party, and it remained narrowly tied to specific offenses, but it was gender-neutral in its application and it was legally available in most states. In fact, not many couples resorted to legal divorce; the era of sharply rising divorce rates was at least another century away. But its availability and eclectic working in case after case under various state laws reveal much about the possibilities, tensions, and choices confronting women in the early republic.

The first forty years of the new nation were characterized by legal, economic, and cultural changes that shaped the lives of men and women throughout the rest of the nineteenth century.

The nature of the changes does not lend itself to the simplified history captured in a timeline, and probably for good reason we have found it most efficient to teach this period first by describing the world of the republican mother and then leaping to the world of the 1830s, comparing two different ideal-typical models. Filling in the intervening ground is an exciting task, however, and one that can be shared in the classroom with students who are prepared to think about the amorphous and complex nature of cultural change. After all, many of these same kinds of long-term trends and processes undergird the significant influences in their own lives today, where ideas about the value of work, sexuality, family life, and the relative equality of the sexes are all still contested and in flux.

Bibliography

Basch, Norma. *Framing American Divorce: From the Revolutionary Generation to the Victorians.* Berkeley: University of California Press, 1999.

Boydston, Jeanne. *Home and Work: Housework, Wages, and the Ideology of Labor in the Early Republic.* New York: Oxford University Press, 1991.

Brekus, Catherine A. *Strangers and Pilgrims: Female Preaching in America, 1740–1845.* Chapel Hill: University of North Carolina Press, 1998.

Cohen, Patricia Cline. *The Murder of Helen Jewett: The Life and Death of a Prostitute in Nineteenth-Century New York.* New York: Knopf, 1998.

Cott, Nancy F. *The Bonds of Womanhood: "Women's Sphere" in New England, 1780–1835.* New Haven: Yale University Press, 1977.

Evans, Sara M. *Born for Liberty: A History of Women in America.* New York: Free Press, 1997.

Juster, Susan. *Disorderly Women: Sexual Politics and Evangelicalism in Revolutionary New England.* Ithaca: Cornell University Press, 1994.

Kerber, Linda K. *No Constitutional Right to be Ladies: Women and the Obligations of Citizenship.* New York: Hill and Wang, 1998.

———. *Toward an Intellectual History of Women: Essays.* Chapel Hill: University of North Carolina Press, 1997.

———. *Women of the Republic: Intellect and Ideology in Revolutionary America.* Chapel Hill: University of North Carolina Press, 1980.

Kerber, Linda K. and Jane De Hart Matthews, eds. *Women's America: Refocusing the Past.* 5th ed. New York: Oxford University Press, 2000.

Klinghoffer, Judith Apter and Lois Elkis. *"'The Petticoat Electors': Women's Suffrage in New Jersey, 1776–1807."* Journal of the Early Republic 12 (1992): 159–93.

Norton, Mary Beth. *Liberty's Daughters: The Revolutionary Experience of American Women, 1750–1800.* Boston: Little, Brown, 1980.

Norton, Mary Beth and Ruth M. Alexander. *Major Problems in American Women's History.* 2d ed. Lexington, MA: D. C. Heath, 1996.

Skemp, Sheila L. *Judith Sargent Murray: A Brief Biography with Documents.* Boston: Bedford Books, 1998.

Ulrich, Laurel Thatcher. *A Midwife's Tale: The Life of Martha Ballard, Based on Her Diary, 1785–1812.* New York: Knopf, 1990.

Woloch, Nancy. *Women and the American Experience.* 2d edition. New York: McGraw-Hill, 1994.

Zagarri, Rosemarie. "The Rights of Man and Woman in Post-Revolutionary America." *William and Mary Quarterly* 55 (1998): 203–30.

———. *A Woman's Dilemma: Mercy Otis Warren and the American Revolution.* Wheeling, IL: Harlan Davidson, 1995.

PATRICIA CLINE COHEN has been a professor of history at the University of California at Santa Barbara for twenty-three years. She has authored two books: *A Calculating People: The Spread of Numeracy in Early America* and *The Murder of Helen Jewett: The Life and Death of a Prostitute in Nineteenth-Century New York.* She is also the co-author of a survey textbook, *The American Promise,* for which she wrote the chapters covering 1754–1840.

From *OAH Magazine of History,* Winter 2000. Copyright © 2004 by Organization of American Historians. Reprinted by permission via the Copyright Clearance Center.

African Americans in the Early Republic

GARY B. NASH

Any teacher using a textbook published before the 1980s would find virtually nothing on African Americans—slave or free, North or South—in the era of the American Revolution and the early republic. Though about 20 percent of the population, African Americans simply did not exist in the pre-1980s story of how the Revolution proceeded and how the search for "life, liberty, and the pursuit of happiness" affected those most deprived of these unalienable rights. Nor did textbooks take any notice of the free black churches, schools, and benevolent societies created by an emerging cadre of black leaders after the Revolution. A cursory examination of pre-1980s texts shows black history beginning when the first Africans arrived in Virginia in 1619 and then jumping magically over about two hundred years until the Missouri Compromise in 1820 produced heated arguments among white legislators over the spread of slavery. While older textbooks treat antebellum slavery and the rise of abolitionism after 1820 in some detail, they leave unnoticed the fast-growing free black communities of the North and upper South.

The outpouring of scholarship on African and African American history in the last third of this century, prompted by the civil rights movement and the opening up of the historical profession, has gradually remedied the astounding erasure of one-fifth of the American population in the nation's formative years. Yet many school textbooks today still lag a decade or more behind current scholarship on African Americans. Today, most students learn something about such figures as Olaudah Equiano, Crispus Attucks, and Richard Allen and have at least some notion that slaves and free blacks fought heartily in the American Revolution, began to throw off the shackles of slavery before the Emancipation Proclamation, and resisted slavery before Nat Turner's rebellion of 1831. Yet there is much still to be learned before the student graduating from high school can claim a basic grasp of both race relations during the nation's formative decades and the role of free and enslaved blacks in the nation's explosive growth. Five African American topics—some historians might add more—ought to be essential parts of the history curriculum that young Americans learn as they study the years between 1760 and 1830.

The Black American Revolution

African Americans, most born in the colonies but many in Africa, were deeply involved in the American Revolution and were deeply affected by it. The earliest black historians, wanting to stimulate racial pride and counter white hostility, focused on the few thousand blacks who fought with white Americans to gain their independence. Crispus Attucks, Salem Poor, and James Forten were typical of those who made blood sacrifices for "the glorious cause." But now, in a latter era when we can be more realistic about the American Revolution, students will readily understand why ten to twenty times as many slaves (along with some free blacks) fought with the British as with the American patriots. While white Americans discouraged or forbade black enlistment in state militias and the Continental Army, the British promised to grant perpetual freedom to any slave (or indentured servant) who fled his or her master to join the British forces.

The wholesale flight to the British, Benjamin Quarles wrote in his mold-breaking *Negro in the American Revolution,* had "one common origin, one set purpose—the achievement of liberty." This book, first published in 1961 and republished with an introduction by this author in 1996, is still the best one-volume account of the African Americans' American Revolution. In ringing phrases, Quarles wrote of how the "major loyalty" of blacks "was not to a place nor a people, but to a principle" and "insofar as he had freedom of choice, he was likely to join the side that made him the quickest and best offer in terms of those 'unalienable rights' of which Mr. Jefferson had spoken." This little secret about African American history ought to become common knowledge, without embarrassment or anger.

Much scholarship since Quarles's book has deepened our understanding of the massive slave rebellion that occurred during the American Revolution and the effect of white rhetoric about unalienable rights and British oppression on early abolitionists, white and black. Teachers wanting to present heroic figures who stood with the Americans can bring alive figures such as James Armistead Lafayette, the double spy who helped win the climactic battle at Yorktown, and the men of Rhode Island's black regiment. But those who struggled for freedom with the British present equally heroic stories, and their travails after the war, as they sought refuge in Nova Scotia and then returned to Africa to join the Sierra Leone experiment, are remarkable examples of endurance and unextinguishable hopes for the future. Sidney Kaplan's *Black Presence in the Era of the American Revolution,* first published in 1976 and republished in an expanded edition with Emma Nogrady Kaplan in 1989, is a teacher's goldmine. Little-known black figures leap off the pages of this fine book, which is studded with short primary sources suitable for classroom use and includes nearly every image of African Americans in the revolutionary generation that has come to light. In addition, part two of PBS's new four-part television series, *Africans in America,* is available for classroom viewing. Accompanied by a teacher-friendly companion volume by Charles Johnson, Patricia Smith, and the WGBH Research Team, the episode is a surefire way to jumpstart classes in both middle schools and high schools[1]. For teachers with advanced students who want to pursue black involvement in the American Revolution, the third section of Ira Berlin's *Many Thousands Gone* provides a comprehensive view of the revolutionary generation of African Americans, free and slave, in all parts of North America.

The Rise of Free Black Communities

One of the big stories untold in most textbooks even today concerns the rise of free black communities after the American Revolution. Blacks released from slavery, and those who made good their flight from bondage, commonly sought new lives in urban centers. In the North, they gathered especially in the seaports, with Philadelphia and New York attracting the largest black populations. They congregated also in Baltimore, Washington DC, Charleston, and smaller southern towns. In these urban places they constructed the foundations of free black life in the United States.

Especially important was the creation of free black churches, which were originally under white ecclesiastical control, but which became autonomous by 1816. Black leaders such as Absalom Jones and Richard Allen in Philadelphia; Peter Spencer in Wilmington, Delaware; and Peter Williams in New York City became not only apostles to their flocks but political spokespersons, entrepreneurs, and teachers. Many mini-biographies of these black founders are included in Kaplan and Kaplan's *Black Presence in the Era of the American Revolution* and in the five-volume *Encyclopedia of African American Culture and History,* edited by Jack Salzman, et al.

Students need to study how much a generation of blacks accomplished in building free black communities organized around churches and schools. How, one might ask, could those recently emerging from slavery (which taught slaves not to think for themselves and not to think of themselves as capable) find the inner resources and external support to create new names, form families, learn to read and write, find employment,

and create neighborhoods and social associations? One of the main themes of this quest for community was the notion that the only secure foundation of free black life was the construction of independent organizations embodying their sense of being a people within a people and relying on their own resources rather than on white benevolence. While coming to grips with this emerging sense of black autonomy and strength, students should recognize that mounting white hostility to free blacks complicated their struggle for family formation, work, education, respectability, civil rights, and justice before the law.

A torrent of scholarship in recent years traces how the Enlightenment ideals of the revolutionary generation crumbled by the early nineteenth century, how discrimination and violence against free blacks increased yet how the free black communities remained vibrant and enterprising. The three largest free black communities—Philadelphia, New York, and Baltimore—were studied respectively by this author in *Forging Freedom,* by Shane White in *Somewhat More Independent,* and by Christopher Phillips in *Freedom's Port.* Although too detailed for most students, they can be mined by teachers interested in explaining community building among free blacks. The surest way to capture the imaginations of students is to view part three of the PBS series *Africans in America* and read the parallel section of the companion book mentioned above.

Early Abolitionism

Most textbooks give only casual references to how the American Revolution fueled a prolonged debate over abolishing slavery. Nonetheless, this was a burning issue for the revolutionary generation and naturally a preoccupation of black American society. More than thirty years ago, Winthrop Jordan wrote, "It was perfectly clear that the principles for which Americans had fought required the complete abolition of slavery; the question was not *if,* but *when* and *how*"[2]. Twenty-four years ago, David Brion Davis wrote brilliantly on the rise of abolitionism—and on the exhaustion of it—in *The Problem of Slavery in the Age of Revolution, 1770–1823.* Both the rise and dissipation of abolitionist fervor ought to be understood in high school American history courses, and selected chapters of these two books can guide classroom discussions.

The North and upper South were the main theaters of abolitionism. Gradual legislated emancipation characterized northern attempts at eradicating chattel bondage while private (and limited) manumission characterized southern discomfort with the peculiar institution. Students need to understand how white economic interest and white abhorrence of the notion of freed slaves mingling on an equal standing with whites dashed revolutionary idealism, thus leaving the issue of slavery to another generation. This lesson of ideology facing off against economic interest and entrenched attitudes provides a weighty lesson for students to consider. The first two essays of this author's *Race and Revolution* discuss this and provide documents for classroom use on the rise and decline of abolitionism.

Two aspects of abolition ought to stick in students' minds. First, the freeing of slaves was not always benevolent, a simple case of morality transcending economic interest. Moreover, freedom came by degrees for emancipated slaves. They did not move from abject slavery to the light of freedom as if moving across the dark side of a river to the bright side. Legal emancipation did not confer full political rights, equal economic opportunity, or social recognition. All of that was denied and contested. Second, abolition was not engineered solely by high-minded whites. It was also produced, especially in the North, by slaves who made it their business to run away and perfect insolence to the point that their masters found slavery more trouble than it was worth.

Every American youngster studies the writing and ratification of the Constitution, but not all consider how the delegates to the 1787 convention in Philadelphia wrestled with the problem of slavery and the slave trade. Sparks will fly in classrooms where the teacher stages a debate pitting those who argue that the convention could—and should—have abolished slavery against those who argue that this was impossible at that point in time. The provocative essays in Paul Finkelman's *Slavery and the Founders* will help teachers construct lively classroom activities. Comparisons of how Washington and Jefferson—both professing to detest slavery and hoping to see it abolished in their own lifetimes—made their own decisions regarding their slave property can also be instructive. Available from the National Center for History in the Schools is a teaching unit utilizing primary documents and lesson plans to allow students to evaluate the positions taken during the congressional debates over slavery in the First Congress.[3]

The Spread of Slavery

Many opponents of slavery (and some defenders of it) believed that the slave population would gradually wither after slave importations ceased. But the first state censuses after the Revolution showed that slavery was growing in spite of a wartime hiatus in importations. When Eli Whitney's invention of the cotton gin in 1793 gave a tremendous boost to the production of short-staple cotton, slavery acquired a powerful new lease on life. The cotton gin gave new incentives for reopening the slave trade and insured that slavery would spread rapidly into the deep South where the demand for field hands grew enormously between 1800 and 1830. Berlin's *Many Thousands Gone* provides a fine account of how lawmakers in the lower South defended the expansion of slave society and how large slaveholders consolidated their power as the region's ruling class.

The growth of slavery amidst gradual emancipation needs to be understood. From about 470,000 slaves in 1770, the population grew to about 720,000 in 1790 and 1,200,000 in 1810 (while the population of free blacks grew from about 60,000 in 1790 to 185,000 in 1810). Also notable, the coming of King Cotton led to massive interregional transfers of slaves. The cotton revolution precipitated the widespread sale of slaves from the upper to lower South—a brutal process involving a kind of new Middle Passage that sundered thousands of slave

families. Students can learn about this through Toni Morrison's poignant historical novel *Beloved* (which is also available in movie form).

Life under slavery is generally studied during the decades preceding the Civil War, but teachers may have time to delve into this as part of the curriculum that deals with the early republic. Some fine, accessible essays and excellent visual material are available in Edward Campbell's edited volume *Before Freedom Came*.

Black Resistance in the New Nation

If Congress did not listen to petitioners who urged the end of slavery; if hard-nosed economic realities about the profitability of slavery submerged idealistic hopes for a new nation cleansed of its most important cancer; if by the early nineteenth century it became clear that the new nation was to be defined as a white man's republic; then how would slaves and free blacks respond, and how would they carry on their lives? Several rich veins of scholarship have explored this question, and some of the new work ought to make its way into precollegiate classrooms.

One topic well worth discussing is the Haitian Revolution of 1791-1804, the long, slave-centered revolt against the powerful and brutal French slave regime in Saint Domingue. Textbooks hardly mention the prolonged revolution in Haiti, yet it was of signal importance. It was the first racial war to overthrow a European colonial power; the first instance of mass self-emancipation by a populous slave society; the first creation of a black republic in the Americas in the midst of the slaveholding West Indies; and the event that made the Louisiana Territory nearly useless to France, since its main importance was supplying the foodstuffs to feed the hundreds of thousands of French slaves in the Caribbean. Ironically, Jefferson's acquisition of the Louisiana Territory vastly extended the American domain suitable for enslaved labor.

Students can also explore how the Haitian Revolution spread the spark of black rebellion to the United States and how Haiti became a beacon of freedom and an inspiration for all who hoped for the overthrow of slavery. Students can also consider how it produced a morbid fear of black insurrection while dampening white manumitting instincts. Jefferson's personal inner conflict is illuminating. As president, he encouraged the black overthrow of slavery in Saint Domingue and applauded black independence. But he refused to recognize the black government when it came to power in 1804 and worked to quarantine or neutralize Haiti commercially in deference to the interests of southern planters.

Another part of the continuing struggle of African Americans for freedom involved open resistance. Gabriel's Rebellion of 1800 in Virginia and Denmark Vesey's plot in 1822 in South Carolina, both inspired in part by the Haitian Revolution, are well known; but many other smaller insurrections and plots deserve attention, particularly the flight of slaves to the British forces in the War of 1812, paralleling the Revolutionary

War attempts by blacks to cash in on British offers of freedom. Much of this resistance is captured in part three of the PBS video series *Africans in America* and in the companion book cited above.

Another aspect of the search for liberty and equality among free and slave, in both the North and South, is the remarkable growth of Afro-Christianity in the early nineteenth century. A transformative process among African Americans living under slavery, it was a resistance movement in its own right, and it had much to do with their ability to endure captivity. Sylvia Frey and Betty Wood's *Come Shouting to Zion* is a rich treatment of this topic. The book pays particular attention to the role of women in fashioning black churches. The northern chapter of this quest for spiritual autonomy and the building of black churches as citadels of social, political, and psychological strength is movingly told by Vincent Harding in chapters three and four of *There is a River*. Many mini-biographies of black church leaders appear in Kaplan and Kaplan's *Black Presence in the Era of the American Revolution* and *The Encyclopedia of African-American Culture and History*.

One final aspect of black resistance that deserves attention involves emigrationist schemes. African Americans, led notably by the mixed-blood merchant and mariner Paul Cuffe, had toyed with immigrating to the African homelands since the 1780s and, after 1804, to Haiti and Canada. But the larger part of the story involves the launching of the American Colonization Society (ACS) in 1816. Historians have argued for many years about the strange mixture of northern clergy, southern slaveowners, and a few free black leaders who came together to promote the voluntary emigration of free blacks to what would become Liberia. The interest of African American leaders was centered in the belief that the rising tide of white hostility to free blacks made repatriation to Africa the only viable option. However, the mass of free blacks correctly understood that the ACS (notwithstanding the fact that some northern clergy who joined the ACS were sincere abolitionists who dwelled on the glory of African Americans returning to their homelands to Christianize black Africa) was for southern leaders a deportation scheme that would remove incendiary free blacks from the United States and provide cover for slavery's expansion.

Most teachers will not have time to explore the mixed motives of the ACS and its limited success. However, at the least they can interest students in how the ACS's emigrationist schemes reflected the crossroads at which the new republic stood. On the one hand, whites who were unwilling to give free blacks real equality and were eager to cleanse the country of them enthusiastically supported the ACS emigrationist efforts. On the other hand, this passion to encourage a back-to-Africa movement galvanized free black leaders who now understood that a new militance and a new inter-city league of black spokespersons were required to keep their revolutionary era hopes alive.

None of the five topics outlined above should be thought of as self-contained *African American* topics. Rather they are *American* history topics. Occupying vastly different social places, white and black Americans were linked together by a common quest for freedom, though freedom had many meanings and required various strategies to achieve. Their lives were intertwined whether on slave plantations, in cities, or on ships at sea. Their productive efforts were part of the development of the expanding nation. Great events outside the United States, such as the French and Haitian Revolutions, left imprints on everybody. While drawing attention to topics vital to the African American experience in the era of the American Revolution and the early republic, this essay is a plea for restoring to memory African American topics that are indispensable elements of the larger American story.

Notes

1. Charles Richard Johnson, et al., *Africans in America: America's Journey through Slavery* (New York: Harcourt Brace and Company, 1998); and *Africans in America: America's Journey through Slavery,* produced by WGBH Educational Foundation, 270 min., PBS Video, 1998, videocassette. Teaching kits are also available through WGBH. For more information or to order, write WGBH, 125 Western Avenue, Boston, MA 02134 or call (617) 300-5400.

2. Winthrop Jordan, *White over Black: American Attitudes Toward the Negro, 1550–1812* (Chapel Hill: University of North Carolina Press, 1968), 342.

3. Copies of the teaching unit, *Congress Debates Slavery, 1790–1800,* are available for $12 from The National Center for History in the Schools, 6265 Bunche Hall, UCLA, 405 Hilgard Avenue, Los Angeles, CA 90095.

Sources Cited

Africans in America: America's Journey through Slavery, produced by WGBH Educational Foundation. 270 min. PBS Video, 1998. Videocassette.

Beloved, produced by Harpo Films and Clinica Estetico. Directed by Jonathan Demme. 172 min. Touchstone Home Video, 1998. Videocassette.

Berlin, Ira. *Many Thousands Gone: The First Two Centuries of Slavery in North America.* Cambridge: Harvard University Press, 1998.

Campbell, Edward D. C., Jr., ed. *Before Freedom Came: African-American Life in the Antebellum South.* Richmond, VA: Museum of the Confederacy, 1991.

Davis, David Brion. *The Problem of Slavery in the Age of Revolution, 1770-1823.* Ithaca: Cornell University Press, 1975.

Finkelman, Paul. *Slavery and the Founders: Race and Liberty in the Age of Jefferson.* New York: M. E. Sharpe, 1996.

Frey, Sylvia and Betty Wood. *Come Shouting to Zion: African American Protestantism in the American South and British Caribbean to 1830.* Chapel Hill: University of North Carolina Press, 1998.

Harding, Vincent. *There is a River: The Black Struggle for Freedom in America.* New York: Harcourt Brace Jovanovich, 1981.

Johnson, Charles Richard, et al. *Africans in America: America's Journey through Slavery.* New York: Harcourt Brace and Company, 1998.

Kaplan, Sidney and Emma Nogrady Kaplan. *The Black Presence in the Era of the American Revolution.* Amherst: University of Massachusetts Press, 1989.

Morrison, Toni. *Beloved.* New York: Knopf, 1987.

Nash, Gary B. *Forging Freedom: The Formation of Philadelphia's Black Community, 1720-1840.* Cambridge: Harvard University Press, 1988.

——. *Race and Revolution.* Madison, WI: Madison House, 1990.

Phillips, Christopher. *Freedom's Port: The African American Community of Baltimore, 1790-1860.* Urbana: University of Illinois Press, 1998.

Quarles, Benjamin. *The Negro in the American Revolution.* 1961. Reprint, Chapel Hill: University of North Carolina Press, 1996.

Salzman, Jack, et al., eds. *Encyclopedia of African-American Culture and History.* 5 vols. New York: MacMillan Library Reference, 1996.

White, Shane. *Somewhat More Independent: The End of Slavery in New York City, 1770-1810.* Athens: University of Georgia Press, 1991.

GARY B. NASH is a professor of history at the University of California, Los Angeles, and is the author of many books and articles on race, class, and society in the early republic, including *Red, White, and Black: The Peoples of Early America* (1974, 4th ed. 2000). A Guggenheim Fellow, and finalist for the Pulitzer Prize for his book *The Urban Crucible,* Nash is a former president of the Organization of American Historians (1994–1995). He served as co-chair for the National History Standards Project and currently directs UCLA's National Center for History in the Schools.

From *OAH Magazine of History,* Winter 2000, pp. 12–16. Copyright © 2000 by Organization of American Historians. Reprinted by permission via the Copyright Clearance Center.

Liberty Is Exploitation
The Force of Tradition in Early Manufacturing

Barbara M. Tucker

The industrial revolution represented a watershed in American history. The transition from agriculture to manufacturing was neither an even nor an easy process. The factory floor became a contested and negotiated place, in which the very shape of the work-place depended upon the outcome of struggles between management and labor and between the demands of the factory system and traditional values observed by families. Change occurred at a different pace in various industries as production moved from the household to the workshop and then to the factory. It was the factory system, however, that had the most dramatic impact on the production process and helped to change the economic and social direction of the new nation.

In the historiography of the early republic, the rise of the factory system has received considerable scholarly attention. Beginning in the 1970s, a plethora of monographs were published on the economic and social transformation of such industries as boots and shoes, textiles, paper, and armaments. The customary concerns of economic and business historians, however, did not dominate the discussion; instead, a "new labor history" emerged. These scholars emphasized the impact of the new industrial order on the people who worked in the shops and factories that appeared between 1790 and 1860 and followed them from their workplaces to their communities, homes, churches, and social activities. Issues of paternalism, class, and gender informed their works.

Alan Dawley and Paul Faler were among the most significant innovators in this changing field. Their work on the boot and shoe industry of Lynn, Massachusetts, partly focused on the stress caused when laborers and shoe manufacturers ceased to share a common work space or ideology. This simple change in manufacturing relations profoundly affected the town of Lynn, its neighborhoods, churches, and political structure.[1]

Other scholars turned to the textile industry, in particular Thomas Dublin, who authored a work that challenged the romanticized view of the Lowell system. With eleven investors, Francis Cabot Lowell had formed the Boston Manufacturing Company in 1813. This was one of the most innovative companies organized during the early republic, a corporation characterized by professional management, large-scale production of yarn and cloth, and a unique labor force comprised of girls and women. Dublin challenged the sentimental view of labor-management relations advanced by others. He argued that the relationship between labor and management was an economic one and that the female workers recognized it as such. Whatever community of interests emerged in Waltham and later Lowell and Lawrence, Massachusetts, was among the girls and women themselves and not between labor and management. "When women workers spoke of independence," Dublin writes, "they referred at once to independence from their families and from their employers."[2] While the Lowell system embraced a new production system, its development did not overspread the entire textile industry and remained largely confined to the regions north of Boston. Throughout most of the country, cloth continued to be produced in homes and shops on hand looms. And spinning mills, not integrated corporations, supplied workers with the necessary yarn. Many of these processes were patterned after the system introduced by Samuel Slater.

Born in England and trained under the progressive factory master Jedediah Strutt, Samuel Slater brought the Arkwright system of yarn manufacturing to the United States. Around 1790 he formed a partnership with William Almy and Obadiah Brown to build a factory for the production of yarn. (Parenthetically, most accounts link Almy with Moses Brown, who placed the ad to which Slater responded. Actually, in this partnership Smith Brown, not Moses Brown, first entered the agreement and was later replaced by Obadiah Brown.) Under their arrangement, Slater built carding engines, water frames, and a carding and roving machine which he temporarily installed in a clothier's shop in nearby Pawtucket, Rhode Island, while Almy and Brown supplied the capital. Boys were hired to operate the equipment; within weeks, he doubled his labor force and eventually moved his operations to a specially built factory. Following a practice adopted in England, young children between seven and twelve years of age were employed to operate the new equipment. Initially they were drawn from local families, but as the need for workers increased. Slater turned to the apprentice system. In 1794 he advertised for "four or five active Lads, about 15 Years of Age to serve as Apprentices in the Cotton Factory."[3]

Local poor law officials answered Slater's advertisement and sent indigent boys to the mills. But apprentices proved problematic. Some resented Slater's control over them and his disciplinary style, while others were appalled by the demanding schedule that required them to work from twelve to sixteen hours a day, six days a week. They learned few skills, received room and board in lieu of wages, and were forced to attend Sunday Schools operated by Slater where they received educational training. Many ran away. By 1797 Slater noted that one Rehoboth boy ran away and another followed, and "again If it is suffered to pass, another will go tomorrow & so on until they are all gone."[4] Another form of labor had to be found.

Slater now turned to poor families throughout the area and invited them to send their children to the mill. This form of pauper labor also presented problems. Slater needed the children but not their parents, who resented Slater's control over their children and complained about the irregularity of wage payments and the lack of light and heat in the factories. Some threatened to keep their children home while others entered the factory and withdrew their children without notice, thereby stopping the machines. Slater was exasperated. He had little control over some of the complaints voiced by the parents. Almy and Brown were responsible for paying the families in cash or in kind, but often they were not able to keep their commitments. Slater protested: "You must not expect much yarn until I am better supplied with hands and money to pay them with several are out of corn and I have not a single dollar to buy any for them." The situation was not rectified and Slater again pleaded with Almy and Brown. Send "a little money if not I must unavoidably stop the mill after this week." He could not "bear to have people come round me daily if sometimes hourly and saying I have no wood nor corn nor have not had any several days. Can you expect my children to work if they have nothing to eaf?[5] In desperation, he threatened to close the mill and sell the machinery.

Pauper labor was not the answer, and Slater turned to the family system. In New England the family was the basic economic unit. The householder still dominated the family economy, and he retained considerable authority within it to discipline wife and children, protect kin, lead the family in prayer, and supervise the educational and moral training of sons and daughters. Men fought and children resisted attempts by Slater to encroach on these prerogatives. To recruit and retain a labor force of children. Slater had to find common ground with householders. He had to effect some sort of compromise with parents whereby their customary values and their social and economic position within the family and the wider society would be safeguarded and respected. Slater sought to strengthen patriarchy, not challenge it. He recruited entire families to work for him, and a division of labor developed based on age and gender. Householders were brought under the control of the factory master, but they were not required to enter the factory and work alongside their children. Instead, Slater employed them in traditional jobs such as night watchman, painter, mason, and later farm hand. He strengthened their position within the family by having householders negotiate and sign contracts for the employment of their children and personally receive all wages earned by them.

Labor contracts suggest the strength and influence householders exerted over manufacturers. At the Slater and Kimball factory, contracts usually were signed annually beginning April 1. Abel Dudley, for example, agreed to work in 1827, and he put five children in the mill: Sumner, Mary, Eliza, Abigail, and Caroline. He stipulated, however, that "Mary and Caroline have the privilege of going to school two months each one at a time and Amos is to work at 4/pr week when they are out."[6] Some contracts included other stipulations: a child was allowed to work with the mule spinner and taught his trade; either party had to give two weeks notice before quitting; householders were to receive extra pay for Sunday work. Thus, in order to recruit and retain a stable labor force, Samuel Slater struck a compromise with New England householders. If Slater respected their traditional prerogatives, they would provide him with a plentiful, tractable supply of workers. For those families who failed to adhere to this understanding. Slater had a solution. The case of Obadiah Greenhill was typical. On April 1, 1827, Greenhill placed five children from nine to seventeen years of age in Slater's factory. On October 6, the family was "Dismissed for manifesting a disposition to make disturbance in the mills amongst the help and for misconduct in general."[7]

The force of tradition that operated in the factories was extended to village, home, and church. The new factory villages Slater established reflected the needs of New England families. Slatersville was one of the first mill villages developed by Slater and served as a model for later manufacturers:

> Like many of the towns of colonial New England, it was built around a broad road that traversed the town center. The smithy, the dry goods stores, the church, and the school were on this road. Predictably, the Congregational church stood in the geographic center of the village and was surrounded by a broad common. Toward the outskirts of the village lived more than six hundred textile workers, farm laborers, merchants, and mechanics. Their homes were one- and two-story detached and semi-detached dwellings that were built parallel to the main road and separated from one another by garden plots. Each dwelling was occupied by a single family. No house stood isolated from the central community. The mill and its outbuildings . . . did not disturb the traditional sense of community. They were built at a short distance from the village and were surrounded by fenced and tilled fields belonging to the company.[8]

The family and the church were the predominant forces in the lives of many residents. Familial and religious doctrines and discipline served as the basis for a well-ordered society and also a well-run factory. Values taught in the home and the church served the needs of the factory masters.

In the nineteenth century, the home became a training ground for a generation of factory hands. The first law of childhood, the one necessary for the proper maintenance of good family government and obviously the one necessary for the proper maintenance of good order within the factory, was unquestioning obedience. All commands had to be immediately and, in fact, cheerfully obeyed. If obedience was the first law of childhood, then deference was the second. According to nineteenth-century educator Heman Humphrey, "children must early be brought under absolute parental authority, and must submit to all the rules and regulations of the family during the whole period of their minority, and even longer, if they choose to remain at home."[9] These values were reinforced by the church.

Samuel Slater was one of the first manufacturers to establish schools for factory children. Called Sunday Schools, they later were brought under the supervision of local churches. In Webster, Massachusetts—a Slater company town—the Methodist Church played a leading role in the discipline of factory children. The written tracts, hymns, and sermons found in the church advanced a familiar message: obedience, deference, industry, punctuality, and temperance. Such lessons prepared the child and adolescent operatives for salvation and also trained them to be good, obedient factory hands. The Webster Sabbath School Constitution reinforced these notions. In part it read:

To be regular in attendance, and punctually present at the hour appointed to open school.

To pay a strict and respectful attention to whatever the teacher or Superintendent shall say or request.

To avoid whispering, laughing and any other Improper conduct.[10]

Manufacturers throughout New England and the Mid-Atlantic states adopted many of the features developed by Slater. Philadelphia, for example, became a center for hand-loom weaving. This occurred even after power looms had been installed in Waltham and Lowell. In the Kensington section of Philadelphia, weavers "turned out cotton cloth on hand frames in tiny red-brick cottages lined up in monotonous rows on grid-like streets." A local resident of the area observed that the "sound of these looms may be heard at all hours in garrets, cellars, and out-houses, as well as in the weavers' apartments."[11] Among these weavers a distinct culture emerged. Workers generally owned their own looms, regulated their own time, and observed traditional feasts and holidays. They were a group of especially independent and proud men. Their craft world was "a man's dominion, the weaver's prowess an element in the constitution of patriarchal family relations."[12] But by the 1840s the industry began to change. Adjacent to their dwellings, some men constructed wooden buildings or sheds, either purchased looms outright and hired weavers to operate them, or opened their sheds to weavers who brought their own equipment with them. By the Civil War, a weaver earned from $3.00 to $4.50 per week, a wage insufficient to support a family.[13] Their children often had to work in the spinning mills. Slater's efforts to preserve the patriarchy of the fathers in effect reduced their offspring to permanent children—as opposed to the apprenticeship model that implied growth and eventual maturity.

While the spinning mills that supplied yarn to the weavers of Kensington were patterned after those started by Slater, there were differences. This was especially true for the treatment of labor. In Philadelphia, where hand loom weaving persisted well into the mid-century, the treatment of young child operatives in textile mills caused a public scandal. In 1837 a Select Committee was formed by the Pennsylvania Senate to investigate conditions of labor, especially the employment of children under twelve in the state's textile mills. One adult worker, William Shaw, commented extensively on the work and treatment of children. Most of the youngest children were employed at carding and spinning and worked from twelve to fourteen hours per day. Shaw commented further: "I have known children of nine years of age to be employed at spinning[;] at carding, as young as ten years. Punishment, by whipping, is frequent; they are sometimes sent home and docked for not attending punctually." Another witness, Joseph Dean, offered similar testimony. At his factory one-third to one-half of the operatives were under the age of twelve. He described the attitudes toward the children: "The children were occasionally punished by a blow from the hand; does not know that the strap was used. . . . Males and females were provided with separate water closets, when provided at all; no pains taken on the subject: sometimes none were provided." Another witness, Robert Craig, described some of the working conditions experienced by the young workers:

"the children must stand all the time at their work, walking backwards and forwards; the children often complain of fatigue; witness has been many of them neglect their work, from exhaustion, and seek repose in sleep; for this, they are generally punished. . . . The greatest evil, in my mind, is that the children, from nine to eleven years old, are required to carry up from one to four stories, a box of bobbins; these boxes weight about sixteen pounds; they are carried on the head."[14]

Some labor leaders and educators—Seth Luther, Horace Mann, and Henry Barnard, among others—called for an end to child labor. While legislation was passed, it failed to solve the problem. In 1842 Massachusetts declared that children under twelve could not work more than ten hours per day. Six years later Pennsylvania passed laws stating that minors could not work over ten hours a day or sixty hours per week. But by special contract, boys and girls over fourteen could work longer.[15] And then, of course, enforcement of these laws became problematic. Who was to enforce the laws and who was to be the final arbiter in determining the age of the children?

By the time child labor laws were passed, conditions within the industry had begun to change. The industry experienced several economic downturns, especially in 1829 and chronically from 1836 to 1844. Companies took the opportunity to reorganize, and Samuel Slater was no exception. In 1829 Slater feared insolvency. He had endorsed notes and was not able to pay them without first liquidating and reorganizing his holdings. He relinquished partial control of his business to his three sons and formed Samuel Slater and Sons. Other changes included the introduction of cost accounting, the employment of paid professional managers, and incorporation. The labor force was not exempt. Family labor and many of the traditional prerogatives associated with it ended. Each hand was hired, paid, assigned jobs, and disciplined by the factory manager. Young people now could contract for themselves, and this had an important impact on the family. Economically independent now, adolescents could negotiate with parents over the price of room and board, education, discipline, dress, marriage partners, and life style. Some left home and moved into boarding houses or traveled to other mill towns looking for work. If men wanted to remain with the company, they now had to enter the mills and labor alongside their women and children, suffering an implicit loss of status. This trend spread throughout the textile industry. The paternalism that once served the needs of labor and management was discarded by manufacturers; increasingly, the Slater system came to resemble Lowell.

Less expensive hands could be found, and by the 1840s French Canadian and Irish immigrants replaced many Yankee families in the mills. Factory owners no long felt compelled to accommodate adults. Next to their factories they erected multi-family tenements and boarding houses. Built side by side along a roadway, the small wooden tenements housed from three to four families plus their boarders. Rooms were small, windows were few, storage space was limited, and garden plots were eliminated altogether. Physically the tenements, boarding houses, and factory now formed a distinct unit; the factory dominated work and home life. Overcrowding occurred, health deteriorated, and mortality rates increased. Deaths from dysentery, convulsions, lung fever, delirium tremors, dropsy, erysipelas, typhus, and of course consumption or tuberculosis were recorded. In the 1840s typhus reached epidemic proportions, striking Webster, Massachusetts, first in 1843, then again in 1844 and 1846. Consumption was endemic, and children often were its victims. Indeed, child mortality rates were high, and young children even succumbed to convulsions and "teething."[16] Several possibilities could account for such infant deaths. To quiet a crying child, parents might give him or her a drug such as laudanum; some of these children could have overdosed on opiates. Or vitamin and mineral deficiencies, including a lack of calcium, magnesium, and vitamin D, might have caused convulsions and resulted in death. As two historians suggest, however, "teething is suspect because nineteenth century physicians observed that the convulsions which ravaged babies often occurred during the teething process and concluded that the sprouting of teeth was somehow responsible—hence 'teething' as a cause of death." It has been argued that the primary source of calcium for children came from mother's milk; during teething, some women ceased to breast feed children and turned to bovine milk. This abrupt shift sometimes triggered convulsions, but people mistakenly blamed the child's death on teething.[17]

By the 1850s manufacturers with clear economic interests and goals considered labor just another cost of production. Paternalism and the force of traditional social relations gave way under changing conditions. Individual hands replaced family units in the mills; manufacturers enlarged their mills and increased their labor supply. Little attention was given to the quality of life in the factory towns. Overcrowding, disease, high mortality rates, frequent labor turnover, crime, and illiteracy came to characterize life in these communities. The factories and villages of 1850 bore scant resemblance to traditional rural manufacturing communities of 1800. In the end, neither innovators such as Lowell nor conservative paternalists such as Slater had been able to prevent the transformation of factory labor into a commodity with a price—the living wage—to be set by supply and demand.

Notes

1. Alan Dawley, *Class and Community: The Industrial Revolution in Lynn* (Cambridge, MA: Harvard University Press, 1976) and Paul G. Faler, *Mechanics and Manufacturers in the Early Industrial Revolution: Lynn, Massachusetts, 1780–1860* (Albany: State University of New York Press, 1981).

2. Thomas Dublin, *Women at Work: The Transformation of Work and Community in Lowell, Massachusetts, 1826–1860* (New York: Columbia University Press, 1979), 95.

3. *Providence Gazette,* October 11, 1794, quoted in Brendan F. Gilbane, "A Social History of Samuel Slater's Pawtucket, 1790–1830" (Ph.D. diss., Boston University Graduate School, 1969), 247. Much of this essay is based on the author's book; see Barbara M. Tucker, *Samuel Slater and the Origins of the American Textile industry, 1790–1860* (Ithaca, NY: Cornell University Press, 1984).

4. Ibid., 78.

5. Ibid., 84.

6. Slater and Kimball vol. 3. contract. Abel Dudley, 1827. Samuel Slater Collection. Baker Library, Harvard University, Cambridge, Massachusetts.

7. Ibid., Obadiah Greenhill, 1827.

8. Tucker, *Samuel Slater and the Origins of the American Textile Industry,* 126.

9. Heman Humphrey. *Domestic Education* (Amherst, MA; J, S. & C. Adams, 1840), 41.

10. "Constitution of the Methodist Episcopal Church Sabbath School," 1861–1863, United Church of Christ, Webster, Massachusetts.

11. Bruce Laurie. *Working People of Philadelphia, 1800–1850* (Philadelphia: Temple University Press, 1980), IL. See also, Edwin T. Freedley. *Philadelphia and Its Manufactures: A Handbook Exhibiting the Development, Variety, and Statistics of the Manufacturing Industry of Philadelphia in 1857* (Philadelphia: Edward Young, 1859). 253.

12. Philip Scranton, *Proprietary Capitalism: The Textile Manufacture at Philadelphia, 1800–1885* (Cambridge: Cambridge University Press, 1983), 195.

13. Freedley, *Philadelphia and Its Manufactures,* 254.

14. Pennsylvania General Assembly. Senate, *Report of the Select Committee Appointed to Visit the Manufacturing Districts of the Commonwealth, for the Purpose of Investigating the Employment of Children in Manufactories, Mr. Peltz, Chairman.* (Harrisburg, PA: Thompson & Clark, Printers. 1838), 12–16.

15. Elizabeth Otey, *Beginnings of Child Labor Legislation in Certain States; a Comparative Study,* vol. VI of *Report on Condition of Woman and Child Wage-Earners in the United*

States. Prepared under the direction of Chas. P. Neill, Commissioner of Labor. 61st. Cong., 2nd. Sess., (Washington, DC: Government Printing Office, 1910), 207–8.

16. Tucker, *Samuel Slater and the Origins of the American Textile Industry,* 232. See also Webster, Massachusetts. Vital Statistics, Deaths. Emory Hough, November 1853 and Lewis Johnson, 1844, 1845.

17. Kenneth F. Kiple and Virginia H. Kiple, "Slave Child Mortality: Some Nutritional Answers to a Perennial Puzzle." *Journal of Social History* 10 (March 1977): 291–92. The Kiples

believe that convulsions and teething as a cause of death were misunderstood. The children had tetany, a disease not recognized at the time.

BARBARA M. TUCKER is Professor of History and Director of the Center for Connecticut Studies at Eastern Connecticut State University. She is the author of *Samuel Slater and the Origins of the American Textile Industry, 1790–1860* and has published articles in such journals as *Labor History, Business History Review, Agricultural History* and *Journal of the Early Republic.*

From Detroit to the Promised Land

Two escaped slaves from Kentucky touched off riots in Detroit and set an international legal precedent.

KAROLYN SMARDZ FROST

Detroit Sheriff John M. Wilson glanced anxiously upward. From the courtroom balcony came the sounds of angry muttering and restless shuffling. Peering down over the railing were dozens of black faces.

Before him stood a young couple, well-dressed and respectful toward Judge Henry Chipman, who occupied the bench of the Wayne County, Courthouse that Saturday morning in 1833. Thornton Blackburn, 21, and his beautiful wife, Ruthie, some nine years his senior, were accused of being fugitives from slavery. According to Michigan law, those claimed as runaways had to prove themselves entitled to free status before a judge or magistrate. While no black could testify on his or her own behalf against a white claimant, the law guaranteed a legal defense to ensure that the genuinely free could not be carried off to a life of bondage. After all, slave catchers, the unscrupulous bounty hunters who captured runaways and returned them to their Southern owners, had been known to kidnap free blacks and sell them into slavery. Detroit city attorney Alexander D. Frazier was tasked with defending the accused.

Despite an impassioned defense by Frazier, the case was not going well for the Blackburns. They had been unable to produce certificates of manumission, the documentation registered in a local courthouse when a Southern slave was legally freed by his or her owner. On the other hand, the Kentucky attorney employed by the Blackburns' owners, Benjamin G. Weir, and Talbot Clayton Oldham, the nephew of Thornton's owner who had traveled to Detroit to identify him, had presented signed affidavits stating that the Blackburns were both "fugitives from labor."

The Blackburns had lived in Detroit for two years after a harrowing escape from Kentucky. Ruthie had been auctioned off to a Louisville merchant named Virgil McKnight—who was suspected of buying groups of Kentucky slaves to then sell to Southern markets. The couple fled in a bold and incredibly dangerous escape in broad daylight. Traveling up the Ohio River by steamboat as far as Cincinnati, they reached free soil on July 4, Independence Day, 1831, before continuing on to Michigan Territory where they settled down. Thornton had trained as a stonemason in his youth and soon found employment. The couple became both respected and popular in Detroit's tiny black community.

A slave's heavy iron shackles, sometimes used as a punishment for running away, weighed down body and spirit.

Shortly after the fugitives reached Michigan, a Louisville native visiting Detroit had recognized Thornton Blackburn on the street. Thomas Rogers knew that Blackburn was Susan Brown's escaped slave but, inexplicably, he withheld information about his discovery for almost two years. When he finally disclosed the Blackburns' whereabouts in late May 1833, Judge John Pope Oldham, Brown's brother-in-law, and McKnight hired Weir, a prominent lawyer and member of the Louisville City Council, to travel to Detroit and present their claim to the Blackburns before the Michigan courts.

Weir and Judge Oldham's son, Talbot, arrived in Detroit on June 13 and demanded the return of Thornton and Ruthie Blackburn. Judge Chipman had little choice in the matter. The federal Fugitive Slave Law of 1793 required that he hand the hapless couple over to their claimants. Likewise, the Northwest Ordinance of 1787, which forbade slavery north and west of the Ohio River, guaranteed that Southern fugitives apprehended in those territories would be returned to their owners. Runaway slaves like the Blackburns faced terrible punishment: Whippings, brandings and mutilation were well-known consequences of flight. Then, most likely, one or both of them would be "sold down the river." Thousands of Kentucky slaves, worth less in the cooler climate of that border state than in the great markets at the mouth of the Mississippi River, had been sold over the years to feed the unending appetite of King Cotton for labor.

Black Detroit was incensed at the prospect. When Judge Chipman pronounced his fateful sentence sending the Blackburns back to bondage, the mood turned ugly. Observers in the courtroom that day later testified that the blacks there threatened to burn Detroit to the ground.

Weir and Oldham had booked passage for themselves and the Blackburns on the steamboat Ohio, scheduled to leave for Buffalo the next day, Sunday. Legally, the Detroit courts and keepers of the peace had no further responsibility, in the matter.

But Sheriff Wilson quite rightly feared the rising racial tension in the city and took the unprecedented step of incarcerating the Blackburns in the city jail. He then set about convincing Ohio's captain to delay sailing until Monday afternoon when most in the black community would be back at work.

Wilson's actions further enraged blacks in the city. They considered him to be acting in the interests of the slaveholders, above and beyond his responsibilities as sheriff. Furthermore, rumors spread that both Wilson and the city jailer, Lemuel Goodall, had been promised $50 by Weir for the safe delivery of Thornton and Ruthie Blackburn to the docks.

By the early 1830s, there were already numerous former slaves living in the nominally free territory of Michigan. Detroit was an important station on what would soon be called the Underground Railroad. If the judge and sheriff willingly handed over the Blackburns to slave agents, then no black man, woman or child living in Michigan Territory was safe. The more militant elements of the community immediately armed themselves and took to the streets.

Angry crowds milled around the jail on Gratiot Street well into Saturday evening. People came from as far away as Fort Malden, Upper Canada, to lend their support. The sheriff's deputy, Alexander McArthur, later testified:

> There were assembled around the said jail a large number of blacks and mulattoes armed with sticks, clubs, knives, pistols, swords, and other unlawful weapons avowing with loud threats their determination to rescue the said Prisoner Thornton Blackburn then in the custody of the said John M. Wilson, Sheriff of the said County. The Sheriff . . . endeavored reasoning with them to persuade them to disperse, but without effect, they telling him that they expected some of them would be killed but that they were determined to rescue the prisoner at all hazards.

Saturday night, after the case had been decided, concerned men and women met at the home of respected local businessman Benjamin Willoughby. Willoughby was an emancipated slave from Kentucky who had lived very close to the place Thornton had been born. He brought his family to Detroit in about 1826, and he and his wife wielded considerable influence within the black community.

Several other people who would later become leaders in the Underground Railroad activities along the Detroit River shore were also present: Madison J. Lightfoot and his wife, Tabitha; George and Caroline French; and John Cook, who owned a profitable hairdressing establishment that served a largely white clientele. Frazier, the white attorney who had defended the Blackburns, and his friend Charles Cleland, the white publisher of the Detroit Courier and also an attorney, were there, too. The group hatched a daring plot to rescue the Blackburns and, at the same time, send a strong message to Michigan's territorial government that returning fugitive slaves to bondage would not be tolerated.

The next day, Sunday, June 16, crowds of armed blacks flocked to the district near the jail. They also gathered at the steamboat docks at the foot of Randolph Street where Ohio bobbed gently at its berth. That afternoon, Tabitha Lightfoot and Caroline French approached Sheriff Wilson. Could they possibly visit Mrs. Blackburn in her cell to pray with her and comfort her before her journey? Wilson, concerned about the possibility of civil unrest, quite likely saw granting the visit as one means for diffusing the tension and agreed.

It was well after dark when two very distressed ladies, covering their faces with veils as they wept, emerged from the jail and hurried home. When the jailer entered Ruthie Blackburn's cell the next morning, he found Caroline French in her place. The editor of the Detroit Courier of June 19 wrote, "By a contrivance that demonstrates that Negroes are not wholly wanting in shrewdness, the female was rescued from jail on Sunday evening and made her escape to Canada where she is now." It was later revealed that she had been taken across the Detroit River on the advice of Frazier, who had visited the Blackburns in their cells and informed them that their only safety lay in reaching the British colony of Upper Canada.

When Weir and Talbot Oldham learned of Blackburn's flight, they approached Judge Chipman to claim Mrs. French in lieu of their rightful prisoner. They intended to sell her as a slave so Ruthie Blackburn's owner, McKnight, could recoup his losses. Fortunately for French, her husband George and Madison Lightfoot worked at the popular Steamboat Hotel in downtown Detroit. Many members of the legal profession frequented the hotel bar, including Judge Charles Larned, who sympathized with French's situation. Larned immediately issued a writ of habeas corpus protecting French and she was freed, but she soon crossed the river and remained in Canada for some months after the incident.

By now, Ruthie Blackburn was safely ensconced with friends at Amherstburg in what is now Ontario, but her husband still remained in prison awaiting his imminent return to slavery.

About 4 o'clock on the same day that Ruthie's escape was discovered, Monday, June 17, Thornton was brought in chains to the door of the jail flanked by Sheriff Wilson and Jailer Goodall. Deputy McArthur and Oldham were also present; Weir had already boarded Ohio. Only a few black men and women were outside the jail, but they were armed and very agitated.

One account, published years later in the February 7, 1870, Detroit Daily Post and probably much embellished, presents an inspiring image of what happened as the carriage arrived to take Thornton to the docks. A crowd of about 200 angry blacks marched up Gratiot Street toward the jail. At their head strode an elderly woman carrying a stake with a white rag tied around it and pointed forward like a spear. The sheriff tried to take the prisoner back inside the jail, but Thornton offered to calm the crowd. Oldham, who had grown up with his aunt's former slave, said that he thought Blackburn might have more influence than would the sheriff. As Thornton came forward, a black man in the crowd tossed him a pistol and said, "Shoot the rascal," meaning Wilson, who then tried to wrest the gun from his prisoner. Thornton fired in the air, igniting what came to be known as the Blackburn Riots of 1833, the first racial riots in Detroit history.

Although no one suspected it at the time, the whole event had been carefully orchestrated. Well known local blacks such as the Lightfoots, Frenches and Willoughbys stayed in the background while a daring group of young men prepared to grab Thornton and carry him off to a boat waiting by the river. All but one were fugitive slaves themselves, and all were readily identified by Wilson and the other officials. The rescuers knew that if they were successful in rescuing Thornton, they could never return from the Upper Canadian shore.

Eminent Detroit historian Norman McRae pieced together the following account of the riot:

Seeing Blackburn in difficulty, members of the mob attacked Sheriff Wilson, while Lewis Austin took Blackburn into the stagecoach that was waiting to transport Blackburn, his captor and the sheriff to the dock. Earlier several women had removed the linchpin from the vehicle in order to disable it. As a result Blackburn was kept inside the coach until two elderly blacks. Daddy Grace and Sleepy Polly, could remove him. Then . . . Blackburn was placed into a horse-drawn cart that disappeared into the nearby woods.

Considering discretion the better part of valor, Goodall, Oldham and McArthur retreated into the jail, leaving Wilson to face the furious crowd alone. The sheriff fired several shots in an effort to halt the violence, but he was pulled to the ground and terribly beaten. Afterward, Wilson could remember little of the day's events, and he died of his injuries a year later. Neither did the rescuers all escape unscathed. According to the Detroit Daily, Post's 1870 retrospective edition—published at the time that Michigan blacks were finally awarded the right to vote—"One Negro, named Louis Austin, was shot in the breast, the ball penetrating the lung, and lodging in the shoulder blade. . . . After two years of long suffering, Louis died, attributing his death to the effects of the wound."

The Daily Post also gave the following description of the escape in which Daddy Grace (or Daddy Walker, accounts vary) took center stage. The numbers are much exaggerated, with most contemporary accounts recording that only 30 or 40 people actually took part in the fray.

During the melee, an old colored man, named "Daddy Walker," who, with his cart and a blind horse, had been impressed into the service, backed up his vehicle to the jail steps, while an old colored woman by the name of "Sleepy Polly," and who never before nor after showed signs of activity, seized hold of Blackburn and dragged him into the cart. . . . Daddy Walker, and the mob, which had been swelled to 400 or 500 persons, immediately drove, post-haste, up Gratiot road with the evident intention of turning toward the river as soon as practicable. . . .

The driver was somewhat reluctant about his task, but a Negro in the cart, holding a drawn sword over his head, urged him and his blind horse to respectable speed. The crowd continued to push up Gratiot road and in answer to inquiries whither the fugitive had been taken, pointed forward and said, "further on." But the cart entered the woods on the north side of the road, about where Russell street now is, and disappeared.

The sound of barking dogs alerted the Blackburn party that a posse had been formed and was in pursuit. They devised a clever ruse to put the dogs off the scent. Sending Daddy Grace and his cart off in one direction as a decoy, the rescuers broke the manacles on Thornton's feet with an axe and wrapped his

chains in bandanas to stop them from rattling. Together they ran through the woods toward the river. They paid the waiting boatman with a gold watch and were safely conveyed across to Sandwich (now part of Windsor), Upper Canada.

Back in Detroit, all was chaos. General Friend Palmer was a youthful eyewitness to the event. "Great excitement ensued; the Presbyterian Church bell rang an alarm, the cry 'To Arms' was shouted through the streets and men with guns, pistols and swords were seen coming from all directions," Palmer wrote in 1906. Wilson lay bleeding and alone on the jailhouse steps until McArthur, Goodall and Oldham ventured out to bring the sheriff inside and dress his wounds. There they remained until the entire mob had dispersed, about 8 o'clock that night.

In the aftermath of the riot, many of the city's African-American residents were rounded up and jailed. Their cases were heard before the mayor's court. Those who were judged innocent still had to provide bail to ensure their good behavior, and then they were freed. At least 10 men, including the aged Daddy Grace, were sentenced to hard labor and served several months in municipal roadwork gangs.

Madison Lightfoot and George French, surely the ringleaders of the plot along with Willoughby, were incarcerated for only a short time, even though Lightfoot was suspected of supplying Thornton with the pistol. Upon his release, French crossed to Upper Canada and remained there with his wife for months; he later returned to Detroit. No suspicion seems to have fallen on the Willoughbys or on Cook, and their names were never mentioned in formal records of the affair. Tabitha Lightfoot was fined $25 as "the prime mover of the riot," a charge she did not dispute.

A curfew was maintained in Detroit for some weeks, and the militia, under War of 1812 veteran General John Williams, was charged with patrolling the streets. Lewis Cass, a former governor of Michigan and President Andrew Jackson's secretary of war, happened to be in town when the incident occurred. He declared martial law and called out federal troops from Fort Gratiot to assist the militia.

Rumors abounded. It was widely believed that blacks from Upper Canada (what is now Ontario) were planning to cross the river en masse and invade Detroit. Contemporary letters attested to the fear felt by the white citizens and made comparisons to the early days of Michigan Territory, when they worried about Indian attacks. A night watch of 16 men was appointed, with orders not to allow any black person to approach the Detroit River bank. Their only catches were a smuggler plying his clandestine trade along the river and the mayor himself who was prowling the streets in search of miscreants and was apprehended by an overzealous picket.

There was a terrible backlash against black Detroiters for the community's support of Thornton and Ruthie Blackburn. People were attacked in the streets, and homes were burned to the ground. Many blacks sold their property for less than it was worth or simply abandoned what they had and fled across the river to Upper Canada. Detroit lost all but a few of its black residents as a result of the 1833 riots and their aftermath, and the population did not again increase until after 1837, when

Looking for Clues

Researching the early lives of fugitive slaves is extremely difficult. Slaveholders' records are usually limited to describing the labor slaves could perform and their potential market value. Furthermore, although African Americans often adopted surnames, part of the intentional dehumanizing process was that slaves were addressed only by their first names, as one would address a child or a pet.

Fortunately for researchers, the Blackburn family had an illustrious surname redolent of old Virginia. The Blackburns of Rippon Lodge, Prince William County, Va., who owned Thornton's mother, Sibby, at the time of her birth were intimate friends of George Washington. Sibby and her children consistently used the name after they were taken to Kentucky as part of the vast westward migration and it was occasionally recorded by whites.

Still, for my first foray into African-American genealogy, I found myself searching for a young man named only "Thornton." To complicate matters, he had been owned, successively, by Kentuckians named "Smith" and "Brown." The search for the Blackburn family's individual members took 20 years, and encompassed information located in more than a dozen states as well as Ontario, Canada.

The most fruitful source was the court records. The Blackburns' escape by steamboat up the Ohio River in 1831 was both bold and perilous. The steamboat captain and the boat's owners were prosecuted for their part in the escape in a case that lasted 15 years and went all the way to the U.S. Supreme Court. The Blackburns' recapture in Detroit and the ensuing civil unrest resulted in a vast array of civil and diplomatic documentation, copies of which were found in the Michigan state archives as well as in the official records of the province of Upper Canada (Ontario). Details of the Blackburns' ownership, their earlier lives as slaves and even their personal appearance come from these all-important records, a unique window on a past that has in so many ways shaped modern North American attitudes to race.

—Karolyn Smardz Frost

Michigan became a state and ratified a constitution repudiating slavery and safeguarding personal liberty.

Immediately after the riots, Detroit's municipal government established a citizens' committee to investigate the events. Its report was published in the Detroit Journal and Advertiser of Friday, July 19, 1833, and included resolutions that reaffirmed support for the federal law regarding fugitive slaves:

That while we hold personal liberty to be a sacred and unalienable right, yet when the property of the master is clearly proven in the slave, it becomes our duty to see that the laws be maintained and that no riotous mob be allowed to violate them.

The report also acknowledged the role of Canadian authorities:

Resolved: that we duly appreciate the prompt and efficient measures adopted by the Civil Authority of the Province of Upper Canada and by our British neighbors in arresting and securing the negroes concerned in the riotous proceedings which occurred in this city.

That statement referred to the fact that the mayor of Detroit had sent a letter to the sheriff of the Western District in Upper Canada, whose administrative center was at Sandwich, demanding the arrest of Thornton Blackburn and his rescuers on the grounds that they had incited a riot and tried to kill the Wayne County sheriff. Blackburn and his friends were arrested and jailed, and Ruthie Blackburn was also taken into custody.

What followed was the first extradition case between Canada and the United States over the thorny issue of fugitive slaves. Sir John Colborne, Upper Canada's abolitionist lieutenant governor, and his attorney general, Robert Simpson Jameson, defended the Blackburns on the grounds that even if they were acquitted of the criminal charges in Michigan, they would still be condemned to a lifetime of slavery. Canada, under British colonial law, could not extradite people to a jurisdiction that imposed harsher penalties than they would have received for the same offense in Canada. Thornton and Ruthie Blackburn remained in Ontario, and the landmark decision set the precedent for all future runaway slave disputes. More than any other incident, the Blackburn case established Upper Canada as the main terminus of the fabled Underground Railroad.

Andrew Jackson Versus the Cherokee Nation

"Old Hickory" had been an Indian fighter, and he continued the struggle as president. His new weapon was the Indian Removal Act, which would force Eastern tribes to relocate west of the Mississippi.

Robert V. Remini

The great Cherokee Nation that had fought the young Andrew Jackson back in 1788 now faced an even more powerful and determined man who was intent on taking their land. But where in the past they had resorted to guns, tomahawks, and scalping knives, now they chose to challenge him in a court of law. They were not called a "civilized nation" for nothing. Many of their leaders were well educated; many more could read and write; they had their own written language, thanks to Sequoyah, a constitution, schools, and their own newspaper. And they had adopted many skills of the white man to improve their living conditions. Why should they be expelled from their lands when they no longer threatened white settlements and could compete with them on many levels? They intended to fight their ouster, and they figured they had many ways to do it. As a last resort they planned to bring suit before the Supreme Court.

Prior to that action, they sent a delegation to Washington to plead their cause. They petitioned Congress to protect them against the unjust laws of Georgia that had decreed that they were subject to its sovereignty and under its complete jurisdiction. They even approached the President, but he curtly informed them that there was nothing he could do in their quarrel with the state, a statement that shocked and amazed them.

So the Cherokees hired William Wirt to take their case to the Supreme Court. In the celebrated *Cherokee Nation v. Georgia* he instituted suit for an injunction that would permit the Cherokees to remain in Georgia without interference by the state. He argued that they constituted an independent nation and had been so regarded by the United States in its many treaties with them.

Speaking for the majority of the court, Chief Justice John Marshall handed down his decision on March 18, 1831. Not surprisingly, as a great American nationalist, he rejected Wirt's argument that the Cherokees were a sovereign nation, but he also rejected Jackson's claim that they were subject to state law.

The Indians were "domestic dependent nations," he ruled, subject to the United States as a ward to a guardian. Indian territory was part of the United States but not subject to action by individual states.

When the Cherokees read Marshall's decision they honestly believed that the Nation had won the case, that Georgia lacked authority to control their lives and property, and that the courts would protect them. The Supreme Court, the Principal Chief told his people, decided "in our favor." So they stayed right where they were, and missionaries encouraged them to stand fast.

But they figured without Andrew Jackson—the man the Cherokees called Sharp Knife—and the authorities of Georgia. In late December 1830, the state passed another law prohibiting white men from entering Indian country after March 1, 1831, without a license from the state. This move was obviously intended to keep interfering clergymen from inciting the Indians to disobey Georgia law. Eleven such missionaries were arrested for violating the recent statute, nine of whom accepted pardons from the governor in return for a promise that they would cease violating Georgia law. But Samuel A. Worcester and Dr. Elizur Butler refused the pardon, and Judge Augustin S. J. Clayton sentenced them to the state penitentiary, "there to endure hard labor for the term of four years." They appealed the verdict and their case came before the Supreme Court.

On March 3, 1832, Marshall again ruled in *Worcester v. Georgia,* declaring all the laws of Georgia dealing with the Cherokees unconstitutional, null, void, and of no effect. In addition he issued a formal mandate two days later ordering the state's superior court to reverse its decision and free the two men.

Jackson was presently involved in a confrontation with South Carolina over the passage of the Tariffs of 1828 and 1832. The state had nullified the acts and threatened to secede from the Union if force were used to make her comply with them. The last thing Jackson needed was a confrontation with another state, so he quietly nudged Georgia into obeying the court order and freeing Butler and Worcester. A number of well-placed officials in both the state and national governments lent a hand and the governor, Wilson Lumpkin, released the two men on January 14, 1833.

With the annoying problem of the two missionaries out of the way, both Georgia and Jackson continued to lean on the Cherokees to get them to remove. "Some of the most vicious and base characters that the adjoining states can produce" squatted on their land and stole "horses and other property" and formed a link with as many "bad citizens" of the Cherokee Nation "as they can associate into their club." Missionaries decried what was happening to the Cherokees. If only "whites would not molest them," wrote Dr. Elizur Butler in *The Missionary Herald.* They have made remarkable progress in the last dozen years and if left alone they can and will complete the process toward a "civilized life."

Ross resolutely resisted any thought of leading his people from their ancient land into a god-forsaken wilderness.

But allowing eastern Indians full control of their eastern lands was virtually impossible in the 1830s. There was not army enough or will enough by the American people to bring it about. As Jackson constantly warned, squatters would continue to invade and occupy the land they wanted; then, if they were attacked, they would turn to the state government for protection that usually ended in violence. All this under the guise of bringing "civilization" to the wilderness.

Even so, the Cherokees had a strong leader who had not yet given up the fight. They were led by the wily, tough, and determined John Ross, a blue-eyed, brown-haired mixed-blood who was only one-eighth Cherokee. Nonetheless he was the Principal Chief, and a most powerful force within the Nation. He was rich, lived in a fine house attended by black slaves, and had influence over the annuities the United States paid to the tribal government for former land cessions. His appearance and lifestyle were distinctly white; in all other respects he was Indian.

From the beginning of Jackson's administration Ross urged his people to stand their ground and remain united. "Friends," he told his people, "I have great hopes in your firmness and that you will hold fast to the place where you were raised. Friends if you all unite together and be of one mind there is no danger." And the Cherokees cheered his determination. They approved wholeheartedly of his leadership and they took comfort in what he said. So, with the Nation solidly behind him, Ross resolutely resisted any thought of leading his people from their ancient land into a god-forsaken wilderness.

Still the Cherokees held out, even though even they had begun to feel the unrelenting pressure. A so-called Treaty Party emerged within the Nation, made up of chiefs and headmen who understood Jackson's inflexible will and had decided to bow to

John Ridge, a leader of the Treaty Party, was assassinated by opponents in 1839.
Source: Library of Congress

his wishes and try to get the best treaty possible. They were led by very capable, hard-headed, and pragmatic men, including the Speaker of the Cherokee National Council, Major Ridge; his son, the educated and politically ambitious John Ridge; and the editor of the Cherokee *Phoenix,* Elias Boudinot.

John Ridge took a leading role in the emergence of the Treaty Party, for when the *Worcester* decision was first handed down he instantly recognized that Chief Justice Marshall had rendered an opinion that abandoned the Cherokees to their inevitable fate. So he went to Jackson and asked him point-blank whether the power of the United States would be exerted to force Georgia into respecting Indian rights and property. The President assured him that the government would do nothing. He then advised Ridge "most earnestly" to go home and urge his people to remove. Dejected, the chief left the President "with the melancholy conviction that he had been told the truth. From that moment he was convinced that the only alternative to save his people from moral and physical death, was to make the best terms they could with the government and remove out of the limits of the states. This conviction he did not fail to make known to his friends, and hence rose the '*Treaty Party.*'"

The members of this Treaty Party certainly risked their lives in pressing for removal, and indeed all of them were subsequently marked for assassination. Not too many years later, Elias Boudinot and John Ridge were slain with knives and tomahawks in the midst of their families, while Major Ridge was ambushed and shot to death.

John Ross, on the other hand, would not yield. As head of the National Party that opposed removal he was shrewd enough to recognize immediately that the President would attempt to play one party off against the other. "The object of the President is unfolded & made too plain to be misunderstood," he told the Nation. "It is to create divisions among ourselves, break down our government, our press & our treasury, that our cries may not be heard abroad; that we may be deprived of the means of sending delegations to Washington City to make known our grievances before Congress . . . and break down the government which you [Cherokees] have, by your own free will & choice, established for the security of your freedom & common welfare."

Under the circumstance, Ross decided to go to Washington and request a meeting with the President in order to try again to arrange some accommodation that would prevent the mass relocation of his people to what was now the new Indian Territory, which Congress had created in 1834 and which eventually became the state of Oklahoma. He was tormented by the knowledge that his people would be condemned to a "prairie badly watered and only skirted on the margin of water courses and poor ridges with copes of wood." Worse, districts would be laid out for some "fifteen or twenty different tribes, and all speaking different languages, and cherishing a variety of habits and customs, a portion civilized, another half civilized and others uncivilized, and these congregated tribes of Indians to be regulated under the General Government, by no doubt white rulers." The very thought of it sent shivers through Ross's entire body.

Since he had fought with Jackson at the Battle of Horseshoe Bend during the Creek War he reckoned that his service during that battle would provide him with a degree of leverage in speaking with the President. And, as Principal Chief, he could speak with the duly constituted authority of the Cherokee Nation as established under the Cherokee Constitution of 1827.

He had another reason for requesting the interview. He had heard a rumor that Jackson had commissioned the Reverend John F. Schermerhorn, an ambitious cleric who had assisted in the removal of the Seminoles from Florida, to negotiate with Ridge and his associates and see if a deal could be worked out that would result in a treaty. Definitely alarmed, Ross asked to speak with the President at which time he said he would submit his own proposal for a treaty.

Jackson never liked Ross. He called him "a great villain." Unlike Ridge and Boudinot, said Jackson, the Principal Chief headed a mixed-blood elite, and was intent on centralizing power in his own hands and diverting the annuities to those who would advance his authority and their economic self-interests. Real Indians were full-blooded Indians, not half-breeds, he declared. They were hunters, they were true warriors who, like Ridge and Boudinot, understood the President's concern for his red children and wished to prevent the calamity of certain annihilation that would ensue if they did not heed his pleas to move west. As for Ross's authority under the Cherokee Constitution, Jackson denied that it existed. He said that this so-called Constitution

Major Ridge, John Ridge's father, was also a member of the Treaty Party. He was killed in an ambush on the same day his son died.

Source: Library of Congress

provided for an election in 1832 and it had not been held. Instead the Principal Chief had simply filled the National Council with his henchmen—another indication, claimed Jackson, of an elitist clique who ruled the Nation and disregarded the interests of the majority of the people.

Despite his feelings about the chief, Jackson decided to grant Ross's request for a meeting. Above all else he wanted Cherokee removal and if that meant seeing this "great villain" and hearing about his proposal for relocating the tribe then he would do it. As a consummate politician, Jackson understood the value of playing one party off against another, so when he granted the interview he directed that Schermerhorn suspend his negotiations with the Treaty Party and wait for the outcome of his interview with the Principal Chief.

Actually Jackson and Ross were much alike. They were both wily, tough, determined, obsessed with protecting the interests of their respective peoples, and markedly dignified and polite when they came together in the White House on Wednesday, February 5, 1834. It was exactly noon when the Principal Chief arrived, and the Great Father greeted him with the respect due Ross's position. The chief returned the compliment. For a few minutes their conversation touched on pleasantries, then they got down to the question at hand and began playing a political game that involved the lives of thousands, both Native Americans and white settlers.

Unfortunately, despite his many talents and keen intelligence, Ross was no match for the President. He simply lacked the resources of his adversary.

The Principal Chief opened with an impassioned plea. "Your Cherokee children are in deep distress," he said, ". . . because they are left at the mercy of the white robber and assassin" and receive no redress from the Georgia courts. That state, he declared, has not only "surveyed and lotteried off" Cherokee land to her citizens but legislated as though Cherokees were intruders in their own country.

Jackson just listened. Then the Principal Chief acted imprudently and made impossible demands on the President. To start, he insisted that in any treaty the Nation must retain some of their land along the borders of Tennessee, Alabama, and Georgia, land that had already been occupied by white settlers. He even included a small tract in North Carolina. He then required assurances that the United States government would protect the Cherokees with federal troops in the new and old settlements for a period of five years.

Jackson could scarcely believe what was being demanded of him. Under other circumstances he would have acted up a storm in an attempt to frighten and cower the chief. But, on this occasion he decided against it. Instead, in a calm and quiet but determined voice, he told Ross that nothing short of an entire removal of the Cherokee Nation from all their land east of the Mississippi would be acceptable.

Having run into a stone wall, Ross headed in another direction. In view of the gold that had recently been discovered in Georgia and North Carolina, he wanted $20 million for all their eastern land plus reimbursement for losses sustained by the Nation for violations of former treaties by the United States. He also asked for indemnities for claims under the 1817 and 1819 Cherokee treaties. The total amount almost equaled the national debt.

On hearing this, Jackson also changed direction. His voice hardened, his intense blue eyes flared, and the muscles in his face tightened and registered his growing displeasure. Obviously the Principal Chief had not caught the President's meaning when he rejected the first demand. Jackson snapped at Ross, rejected the proposal as "preposterous" and warned him that the Great Father was not to be trifled with. If these demands were the best the chief could offer then there was no point in continuing the discussion.

That brought Ross up short. Completely surprised by Jackson's reaction he protested his sincerity, and to prove it he offered to accept any award the Senate of the United States might recommend. Apparently the chief was attempting to set up a bidding contest between the upper house and the chief executive. Surprisingly, Jackson accepted the offer and assured Ross that he would "go as far" as the Senate in any award that might be proposed. And on that conciliatory note the interview ended.

In less than a week Ross received his answer about what the Senate would offer. John P. King of Georgia chaired the Committee on Indian Affairs that considered the question. That was bad enough. Then the committee came up with an offer of $5 million. The figure shocked the Principal Chief. Jackson probably knew beforehand what would happen and therefore agreed

to Ross's suggestion. Now the Indian was faced with rejecting the money outright or accepting this paltry sum and thereby losing credibility with his people. Naturally he chose the former course. He claimed he had been misunderstood, that he could not possibly agree to such an amount, and that his reputation among the Cherokees would be shattered if he consented to it. He left Washington an angry and bitter man.

Having disposed of Ross, Jackson turned back to Schermerhorn and instructed him to renew the negotiations with the Treaty Party. With little difficulty the cleric managed to arrange a draft removal treaty signed on March 14, 1835, by Schermerhorn, John Ridge, Elias Boudinot, and a small delegation of Cherokees. After due notice the treaty was submitted to the Cherokee National Council at New Echota, Georgia, for approval and sent to the President for submission to the Senate. The draft stipulated that the Cherokees surrender to the United States all its land east of the Mississippi River for a sum of $5 million, an amount that one modern historian has called "unprecedented generosity." This cession comprised nearly 8 million acres of land in western North Carolina, northern Georgia, northeastern Alabama, and eastern Tennessee. A schedule of removal provided that the Cherokees would be resettled in the west and receive regular payments for subsistence, claims, and spoliations, and would be issued blankets, kettles, and rifles.

At approximately the same time this draft treaty was drawn up and considered at New Echota, a large delegation of Cherokee chiefs—in the desperate hope that their assembled presence would make a difference and prevent the treaty from going forward to the Senate—went to Washington and asked to speak to their Great Father. In contrast to his grudging granting of Ross's request, Jackson was anxious to meet the delegation and give the chiefs one of his celebrated "talks."

The Indians arrived at the White House at the designated hour, and Jackson treated them with marked respect, as though they really were dignitaries of a foreign nation. Yet he did not remotely say or do anything that would indicate an acceptance of their independence or sovereignty. Once the Indians had assembled they faced the President as he began his talk.

"Brothers, I have long viewed your condition with great interest. For many years I have been acquainted with your people, and under all variety of circumstances, in peace and war. Your fathers are well known to me. . . . Listen to me, therefore, as your fathers have listened. . . ."

Jackson paused. He turned from side to side to look at and take in all the Cherokees standing around him. After a few moments he began again.

"You are now placed in the midst of a white population. . . . You are now subject to the same laws which govern the citizens of Georgia and Alabama. You are liable to prosecutions for offenses, and to civil actions for a breach of any of your contracts. Most of your people are uneducated, and are liable to be brought into collision at all times with your white neighbors. Your young men are acquiring habits of intoxication. With strong passions . . . they are frequently driven to excesses which must eventually terminate in their ruin. The game has disappeared among you, and you must depend upon agriculture and the mechanic arts for support. And yet, a large portion of your people have acquired little or no property in the soil itself. . . . How, under these circumstances, can you live in the country you now occupy? Your condition must become worse and worse, and you will ultimately disappear, as so many tribes have done before you."

They had two years—that is, until May 23, 1838—to cross over the Mississippi and take up their new residence in the Indian Territory.

These were his usual arguments, but he judged them essential for success.

You have not listened to me, he scolded. You went to the courts for relief. You turned away from your Great Father. And what happened? After years of litigation you received little satisfaction from the Supreme Court and succeeded in earning the enmity of many whites. "I have no motive, Brothers, to deceive you," he said. "I am sincerely desirous to promote your welfare. Listen to me, therefore, while I tell you that you cannot remain where you are now. . . . It [is] impossible that you can flourish in the midst of a civilized community. You have but one remedy within your reach. And that is to remove to the West and join your countrymen, who are already established there." The choice is yours. "May the great spirit teach you how to choose."

Jackson then concluded by reminding them of the fate of the Creeks, that once great and proud Nation. How broken and reduced in circumstances their lives had now become because they resisted. It was a not-so-subtle threat that also struck home. "Think then of these things," he concluded. "Shut your ears to bad counsels. Look at your condition as it now is, and then consider what it will be if you follow the advice I give you."

That ended the talk, and the Indians filed from the room more disappointed and depressed than ever. Jackson would not budge, and they knew their kinsmen were dead set against removal. It was a stalemate that could end only in tragedy.

Meanwhile Schermerhorn called "a council of all the people" to meet him at New Echota in Georgia during the third week of December 1835 to approve the draft treaty, making sure that a large contingent of Treaty Party members attended. Like Jackson, he had the temerity to warn other Cherokees that if they stayed away their absence would be considered a vote of consent for the draft.

Despite the threat and the warning, practically the entire Nation stayed away. As a consequence the treaty was approved on December 28 by the unbelievably low number of 79 to 7. The numbers represented only the merest fraction of the Nation. A vast majority—perhaps fifteen-sixteenths of the entire population—presumably opposed it and showed their opposition by staying away. The entire process was fraudulent, but that hardly mattered. Jackson had the treaty he wanted, and he did not hesitate to so inform the Senate.

The Treaty of New Echota closely, but not completely, resembled the draft treaty in that the Cherokees surrendered all their eastern land and received $4.5 million in return. They would be paid for improvements, removed at government expense, and maintained for two years. Removal was to take place within two years from the date of the treaty's approval by the Senate and President.

A short while later some 12,000 Cherokees signed a resolution denouncing the Treaty of New Echota and forwarded it to the Senate. Even the North Carolina Cherokees, in a separate action, added 3,250 signatures to a petition urging the Senate to reject it. But Jackson was assured by the Treaty Party that "a majority of the people" approved the document "and all are willing peaceable to yield to the treaty and abide by it." Such information convinced the President that the Principal Chief and his "half breed" cohorts had coerced the Cherokees into staying away from New Echota under threat of physical violence.

At New Echota the Treaty Party selected a Committee of Thirteen to carry the treaty to Washington and they were empowered to act on any alteration required by the President or the U.S. Senate. This Committee invited Ross to join the group and either support the treaty or insist on such alterations as to make it acceptable. "But to their appeal [Ross] returned no answer," which further convinced the President that the treaty represented the genuine interests and the will of the majority of Cherokees.

Militiamen charged into the Cherokee country and drove the Cherokees from their cabins and houses.

Although Henry Clay, Daniel Webster, Edward Everett, and other senators spoke fervently against the treaty in the Senate, a two-thirds majority of 31 members voted for it and 15 against. It carried by a single vote on May 18. Jackson added his signature on May 23, 1836, and proclaimed the Treaty of New Echota in force.

And they had two years—that is until May 23, 1838—to cross over the Mississippi and take up their new residence in the Indian Territory. But every day of that two-year period John Ross fought the inevitable. He demanded to see the President and insisted that Jackson recognize the authority of the duly elected National Council, but Sharp Knife would have none of him and turned him away. Back home the Principal Chief advised his people to ignore the treaty and stay put. "We will not recognize the forgery palmed off upon the world as a treaty by a knot of unauthorized individuals," he cried, "nor stir one step with reference to that false paper."

Not everyone listened to him. They knew Andrew Jackson better. Some 2,000 Cherokees resigned themselves to the inevitable, packed their belongings, and headed west. The rest, the vast majority of the tribe, could not bear to leave their homeland and chose to hope that their Principal Chief would somehow work the miracle that would preserve their country to them.

But their fate could not have been worse. When the two-year grace period expired and Jackson had left office, his hand-picked successor, President Martin Van Buren, ordered the removal to begin. Militiamen charged into the Cherokee country and drove the Cherokees from their cabins and houses. With rifles and bayonets they rounded up the Indians and placed them in prison stockades that had been erected "for gathering in and holding the Indians preparatory to removal." These poor, frightened and benighted innocents, while having supper in their homes, "were startled by the sudden gleam of bayonets in the doorway and rose up to be driven with blows and oaths along the weary miles of trail which led to the stockade. Men were seized in the fields, women were taken from their wheels and children from their play." As they turned for one last glimpse of their homes they frequently saw them in flames, set ablaze by the lawless rabble who followed the soldiers, scavenging what they could. These outlaws stole the cattle and other livestock and even desecrated graves in their search for silver pendants and other valuables. They looted and burned. Said one Georgia volunteer who later served in the Confederate army: "I fought through the Civil War and have seen men shot to pieces and slaughtered by thousands, but the Cherokee removal was the cruelest I ever saw."

In a single week some 17,000 Cherokees were rounded up and herded into what was surely a concentration camp. Many sickened and died while they awaited transport to the west. In June the first contingent of about a thousand Indians boarded a steamboat and sailed down the Tennessee River on the first lap of their westward journey. Then they were boxed like animals into railroad cars drawn by two locomotives. Again there were many deaths on account of the oppressive heat and cramped conditions in the cars. For the last leg of the journey the Cherokees walked. Small wonder they came to call this 800-mile nightmare "The Trail of Tears." Of the approximately 18,000 Cherokees who were removed, at least 4,000 died in the stockades along the way, and some say the figure actually reached 8,000. By the middle of June 1838 the general in charge of the Georgia militia proudly reported that not a single Cherokee remained in the state except as prisoners in the stockade.

At every step of their long journey to the Indian Territory the Cherokees were robbed and cheated by contractors, lawyers, agents, speculators, and anyone wielding local police power. Food supplied by the government disappeared or arrived in short supply. The commanding officer, General Winfield Scott, and a few other generals "were concerned about their reputation for humaneness," says one modern historian, "and probably even for the Cherokee. There just wasn't much they could do about it." As a result many died needlessly. "Oh! The misery and wretchedness that presents itself to our view in going among these people," wrote one man. "Sir, I have witnessed entire families prostrated with sickness—not one able to give help to the other, and these poor people were made the instruments of enriching a few unprincipled and wicked contractors."

And this, too, is part of Andrew Jackson's legacy. Although it has been pointed out many times that he was no longer President of the United States when the Trail of Tears occurred and had never intended such a monstrous result of his policy, that hardly excuses him. It was his insistence on the speedy removal of the Cherokees, even after he had left office, that brought about this horror. From his home outside Nashville he regularly badgered Van Buren about enforcing the treaty. He had become obsessed about removal. He warned that Ross would exert every effort and means available to him to get the treaty rescinded or delayed and that, he said, must be blocked. But the new President assured him that nothing would interfere with the exodus of the Cherokees and that no extension of the two-year grace period would be tolerated under any circumstance.

Principal Chief John Ross also shares a portion of blame for this unspeakable tragedy. He continued his defiance even after the deadline for removal had passed. He encouraged his people to keep up their resistance, despite every sign that no appreciable help would be forthcoming from the American people or anyone else; and he watched as they suffered the awful consequences of his intransigence.

Despite the obscene treatment accorded the Cherokees by the government, the tribe not only survived but endured. As Jackson predicted, they escaped the fate of many extinct eastern tribes. Cherokees today have their tribal identity, a living language, and at least three governmental bodies to provide for their needs. Would that the Yemassee, Mohegans, Pequots, Delawares, Narragansetts, and other such tribes could say the same.

ROBERT V. REMINI is the author of a three-volume biography of Andrew Jackson as well as biographies of Daniel Webster and Henry Clay and many other books about Jacksonian America.

Excerpted from *Andrew Jackson and His Indian Wars* by Robert V. Remini. Copyright © Robert V. Remini, 2001. Reprinted by arrangement with Viking Penguin, a division of Penguin Putnam, Inc.

Storm over Mexico

Godfrey Hodgson tells the colourful story of Jane McManus, political journalist, land speculator, pioneer settler in Texas and propagandist who believed that the United States had a 'manifest destiny' to rule Mexico and the Caribbean.

GODFREY HODGSON

At the height of the Furore over the boundary question in Texas that led to the declaration of war against Mexico on May 11th, 1846, George Bancroft, the famous historian who was President Polk's Secretary of the Navy, received a long letter in Washington telling him how to do his job and claiming,

> I mean to show you that I can call out an expression of public sentiment (and create it too) that Mr Polk would be wise to respect.

The letter was signed 'Storms'.

'Who is Storms?' Bancroft wrote to his colleague William Marcy, the Secretary of War. 'She', Marcy replied, 'is an outrageously smooth and keen writer for the newspapers'.

It was not common for women to write for the newspapers in the mid-nineteenth century, and almost unprecedented for them to do so in as confident and aggressive a tone as did the woman who called herself 'Storms'.

But then she wrote and lived, at a furious pace, under several names. She was born Jane Maria Eliza McManus. She married Allen Storm, and so could claim the vaguely ominous 'Storms'. Sometimes she signed her work plain, unisex 'Montgomery', and sometimes she came out as 'Cora Montgomery' or 'Corinne Montgomery'. After her second marriage she could boast the magnificent appellation Jane Eliza McManus Storm Cazneau.

Under any name, she was one of the most formidable women of the antebellum American South, a complete rebuttal of the stereotype of white-skinned Southern ladies at home only in nursery and drawing room. She was Scarlett O'Hara and Rhett Butler in one: a single mother who became one of the first women political journalists, a war correspondent, diplomat, secret agent, explorer, speculator and adventurer.

She was in tune with Young America, an amorphous movement of American nationalists (mostly Democrats) advocating southern expansion, free trade and in sympathy with the European revolutions of 1848. Mostly the Young Americans were Democrats with an interest in slavery. In the 1840s, as the young republic challenged British power in Canada, Oregon and the Caribbean, Spanish rule in Cuba, and Mexican ownership of Texas, New Mexico, Arizona and California, Americans thrilled to the idea of 'manifest destiny'. This brilliant slogan first appeared in the *Democratic Review,* organ of the Young America movement, in an anonymous editorial that appeared in the summer of 1845. American destiny, it proclaimed, was to bring the benefits of freedom (an ideal that did not rule out slavery) to the whole of North America, and to Central America and the Caribbean as well. The piece called boldly for 'opposition to the annexation of Texas to cease'. It denounced the behaviour of 'England, our old rival and enemy' for

> . . . limiting our greatness and checking the fulfilment of our manifest destiny to overspread the continent allotted by Providence for the free development of our yearly multiplying millions.

The article and phrase, 'manifest destiny' has long been attributed to the Democratic Review's editor John L. O'Sullivan; however, Storms' biographer Professor Linda S. Hudson, has suggested (2001) that Jane was the author. She has used a grammar-checking computer programme, to argue that the style of the 'manifest destiny' article resembles Jane's far more closely than O'Sullivan's. But even if she did not coin the phrase, Jane was certainly one of the chief propagandists for 'manifest destiny', and a vigorous champion of American annexation of Texas, Cuba, the Dominican Republic, Nicaragua and most, if not all, of Mexico.

Jane McManus was born in 1807 near Troy, in the Hudson River valley in upstate New York. Her family had long been settled in North America on both sides. Her father's people came originally from Ireland, but had been living in America since the early eighteenth century, and although Jane later converted to Catholicism she was brought up as a Protestant. Her mother's family, whose name was Kuntz, Americanized as Coons, were German, Protestant refugees from the Catholic Rhineland.

Jane's father, William Telemachus McManus, was briefly a member of Congress. He fought as an officer against the British in the local militia in the War of 1812. Then he returned to Troy to work as a lawyer and businessman. He was also involved in the business affairs of the local Indian tribe, the Mohicans. Jane's 'most striking physical trait', writes Professor Hudson, 'was her dark complexion', and Hudson speculates that she may have been of Native American descent.

She was well-educated at Emma Willard's Troy Female Academy, one of the earliest colleges for women. The coming of the Erie Canal made Troy prosperous, and for a time the McManus family flourished. But Jane's father was hard-hit by the nationwide Panic of 1819, which broke the Farmers' State Bank in Troy, in which the McManus family held both stock and accounts. In 1825, at the age of eighteen, Jane had married Allen Storm, a pupil in her father's law office, and in 1826 she gave birth to a son, William McManus Storm. By 1832, however, the marriage had failed and Jane had resumed her maiden name.

Like other early nineteenth-century Americans on the fringe of the frontier, the McManus family were passionate speculators in land. The dream of a vast fortune in the newly settled southwestern frontier, then expanding from Louisiana and Tennessee into Texas, and the Caribbean is one of the keys to Jane's whole career. Her political and business dreams were fused together. All her life she hoped to create a great fortune, and also to bring what she saw as the priceless boon of republican freedom to those not lucky enough to live in the United States.

Jane was first introduced to the potential of Texas, then part of the Mexican state of Coahuila y Texas, when her father became involved with his friend, the spectacular swordsman, rebel and former US vice-president, Aaron Burr, and others in the Galveston Bay and Texas Land Company in 1832. She went to work keeping the books of the Galveston Bay and Texas Land Company in New York and before long was visiting Aaron Burr, fifty years her senior, at his law office in Jersey City, across the Hudson from New York. She was widely said to be Burr's mistress and was cited in his divorce in 1835. Hearsay evidence was given that Burr was seen standing in front of a seated Jane McManus, his trousers lowered.

Late in 1832, Jane and her brother Robert travelled to Texas and acquired rights to two enormous tracts, one on the Gulf of Mexico, and the other near the present site of Waco, Texas. She also tried, without success, to bring several hundred German settlers into Texas.

It was only after these speculative land ventures failed that Jane became a journalist. Her early adventures in Texas left her with two lifelong assets: she learned fluent Spanish and she acquired a set of contacts with many powerful people on the frontier including the founders of the Republic of Texas, among them Sam Houston (who became its first president in October 1836) and his successor, Jane's partner in a lively exchange of letters, the sonorously named Mirabeau Bonaparte Lamar.

Jane's first journalistic assignment came from Horace Greeley, editor of the *New Yorker,* who gave her a choice assignment: to

travel to the Mediterranean and the Ottoman empire. She visited Smyrna, Aleppo, Tangier and Cadiz, among other places. One of those she interviewed was the aged Lady Hester Stanhope, an indomitable English aristocrat who had married a Muslim and lived in the Syrian desert.

Back in the US in 1839, Jane wrote for a number of papers, two of them in particular: the *New York Sun,* then owned by Moses Yale Beach, and John O'Sullivan's *Democratic Review.* Both were enthusiastic campaigners for 'manifest destiny' and in particular for its southern form, annexation of Texas—even if that meant war with Mexico.

'Manifest Destiny' supporters were eyeing other parts of the continent as well. Anti-British feeling, focused on British rule in Canada, was stoked by the fact that the Hudson's Bay Company's presence in Oregon blocked American settlement in that promising territory. In 1846 the New York papers got up an agitation under the slogan 'Fifty-four forty or fight!' This meant that the United States should demand a frontier at 54° 40' of latitude, many miles north of the present border at the 49th degree, or make war on British Canada.

Americans insisted that their desire to occupy the whole continent was something quite different to European imperialism. 'What has Belgium, Silesia, Poland or Bengal to do with Texas?', wrote the *New York Morning News* in 1845:

> Acquisitions of territory in America, even if accomplished by force of arms, are not to be viewed in the same light as the invasions and conquests of the states of the old world.

Two philosophical differences were claimed by the leading American historian of the Manifest Destiny movement, Frederick Merk. American expansion would be republican: it would involve no monarch, no aristocracy, no established church. And it would be democratic in an economic, as well as political, sense. The chief evil of Europe and the blight of England and Ireland, wrote the *Democratic Review,* was that the people did not own the land. This was a doctrine that appealed to would-be pioneers, but also to land speculators such as Jane.

By the 1840s, settlement had poured into the Ohio and Mississippi valleys and was rapidly filling up the cotton lands of the South. The vast, almost empty territory of Mexico—which reached far to the north of modern Mexico—lay ahead. Forward-looking southerners were already conscious that if the slaveholding South lost the battle over free soil in the mid-West and the plains states, the South would lose representation in Congress and therefore political power in Washington. Eventually, the South's 'peculiar institution', slavery itself, might be banned. Ambitious spirits dreamed of creating a great slave empire in central America and the Caribbean to balance what the South might lose in the American West. Jane McManus, New York bred though she was, was one of these.

The *New York Sun,* a penny paper, was the first in America to achieve something like a mass circulation: around 50,000 in the 1840s. Its publisher, Moses Yale Beach, was a businessman and banker as well as a newspaper man. He was a strong supporter of President Polk's war against Mexico. War broke out in 1846 after an American force moved into disputed territory between the Nueces river and the Rio Grande. The Polk administration was keen to annex at least Texas and other Mexican territory if it could.

In November 1846 Beach and the Roman Catholic bishop of New York John Hughes, received word from contacts in Texas and from the Mexican clergy that a negotiated peace might be possible. Jane McManus played a key part in setting up the secret mission, and Beach asked her to travel with him as interpreter and adviser, chaperoned by his daughter Drusilla. Beach had authority from the President to negotiate a peace settlement. His 'fee' was to be a grant of transit rights across the Isthmus of Tehuantepec, in the southern 'waist' of Mexico. Beach saw the mission essentially as a business opportunity. He wanted the concession to build a canal across the isthmus of Tehuantepec, and also banking concessions in Mexico. For Jane it was a superb journalistic break, and at the same time a chance to forward her dream of spreading American ideals to as much of Mexico and the Caribbean as possible.

Beach, Jane and Drusilla travelled via Havana, to conceal the purpose of their journey. The Havana correspondent of the New Orleans *Picayune* newspaper reported that Beach was on his way to Mexico with 'his wife and daughter'. The party reached Mexico City in late January 1847.

While General Zachary Taylor, (who later succeeded Polk as 12th President in 1849), was fighting one Mexican army in the north where he earned a hard-won victory against the Mexicans in the Battle of Buena Vista of February 22nd-23rd. General Winfield Scott, in turn, was besieging the highly fortified city of Vera Cruz on the east coast of Mexico. Moses Beach was trying to persuade the Mexicans to allow the United States to annex their entire country. Beach met bankers and politicians in Mexico, and also prelates of the Mexican church. He also laid out $40,000 of his own money in vain to back one side in what was becoming a Mexican civil war.

Storms, meanwhile, was filing stories for the *Sun* that argued the case for the United States to annex the whole of Mexico. If this could not be achieved, she was prepared to settle for limited annexation of some provinces.

By March 21st, the Mexican dictator, Santa Ana, had returned to Mexico City after the defeat at Buena Vista, where he assumed the presidency. The Beaches and Jane made their way to Vera Cruz, where on March 27th the fortress surrendered to General Scott, a story she was able to report. This made her America's first woman war correspondent.

By May 1847 Jane had returned to Washington, where she saw President Polk. She was bitterly disappointed that he had already sent out a new mission in place of Beach to negotiate peace with Mexico, under Nicholas P. Trist, chief clerk of the State Department. Trist's negotiations with the former President Herrera at the end of August ended in disappointment for the Americans and an end to the armistice that had facilitated them.

However, on February 2nd, 1848, Trist, with a victorious army at his back but unauthorised by his government, forced on the Mexicans the Treaty of Guadalupe Hidalgo. By this treaty Mexico agreed to sign over one-third of its territory, including California, Arizona and New Mexico, in exchange for $15 million and a further $3,250,000 in claims by its citizens. The treaty came into effect on July 4th.

Congress and the cabinet seriously debated the 'All Mexico' plan, as it was called. It was defeated, not least because neither leaders nor public in the United States was ready to incorporate eight million new citizens, Spanish-speaking, Roman Catholic and mostly non-white.

Jane now turned her attention to Cuba whose potential greatly interested her. Writing as 'Montgomery' in the *Sun,* even before the Mexican War began, she had called for the annexation of Cuba (and also Canada). Unlike Mexico, which had won its independence in a war that began in 1810, Cuba was still a Spanish colony. She wrote fifteen 'tropical sketches' denouncing the poor conditions caused by Spanish exploitation and neglect of Cuba.

In January 1848, she had accepted the position of editor of *La Verdad* (Spanish for 'Truth') a weekly published in New York and financed by wealthy Cuban liberal exiles. But a romantic plan to turn Cuba into an independent republic that could later be annexed like Texas eventually failed. On September 7th, 1849, President Zachary Taylor sent the US Navy to turn back the exiles as they sailed to liberate Cuba.

For the rest of her life Jane continued to preach America's manifest destiny, not only to expand to the Pacific, but also to acquire a tropical domain. In 1849 at the age of forty-two, she married an old friend, General William Cazneau. They had met in Texas and both shared a romantic vision of American expansion, and an ambition to make a fortune out of land speculation.

As Cazneau travelled ceaselessly in the service of one scheme after another, Jane settled down at Eagle Pass, a rough frontier village three hundred miles up the Rio Grande from the Gulf. In the book she wrote about her life there, she described the life of an Old Testament matriarch with her flocks and herds. She got to know Native American chiefs with names like Crazy Bear, Gopher John and Wild Cat, whose interpreter was an African-American called John Horse. Life on the frontier had its idyllic moments for Jane as she rode her black pony, Chino, and bathed naked in the river. But she recognized the hardships and dangers for frontier women as well.

She got to know and sympathized with the Indians who had escaped across the border from peonage in Mexico, and the runaway American slaves heading in the opposite direction. Her attitude to slavery was complicated. She sympathized with the plight of individual slaves, and with the Indian peons. She hoped slavery would be ended in time by sending American slaves to colonies in the Caribbean. She disapproved of the Southern secession and was hired by William H. Seward, Abraham Lincoln's Secretary of State, to write propaganda against the South, which she did, like everything else, with gusto. No doubt her position was affected by the patronage of Seward. But Seward and she were both expansionists who feared that the war would weaken the United States and prevent further American thrusts into the Caribbean.

However, she was also contemptuous of abolitionists. In 1851 she and her husband travelled to Morocco to buy camels, which she hoped (unsuccessfully) to introduce into the south-west of the United States. There is even a hint that this project may have disguised a slaving expedition. And she was a supporter of the notorious 'filibuster', William Walker, who tried to set up a slave-holding empire in Central America in the 1850s.

The truth is that two things bulked larger in her mind than the abolition of slavery. One was her own and her husband's speculative investments in Texas land, and in real estate and mines in the Dominican Republic, Jamaica and Nicaragua. The other was her passionate belief in the destiny and ideals of the United States, which—as for many in her generation—implied an inveterate suspicion of Britain and a determination to oppose British interests and influence throughout the Caribbean.

From 1855 until their deaths, with one short interval, she and her husband lived on an estate, Esmeralda, in the Dominican Republic. General Cazneau had been appointed as a secret American agent there by President Buchanan. His job was to report events, and he also lobbied for an American coaling station and port at Santana Bay. For a time they moved, in spite of Jane's hostility to all things British, to a beautiful estate in Jamaica, Keith Hall, where she continued, in spite of failing eyesight, to write up-beat accounts of life in the tropics.

Jane's death was as stormy as her life. In 1878 she set out for Santo Domingo on a 'rattletrap' steamer, the *Emily B. Souder.* She was caught in what proved to be the biggest storm ever recorded in the western Atlantic up to that time. She was drowned at the age of almost seventy-two.

Jane McManus Storm Cazneau's two dreams, of making a great fortune while bringing the benefits of American freedom to Mexico and the Caribbean, were both only partly successful. Yet she had a remarkable degree of influence on the mid-nineteenth-century course of American foreign policy. It came from her ability to impress powerful men, from Burr and Houston to Beach, Polk and Seward, with her romantic vision of America's 'manifest destiny' to bring its own version of a 'freedom' (one that permitted slavery) to the Spanish-speaking lands and islands to the South.

GODFREY HODGSON is an Associate Fellow of the Rothermere American Institute at Oxford University. He is the author of *More Equal Than Others* (Princeton University Press, 2004).

This article first appeared in *History Today,* March 2005, pp. 34–39. Copyright © 2005 by History Today, Ltd. Reprinted by permission.

UNIT 4

The Civil War and Reconstruction

Unit Selections

Key Points to Consider

- What was the Underground Railroad? What did it say about slavery that thousands of blacks risked brutal punishment or death seeking freedom? What did it say to white Southerners that many Northerners were willing to defy existing laws to assist the fugitives?

- John Brown's raid on Harpers Ferry involved a small band of zealots. Why did this act create such a furor both in the North and South? What seemed to be at stake?

- The Civil War began as a struggle over national unity, but became a conflict over the institution of slavery. What were the obstacles to issuing an emancipation proclamation earlier than Lincoln did? Why did emancipation precipitate a "constitutional dilemma?"

- Black Northern troops performed valiantly in the doomed assault against Fort Wagner. What were they trying to prove to the world?

- Discuss the United States government's policies toward American Indians during the 19th Century. What role did the buffalo play in the cultures of Plains Indians? Why did Indians resist moving to reservations?

- The last article in this volume analyzes the Civil War, Emancipation and Reconstruction "on the world stage." What is meant by this phrase? Why were so many people around the globe interested in what happened in the United States during these years?

Student Web Site
www.mhcls.com/online

Internet References
Further information regarding these Web sites may be found in this book's preface or online.

The American Civil War
http://sunsite.utk.edu/civil-war/warweb.html
Anacostia Museum/Smithsonian Institution
http://www.si.edu/archives/historic/anacost.htm
Abraham Lincoln Online
http://www.netins.net/showcase/creative/lincoln.html

Gilder Lehrman Institute of American History
http://www.digitalhistory.uh.edu/index.cfm?
Secession Era Editorials Project
http://history.furman.edu/~benson/docs/dsmenu.htm

Sectionalism plagued the United States from its inception. The Constitutional proviso that slaves would count as three-fifths of a person for representational purposes, for instance, or that treaties had to be passed by two-thirds majorities grew out of sectional compromises. Manufacturing and commercial interests were strong in the North. Such interests generally supported high tariffs to protect industries, and the construction of turnpikes, canals, and railroads to expand domestic markets. The South, largely rural and agriculture, strongly opposed such measures. Southerners believed that tariffs cost them money and lined the pockets of Northern manufacturers. They had little interest in what were known as "internal improvements." Such differences were relatively easy to resolve because there were no moral issues involved, and matters such as tariffs aroused few emotions in the public.

The question of slavery added a different dimension. Part of the quarrel involved economic considerations. Northerners feared that the spread of slavery would discriminate against "free" farming in the west. Southerners just as adamantly believed that the institution should be allowed to exist wherever it proved feasible. Disputes in 1820 and again in 1850 resulted in compromises that papered over these differences—but they satisfied no one. As time wore on, more and more Northerners came to regard slavery as sinful, an abomination that must be stamped out. Southerners, on the other hand, grew more receptive to the idea that slavery actually was beneficial to both blacks and whites and was condoned by the Bible. Now cast in moral terms, the issue could not be resolved in the fashion of tariff disputes by splitting differences.

Two articles in this unit deal with the increasingly emotional atmosphere during the run up to the Civil War. "Free at Last" describes how the Underground Railroad functioned as an escape route for runaway slaves. White Southerners detested and feared its existence for two reasons beyond the sheer number of escapees, which some scholars estimate to be around 150,000. First, it revealed the fallacy of Southern arguments that slavery was a benevolent institution and that slaves were a happy, contented lot. Second, it seemed clear that whatever politicians might say, large numbers of Northerners were willing to break the law in order to undermine the "peculiar institution." "A Day to Remember" describes this widely publicized act that touched off an explosion of feverish charges and countercharges by both sides. The tendency in the North to treat Brown as a martyr, confirmed Southern suspicions that abolitionists meant to destroy slavery by violence if necessary.

Moderates in the two national parties, the Whigs and Democrats, tried to keep the slavery question from tearing the country in two. Though suffering some defections, the Democrats managed to stay together until the elections of 1860. The Whigs,

however, fell apart during the 1850s. The emergence of the Republican Party, with its strength almost exclusively based in the North, signaled the beginning of the end. Southerners came to regard the Republicans as the party of abolitionism. Abraham Lincoln, Republican presidential candidate in 1860, tried to assure Southerners that although he opposed the spread of slavery he had no intentions of seeking to abolish the institution where it already existed. He was not widely believed in the South. Republican victory in 1860 seemed to them, or at least to the hotheads among them, to threaten not just slavery but the entire Southern way of life. One by one Southern states began seceding, and Lincoln's unwillingness to let them destroy the union led to the Civil War.

"New York City's Secession Crisis" analyzes this little-known event. To many New York merchants and other business people the city's prosperity depended on the continued existence of slavery. Some leading citizens in New York actually proposed that the city secede from the Union and reach an accommodation with the South.

Once the war got underway, many on both sides believed it would be over quickly. They were wrong. What began as a limited conflict turned into total war against resources and morale. In addition to military operations, the North with its superior navy sought to cripple the Southern economy by blockading its ports. Unable to purchase imported goods, Southerners had to live amidst shortages of all kinds.

The Civil War began as a struggle over national union, but ultimately became a conflict over the continued existence of slavery. "Lincoln and the Constitutional Dilemma of Emancipation" analyzes the many obstacles that prevented Abraham Lincoln from issuing the preliminary Emancipation Proclamation before he did. Among the most important factors in Lincoln's mind was the Constitution's protection of property rights. Although he knew he would be criticized by some for not going far enough, he also knew he would be condemned for having exceeded his executive powers. Author Edna Greene Medford argues that Lincoln satisfied himself that he was acting within his Constitutional powers.

Although many white Northerners opposed slavery, they believed that Blacks lacked the courage and intelligence to be suitable as combat soldiers. Men of the 54th Massachusetts Regiment were determined to disprove such beliefs. Their heroism in the bloody assault on Fort Wagner in South Carolina showed the world "that black troops could fight—and die—for the Union." Unfortunately this would turn out to be a lesson not learned, for Blacks would have to prove themselves over and over in subsequent wars.

A struggle took place after the war ended over how the South would be reintegrated into the Union. The most important issue was what status Blacks would have in the postwar society. Moderates such as Lincoln wished to make Reconstruction as painless as possible even though this meant continued white domination of Southern states. Radical Republicans sought to grant freed people the full rights of citizenship, and were willing to use force to attain this goal. Southern whites resisted "Radical Reconstruction" any way they could, and ultimately prevailed when Northern will eroded. "The American Civil War, Emancipation, and Reconstruction on the World Stage" analyzes the events of these years and writes that they "embodied struggles that would confront people on every continent."

White encroachment on Indian lands continued up to and after the Civil War. Railroads constructed after the conflict ended speeded this process. "How the West Was Lost," describes the westward expansion that disrupted and demoralized Indian tribal culture. One of the worst catastrophes for the plains Indians was the destruction of the once huge buffalo herds that provided them with everything from food and clothing to weapons. The Indians fought back from time to time but confronted overwhelming odds. In the end most tribes were forced onto reservations where they became little more than wards of the state. To its great discredit the United States made and broke countless treaties with the Indians over the years.

Free at Last

A new museum celebrates the Underground Railroad. The secret network of people who bravely led slaves to liberty before the Civil War.

FERGUS M. BORDEWICH

The phone rang one drizzly morning in Carl Westmoreland's office overlooking the gray ribbon of the Ohio River and downtown Cincinnati. It was February 1998. Westmoreland, a descendant of slaves, scholar of African-American history and former community organizer, had recently joined the staff of the National Underground Railroad Freedom Center. Then still in the planning stages, the center, which opened this past August in Cincinnati, is the nation's first institution dedicated to the clandestine pre-Civil War network that helped tens of thousands of fugitive slaves gain their freedom.

The caller, who identified himself as Raymond Evers, claimed that a 19th-century "slave jail" was located on his property in northern Kentucky; he wanted someone to come out to look at it. As word of the center had gotten around, Westmoreland had begun to receive a lot of calls like this one, from individuals who said their house contained secret hiding places or who reported mysterious tunnels on their property. He had investigated many of these sites. Virtually none turned out to have any connection with the Underground Railroad.

"I'll call you back tomorrow," Westmoreland said.

The next day, his phone rang again. It was Evers. "So when are you coming out?" he asked. Westmoreland sighed. "I'm on my way," he said.

An hour later, Westmoreland, a wiry man then in his early 60s, was slogging across a sodden alfalfa pasture in Mason County, Kentucky, eight miles south of the Ohio River, accompanied by Evers, 67, a retired businessman. The two made their way to a dilapidated tobacco barn at the top of a low hill.

"Where is it?" Westmoreland asked.

"Just open the door!" Evers replied.

In the darkened interior, Westmoreland made out a smaller structure built of rough-hewn logs and fitted with barred windows. Fastened to a joist inside the log hut were iron rings: fetters to which manacled slaves had once been chained. "I felt the way I did when I went to Auschwitz," Westmoreland later recalled. "I felt the power of the place—it was dark, ominous. When I saw the rings, I thought, it's like a slave-ship hold."

At first, Westmoreland had difficulty tracking down the history of the structure, where tobacco, corn and farm machinery had been stored for decades. But eventually Westmoreland located a Mason County resident who had heard from his father, who had heard from his grandfather, what had gone on in the little enclosure. "They chained 'em up over there, and sold 'em off like cattle," the Mason County man told Westmoreland.

At Westmoreland's urging, the Freedom Center accepted Evers' offer to donate the 32- by 27-foot structure. It was dismantled and transported to Cincinnati; the total cost for archaeological excavation and preservation was $2 million. When the Freedom Center opened its doors on August 23, the stark symbol of brutality was the first thing that visitors encountered in the lofty atrium facing the Ohio River. Says Westmoreland: "This institution represents the first time that there has been an honest effort to honor and preserve our collective memory, not in a basement or a slum somewhere, but at the front door of a major metropolitan community."

By its own definition a "museum of conscience," the 158,000-square-foot copper-roofed structure hopes to engage visitors in a visceral way. "This is not a slavery museum," says executive director Spencer Crew, who moved to Cincinnati from Washington, D.C., where he was director of the Smithsonian Institution's National Museum of American History. "Rather, it is a place to engage people on the subject of slavery and race without finger-pointing. Yes, the center shows that slavery was terrible. But it also shows that there were people who stood up against it."

Visitors will find, in addition to the slave jail, artifacts including abolitionists' diaries, wanted posters, ads for runaways, documents granting individual slaves their freedom and newspapers such as William Lloyd Garrison's militant *Liberator*, the first in the United States to call for immediate abolition. And they will encounter one of the most powerful symbols of slavery: shackles. "Shackles exert an almost mystical fascination," says Rita C. Organ, the center's director of exhibits and collections. "There were even small-sized shackles for children. By looking at them, you get a feeling of what our ancestors must have felt—suddenly you begin to imagine what it was like being huddled in a coffle of chained slaves on the march."

Additional galleries relate stories of the central figures in the Underground Railroad. Some, like Frederick Douglass and Harriet Tubman, are renowned. Many others, such as John P. Parker, a former slave who became a key activist in the Ohio underground, and his collaborator, abolitionist John Rankin, are little known.

Other galleries document the experiences of present-day Americans, people like Laquetta Shepard, a 24-year-old black West Virginia woman who in 2002 walked into the middle of a Ku Klux Klan rally and shamed the crowd into dispersing, and Syed Ali, a Middle Eastern gas station owner in New York City who prevented members of a radical Islamic group from setting fire to a neighborhood synagogue in 2003. Says Crew, "Ideally, we would like to create modern-day equivalents of the Underground Railroad conductors, who have the internal fortitude to buck society's norms and to stand up for the things they really believe in."

The center's concept grew out of a tumultuous period in the mid-1990s when Cincinnati was reeling from confrontations between the police and the African-American community and when Marge Schott, then the owner of the Cincinnati Reds, made comments widely regarded as racist. At a 1994 meeting of the Cincinnati chapter of the National Conference of Christians and Jews, its then-director, Robert "Chip" Harrod, proposed the idea of a museum devoted to the Underground Railroad. Since then, the center has raised some $60 million from private donations and another $50 million from public sources, including the Department of Education.

The term underground railroad is said to derive from the story of a frustrated slave hunter who, having failed to apprehend a runaway, exclaimed, "He must have gone off on an underground road!" In an age when smoke-belching locomotives and shining steel rails were novelties, activists from New York to Illinois, many of whom had never seen an actual railroad, readily adopted its terminology, describing guides as "conductors," safe houses as "stations," horse-drawn wagons as "cars," and fugitives as "passengers."

Says Ira Berlin, author of *Many Thousands Gone: The First Two Centuries of Slavery in North America:* "The Underground Railroad played a critical role, by making the nature of slavery clear to Northerners who had been indifferent to it, by showing that slaves who were running away were neither happy nor well-treated, as apologists for slavery claimed. And morally, it demonstrated the enormous resiliency of the human spirit in the collaboration of blacks and whites to help people gain their freedom."

Thanks to the clandestine network, as many as 150,000 slaves may have found their way to safe havens in the North and Canada. "We don't know the total number and we will probably never know," says James O. Horton, a professor of American studies and history at George Washington University in Washington, D.C. "Part of the reason is that the underground was so successful: it kept its secrets well."

By the 1850s, activists from Delaware to Kansas had joined the underground to help fugitives elude capture. Wrote abolitionist Gerrit Smith in 1836: "If there be human enactments against our opening our door to our colored brother. . . . We must obey God."

As the nation's second great civil disobedience movement—the first being the actions, including the Boston Tea Party, leading to the American Revolution—the Underground Railroad engaged thousands of citizens in the subversion of federal law. The movement provoked fear and anger in the South and prompted the enactment of draconian legislation, including the 1850 Fugitive Slave Law, which required Northerners to cooperate in the capture of escaped slaves. And at a time when proslavery advocates insisted that blacks were better off in bondage because they lacked the intelligence or ability to take care of themselves, it also gave many African-Americans experience in political organizing and resistance.

"The Underground Railroad symbolized the intensifying struggle over slavery," says Berlin. "It was the result of the ratcheting up of the earlier antislavery movement, which in the years after the American Revolution, had begun to call for compensated emancipation and gradualist solutions to slavery." In the North, it brought African-Americans, often for the first time, into white communities where they could be seen as real people, with real families and real feelings. Ultimately, Berlin says, "the Underground Railroad forced whites to confront the reality of race in American society and to begin to wrestle with the reality in which black people lived all the time. It was a transforming experience."

For blacks and whites alike the stakes were high. Underground agents faced a constant threat of punitive litigation, violent reprisal and possible death. "White participants in the underground found in themselves a depth of humanity that they hadn't realized they had," says Horton. "And for many of them, humanity won out over legality." As New York philanthropist Gerrit Smith, one of the most important financiers of the Underground Railroad, put it in 1836, "If there be human enactments against our entertaining the stricken stranger—against our opening our door to our poor, guiltless, and unaccused colored brother pursued by bloodthirsty kidnappers—we must, nevertheless, say with the apostle: 'We must obey God rather than man.'"

From the earliest years of American bondage—the Spanish held slaves in Florida in the late 1500s; Africans were sold to colonists at Jamestown in 1619—slaves had fled their masters. But until British Canada and some Northern states—including

Pennsylvania and Massachusetts—began abolishing slavery at the end of the 18th century, there were no permanent havens for fugitives. A handful of slaves found sanctuary among several Native American tribes deep in the swamps and forests of Florida. The first coordinated Underground Railroad activity can be traced to the early 19th century, perhaps when free blacks and white Quakers began to provide refuge for runaways in and around Philadelphia, or perhaps when activists organized in Ohio.

The process accelerated throughout the 1830s. "The whole country was like a huge pot in a furious state of boiling over," recalled Addison Coffin in 1897. Coffin served as an underground conductor in North Carolina and Indiana. "It was almost universal for ministers of the gospel to run into the subject in all their sermons; neighbors would stop and argue pro and con across the fence; people traveling along the road would stop and argue the point." Although abolitionists initially faced the contempt of a society that largely took the existence of slavery for granted, the underground would eventually count among its members Rutherford B. Hayes, the future president, who as a young lawyer in the 1850s defended fugitive slaves; William Seward, the future governor of New York and secretary of state, who provided financial support to Harriet Tubman and other underground activists; and Allan Pinkerton, founder of the Pinkerton Detective Agency, who in 1859 helped John Brown lead a band of fugitive slaves out of Chicago and on to Detroit, bound for Canada. By the 1850s, the underground ranged from the northern borders of states including Maryland, Virginia and Kentucky to Canada and numbered thousands among its ranks from Delaware to Kansas.

But its center was the Ohio River Valley, where scores of river crossings served as gateways from slave states to free and where, once across the Ohio, fugitives could hope to be passed from farm to farm all the way to the Great Lakes in a matter of days.

In practice, the underground functioned with a minimum of central direction and a maximum of grass-roots involvement, particularly among family members and church congregations. "The method of operating was not uniform but adapted to the requirements of each case," Isaac Beck, a veteran of Underground Railroad activity in southern Ohio, would recall in 1892. "There was no regular organization, no constitution, no officers, no laws or agreement or rule except the 'Golden Rule,' and every man did what seemed right in his own eyes." Travel was by foot, horseback or wagon. One stationmaster, Levi Coffin, an Indiana Quaker and Addison's uncle, kept a team of horses harnessed and a wagon ready to go at his farm in Newport (now Fountain City), Indiana. When additional teams were needed, Coffin wrote in his memoir, posthumously published in 1877, "the people at the livery stable seemed to understand what the teams were wanted for, and they asked no questions."

On occasion, fugitives might be transported in hearses or false-bottomed wagons, men might be disguised as women, women as men, blacks powdered white with talc. The volume of underground traffic varied widely. Levi Coffin estimated that during his lifetime he assisted 3,300 fugitives—some 100 or so annually—while others, who lived along more lightly traveled routes, took in perhaps two or three a month, or only a handful over several years.

The underground clarified the nature of slavery (fugitives brought ashore in Philadelphia in 1856) to Northerners. As the railroad accelerated, "the whole country," wrote conductor Addison Coffin in 1897, "was like a huge pot in a state of boiling over."

One of the most active underground centers—and the subject of a 15-minute docudrama, *Brothers of the Borderland,* produced for the Freedom Center and introduced by Oprah Winfrey—was Ripley, Ohio, about 50 miles east of Cincinnati. Today, Ripley is a sleepy village of two- and three-story 19th-century houses nestled at the foot of low bluffs, facing south toward the Ohio River and the cornfields of Kentucky beyond. But in the decades preceding the Civil War, it was one of the busiest ports between Pittsburgh and Cincinnati, its economy fueled by river traffic, shipbuilding and pork butchering. To slave owners, it was known as "a black, dirty Abolition hole"—and with good reason. Since the 1820s, a network of radical white Presbyterians, led by the Rev. John Rankin, a flinty Tennessean who had moved north to escape the atmosphere of slavery, collaborated with local blacks on both sides of the river in one of the most successful underground operations.

The Rankins' simple brick farmhouse still stands on a hilltop. It was visible for miles along the river and well into Kentucky. Arnold Gragston, who as a slave in Kentucky ferried scores of fugitives across the then 500- to 1,500-foot-wide Ohio River, later recalled that Rankin had a "lighthouse in his yard, about thirty feet high."

Recently, local preservationist Betty Campbell led the way into the austere parlor of the Rankin house, now a museum open to the public. She pointed out the fireplace where hundreds of runaways warmed themselves on winter nights, as well as the upstairs crawl space where, on occasion, they hid. Because the Rankins lived so close to the river and within easy reach of slave hunters, they generally sheltered fugitives only briefly before leading them on horseback along an overgrown streambed through a forest to a neighboring farmhouse a few miles north.

"The river divided the two worlds by law, the North and the South, but the cultures were porous," Campbell said, gazing across the river's gray trough toward the bluffs of Kentucky, a landscape not much altered since the mid-19th century. "There were antislavery men in Kentucky, and also proslavery men here in Ohio, where a lot of people had Southern origins and took slavery for granted. Frequently, trusted slaves were sent from Kentucky to the market at Ripley."

For families like the Rankins, the clandestine work became a full-time vocation. Jean Rankin, John's wife, was responsible for seeing that a fire was burning in the hearth and food kept on the table. At least one of the couple's nine sons remained on call, prepared to saddle up and hasten his charges to the next way station. "It was the custom with us not to talk among ourselves about the fugitives lest inadvertently a clue should be obtained of our modus operandi," the Rankins' eldest son, Adam, wrote years later in an unpublished memoir. " 'Another runaway went through at night' was all that would be said."

One Rankin collaborator, Methodist minister John B. Mahan, was arrested at his home and taken back to Kentucky, where after 16 months in jail he was made to pay a ruinous fine that impoverished his family and likely contributed to his early death. In the summer of 1841, Kentucky slaveholders assaulted the Rankins' hilltop stronghold. They were repulsed only after a gun battle that left one of the attackers dead. Not even the Rankins would cross the river into Kentucky, where the penalty for "slave stealing" was up to 21 years' imprisonment. One Ripley man who did so repeatedly was John P. Parker, a former slave who had bought his freedom in Mobile, Alabama; by day, he operated an iron foundry. By night, he ferried slaves from Kentucky plantations across the river to Ohio. Although no photograph of Parker has survived, his saga has been preserved in a series of interviews recorded in the 1880s and published in 1996 as *His Promised Land: The Autobiography of John P. Parker.*

On one occasion, Parker learned that a party of fugitives, stranded after the capture of their leader, was hiding about 20 miles south of the river. "Being new and zealous in this work, I volunteered to go to the rescue," Parker recalled. Armed with a pair of pistols and a knife, and guided by another slave, Parker reached the runaways at about dawn. He found them hidden in deep woods, paralyzed with fear and "so badly demoralized that some of them wanted to give themselves up rather than face the unknown." Parker led the ten men and women for miles through dense thickets.

As many as 150,000 slaves may have gained freedom. "We will probably never know [the total]," says historian James O. Horton. "Part of the reason is that the underground was so successful: it kept its secrets well."

With slave hunters closing in, one of the fugitives insisted on setting off in search of water. He had gone only a short way before he came hurtling through the brush, pursued by two white men. Parker turned to the slaves still in hiding. "Drawing my pistol," he recalled, "I quietly told them that I would shoot the first one that dared make a noise, which had a quieting effect." Through thickets, Parker saw the captured slave being led away, his arms tied behind his back. The group proceeded to the river, where a patroller spotted them.

Though the lights of Ripley were visible across the water, "they might as well have been [on] the moon so far as being a relief to me," Parker recalled. Bloodhounds baying in their ears, the runaways located a rowboat quickly enough, but it had room for only eight people. Two would have to be left behind. When the wife of one of the men picked to stay behind began to wail, Parker would recall, "I witnessed an example of heroism that made me proud of my race." One of the men in the boat gave up his seat to the woman's husband. As Parker rowed toward Ohio and freedom, he saw slave hunters converge on the spot where the two men had been left behind. "I knew," he wrote later, "the poor fellow had been captured in sight of the promised land."

Parker carried a $2,500 price on his head. More than once, his house was searched and he was assaulted in the streets of Ripley. Yet he estimated that he managed to help some 440 fugitives to freedom. In 2002, Parker's house on the Ripley waterfront—restored by a local citizens' group headed by Campbell—opened to the public.

On a clear day last spring, Carl Westmoreland returned to the Evers farm. Since his first visit, he had learned that the slave jail had been built in the 1830s by a prosperous slave trader, John Anderson, who used it to hold slaves en route by flatboat to the huge slave market at Natchez, Mississippi, where auctions were held several times a year. Anderson's manor house is gone now, as are the cabins of the slaves who served in his household, tended his land and probably even operated the jail itself.

"The jail is a perfect symbol of forgetting," Westmoreland said at the time, not far from the slave trader's overgrown grave. "For their own reasons, whites and blacks both tried to forget about that jail, just as the rest of America tried to forget about slavery. But that building has already begun to teach, by causing people to go back and look at the local historical record. It's doing its job." Anderson died in 1834 at the age of 42. Westmoreland continued: "They say that he tripped over a grapevine and fell onto the sharp stump of a cornstalk, which penetrated his eye and entered his brain. He was chasing a runaway slave."

FERGUS M. BORDEWICH is the author of *Bound for Canaan: The Underground Railroad and the War for the Soul of America,* to be published in April by Amistad/HarperCollins.

A Day to Remember

October 16, 1859: John Brown Raids Harpers Ferry

CHARLES PHILLIPS

Before the Civil War, Harpers Ferry was a small Southern town—a clump of homes and hotels, shops and saloons that sat on a pretty hillside where the Shenandoah and Potomac rivers meet. It also had forges, machine works and stock-making shops that produced guns for the Federal government, and many of the weapons were stored in a U.S. arsenal there.

For the 22 men who made their way down from the Maryland Heights and across the Potomac through the cold drizzle of the moonless Sunday night of October 16, 1859, however, Harpers Ferry was to be the staging point from which to launch Armageddon. Sixteen of the men were white, as was their leader, and five were free black men; all were armed. They tramped solemnly behind a creaking wagon. Up front slumped a figure whose long beard and piercing gaze put folks in mind of some Old Testament prophet, if not the wrathful Jehovah himself. He was the radical abolitionist John Brown, and he had chosen this Sunday evening to spark the rebellion he believed would destroy the Slave Power, his sobriquet for a United States government that he felt was dominated by the slave-holding South.

Brown had begun planning his attack in 1857, after moving back East from Kansas, where he had served as the self-appointed captain of the violent antislavery forces pouring into that territory. There, in an attempt to staunch the virulent proslavery immigration sparked by the Kansas-Nebraska Act, Brown had led a band of six men, including four of his sons, in an 1856 raid against a pioneer settlement of Southerners along Pottawatomie Creek. At Brown's command, the raiders brutally murdered five settlers. Other depredations followed in the spreading fight over the slavery issue: More than 200 people had been killed in "Bloody Kansas" by the end of the year, and Brown fled with a price on his head. Though a fugitive, he traveled openly around the Northeast, and especially to Boston, drumming up support for his cause.

Over the years, Brown, a debt-ridden Ohio farmer with a New England Puritan pedigree stretching back—or so he claimed—to *Mayflower,* had become associated with several prominent abolitionists. They included such Boston Brahmins as Samuel Gridley Howe (educator and the first director of the Perkins School for the Blind), Thomas Wentworth Higginson (former minister turned writer), Theodore Parker (theologian and scholar), Franklin Sanborn (founder of a high-toned prep school) and George L. Stearns (a Boston merchant), as well as Gerrit Smith (scion of a wealthy New York family). Though Brown had other supporters, these men, the Secret Six, raised funds for him, bought guns for him and supplied his family with a house in the Adirondacks in New York.

There in the mountains, John Brown developed his scheme. He would take Harpers Ferry. Since the place contained U.S. government installations, he knew that word of his rebellion would quickly spread far and wide. Surely, he thought, thousands of slaves, freedmen and antislavery whites would rally to his cause, and Harpers Ferry could supply the guns and ammunition to arm them all. Once a large enough force had gathered, Brown planned to break out and terrorize his way south through Virginia, Tennessee and Alabama hoping more and more slaves would join his rebellion as they went.

Probably none of the Secret Six knew his plan in any detail. Brown did not tell his own men—not even two of his sons, Oliver and Watson—the entire plan until the night before the raid, after which he had to deploy the full force of his overbearing personality to persuade them all to continue. He had, however, revealed everything to the famed abolitionist Frederick Douglass and an escaped slave named Shields Green when they met with Brown a few days earlier in a quarry outside Chambersburg, Pa. Brown was hoping that Douglass, a supporter, would use his prestige to summon slaves to join the uprising after it started. But Douglass could see the folly of the scheme and tried to persuade Brown to call it off. When Douglass left to return home to Rochester, N.Y., Green elected to stay and risk his life. "I believe I'll go with the old man," the fugitive said.

On October 16, 1859, from their headquarters on a rented farm in Maryland, John Brown's band of guerrilla fighters invaded Harpers Ferry. Two of his young Bloody Kansas veterans, John E. Cook and Charles P. Tidd, disappeared into the woods to find and cut telegraph lines east and west of town. Brown motioned two others, Aaron D. Stevens and John H. Kagi, forward. They dashed onto the covered railroad and wagon bridge that led across the river into town and captured the night watchman, who thought it was all a joke until he saw the rifles and the expressions on their faces. The other attackers quickly came up and deployed across the Shenandoah bridge.

The free mulatto Dangerfield Newby (who dreamed of rescuing his enslaved wife and children), young William Thompson and Brown's son Oliver were left to guard the bridges, while the others slipped through the nearly deserted streets past a well-lit hotel (the Wager House) and saloon (the Galt House). On Potomac Street, they took the watchman of the government shops by surprise and secured both the armory and the arsenal. The guard, pinned against the gate, shivered as he heard the scary old man leading this wild bunch say to him: "I came here from Kansas and this is a slave state. I have possession now of the United States armory, and if the citizens interfere with me I must only burn the town and have blood."

As Brown brought his wagon into the armory yard, his troops grabbed a few people out on the streets as hostages, herding them inside the firehouse next to the gate. Then Brown led a party up Shenandoah Street to seize Hall's Rifle Works, taking another prisoner along the way. Kagi and a young black student from Oberlin College named John A. Copeland manned the rifle works, where they were later reinforced by another of Brown's black followers, Lewis S. Leary.

It was all going according to plan. Brown had taken his prime targets. Now in charge of millions of dollars' worth of Federal guns and ammo, he dispatched raiders to spread throughout the area and raid plantations, take hostages and free slaves. Around midnight, the special detachment returned with some 10 liberated slaves and three hostages, most prominent among them Colonel Lewis Washington, a local planter. The colonel carried a splendid saber that he had inherited from his great uncle, George Washington. (The blade was reportedly a gift from Frederick the Great to the first American president.) Brown confiscated it in the name of the revolution and made it his own "terrible swift sword."

Then things went wrong. Shortly after midnight, Brown's guards fired at the just-arrived relief night watchman for the Potomac bridge, and he—bleeding from a flesh wound to the head—bolted for the Galt House. The raiders barely had time to build a barricade across the bridge before an express train from Wheeling, Va., came rolling in. The wounded watchman rushed out to warn the conductor that he had been shot by invaders. The train's engineer and another railroad employee walked down the track to investigate, only to be driven back by gunfire. The conductor backed the train and stopped, out of rifle range. Passengers, their faces pressed against car windows, peered into the gloom.

Just then Hayward Shepherd, the station's baggage master, came down the tracks looking for the night watchman. The raiders shouted, "Halt!" When Shepherd headed back the way he had come, they shot him. He staggered and fell before the wounded night watchman could reach him. Dragged back into the station, Shepherd later died there in agony. (There was irony in Hayward Shepherd's death—the first fatality of John Brown's raid was a free black man.)

Shortly after Shepherd was mortally wounded, the anxious Dangerfield Newby gunned down a well-to-do grocer named Thomas Boerly—an Irishman popular with locals. Gushing blood, Boerly fell to the street and died. By early Monday morning, October 17, the shooting and shouting had awakened the town. Its denizens mobbed the streets armed with pickaxes and squirrel guns, jabbering about murder and insurrection as the Lutheran church bell tolled the alarm.

Brown had meanwhile allowed the express train to travel on, perhaps thinking it would spread the word to his hoped-for supporters. It proved a mistake. When the train reached first Monocacy and then Frederick, Md., the rumors of black rebellion and rampage blazed through the countryside. The Slave Power's greatest fear, constantly nagging at the collective mind of the South, especially since Nat Turner's uprising in Virginia in 1831, seemed to have come to pass. From every village and town within 30 miles, men formed militias and struck out for Harpers Ferry.

By 11 A.M. on the 17th the town was embroiled in a running battle as farm boys and townsfolk took up positions and fired on the firehouse and armory where Brown and his troops had ensconced themselves. To Osborne F. Anderson, one of the five blacks involved in the raid, the old man seemed "puzzled" by the speed and size of the mobilization against him and by the lack of response from the local slave population. As Kagi and others counseled flight, Brown dithered, even taking time to order breakfast from the Wager House for his growing number of hostages.

While his confused men milled about the confines of the armory, Brown dispatched Cook and Tidd to take the liberated slaves and hook up with his son Owen, in charge of Brown's rear guard back at the farm. Still the abolitionist waited for the general uprising on which he had based his scheme. Instead of rebel slaves rallying to his side, however, white militias from nearby Charlestown, Va., joined the counterattack.

By the time those units came charging across the bridge with their rifles blazing, John Brown had waited too long. They routed Brown's sentinels, secured control of both bridges and took up a position behind the barricaded Wager House, thus cutting off the invaders' only line of retreat into Maryland. In the course of the attack, Dangerfield Newby became Brown's first casualty. Shot in the throat making a run for the armory, he died in the street, where an angry crowd beat his lifeless body, poked sticks into his bullet wound, sliced off his ears, castrated him and then fed him to some hogs. Brown sent Will Thompson out under a truce flag to negotiate a cease-fire. The holed-up abolitionist would release his 30-odd prisoners if the militia let him and his men go free. The crowd arrested Thompson and locked him up in the Galt House. Brown next sent out his son Watson and Stevens with the armory's acting superintendent under a white flag, but the mob fired on and wounded the two invaders. Watson crawled back to the firehouse (where he later died an agonizingly painful death at his father's side), but Stevens lay in the gutter bleeding. One of Brown's prisoners, a man named Joseph Brau, volunteered to help. He carried the wounded man to the railroad station, saw that he got medical attention, then—amazingly—returned to captivity.

As the crowd liquored up at the Galt House and grew ever more profane and threatening, the youngest of Brown's recruits, William Leeman, snapped. He fled across the armory yard, leaped over the gate and ran for his life toward the Potomac. Militiamen chased Leeman down and shot him dead. His body lay on a little islet in the river for much of the day as others used it for target practice. Then, riddled with bullets, it slipped into the water and floated away.

Newby, Stevens, Leeman and Watson Brown—so it went; the casualties mounted. At about 2 P.M., the raiders killed a slave owner named George Turner, further infuriating the mob. Angry citizens stormed Hall's Rifle Works, killing Kagi, mortally wounding Leary and capturing Copeland as all three tried to escape across the Shenandoah. When one of Brown's troops, Edwin Coppoc—a Quaker boy from Iowa—gunned down the town's kindly old mayor, Fontaine Beckham, a mob led by one of Beckham's relatives dragged Will Thompson from the Galt House, shot him in the head and dumped him into the Potomac, where—like Leeman—his body was used for target practice.

Meanwhile, news of a slave revolt had spread throughout Maryland and Virginia. In Baltimore five more militia companies boarded a special train bound for Harpers Ferry. President James Buchanan ordered three artillery companies and 90 Marines to the town, and then dispatched Lt. Col. Robert E. Lee of the 2nd Cavalry to take charge of the forces at Harpers Ferry.

On the morning of October 18, as the remaining raiders—Brown, Edwin Coppoc, Jeremiah C. Anderson, Dauphin hompson and Shields Green—watched from their gun holes, the Marines deployed in front of the engine house, much to the approval of some 2,000 spectators lining the sidewalks and streets. Lee, 40 feet away, sent his flamboyant second-in-command, James Ewell Brown (J.E.B.) Stuart, up to the door under a white flag. As the old man took Lee's demand for unconditional surrender, Stuart—who had served in Kansas—recognized him as the firebrand abolitionist with a price on his head. When Brown rejected Lee's conditions, Stuart jumped aside and waved his hat. Marines stormed the door, and the crowd let go a loud cheer. The Marines killed Anderson and Dauphin Thompson, wounded the others and crippled Brown with a sword. But the abolitionist lived, and Lee ordered a doctor to tend to Brown's wounds.

The state of Virginia charged John Brown with treason, conspiracy and murder. During his trial and after he was convicted and sentenced to die by hanging, the old man acquitted himself well in the eyes of many, even some among his Southern prosecutors. By the calm sureness with which he accepted the loss of his two sons during the raid and his own fate afterward, indeed, Brown seemed to welcome his martyrdom.

While Northern abolitionists at length held up John Brown as the new standard of their cause, Southerners reacted with alarm. For Northerner and Southerner alike, Brown's raid exacerbated the tensions that threatened to tear the country apart, leading Americans to ever more readily embrace violence. Harpers Ferry was one of the flash points that turned a virulent social debate into a civil war.

From *American History,* October 2005, pp. 16–18, 72–73. Copyright © 2005 by Weider History Group. Reprinted by permission.

New York City's Secession Crisis

Strong economic ties to the South tempted Gotham to consider a break from the Union in 1861.

CHUCK LEDDY

On December 20, 1860, in the wake of the election of Abraham Lincoln, the words that would ignite a war rang out at a state convention in South Carolina: "the union now subsisting between South Carolina and other States . . . is hereby dissolved." Soon six other Southern states would also leave the Union. And if a colorful but corrupt mayor had had his way, they would have had some unlikely company.

New York City, the North's largest and wealthiest metropolis, seriously considered exiting the Union only two weeks after South Carolina had done so. Several of the city's most influential political and business leaders proposed to separate it from the United States in the months prior to the Civil War, and worked tirelessly—though unsuccessfully—to achieve a negotiated accommodation with secessionists from the Southern states.

On January 6, 1861, New York City's Democratic Mayor Fernando Wood addressed the Common Council in his annual State of the City speech. Wood described how the city's "great trading and producing interests" were presently "prostrated by a monetary crisis." Southern secession threatened commercial relationships upon which New York City's wealth had historically depended. Wood's solution to the crisis was simple. "[W]hy should not New York City . . . become also equally independent? As a free city . . . she would have the whole and united support of the Southern States. . . ." Wood intended to call the independent city-state, comprising Manhattan, Staten Island and Long Island, "Tri-Insula," meaning "three islands" in Latin. Once separated, it would he free to continue its extraordinarily lucrative cotton trade with the seceded South.

Business relationships between New York City and the South had grown strong in the four decades prior to the Civil War. Mayor Wood, during his campaign for a third term as mayor in 1859, put it simply: "The South is our best customer. She pays the best prices, and pays promptly." Cotton had become the nation's top export, accounting for more than half of all American exports, and New York City was America's undisputed center of the trade. New York City merchants directly

benefited from slave labor, and in the antebellum years worked constantly to keep the growing slavery crisis from boiling over into a civil war that would devastate their bottom lines.

Historian Philip S. Foner, in his book *Business and Slavery: New York Merchants and the Irrepressible Conflict,* explains that "New York dominated every single phase of the cotton trade from plantation to market." Southern planters financed their operations through New York City banks, negotiated contracts with New York City business agents, transported their crops on New York City ships, insured them through New York City brokers and purchased equipment and household goods from New York City merchants. According to Foner, the South pumped approximately $200 million annually into Gotham's economy. James De Bow, an economist, statistician and editor of the widely circulated Southern magazine De Bow's Review, estimated at the time that New York City businessmen received 40 cents for every dollar spent on Southern cotton.

Southern planters regularly traveled to New York to purchase luxury items, married into New York's leading merchant families, vacationed at Saratoga and socialized with their Northern business partners. One of New York's top financiers of the cotton trade, August Belmont, was related by marriage to Louisiana Congressman James Slidell, later a Confederate diplomat. Through Slidell, Belmont was connected to the South's leading politicians and planters. During the secession crisis of 1860-61, Belmont would become a vocal leader in New York City's continuous efforts to negotiate a solution.

Mayor Wood, himself a former merchant, clearly understood that New York City's prosperity depended on the enslavement of 4 million African Americans, admitting in 1859 that "the profits . . . depend upon the products only to he obtained by continuance of slave labor. . . ." The connections between New York City's merchants and Southern cotton growers were everywhere. Three Lehman brothers were cotton brokers in Alabama before moving north to help establish the New York Cotton Exchange. Today, Lehman Brothers is a major Wall Street investment firm. Shipping magnate John Jacob Astor's ships hauled Southern cotton. J.P. Morgan studied the cotton trade as a young man.

These strong economic ties had obvious political ramifications. New York merchants were overwhelmingly Democratic, in sympathy with the South and the institution of slavery. When the American Anti-Slavery Society held its annual convention in New York City in 1859, for example, the Democratic New York Herald described the visiting abolitionists as "a little set of crazy demagogues and fanatics."

One New York City merchant bluntly explained the merchant community's attitude toward slavery to Syracuse abolitionist Samuel May: "Mr. May, we are not such fools as not to know that slavery is a great evil, a great wrong. But a great portion of the prosperity of the Southerners is invested under its sanction; and the business of the North, as well as the South, has become adjusted to it. There are millions upon millions of dollars due from Southerners to the merchants and mechanics alone, the payment of which would be jeopardized by any rupture between the North and the South. We cannot afford, sir, to let you and your associates endeavor to overthrow slavery. It is not a matter of principles with us. It is a matter of business. . . ." Abolitionists, in short, were rocking a boat that was making New York City's merchants rich.

During the 1860 presidential campaign, Mayor Wood and New York's merchant community fanned fears of "Black Republican" control in Washington. The New York Daily News, edited by the mayor's brother, Benjamin Wood, shamelessly appealed to working class racism by warning workers that "if Lincoln is elected you will have to compete with the labor of four million emancipated negroes." Many businessmen also warned their employees that if Lincoln won in November, the South would soon bolt the Union, taking away its lucrative business and leaving New York City workers without jobs. The anti-Lincoln vote in New York City was 62 percent. But Republican strength upstate outweighed Democratic gains in the metropolis. Lincoln won the state and the election, triggering a nightmare scenario for the South and the New York City merchants who depended upon its trade.

In early December 1860, New York merchants planned to assemble and discuss rumors of South Carolina's secession and the possible loss of Southern trade. Two hundred invitations were sent out for the December 15 meeting at 33 Pine Street, the offices of a cotton merchant near Wall Street. Over 2,000 worried merchants showed up, a veritable "Who's Who" of the city's commercial establishment, determined to show their solidarity with the South and seek an alternative to Southern secession.

Hiram Ketchum, a prominent lawyer, spoke for many New York City merchants at the Pine Street meeting when he begged the South to "give us time to organize and combine, and we will put down any parry that attempts to do what the South fears the Republican Party will do. . . . We can right the wrong in the Union, only give us time." But after decades of cobbled-together, last-second compromises, the South was sick and tired of waiting. Five days after the massive Pine Street meeting, South Carolina seceded from the Union. With about $200 million in outstanding Southern debt still owed New York City,

its merchants trembled at the possibility that this massive deficit might be ignored, and the lucrative Southern trade cut off.

In late December, a delegation of 30 New York City merchants journeyed to Washington to sound out lame-duck President James Buchanan about how he planned to respond to South Carolina's secession. The merchants stood in stunned silence as Buchanan answered their anxious questions by shaking his head and uttering: "I have no power in the matter. I have no power in the matter." President-elect Lincoln remained silent on the issue, biding his time until he took power in March. The worried merchants next turned to Congress, lobbying in support of the recently introduced Crittenden Compromise, which included constitutional amendments intended to protect slavery in the South forever. (Ultimately, the compromise was narrowly defeated in the Senate, a few days before Lincoln's March 4 inauguration.)

The secession crisis was proving to be the expected body blow for New York City's cotton-dependent economy. Many Southerners, long resentful of what they regarded as Gotham's exploitation of cotton growers, cared little about the city's dilemma. When the London Times asked editor James De Bow what would happen to New York City without the South, he gleefully replied: "The ships would rot at her docks; grass would grow in Wall Street and Broadway, and the glory of New York . . . would be numbered with the things of the past."

The city would not wait idly for that disaster to happen. Wood's proposal that New York City leave the Union in order to continue trading with the South—taking with it the hefty 67 percent of the federal revenue that was the city's contribution—came shortly after. Wood blamed the secessionist crisis on Republican abolitionists in Albany and New England, and also castigated Albany for its interference with his city's government.

Wood had a history of bad blood with the stare government. The mayor "set the pattern for the institutionalized corruption that plagued nineteenth-century New York politics," according to Melvin Holli, author of The American Mayor. In the 1856-57 session of the state Legislature, the Albany Republicans had voted to slash Wood's term as mayor in half. Moreover, Albany had created a new law enforcement entity, the Metropolitan Police, to replace the Wood-controlled Municipal Police. Legislators believed that Wood's men had become so corrupt and disorganized that they had to intervene. The two police forces clashed in front of City Hall in 1857, and the Metropolitan Police arrested a rebellious Wood for inciting a riot for refusing to disband "his" police force.

Republican reaction to Wood's secession proposal was predictably hostile. Pro-Lincoln editor Horace Greeley concluded in the New York Tribune that "Fernando Wood evidently wants to be a traitor." Still, Wood's proposal would remain a subject of debate until the first shots were fired at Fort Sumter

Although Wood's proposal received support among some merchants as one possible option to forestall the commercial crisis, city merchants continued to lobby Congress for a legislative resolution, such as that embodied by the Crittenden Compromise. In late January 1861, a second delegation of New York

City businessmen traveled to Washington seeking a compromise to the secession crisis, this time carrying a petition signed by over 40,000 city merchants. The delegation strongly hinted that Wall Street would withhold financial support from the Union unless an agreement with the South was reached. These veiled threats infuriated the Republican press, which viewed them as tantamount to blackmail. Greeley condemned the "mercantile howl" and claimed that the public possessed "a wider range of vision than the shelves of dry goods and warehouses of cotton" and didn't need these unscrupulous, pro-slavery "money men" to finance the Union cause.

This second New York merchant delegation also left Washington empty-handed, reporting that the escalating crisis was "apparently insurmountable." The New York Herald expressed disappointment, complaining that "the Southern trade is reduced to nothing, and everything seems to be going to the dogs." To make matters worse, the Republican Congress soon passed a tariff favoring Northern manufacturers, and the Confederacy followed suit in March by erecting tariff walls to protect Southern trade. Wood's dream of an independent New York City able to trade freely and peaceably with everyone suffered a severe setback.

President-elect Lincoln soon arrived into this atmosphere of doom and gloom within New York City's commercial circles. Hoping to quell secessionist sentiment in the city, he had breakfast on February 20 with 100 of the city's leading businessmen, nearly all of whom either favored compromising with the South or supported Gotham's right to secede. In his comments, Lincoln did his best to be noncommittal on secession while stating his support for the law and the Union. When someone pointed out to Lincoln all the millionaires gathered in the room, underscoring their financial muscle, he wryly snapped back: "I'm a millionaire myself. I got a minority of a million in the votes last November."

Lincoln met with Mayor Wood at City Hall later the same day and in his public remarks seemed to criticize Wood's secessionist proposal without directly mentioning it. "There is nothing," said Lincoln, "that can ever bring me to willingly consent to the destruction of this Union, under which not only the commercial city of New York, but the whole country has acquired its greatness." What went on behind closed doors, and whether or not Lincoln promised to give special treatment to New York City's commercial interests, is unknown.

When Lincoln gave his long-anticipated Inaugural Address on March 4, he attempted to set a conciliatory tone while holding firm to the principal that "the Union of these states is perpetual." Tellingly, Lincoln asserted that "the central idea of secession is the essence of anarchy." Lincoln also promised to protect federal property, an indirect reference to the stalemate at Fort Sumter in South Carolina, a political headache he had inherited from the outgoing Buchanan.

In March 1861, faced with high tariffs, a new president seemingly set against recognizing the right of secession and the real possibility of the Confederacy's repudiation of its debts to New York City, Mayor Wood's dream of an independent, free-trading "Tri-Insula" was tottering on the ropes. The knockout blow came

a few weeks later. Early on the morning of April 12, 1861, Confederate shells burst out over Fort Sumter. The following day Major Robert Anderson surrendered the garrison to Confederate forces. The Civil War had begun, ending any realistic possibility of a negotiated settlement—or an independent New York City.

Patriotic fervor spread quickly throughout the North, and a bipartisan rallying ensued around President Lincoln. On April 20, a crowd of between 100,000 to 250,000 people thronged New York's Union Square to hear patriotic speeches. Wood, caught up in the flag-waving, had even issued a vague proclamation supporting the Union in the days after Fort Sumter. Republicans and other New Yorkers remained skeptical of his supposed change of heart. Prominent attorney George Templeton Strong, who would later work for Lincoln as treasurer of the U.S. Sanitary Commission, wrote about Wood's apparent transformation in his diary on April 15: "The cunning scoundrel [Wood] sees which way the cat is jumping."

On April 21, Lincoln disbursed $2 million into the hands of a New York City business organization to purchase arms and supplies, and New York City businessmen would continue to grow rich financing the Union war effort over the next four years. In a moment of supreme irony, Wood sat down to write a letter to Lincoln on April 29, 1861, and made a proposal utterly unlike his one of January 6: "I beg to tender my services in any military capacity consistent with my position as Mayor of New York." Lincoln, not needing another inexperienced political general, particularly one of questionable loyalty, ignored the offer.

On April 30, the Richmond Dispatch spoke for much of the South in denouncing the sudden transformation of the once-friendly Wood and his metropolis: "We could not have believed, nothing could have persuaded us, that the city of New York, which has been enriched by Southern trade, and had ever professed to be true to . . . the South, would in one day he converted into our bitterest enemy, panting for our blood, fitting out fleets and armies, and raising millions for our destruction."

The Mayor was far from finished in his duplicity. He ran for reelection later in 1861, roundly criticizing Lincoln and his use of war powers. After one anti-Republican speech, the local U.S. marshal was so outraged that he asked Secretary of State William Seward for permission to arrest Wood. Wood lost his reelection bid, but soon won a seat in Congress, where he became a leading Copperhead and a constant thorn in Lincoln's side. Whenever the war went badly Wood could always be counted on to criticize the Republican administration, and he was particularly outspoken when Lincoln shifted the focus of the conflict from preserving the Union to emancipating the slaves. He also voted against the 13th Amendment, which guaranteed freedom to former slaves.

When Congressman Wood tried to visit Lincoln at the White House in mid-December of 1863, the exasperated president sent him away, commenting to an aide: "I am sorry he is here. I would rather he should not come about here so much. Tell Mr. Wood I have nothing yet to tell him. . . ."

New York City would remain a center of Copperhead sentiment. Rioting broke out at a draft office on July 13, 1863, after

Lincoln instituted a conscription act and soon boiled over into the worst episode of public unrest in American history. The mob's focus eventually expand-ed from targeting draft officials and wealthy Republicans to targeting African Americans. An officer in charge of mustering new recruits blamed the rioting on Democratic politicians, though he did not name Wood specifically: "The authorities in Washington do not seem able or willing to comprehend the magnitude [of] the opposition to the government which exists in New York. There's no doubt that most, if not all, of the Democratic politicians are at the bottom of this riot."

Although New York City and its opportunistic mayor never officially left the Union, keeping the city fighting for the Union cause would be a constant source of anxiety for President Lincoln. The frustrations expressed by Wood on January 6, 1861, would not disappear, but would be transformed into the type of political sniping that Lincoln famously termed "the fire in the rear."

CHUCK LEDDY, who writes from Quincy, Mass., is the author of several articles on the Civil War and American history.

Lincoln and the Constitutional Dilemma of Emancipation

EDNA GREENE MEDFORD

> The President shall be Commander in Chief of the Army and Navy of the United States, and of the Militia of the several States, when called into the actual Service of the United States.
>
> —U. S. Constitution, Article II, Section 2

On the afternoon of January 1, 1863, following nearly two years of bloody civil war, Abraham Lincoln set in motion events that would reconnect the detached cord of Union and that would begin to reconcile the nation's practices to its avowed democratic principles. Interpreting Article II, Section 2 of the Constitution broadly, the president used his war powers to proclaim freedom for those enslaved laborers caught in the dehumanizing grip of one of the Confederacy's most sacrosanct institutions. His bold move challenged prevailing notions of presidential prerogative and triggered criticism from his supporters as well as his opponents. While many abolitionists bemoaned the limited scope of the president's actions, alleging that he freed those persons over whom he had no control, while exempting from his edict those under Union authority, his more conservative critics charged that he had exceeded the powers the Constitution invested in the executive.

Lincoln anticipated the criticism. He knew that most abolitionists would be satisfied with nothing less than universal emancipation and that, contrarily, pro-South forces would find in his actions reason to brand him a betrayer of American liberties. Given that slavery evoked such polarization in the North, he realized that whatever action he took on the institution posed considerable danger to the goal of the war—preservation of the Union.

Although influenced by the practical considerations of containing the rebellion—that is, not losing any more slaveholding states to the Confederacy—Lincoln's greatest challenge regarding emancipation was to achieve it without violating constitutional guarantees. He understood slavery to be the cause of the war but he believed that the Constitution denied the president any easy solution for its eradication. Whatever his personal views on slavery (and there is incontrovertible evidence that he hated the institution on moral grounds as well as practical rea-

sons), law and custom had deemed enslaved people property.[1] Because the Constitution protected property rights, Lincoln felt compelled to operate within those constraints. As war propelled him inexorably toward emancipation, he sought authority to do so within the framework that the Constitution provided.

The Civil War began as a struggle over national union, one half of the American people believed it indissoluble and fought to preserve it, while the other half wished to withdraw from it and secure their own identity. Northern attempts at appeasement and diplomacy having failed, war became the only recourse for a president convinced that secession was unconstitutional. Hence, in his first official act after hostilities commenced, Lincoln called up the state militias "to maintain the honor, the integrity, and the existence" of the nation.[2] The decision had not been an easy one. When he spoke before Congress in special session on July 4, 1861, he explained that.

"It was with the deepest regret that the Executive found the duty of employing the war-power, in defense of the government, forced upon him. He could but perform this duty, or surrender the existence of the government."[3]

Defense of the government ultimately led Lincoln to strike at the heart of the South's reason for challenging national union. It would prove even harder than prosecuting the war itself, because the Constitution—compromise document that it was—reflected the ambivalence of the framers over the issue of slavery. Lincoln had acknowledged "not grudgingly, but fully, and fairly," the constitutional rights of the slaveholder, but the treatment of slavery in the Constitution suggested to him that the framers had deliberately paved the way for the institution's eventual extinction.[4] The founding fathers and the earliest Congress were hostile to slavery; they tolerated it "only by necessity," he argued. The framers even excluded the words "slave" and "slavery" from the Constitution and chose instead to refer to those held in bondage as "persons" from whom "service or labor may be due." This was a deliberate attempt, thought Lincoln, to keep the idea of "property in man" out of this democratic document.[5] The founding fathers hid it away "just as an afflicted man hides away . . . a cancer, which he does not cut out at once, lest he bleed to death."[6] Hence, the Supreme Court's ruling in *Scott v. Sandford*, which declared that slaveholders could not be prohibited from taking their chattel wherever they wished, was "based upon a mistaken statement of fact . . . that the right of property in a slave is distinctly and expressly affirmed in the Constitution." That document was "literally silent" about any right of slaveholders to take their human property into the territories.[7]

Lincoln had always believed that Congress could prevent slavery from spreading into the territories, over which it had jurisdiction. But the government, he believed, did not have the constitutional authority to touch the institution where it had already been established. Indeed, the 1860 Republican platform on which he was elected to the presidency declared:

That the maintenance inviolate of the rights of the States, and especially the light of each State to order and control its own domestic institutions according to its own judgment exclusively, is essential to that balance of power on which the perfection and endurance of our political fabric depend.[8]

Lincoln did not stand down from this position when in the weeks following his election several southern states seceded and formed the Confederate States of America. Far from seizing upon this as an opportunity to move against slavery, the newly elected president attempted to reassure the secessionists and their non-seceding slaveholding brothers that he had "no purpose, directly or indirectly, to interfere with the institution of slavery in the States where it exists. I believe I have no lawful right to do so, and I have no inclination to do so." Lincoln promised that "all the protection which, consistently with the Constitution and the laws, can be given, will be cheerfully given to all the States when lawfully demanded as cheerfully to one section, as to another."[9] It was a position he held throughout the war.

In promising to uphold the laws, Lincoln was speaking primarily about enforcement of the Fugitive Slave Act, passed in 1850 as one of the compromises after the war with Mexico resulted in the ceding of millions of acres to the United States. The Missouri Compromise had maintained a balance of free and slave states since 1820, but this new acquisition threatened to give advantage to one section over the other. In an effort to stay the rising crisis, Congress had proposed a series of measures that would appease each region. The Fugitive Slave Act aimed to assure southerners that the northern people would be equally obligated to protect the rights of the slaveholder. The law imposed fines on anyone who refused to assist in the apprehending of a fugitive or who facilitated any effort to prevent recovery. This attempt by Congress to resolve the conflict may have pleased the South, but it evoked anger and frustration among northerners who had no desire to become slave catchers.[10]

After the secessionist attack on Fort Sumter ignited armed conflict, Lincoln's declaration of noninterference met with increased criticism within the Union and initiated direct challenge to the administrations position. Undeterred by the president's pledge, enslaved African Americans had themselves seized the opportunity to obtain their freedom by flight. As Union troops advanced on the Confederacy, fugitives from slavery met them and offered loyalty, labor, and information in exchange for asylum. Even in the ostensibly loyal border states, black men and women sought to secure freedom as the chaos of war blurred distinctions between rebel and Unionist slaveholders.[11]

Without specific guidelines for dealing with fugitives, Union Commanders in the field implemented their own solutions. Some of them saw the advantage to sheltering runaways and chose to employ them in erecting defense against southern forces or utilized them in a variety of noncombatant occupations. General Benjamin Butler's declaration that these fugitives were contraband of war encouraged other commanders to embrace the designation.[12] But for every General Butler there was a Henry Halleck who barred fugitive slaves from the camps under his command. In the first months of the war, the Lincoln administration chose not to make any additional public pronouncements on the issue of fugitives, but the president, eager to keep the conflict contained and of short duration, privately queried the general-in-chief, Winfield Scott, if it "would be well to allow owners to bring back [slaves] which have crossed the Potomac" with Union troops.[13] As a consequence, runaways were banned from the Union camps of the Department of Washington and were prohibited from following soldiers on the move.[14]

Congress's attempt to turn the South's "peculiar institution" to the North's advantage and the emancipating actions of commanders in the field left Lincoln less than enthusiastic and, in some instances, downright perturbed. In August 1861, Congress had passed the First Confiscation Act, which provided for seizure of any property (including enslaved persons) that had been used to wage war against the government. The act did not address the status of the confiscated slaves once the war was over. Yet, concerned that such action would strengthen the resolve of the rebels and would likely be overturned by constitutional challenge, Lincoln reluctantly signed the measure and made little effort to enforce it.[15]

General John C. Frémont's proclamation of August 30 gave Lincoln even greater concern. As commander of the Department of the West, Frémont declared martial law in Missouri and issued a proclamation stipulating that "the property, real and personal, of all persons in the state of Missouri who shall take up arms against the United States . . . is declared to be confiscated and their slaves are hereby declared freemen."[16] Frémont's proclamation differed from the First Confiscation Act in that property could be seized without having been employed against the Union. Moreover, the human property thus confiscated was declared free. Citing concern that the decree might "alarm our southern Union friends, and turn them against us—perhaps ruin our rather fair prospect for Kentucky," Lincoln asked, and later commanded, the unyielding Frémont to place his proclamation in conformity with Congress' confiscation measure.[17]

In a letter written in late September to friend Orville H. Browning, fellow Republican and U.S. senator from Illinois, Lincoln reiterated these political concerns, especially the importance of securing the loyalty of Kentucky. But it was the constitutional question that was paramount. Lincoln argued that the general's proclamation, specifically the part which stipulated the liberation of the slaves, was "purely political, and not within the range of military law, or necessity." He challenged the notion that:

"If a commanding General finds a necessity to seize the farm of a private owner, for a pasture, an encampment, or a fortification, he has the right to do so . . . as long as the necessity lasts. . . . But to say the farm no longer belong to the owner, or his heirs forever, and this as well when the farm is not needed for military purposes as when it is, is purely political, without the savor of military law about it."[18]

Lincoln believed that this applied to slaves as well. Human property could be confiscated, "But when the need is past, it is not for [the confiscator] to fix their permanent future condition. That must be settled according to laws made by law-makers, and not by military proclamations. . . . Can it be pretended that it is any longer the government of the U.S. . . . wherein a General, or a President, may make permanent rules of property by proclamation?."[19]

When eight months later, General David Hunter, commander of the Department of the South, declared martial law and freed the slaves within the three states under his jurisdiction, an exasperated Lincoln rescinded the order, declaring that as president he would "reserve to myself" the question of whether or not as commander in chief he had authority to emancipate the slaves.[20]

Contrary to his response to the emancipating actions of commanders in the field, Lincoln did not challenge Congress's authority to free enslaved people in the District of Columbia when on April 11, 1862, that body approved a measure to emancipate "persons held to service or labor" in the city. As a federal enclave, Washington was under the jurisdiction of Congress, and hence, it had the constitutional authority to end slavery there. The city had been steadily moving toward eradication of the institution for some time, and so fewer than 3,200 African Americans out of a total black population of 11,000 were affected directly.[21] Nevertheless, many white Washingtonians challenged Congress's actions because they thought the maximum amount of three hundred dollars per slave was inadequate compensation and because they imagined that a free city would quickly become overrun with fugitives from slavery in Maryland and Virginia.[22]

But acknowledgement of constitutional authority did not suggest that the District Emancipation Bill was to Lincoln's liking. Weeks before, he had proposed a plan for gradual, compensated emancipation, implemented by the border states. In this way, constitutional constraints would be recognized while emancipation would sever the bond between the slaveholding Union states and their sisters in rebellion.[23] But none of those states had exhibited much interest. Hence, when Congress stepped in to implement emancipation for the District of Columbia, Lincoln was somewhat ambivalent. While the measure was making its way through Congress, he expressed his uneasiness "as to the time and manner of doing it." He preferred the initiative to come from one of the border states, but if this could not be achieved quickly, he hoped that the bill would stipulate an emancipation that was gradual, provided compensation to the owners, and was voted on by the people of the District.[24]

When Lincoln signed the District Emancipation Bill after delaying for five days, he sent a message to Congress that officially voiced his concerns. The president reminded them that he had "ever desired to see the national capital freed from the institution in some satisfactory way."[25] But he proposed an "amendatory or supplemental act" that would guarantee sufficient time for which to file claims for compensation. Moreover, he hinted at "matters within and about this act, which might have taken a course or shape, more satisfactory to my jud[g]ment."[26] Presumably, he was disturbed that emancipation had been carried out absent any opportunity for District residents to shape it as they did not have a vote.

One last action on the part of Congress would address the issue of emancipation of enslaved people before Lincoln issued his preliminary proclamation in September 1862. In July, Congress had passed the Second Confiscation Act. The measure, intended "to suppress Insurrection, to punish Treason and Rebellion, to seize and confiscate the Property of Rebels," provided for the freeing of all slaves of persons who were "adjudged guilty" of committing treason against the United States.[27] Again, certain features of the bill disturbed Lincoln, and again he responded by submitting written objections to Congress. While expressing his pleasure that loyal Unionist slaveholders were not touched by the measure and that persons charged with treason would enjoy "regular trials, in duly constituted courts," the president found it 'startling' that Congress could free a slave who resided in a state unless "it were said the ownership of the slave had first been transferred to the nation, and that congress had then liberated him." But what troubled Lincoln most about the Second Confiscation Act was the idea that forfeiture of title to the slave extended beyond the life of the rebel owner. The act, Lincoln believed, violated Article III, Section 3 of the Constitution that stipulated: "The Congress shall have Power to declare the Punishment of Treason, but no Attainder of Treason shall work Corruption of Blood, or Forfeiture except during the Life of the Person attainted."[28] The enforcement of the Second Confiscation Act would do just that by denying the property rights of the heirs of the person committing treason. Lincoln's objections led Congress to pass a joint resolution that disallowed any "punishment or proceedings under the act that would lead to forfeiture beyond the offender's natural life."[29]

The president's concerns regarding the Second Confiscation Act were no trivial matter. He was only two months away from issuing his Preliminary Emancipation Proclamation, which would announce his intention to make "forever free" those slaves in states and parts thereof still in rebellion by January 1, 1863. While the Constitution did not expressly give the president the authority to free slaves, Lincoln claimed such authority through the war powers. "The Constitution invests its Commander-in-Chief with the law of war, in time of war," he declared. "By the law of war, property, both of enemies and friends, may be taken" or destroyed if doing so hurts the enemy and helps the cause.[30] Hence, Lincoln claimed the right to issue the proclamation as a "fit and necessary war measurer."[31] By claiming military necessity, he sidestepped the constitutional concerns that had attended Congress's effort to legislate freedom under the clause regulating punishment for treason.

Despite objections to the proclamation, Lincoln declined to rescind the decree. "The promise [of freedom] being made, must be kept," he declared.[32] But his resoluteness masked the fear that his decree would face legal challenge. Moreover, he recognized that while freeing enslaved people in the Confederacy, slavery as an institution had not been abolished. Hence, during the summer of 1864, he joined Congress in pressing for the passage of a constitutional amendment banning slavery. When in February 1865, Congress passed the Thirteenth Amendment and submitted it to the states for ratification, Lincoln declared it "a King's cure for all the evils."[33] Interestingly, shortly thereafter, he drafted a recommendation to Congress that proposed that compensation payments be made to all the slaveholding states—including those currently in the Confederacy—provided the states were not in rebellion by April. The recommendation was never delivered to Congress because the president's cabinet unanimously rejected it.[34]

As he moved toward emancipation, Lincoln looked to the Constitution for guidance, ever careful to conform to what he believed were the guarantees of that document. Since enslaved people were deemed property, he felt it imperative to address the legality of efforts to liberate them from the perspective of the constitutional rights of the slaveholder. Although he acknowledged the humanity (albeit inferior to whites, in his estimation) of black men and women, issues of emancipation within the context of constitutional constraints precluded any humanitarian sentiment as a part of "official duty." "What I do about slavery, and the colored race, I do because I believe it helps to save the Union," he had declared. "[A]nd what I forbear, I forbear because I do not believe it would help to save the Union."[35] Despite the limitations it placed on presidential emancipation, the Constitution had given him the authority to save the Union and begin the destruction of slavery throughout the nation.

Notes

1. In his speech on the Kansas-Nebraska Act at Peoria, Illinois, on October 16, 1854. Lincoln had declared: "I hate [slavery] because of the monstrous injustice . . . I hate it because it deprives our republican example of its just influence in the world—enables the enemies of free institutions . . . to taunt us as hypocrites." See "Speech at Peoria," in *The Collected Works of Abraham Lincoln* (hereinafter cited as *Collected Works*). 8 vols., ed. Roy P. Basler (New Brunswick, NJ: Rutgers University Press. 1953), 2:255.

2. "By the President of the United States a Proclamation, April 15, 1861," *Collected Works,* 4:331–32.

3. "Message to Congress in Special Session, July 4, 1861," in *Collected Works,* 4:421.

4. Speech at Peoria, October 16, 1854, *Collected Works,* 2:256.

5. Address at Cooper Institute, February 27, 1860, *Collected Works,* 3:545.

6. Speech at Peoria, October 16, 1854, *Collected Works,* 2:274.

7. Address at Cooper Institute, February 27, 1860, *Collected Works,* 3:543–44.

8. Quoted in First Inaugural Address, 1861, *Collected Works,* 4:263.

9. Ibid.

10. For discussion of the Fugitive Slave Act and the Compromise of 1850, see Stanley W. Campbell, *The Slave Catchers: The Enforcement of the Fugitive Slave Law, 1850–1860* (Chapel Hill, NC: University of North Carolina Press. 1968).

11. See Harold Holzer, Edna Greene Medford, and Frank Williams, *The Emancipation Proclamation: Three Views* (Baton Rouge: Louisiana State University Press. 2006), 6–9.

12. Three fugitives from a rebel master sought asylum at Fortress Monroe (Virginia) in late May 1861, claiming that they were about to be taken out of Virginia and employed against the Union. As commander of the fort, Butler declared the men "contraband of war" and set them to labor for the Union. "Benj. F. Butler to Lieut. Gen. Winfield Scott. May 24, 1861." *The War of the Rebellion: A Compilation of the Official Records of the Union and Confederate Armies* (hereinafter O.R.), 128 vols. (Washington: Government Printing Office, 1880–1901), ser. 2, 1:752.

13. Lieutenant Colonel Schuyler Hamilton to Brigadier General Irwin McDowell, Washington, July 16, 1861, *O.R.,* ser. 2, 1:760.

14. General Orders, No. 33, July 17, 1861, Headquarters Department of Washington, in *O.R.,* ser. 2, 1:760.

15. See Allen C. Guelzo, *Lincoln's Emancipation Proclamation: The End of Slavery in America* (New York: Simon and Schuster, 2004), 45.

16. Proclamation of John C. Frémont, August 30, 1861, *O.R.,* ser 1, 3:467.

17. To John C. Frémont, September 2, 1861, *Collected Works,* 4:506.

18. To Orville H. Browning, September 22, 1861, *Collected Works,* 4:531.

19. Ibid.

20. "Revocation of the Hunter Proclamation," *Collected Works,* 5:222.

21. Constance McLaughlin Green, *The Secret City: A History of Race Relations in the Nation's Capital* (Princeton: Princeton University Press, 1967), 33. At 1860, the total population of the District (including Washington and Georgetown) was just over 75,000.

22. Ibid., 59–60.

23. Message to Congress, March 6, 1862, *Collected Works,* 5:145.

24. Letter to Horace Greeley, March 24, 1862, *Collected Works,* 5:169.

25. Message to Congress, April 16, 1862, *Collected Works,* 5:192.

26. Ibid.

27. See Holzer, Medford and Williams, *The Emancipation Proclamation: Three Views,* 137–40.

28. To the Senate and House of Representatives, July 17, 1862, *Collected Works,* 5:329.

29. Ibid.

30. To Hon. James C. Conkling, August 26, 1863, *Collected Works,* 6:408.

31. The Final Emancipation Proclamation, *Collected Works,* 6:29. See also Daniel Farber, *Lincoln's Constitution* (Chicago: University of Chicago Press. 2003), 152–57.

32. To Hon. James C. Conkling, August 26, 1863, *Collected Works,* 6:409.

33. "Response to a Serenade," February 1, 1865, *Collected Works,* 8:255.

34. "Message to the Senate and House of Representatives," February 5, 1865, *Collected Works,* 8:261.

35. Letter to Horace Greeley, August 22, 1862, *Collected Works,* 5:388–89.

EDNA GREENE MEDFORD is associate Professor and director of Graduate Studies in the Department of History at Howard University. Specializing in nineteenth-century African American history, she also teaches both graduate and undergraduate courses in Civil War and Reconstruction, Colonial America, the Jacksonia's Era, and Comparative Slavery. She has published more than a dozen articles and book chapters on African Americans, especially during the one of the Civil War. Her publications include the coauthored work, *The Emancipation Proclamation: Three Views,* Baton Rouge: Louisiana State University Press, 2006.

A Gallant Rush for Glory

For the men of the 54th Massachusetts, the assault on a Confederate fort outside Charleston was much more than just another battle. It was their chance to show the world that black troops could fight—and die—for the Union.

WILLIAM C. KASHATUS

Before Union forces could capture Charleston, South Carolina, they first had to take Fort Wagner, a Confederate stronghold guarding the harbor's entrance. So shortly after 6:30 p.m. on July 18, 1863, Union Colonel Robert Gould Shaw readied 600 men of the 54th Massachusetts Regiment for an assault on the fort. Shaw, the 25-year-old son of Boston abolitionists, was white, as were all his officers. The regiment's men were black.

The 54 would spearhead a three-pronged attack aimed at capturing the necklace of heavily fortified islands that dotted Charleston harbor. If they could take Fort Wagner, the Federals would launch a major assault on nearby Fort Sumter. From there, it would only be a matter of time before Charleston fell. But capturing Fort Wagner would be no easy task.

At first glance, the fort appeared to be little more than a series of irregular, low sand hills. In fact, it was much more formidable than that. A timber and sandbag foundation beneath the sand-covered hills allowed the structure to absorb artillery fire without any significant damage. The fort had 11 heavy guns mounted in fixed positions behind the parapets, while smaller wheeled cannon could be quickly repositioned where needed. Defending it were 1,300 men from the 51st and 31st North Carolina Regiments as well as several companies of South Carolina artillerymen.

Fort Wagner sat in the middle of Morris Island's northern sandy peninsula. Four batteries at the island's northern tip guarded the entrance to Charleston harbor. The largest of these batteries was Battery Gregg, whose guns faced the ocean and covered the harbor mouth. South of the batteries, a deep moat with a sluice gate and three guns bounded Fort Wagner along its northern sea face. To the east lay the Atlantic Ocean, and on its western boundary were the impassable marshes of Vincent's Creek. On its southern side the fort had guns and mortars for direct and flanking fire on any advancing troops. The only possible assault approach was east of the fort, along a slim stretch of sand, narrow even at low tide. Shaw and his troops would have to launch their attack on the seemingly impregnable fort from there.

Colonel Shaw readied his men on the beach. Tightly wedged together, elbow to elbow, the soldiers of the 54th began their gallant rush, determined to disprove the popular belief among

Shaw came from a prominent New England anti-slavery family, but he was initially hesitant about accepting command of the 54th. Once in command of the black regiment, he encountered considerable scorn from other white officers.

Source: Usamhi

whites that Negroes were an inferior race, lacking the courage and intelligence of combat-ready soldiers.

The onset of the Civil War set off a rush by free black men to enlist in the U.S. military, but a 1792 law barred "persons of color from serving in the militia." Also, strong opposition in the North as well as a widespread prejudice that blacks were intellectually and socially inferior limited their involvement in the war to driving supply wagons, burying the battle dead, and building railroads.

Yet public opinion slowly began changing. Northern morale faltered after Union forces suffered a series of military defeats, and fewer white men were willing to join the army. Pressured by this turn of events, on July 17, 1862, Congress passed a Confiscation Act that declared all slaves of rebel masters free as soon as they came into Union lines, and a Militia Act that empowered the president to "employ as many persons of African descent" in "any military or naval service for which they may be found competent." Congress also repealed the 1792 law.

On August 25, 1862, the War Department authorized Brigadier General Rufus Saxton, military governor of the Union-controlled South Carolina Sea Islands, to raise five regiments of black troops for Federal service, with white men as officers. Volunteers came forward slowly at first, but by November 7 the regiment had reached its quota and was mustered in as the 1st South Carolina Volunteer Regiment under the command of Massachusetts abolitionist Colonel Thomas Wentworth Higginson. A second regiment followed, led by Colonel James Montgomery.

Still, President Abraham Lincoln refused to raise a large black army on political grounds. "To arm the Negroes would turn 50,000 bayonets from the loyal Border States against us that were for us," he told his abolitionist critics. Black leaders continued to urge the necessity of enlisting black troops, realizing that if the black man proved his patriotism and courage on the battlefield, the nation would be morally obligated to grant him first-class citizenship. No one expressed those sentiments more eloquently than Frederick Douglass, a former slave and the nation's most prominent black abolitionist. He insisted that "once the black man gets upon his person the brass letters 'U.S.', a musket on his shoulder and bullets in his pocket, there is no power on earth which can deny that he has earned the right to citizenship in the United States."

Debate continued within the Union command until January 1, 1863, when President Lincoln signed the Emancipation Proclamation. Having freed, by executive order, those slaves in the South, Lincoln could no longer deny the black man the opportunity to fight. Now the Civil War was being fought not only to preserve the Union, but for the freedom of all the American people, white and black. The success of the 1st and 2nd Carolina Colored Troops only reinforced that position. Higginson and Montgomery had already led their black troops on several successful raids into the interior of Georgia and Florida, and in March 1863 they captured and occupied Jacksonville.

On February 13, 1863, Senator Charles Sumner of Massachusetts introduced a bill proposing the "enlistment of 300,000 colored troops." Although the bill was defeated, abolitionist governor John A. Andrew of Massachusetts requested and received authorization from Secretary of War Edwin M. Stanton to organize a colored regiment of volunteers to serve for three years.

Massachusetts had a small black population, and only 100 men volunteered during the first six weeks of recruitment. Disillusioned by the turnout, Andrew organized a committee of prominent citizens and Negro leaders to supervise the recruitment effort. Within two months the committee collected $5,000 and established a line of recruiting posts from Boston to St. Louis, resulting in the recruitment of 1,000 black men from throughout the Union who became part of the 54th Regiment Massachusetts Volunteer Infantry, Colored, the first black regiment raised in the free states. Toward the end of the second recruiting month, volunteers arrived at the rate of 30 to 40 each day, and Andrew soon had enough men to form a second black regiment, the 55th Massachusetts.

For the 54th's commander, Governor Andrew turned to Robert Gould Shaw, captain of the Massachusetts 2nd Infantry. Charming and handsome, Shaw came from a wealthy and socially prominent Boston abolitionist family. His parents Francis and Sarah had joined the American Anti-Slavery Society in 1838, and by 1842 Francis was working with the Boston Vigilance Committee to help runaway slaves gain their freedom. Robert entered Harvard University in 1856 but abandoned his studies during his third year and moved to New York to work in his uncle's mercantile office. Shaw joined an exclusive militia regiment, the 7th New York National Guard, where he talked about what he would do if the South made trouble. Shaw did not possess the strong anti-slavery calling of his parents, but he was fiercely patriotic. When the Civil War began, he was primed to take revenge on the South. To Shaw, the South was the transgressor, and if it took the end of slavery to redeem the honor of America, then he was willing to fight for that. When the 7th disbanded, Shaw accepted a commission in the 2nd Massachusetts Infantry. During his 20 months there, Captain Shaw received a minor wound at Antietam, during the single bloodiest day of the war.

When Governor Andrew asked the young captain to lead a black volunteer infantry, Shaw was hesitant. The prospect of heading a regiment of armed blacks would not be popular among the white ranks. Nor did he want to abandon the men of the 2nd Infantry. Shaw initially refused the position but changed his mind after much discussion with his parents. In a February 1863 letter to his future wife, Annie Haggerty, Shaw wrote, "You know how many eminent men consider a negro army of the greatest importance to our country at this time. If it turns out to be so, how fully repaid the pioneers in the movement will be, for what they may have to go through. . . . I feel convinced I shall never regret having taken this step, as far as I myself am concerned; for while I was undecided I felt ashamed of myself, as if I were cowardly." Shaw received a promotion to major on April 11, 1863, and attained the rank of colonel the following month. Colonel Shaw would now have to navigate the turbulent forces of discrimination that existed within the Union Army.

The men of the 54th trained near Boston at Readville, under the constant scrutiny of white soldiers, many of whom believed black soldiers lacked the stomach for combat. Yet the negative perceptions seemed only to inspire a sense of unity within the ranks of the regiment and their white officers.

Contrary to recruitment promises, the soldiers of the 54th were paid only $10.00 per month, $3.00 less than the white troops. Shaw had become so committed to his men that he wrote to Governor Andrew, insisting that his entire regiment, including white officers, would refuse pay until his soldiers were "given the same payment as all the other Massachusetts troops." Yet Congress did not enact legislation granting equal pay to black soldiers until June 15, 1864.

Shortly after the 54th was mustered into service, the Confederate Congress passed an act stating its intention to "put to death" if captured, "any Negro" as well as "white commissioned officer [who] shall command, prepare or aid Negroes in arms against the Confederate States." The directive only served to strengthen the resolve of the black soldiers.

On May 18 Governor Andrew traveled to the camp to present Shaw with the regimental flags. He made the trip with 3,000 other visitors, including such prominent abolitionists as Frederick Douglass, William Lloyd Garrison, and Wendell Phillips. Douglass had a strong personal link with the 54th—two of his sons, Lewis and Charles, had joined the unit. Andrew presented the flags to Shaw. "I know not, Mr. Commander, in all human history, to any given thousand men in arms, has there been committed a work at once so proud, so precious, so full of hope and glory as the work committed to you," the governor said.

Ten days later the 54th Regiment of Massachusetts Volunteer Infantry marched through the streets of downtown Boston,

Massachusetts Governor John A. Andrew advocated the enlistment of black men into the Union Army. After President Lincoln issued the Emancipation Proclamation on January 1, 1863, Andrew approached Secretary of War Edwin Stanton and obtained authorization to raise a black Massachusetts regiment.

Source: Usamhl

greeted by the cheers of thousands who assembled to see them off at Battery Wharf. It was an impressive spectacle. Shaw, atop his chestnut brown horse, led the way. Close behind marched the color bearers, followed by young black soldiers, handsomely clad in their sharp, new uniforms.

The dress parade gradually made its way to the wharf and boarded the *De Molay* bound for Port Royal Island, South Carolina. There the regiment reported to the Department of the South. Once the men arrived, however, reality set in when they were relegated to manual labor. Not until June 8, when Shaw and his men joined Colonel James Montgomery and the black troops of his 2nd South Carolina Colored Volunteers on an "expedition" to Georgia, did they see any action, and that was during a pointless raid on the small town of Darien. After plundering the 100 or so residences, three churches, the market-house, courthouse, and an academy, Montgomery ordered Darien set afire. Begrudgingly, Shaw directed one of his companies to torch the town. Fanned by a high wind, the flames eventually destroyed everything but a church and a few houses.

Afterward, Shaw wrote to lieutenant Colonel Charles G. Halpine, the acting adjutant general of the department, to condemn this "barbarous sort of warfare." Shaw knew his complaint could result in his arrest or even court-martial, but he felt compelled to express his feelings. He later learned that Montgomery had acted in accordance with the orders of his superior officer, General David Hunter. Soon after the Darien raid, President Lincoln relieved Hunter of his command.

The sacking of Darien and the manual labor his troops were compelled to do disheartened Shaw. "Our whole experience, so far, has been in loading and discharging vessels," he wrote to Brigadier General George C. Strong, commander of Montgomery's brigade. "Colored soldiers should be associated as much as possible with the white troops, in order that they may have other witnesses beside their own officers to what they are capable of doing." That opportunity finally arrived on the morning of July 16, 1863. Fighting alongside white troops on James Island, Shaw's men acquitted themselves well in a sharp skirmish. That same night they ferried to Morris Island, where battle lines had already been drawn for the anticipated attack on Fort Wagner. Despite their exhaustion, hunger, and wet clothes, the men of the 54th were determined to fight on.

When General Strong, now Shaw's brigade commander, heard of the of the 54th on James Island, he asked the colonel if he and his regiment would lead the attack on Fort Wagner. Shaw and his men readily agreed and prepared to lead the charge across a narrow beach obstructed by felled branches, crisscrossed wire, and a deep moat—all of which were constructed to slow the attackers, making them vulnerable to enemy fire. Eight all-white units were to follow. All day long, Union artillery bombarded Fort Wagner in an effort to soften the Confederate defense and minimize the bloodshed that would inevitably follow. Late in the day Shaw arranged the 600 able-bodied men of his regiment into two wings of five companies each and moved them slowly up the beach. He assigned Company B to the right flank, using the surf as its guide. The other companies lined up on its left.

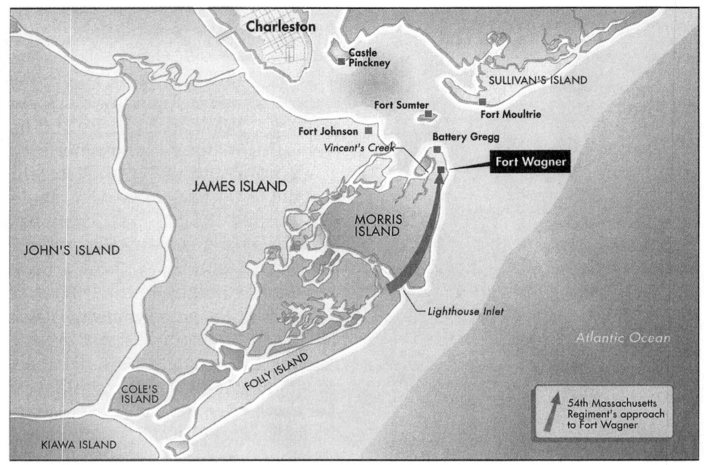

The 54th Regiment approached Fort Wagner along a narrow stretch of beach by the Atlantic Ocean.

Source: Map by Rick Brownlee

At dusk, General Strong addressed Shaw and his men. Pointing to the flag bearer, he said: "If this man should fall, who will pick up the flag?" Shaw stepped forward. "I will," he said. Addressing his troops with final words of inspiration, Shaw reminded them: "The eyes of thousands will look on what you do tonight." Then, drawing his sword, the young Boston Brahmin barked: "Move in quick time until within a hundred yards of the fort, then, double-quick and charge!" Quickstep became double-quick, and then a full run, as Confederate riflemen on the ramparts of the fort let loose a torrent of fire upon the Union soldiers. Men fell on all sides, but those who were able continued the charge with Shaw in the lead.

Company B passed through the moat to the base of the fort where canister, grenades, and small arms fire rained down on them. Surrounded by bloodshed, the 54th commander realized that he could not retreat, and he ordered the final assault on the fort. Shaw somehow managed to reach the parapet before a Confederate bullet pierced his heart.

"Men fell all around me," Lewis Douglass later wrote. "A shell would explode and clear a space of twenty feet, our men would close up again, but it was no use we had to retreat, which

was a very hazardous undertaking. How I got out of that fight alive I cannot tell, but I am here."

The intense fire mowed down the color bearers. Sergeant William Carney, a barrel-chested 23-year-old, seized the national flag and planted it upon the fort's parapet. The men of the 54th fought gallantly for about an hour until Confederate guns forced them to abandon their position. Before retreating, Carney once again grasped the flag, and despite bullets in the head, chest, right arm, and leg, he returned it to Union lines. His heroism earned him the distinction of being the first of 21 black men during the war to earn the Medal of Honor.

Subsequent waves of Federal troops tried for two hours to take the fort but failed, and casualties mounted by the hundreds. At the end of the assault, the Union had lost 1,515 killed, wounded or missing. Of that number, 256 were black soldiers from the 54th Massachusetts.

The following morning revealed a grisly scene. The dead lay in contorted positions along the beach, their fingers and legs stiffened from rigor mortis. The soft but painful cries and moans of the dying could be heard, begging for help.

A few days after the siege, a Union party under a flag of truce requested the return of Shaw's body. Brigadier General Johnson

Hagood, Fort Wagner's new commander, reportedly answered, "We buried him in the trench with his niggers." Learning of Hagood's reply, Colonel Shaw's father declared, "I can imagine no holier place than that in which he is, among his brave and devoted followers, nor wish for him better company."

From a military standpoint, the assault on Fort Wagner proved to be a costly failure. The blame rested on the shoulders of commanding general Quincy A. Gillmore and his commander in the field, Brigadier General Truman Seymour, who had not ordered the usual preparations for such an assault—no one sent out guides to check the terrain in advance or dispatched lines of skirmishers to soften the enemy. Nor had the 54th ever practiced storming a fort. Nevertheless, the assault proved to be a turning point for black soldiers, serving to dismiss any lingering skepticism among whites about the combat readiness of African Americans. "I have given the subject of arming the Negro my hearty support," General Ulysses S. Grant wrote to President Lincoln in August. "They will make good soldiers and taking them from the enemy weakens him in the same proportion they strengthen us."

When other Union generals remained recalcitrant, Lincoln responded swiftly. "You say you will not fight to free Negroes," he said. "Some of them seem to be willing to fight for you. When victory is won, there will be some black men who can remember that, with silent tongue and clenched teeth, and steady eye and well-poised bayonet, they have helped mankind on to this great consummation. I fear, however, that there will also be some white ones, unable to forget that with malignant heart and deceitful speech, they strove to hinder it."

WILLIAM C. KASHATUS is a professional historian at Chester County Historical Society, West Chester, Pennsylvania.

From *American History,* October 2000, pp. 22–28. Copyright © 2000 by Primedia Enterprises. Reprinted by permission.

How the West Was Lost

Chris Smallbone

At the beginning of the nineteenth century the United States neither owned, valued nor even knew much about the Great Plains. This vast tract of grassland which runs across the centre of the continent was described as the 'Great American Desert', but by the end of the century the United States had taken it over completely. As the 'new Americans' (many of them black) pushed the frontier to the west, they established their culture at the expense of that of the indigenous peoples, then known to the incomers as 'Indians'.

The great natural resource of the Plains was the buffalo, which migrated in vast herds. The peoples of the Great Plains hunted and ate the buffalo, made tepees from their hides and utilized most other parts to make tools, utensils and weaponry. Some of them, for example the Mandan and Pawnee, lived in semi-permanent villages; others, like the Lakota and Cheyenne, lived a nomadic life. When necessary, as in life or death situations of war or in securing food in the hunt or moving camp they could be very organized and disciplined, but normally life was very loosely structured. Different peoples or nations were distinguished by language or dialect and in variations of customs and beliefs. But all depended upon nature for survival and had a spiritual approach to it.

Before the arrival of the new Americans the native groups were often in conflict with neighbouring peoples for resources such as horses and land. The latter resulted in some movement in their patterns of settlement. Thus, the Cheyenne and Arapaho had divided into northern and southern groups in the 1820s. Some Cheyenne and Arapaho moved south, following reports of large numbers of wild horses and vast buffalo herds in the land south of the Platte River, while others remained north of the Platte near the Black Hills where they effectively became a separate group, closely allied with the Lakota. Other peoples, such as the Pawnee, Crow and Arikara (or Rees), had become enemies of the Lakota when supplanted by them earlier in the century. The northern Cheyenne and Arapaho were an exception, most other peoples in the northern Plains were enemies of the Lakota. Indeed the name for them adopted by the new Americans, Sioux, was the Ojibwe word for enemy. In the mid-eighteenth century the Lakota had moved gradually westwards from what was to be Minnesota, defeating other peoples as they went and pushing them into new hunting grounds.

In 1840, when the Oregon Trail from Independence, Missouri to the Pacific was first used, the frontier of the United States was roughly at the line of the Mississippi-Missouri, only about one third of the way across the continent. Just two generations later, by 1890, the indigenous peoples had been supplanted and the western frontier no longer existed. Apart from one or two later additions, today's map of the United States was firmly in place.

To understand how this took place one needs to step outside the strict chronology of the events. The new Americans split the Plains environment and those who depended upon it into two. This began in the 1840s with the overland trails to Oregon and California, initiating the age of the Wagon Train, and was cemented by the completion of the transcontinental and Kansas Pacific Railroads in the late 1860s. A series of treaties were signed, confining the native Americans to ever-smaller areas, and every opportunity was taken for incursion into these areas by prospectors, hunters, and settlers, supported by soldiers.

Even before the trails were opened, trading posts were established at key communications points, such as at the confluence of the North Platte and Laramie rivers in Wyoming, where fur traders Robert Campbell and William Sublette built Fort William in 1834. In 1849 it was bought by the US military to protect and supply emigrants travelling the Oregon Trail and renamed Fort Laramie. In the early 1840s relationships between the travellers and the native Americans on the trail had been good, but as the decade wore on relations became more tense, especially as numbers of the emigrants escalated with the California Gold Rush in 1849. Numbers of those seeking a quick fortune far exceeded those steadier individuals who wished to raise crops in the western coastlands of Oregon and California. As these numbers increased so did incidents between the two cultures. The settlement of the Plains did not become a problem for the native Americans until later, especially in the post-Civil War expansionist mood, when the 'sodbusters' were spurred on by the offer of free land through the Homestead Act of 1862. In the late 1840s the concern for the native Americans was that traffic down the Oregon Trail was keeping the buffalo from their traditional habitat in this area. As the numbers of incidents increased the government sought to alleviate the problem by attempting to keep the native Americans away from the trail. In doing so they used a method already used to legitimize riding roughshod over the eastern native Americans: the Treaty.

The various treaties between the US and the indigenous peoples of the west were of as little value as they had been in the east. In 1851 the US Indian agent Thomas Fitzpatrick invited all of the peoples of the Plains to a meeting in the vicinity of Fort Laramie. It was attended by members of the Lakota (Sioux), Cheyenne, Arapaho, Shoshone, Assiniboine, Crow, Mandan, Hidatsa, and Arikara nations. All these peoples still ranged widely across the central Plains, whereas the Comanche and the Kiowa, who did not attend the Fort Laramie meeting, were far in the south, in the vicinity of the Santa Fe Trail, and a separate treaty was signed at Fort Atkinson with them two years later.

By the 1851 Treaty of Fort Laramie, the government bound 'themselves to protect the aforesaid Indian nations against the commission of all depredations by the people of the said United States' and promised annuity goods for fifty years (later amended by the Senate to fifteen years). The native American chiefs guaranteed safe passage for settlers along the Platte River, and accepted responsibility for the behaviour of their followers in specified territories and recognized 'the right of the United States government to establish roads, military and other posts'. However, military posts already existed on the Oregon Trail: Fort Kearny had already been established in Nebraska as a stopping-off point and garrison in 1848, Fort Bridger in Wyoming as a fur-trading post in 1843, as well as Fort Laramie itself. Nor was the United States army a disciplined force: as emigrant William Kelley commented on the troops at Fort Kearny:

A most unsoldierly looking lot they were: unshaven, unshorn, with patched uniforms and a lounging gait. The privates being more particular in their inquiries after whiskey, for which they offered one dollar the half-pint; but we had none to sell them even at that tempting price.

It is not surprising that conflicts arose with native Americans.

Also, noble words meant little when the arbiters of 'justice' attempted to mete it out in a summary manner. Only three years after the treaty, Lieutenant Grattan attempted to bully Conquering Bear's Lakota into giving up a visitor who was accused of helping himself to a lame cow. His troops were annihilated, which led to retaliatory action by the Army, when any available native Americans were punished, regardless of whether they had been involved in the original action. This approach reflected the Army's attitude generally, as indeed had Grattan's action in the first place.

However little value could be placed on the promises in the treaties, their terms stand as clear indicators of the new Americans perceptions of how to deal with what they called the 'Indian Problem', at any one point. The Treaty of 1851 was an attempt to protect travellers on the Oregon Trail, which had become of high importance as a result of the discovery of gold in California in 1848. However, the commitment to protecting 'Indian nations' from 'depredations' by US citizens was of far lower priority to the new Americans and was never properly enforced.

Similarly in a treaty signed in 1861 at Fort Lyon in the southern Plains, the Cheyenne promised to remain in the vicinity of the Arkansas River and not to interfere with the gold-miners along the Smoky Hill Trail from Kansas City to Denver attracted to the area from 1858 onwards. Yet only three years later, in November 1864, an estimated 200 peaceful men, women and children of the Southern Cheyenne and Arapaho were massacred by the Third Colorado Regiment of volunteers and regular troops at Sand Creek. The leader of the outrage, John Chivington, fed the bloodlust of his troops, and was fond of the chilling phrase which rationalized the killing of infants: 'Nits make Lice'.

The idea of limiting to set areas peoples accustomed to a free-ranging existence following their source of life—the buffalo herds—was as unrealistic as it was racist. The concept of the native Americans' land being restricted to a reservation dated from the earliest treaties, and was consolidated in the 'removal' of eastern peoples into Indian Territory (later Oklahoma) in the 1830s under the direction of President Andrew Jackson. The National Park concept is generally credited to artist George Catlin, known for his paintings of native Americans. In 1832 he advocated that the wilderness might be preserved, 'by some great protecting policy of government . . . in a magnificent park . . . A nation's Park, containing man and beast, in all the wild and freshness of their nature's beauty!' In 1864, Congress donated Yosemite Valley to California for preservation as a state park. The second great Park, Yellowstone, was founded in 1872, during the presidency of Ulysses S. Grant, who developed an 'Indian Peace Policy' at this time which aimed to 'civilize' them. By 1876 this policy had increased the number of houses seven-fold, the acres under cultivation sixfold, the ownership of live-stock by fifteen times, and tripled the number of teachers and schools. The concept of the reservation was surely similar to that of National Parks and as such was recognition that the new Americans saw the native Americans as no more or less significant than the flora and fauna.

The native Americans unleashed a robust raiding campaign in response to the massacre at Sand Creek which interfered with the US government's wish to expand and consolidate economically after of the Civil War (1862-65). The Union-Pacific and Kansas-Pacific railroads were built across the Plains in the 1860s. To confine the Southern Cheyenne and Arapaho and to protect the settlers, travellers, railroad workers and miners, the US government perceived the need for another treaty later in the decade and despatched a 'Peace Commission'. This resulted in the treaty of Medicine Lodge Creek, signed in 1867 between the US Army and 5,000 Southern Cheyenne, Arapaho, Comanche, Kiowa and Kiowa-Apache. Under its terms the indigenous peoples gave up their claims to 90 million acres in return for reservations in central Indian Territory (Oklahoma). Yet just four years later, after a method of tanning the buffalo hides to produce a good-quality leather was developed, the buffalo-hunters moved in. They annihilated the buffalo, in a wasteful and devastating manner, in a few short years. In 1872-73 three million buffalo perished and by 1874 the hunters had moved so far south that the Treaty of Medicine Lodge Creek was a dead letter. All the land given to the Cheyenne and Arapaho had been stripped of the buffalo on which they depended. This was recognized by General Philip Sheridan when he said of the buffalo hunters:

These men have done (more) in the last two years, and will do more in the next year to settle the vexed Indian question, than the entire regular army has done in the last thirty years.

The sorry remnants of the Southern Cheyenne and Arapaho united with the Comanche and Kiowa, and fought back in a last-ditch attempt at resistance: the Red River War (1874-75). Now without the animal that had long been their prime source of existence, they were harried and starved into submission. They were encircled in the Texas Panhandle by five columns of troops, who came at the native Americans from all directions, keeping them on the move, giving them no rest. The troops burned and destroyed whatever possessions they left behind, including tepees and winter food stores, as they hastily withdrew their families to safety. A small group of a few dozen warriors still roaming free despite constant harassment came into Forts Sill and Reno in Oklahoma in 1875, where they were humiliated, and seventy-one men and one woman, many indiscriminately chosen, were transported to prison in Miami, Fort Marion.

As the land available to the native Americans shrank, some chiefs refused to accept this and fought back against the Army. This allowed the new Americans to claim that the native American leaders could not control their followers and any agreements were therefore broken. This development supported the new American claim to Manifest Destiny whereby they justified their behaviour as the act of 'taming' a savage wilderness. Later commentators refined this argument to suggest that the native Americans had no cultural tradition of commitment to a permanent system of leadership and government.

It was undoubtedly true that the indigenous peoples functioned with loose social structures based on respect being given to an individual based on their qualities rather than on the office they hold, with no lasting obligation to follow their leaders' directives. However, the new Americans did not show themselves to be any more committed to acting upon agreements or attempting to enforce the rule of law. For as long as the land was seen as a useless desert, the new Americans were content to leave it to the native Americans. However, as soon as something of value was discovered—usually precious metals but, also the buffalo once the market had been established for their hides—the new Americans themselves violated the treaties with impunity. Thus when buffalo-hunters went to Fort Dodge in 1872 to ask if they could hunt south of the Cimarron, thereby violating the Treaty of Medicine Lodge Creek, Colonel Irving Dodge had replied,

Boys, if I were a buffalo hunter, I would hunt where the buffalo are.

While in the southern Plains the native Americans were driven south, confined to ever-smaller areas and ultimately defeated, those in the north were more successful at repelling the invaders in the short term. The Lakota were themselves usurpers, for they had moved into the northern Plains in the late eighteenth century from the north and displaced peoples such as the Crow, Pawnee and Arikara, who remained so hostile to them that they proved willing to ally with the Army against the Lakota. As in the south, miners moved into the area, despite the Treaty of 1851 and this resulted in armed conflict. When gold was discovered in Virginia City, Montana, in 1862, Forts Phil Kearney and C.F. Smith were built to protect miners using the Bozeman Trail taking them north from the Oregon Trail. Helped by Crazy Horse, the Lakota chief Red Cloud led his Lakota

and Northern Cheyenne warriors in a war in the Powder Valley of Wyoming in 1866-68 which culminated in these forts being evacuated and burned. A second Treaty of Fort Laramie (1868) followed, very much on terms dictated by the native Americans which reaffirmed the principles set out in the earlier treaty of 1851. It granted the Lakota a large area in Dakota including the Black Hills, important for hunting, a source of lodge poles and an area sacred to them: the US army withdrew from the forts they had built and they were burned by the exuberant Lakota and northern Cheyenne.

Yet the advantage was to be short-lived; once again the discovery of gold by an expedition led by George Armstrong Custer in 1874, was to result in the rules being rewritten. Attempts to hoodwink the native Americans into selling the Black Hills in 1875 met with a rebuff: commissioners were told by Red Cloud that the asking price was $600,000,000, a figure so far in excess of the Commissioners' valuation that it rendered negotiation futile. Tactics rehearsed in the southern Plains were now re-enacted in the north. Lakota and Northern Cheyenne were given notice to 'come in' to Fort Robinson in Nebraska: those not doing so would be deemed 'hostile'. Three encircling columns under Generals Gibbon, Crook and Terry were assembled to harry and destroy. However, the Lakota chose to fight. This surprised the arrogant Custer who commanded Terry's troops but who underestimated his foe and chose to ride the glory trail in defiance of all logic. In the south the tactics of relentless pursuit had worked, not because of fatalities experienced by the native Americans, but because when their homes were attacked the priority of the warriors was to get their families to safety. Their abandoned possessions could then be commandeered or destroyed. The choice of Custer fitted with the expectation that the Lakota and northern Cheyenne would try to escape as had happened in the south. In September 1867 he had been court-martialled for deserting his command, ordering deserters to be shot, damaging army horses, failing to pursue Indians attacking his escort and not recovering bodies of soldiers killed by Indians; but it was his reckless direct approach appealed to his superiors.

However the Lakota and their allies proved more than a match for their enemies. At the battle against General Crook at the Rosebud River in June 1876, it was only a rearguard action fought by a Crow contingent supporting the Army which enabled General Crook to withdraw, and ten days later Custer's force was wiped out at the Little Big Horn by Lakota and Northern Cheyenne warriors.

When the news of Custer's defeat hit the newsstands in the east, the country was in the midst of centenary celebrations. A shocked nation recoiled; public opinion hardened and resources were found to put more troops in the field. The victors of the Little Big Horn were driven north into Canada.

While in most cases incursions onto land 'granted' to the native Americans in both areas was linked in both northern and southern Plains to the discovery of gold, the eventual supplanting of groups in the south was not. Here it was as a result of the native Americans fighting back after their source of life, the buffalo, had been decimated on the very land that had been promised to them less than a decade previously. The defeat in the south came at the end of a long line of losses that followed each discovery by the new Americans that the land of the Great Plains was not as useless as they had first thought. The native Americans were driven south by the slaughter of the buffalo. The buffalo had been wiped out by 1878 in the south, and two years later the hunters moved in on the northern herd, protected by the post-Little Big Horn US military campaign against the victors. By 1884 few buffalo remained, and in 1885 they were virtually extinct. On the northern Plains, although the Lakota and their allies achieved some military successes, they were ultimately to suffer the same fate: the loss of land promised to them. They were driven further away from the heart of the Great Plains. The Oregon Trail and the railroad which carried travellers, information and goods to link east and west of the nation, was also the dividing line between north and south for the vast buffalo herd and the native Americans who relied on them.

The result for all native Americans of Plains was the same: confinement on reservations. A law was passed in 1871 which formally ended the practice of treaties which had considered the native Americans to be separate nations from the United States. Native American culture was undermined by the practice of removing young children from their families to be 'educated' in residential schools where they were beaten if they spoke their native tongue. Finally in 1887 a law was passed under which the president of the United States was given the power to divide up the reservations, which resulted in another boom-time for the land speculators. Gold, the bison and protecting travellers provided short term reasons for conflict, but ultimately in the clash of cultures, as Red Cloud, Oglala Lakota, observed:

> The white man made us many promises, more than I can ever remember, but they never kept but one; they promised to take our land and they took it.

This article first appeared in *History Today,* April 2006, pp. 42–49. Copyright © 2006 by History Today, Ltd. Reprinted by permission.

America's Birth at Appomattox

ANNE WORTHAM

It would of course be easy to make too much of the general air of reconciliation. . . . And yet by any standard this was an almost unbelievable way to end a civil war, which by all tradition is the worst kind of war there is.[1]

—Bruce Catton

On April 9, 1865, eighty-nine years after the Continental Congress declared the independence of "thirteen United States of America," the United States of America was born at the residence of farmer Wilmer McLean in the hamlet of Appomattox Courthouse, Virginia. Civil War historian James Robertson has said, "Lee signed not so much terms of surrender as he did the birth certificate of a nation—the United States—and the country was born in that moment."[2] An American nationality in the sense of a general feeling of being American above all else did not yet exist when Grant and Lee put their names to the surrender document. But there were at work nineteenth-century values, ideas, and attitudes that transcended sectional loyalties, that remained intact throughout the war, and made possible the birth of the United States as a nation.

I will look at the function of friendship, battlefield comradeship and courtesy, and shared nationality in that process; and argue that these qualities of association—as well as the high value the combatants placed on courage, duty, honor, and discipline—enabled the Federals and Confederates to achieve what Robert Penn Warren called "reconciliation by human recognition." I intend to show how reconciliation was played out in numerous meetings between Union and Confederate officers and soldiers at Appomattox between April 9, 1865, when Lee surrendered, and April 12, when the Confederates stacked their arms, folded their flags, and were paroled.

Lincoln's Attitude

We are not enemies, but friends. . . . Though passion may have strained, it must not break our bonds of affection. The mystic chords of memory, stretching from every battlefield, and patriot grave, to every living heart, and hearthstone, all over this broad land, will yet swell the chorus of the Union, when again touched, as surely they will be, by the better angels of our nature.

—Abraham Lincoln

Reconciliation was an explicit policy goal of Abraham Lincoln's, which he made clear to Generals Grant and Sherman and Adm. David Dixon Porter in a conference aboard the *River Queen* at City Point, Virginia, after his visit to the front on March 27, 1865. Lincoln knew that unless "the better angels of our nature" could be asserted by unambiguous action at war's end, there was no hope for the new birth of freedom and the national community he believed was possible. The problem for Lincoln was how to simultaneously end the war and win the peace. As Bruce Catton puts it, he argued that the Union's aim should be not so much to subdue the Confederacy as to checkmate those forces of malice and rancor that could jeopardize peace. For if the North won the war and lost the peace, there would be no way to realize his hope that "the whole country, North and South together, [would] ultimately find in reunion and freedom the values that would justify four terrible years of war."[3]

In the only existing documentation of the meeting, Admiral Porter wrote:

My opinion is that Mr. Lincoln came down to City Point with the most liberal views toward the rebels. He felt confident that we would be successful, and was willing that the enemy should capitulate on the most favorable terms. . . . He wanted peace on almost any terms. . . . His heart was tenderness throughout, and, as long as the rebels laid down their arms, he did not care how it was done.[4]

Lincoln knew that the peace and reconciliation he envisioned would not stand a chance without generous surrender terms. He expected Grant, "the remorseless killer," and Sherman, "destruction's own self," to "fight without mercy as long as there must be fighting, but when the fighting stopped they [must] try to turn old enemies into friends."

> **Lincoln knew his fellow citizens, and he was confident that while they were politically disunited, the raw material of reconciliation resided in their hearts.**

But could reconciliation be coaxed out of defeat? There were reasons to think it possible. Lincoln knew his fellow citizens, and he was confident that while they were politically disunited, the raw material of reconciliation resided in their hearts. Indeed, friendliness and respect were present within the armies, and there was now less bitterness between them than when the war began. Yet another resource was the extraordinary resilience of the friendships between the former West Pointers leading those armies. Finally, whether he knew it or not, but must have sensed, Lincoln had a most reliable resource in the antisecessionist gray commander himself, Robert E. Lee—but not until he was defeated.

West Point 1: A Cheerful Colloquy

If one would have a friend, one must be willing to wage war for him: and in order to wage war, one must be capable of being an enemy. . . . In one's friend, one shall find one's best enemy.

—Frederich Nietzsche

"The soldiers did not need to be told that it would be well to make peace mean comradeship. All they needed was to see somebody try it," writes Catton.[5] Well, on Palm Sunday, April 9, 1865, there were plenty of occasions to see the vanquished and the victorious extend the hand of friendship. On the morning of that dramatic day, white flags of truce were held aloft as messengers rode between the lines, and a cease-fire was in place until the anticipated surrender meeting between Grant and Lee. By late morning the contending armies stood on either side of the town, with their picket lines out, their guns silent, nervously contemplating the meaning of surrender and ever alert for the resumption of hostile fire. But gathered on the steps of the Appomattox Courthouse, awaiting the arrival of the two commanding generals, was a curious group of Union and Confederate generals, most of them West Point graduates, and many of them from the same graduating classes.

As historian Frank Cauble points out, because of the more significant surrender meeting that everyone was anticipating, this earlier conference of officers has been largely overlooked and seldom mentioned in Civil War histories. However, the sight of these former combatants was "a singular spectacle," wrote New York reporter L.A. Hendrick.

There were mutual introductions and shaking of hands, and soon was passed about some whiskey (General [Romeyn] Ayres furnished the whiskey and he alleges it was a first class article) and mutual healths were drank and altogether it was a strange grouping. The rebel officers were all elegantly dressed in full uniform. Gradually the area of the conference widened. From the steps the conferring party got into the street, and before it closed some were seated on the steps, and others, for lack of more comfortable accommodations, chatted cosily, seated on a contiguous fence.[6]

Gen. Joshua Chamberlain overheard two West Point classmates who had been combatants for four years renewing an old

acquaintance. "Well Billy, old boy, how goes it?" the Union officer said. "Bad, bad, Charlie, bad I can tell you; but have you got any whiskey?"[7]

When we consider the pain, suffering, and death these men had inflicted upon one another and their comrades, how are we to explain their apparent lack of resentment and bitterness?

When we consider the pain, suffering, and death these men had inflicted upon one another and their comrades, how are we to explain their apparent lack of resentment and bitterness? How could one so easily drink of the cup of fraternity with someone who has been shooting at him and his comrades—and sometimes hitting the mark—for four years? Can vanquished and victor really be friends?

Well, yes—if the fellow who had been shooting at you was a friend before he was your enemy, and if he was bound to you by that precious ethos called the "spirit of West Point." Vindictiveness was not the order of the day for these men. They just wanted it over. Indeed, two months before, on February 25, Union Gen. Edward Ord met under a flag of truce with his former classmate, Confederate Gen. James Longstreet, and discussed the possibility of Lee and Grant declaring peace on the field. Now, as the officers waited for Grant and Lee, John Gibbon, a North Carolinian whose three brothers fought for the Confederacy, proposed that if Grant and Lee couldn't come to terms and stop the fighting, they should order their soldiers to fire only blank cartridges to prevent further bloodshed. By noon, when Grant still had not appeared, the West Pointers rode back to their respective lines, all hoping, as Gibbon said, "that there would be no further necessity for bloodshed."

Conditional Surrender

Another year would go by before President Andrew Johnson, on April 2, 1866, proclaimed "that the insurrection . . . is at an end and is henceforth to be so regarded." But Grant and Lee's task of reconciliation could not wait for the U.S. government's official certification of the end of the war. They knew it had to begin with the surrender terms themselves. Grant finally arrived from the field between 1:30 and 2:00 and entered the McLean house where Lee was waiting. By 3:00 the surrender documents were signed, the two commanders had shaken hands, and Lee had mounted Traveller and returned to his lines. At 4:30 Grant telegraphed Washington, informing the secretary of war that Lee had surrendered "on terms proposed by myself."

They agreed that all officers and men of the Army of Northern Virginia should be paroled and disqualified from taking up arms against the government of the United States until properly exchanged; that they should turn over all arms, artillery, and public property to the Union army; but that officers should

Gen. Ulysses S. Grant standing at Cold Harbor, Virginia, in June 1864 (National Archives).

not be deprived of their sidearms, horses, and baggage. In stating that "each officer and man will be allowed to return to their homes not to be disturbed by United States authority so long as they observe their paroles and the laws in force where they may reside," Grant effectively made it impossible for Lee to be tried for treason.

Lee asked that those of the enlisted men who owned their horses be permitted to keep them. At first Grant rejected this request, but then he changed his mind. Since this was the last battle of the war, the men needed their horses to put in their spring crops, and since the United States did not want the horses, he said he would instruct the parole officers to "let every man of the Confederate army who claimed to own a horse or mule to take the animal to his home." It was ironic that for four years Grant had tried to kill these men, and now he didn't want to stand in the way of their planting their crops so they could live. But Grant now saw himself as an instrument for a lasting peace. He extended his generosity further by ordering his army to share its rations with the hungry rebels.

The surrender terms were entirely consistent with the policy of reconciliation that Lincoln had articulated back in March. According to Admiral Porter, when Lincoln learned of the surrender terms, he was "delighted" and exclaimed "a dozen times, 'Good!' 'All right!' 'Exactly the thing!' and other similar expressions." Confederate Porter Alexander was also moved by Grant's generosity at Appomattox and wrote later: "Gen. Grant's conduct toward us in the whole matter is worthy of the very highest praise & indicates a great & broad & generous mind. *For all time it will be a good thing for the whole United States, that of all the Federal generals it fell to Grant to receive the surrender of Lee*" (emphasis in the original).[8]

Union soldiers like Maj. Holman Melcher of the 20th Maine were also impressed by Grant's magnanimity and resolved to follow his example. In a letter to his brother, Melcher noted that "the good feeling between the officers and men of the two armies followed General Grant [who] set us the example by his conduct at the surrender." He went on to "confess" what no doubt many Union officers and soldiers felt—that "a feeling of indignation would rise within me when I would think of all the bloodshed and mourning these same men had caused. But it is honorable to be magnanimous to a conquered foe. And as civilized men and gentlemen, we strive to keep such feelings of hatred in subjection."[9]

Melcher's attitude confirmed Lincoln's insight that, as Catton puts it, "if the terms expressed simple human decency and friendship, it might be that a peace of reconciliation could get just enough of a lead so that the haters could never quite catch up with it." But it would require just the level of self-control that Melcher imposed on himself.

Having signed the certificate of birth, Grant and Lee still had to attend to the business of delivering a deathblow to the idea of secession while simultaneously injecting some vitality into the promise of this new beginning. They did so by word and deed. When news of the surrender reached the Union lines, the men began to fire a salute and cheer, but Grant issued orders forbidding any demonstrations. He wrote later that "the Confederates were now our prisoners, and we did not want to exult over their downfall." While Grant taught his men to resist acts of humiliation, Lee's assignment was to instill stoic dignity.

The Confederates could not believe what had transpired. Orderly Sgt. James Whitehorne of the 12th Virginia, wrote in his diary, "I was thunderstruck. . . . What would Jackson, Stuart, or—any of [those who had been killed fighting under Lee] say about us? . . . It is humiliating in the extreme. I never expected to see men cry as they did this morning. All the officers cried and most of the privates broke down and wept like children and Oh, Lord! I cried too."

The emotions of the weary and humiliated men in Lee's tattered army ranged from bitterness and anger to sadness and acceptance. But they were relieved when they learned that they would be paroled and free to go home rather than sent to Northern prisons. They were also grateful for the much-needed rations. But men need more than rations; they need meaning. And only Robert E. Lee, their beloved Marse Robert, could satisfy that most pressing of human needs by reinforcing their sense of honor, legitimating their pride, and redirecting their tired fury.

Having signed the certificate of birth, Grant and Lee still had to attend to the business of delivering a deathblow to the idea of secession while simultaneously injecting some vitality into the promise of this new beginning.

In his farewell order to the army, Lee praised their "four years of arduous service, marked by unsurpassed courage and fortitude," told them that they were brave and had "remained steadfast to the last," and urged them to peacefully return to their homes, taking with them "the satisfaction that proceeds from the consciousness of duty faithfully performed." He ended by honoring them: "With an increasing admiration of your constancy and devotion to your country, and a grateful remembrance of your kind and generous consideration for myself, I bid you all an affectionate farewell."[11]

What Lee accomplished in his address, says Bruce Catton, was to set the pattern, to give these men the right words to take with them into the future. "Pride in what they had done would grow with the years, but it would turn them into a romantic army of legend and not into a sullen battalion of death."

There were Federals, like General Chamberlain, who would not begrudge the Confederates the sentiments that Lee tried to instill in them. Although he believed they were wrong in their beliefs, "they fought as they were taught, true to such ideals as they saw, and put into their cause their best." Reflecting on the parade of Confederates stacking their arms and flags, Chamberlain, who was appointed to command the formal surrender of arms, said: "For us they were fellow-soldiers as well, suffering the fate of arms. We could not look into those brave, bronzed faces, and those battered flags we had met on so many fields where glorious manhood lent a glory to the earth that bore it, and think of personal hate and revenge."[12]

West Point 2: Sam Grant's Comrades

The next day, April 10, some of Grant's generals asked for permission to enter the Confederate lines to meet old friends. As he sat on the porch of the McLean house waiting for his officers to prepare his army to leave Appomattox, they began arriving with many of Grant's old comrades. Along with Phil Sheridan, John Gibbon, and Rufus Ingalls came the beloved Confederate Cadmus Wilcox, who had been best man at Grant's wedding. Confederate Henry Heth, who had been a subaltern with Grant in Mexico, was joined by his cousin George Pickett, who also knew Grant from Mexico. Pickett and Heth were friends of Gibbon, whose Union division bore the brunt of Pickett's charge at Gettysburg. Federal George Gordon and a number of others also came along.

Grant talked with them until it was time to leave. He later wrote that the officers "seemed to enjoy the meeting as much

as though they had been friends separated for a long time while fighting battles under the same flag. For the time being it looked very much as if all thought of the war had escaped their minds."[13] No doubt somewhere deep in their hearts were the sentiments of the West Point hymn traditionally sung at the last chapel service before graduation:

> When shall we meet again?
> Meet ne'er to sever?
> When will Peace wreath her chain
> Round us forever?
> Our hearts will ne'er repose
> Safe from each blast that blows
> In this dark vale of woes,—
> Never—no, never.[14]

These friends were a band of brothers whom historian James McPherson describes as "more tightly bonded by hardship and danger in war than biological brothers." Now, on this spring day in April, the guns were quiet, and, as historian John Waugh points out, they "yearned to know that they would never hear their thunder or be ordered to take up arms against one another again."

By the time Longstreet arrived to join other Confederate and Union commissioners appointed to formulate the details of the surrender ceremony, Grant had apparently moved inside to a room that served as his temporary headquarters. When Longstreet walked by on the way to the room where the commissioners were meeting, Grant looked up and recognized him. He rose from his chair and, as Longstreet recalled, "with his old-time cheerful greeting gave me his hand, and after passing a few remarks offered a cigar, which was gratefully received."[15] Grant, addressing Longstreet by his nickname, said jokingly, "Pete, let us have another game of brag, to recall the days which were so pleasant to us all."[16] The two men had been best friends since West Point. They had served together for a time in the same regiment at Jefferson's Barracks, Missouri. Longstreet introduced Julia Dent, his distant cousin, to Grant and was present at their marriage vows. Three years after Appomattox, in 1868, Longstreet endorsed Grant's presidential candidacy and attended his inauguration.

Three years after Appommatox, in 1868, Longstreet endorsed Grant's presidential candidacy and attended his inauguration.

"The mere presence of conflict, envy, aggression, or any number of other contaminants does not doom or invalidate a friendship," says professor of English Ronald Sharp.[17] Much of the behavior of the West Pointers can be explained by the enormous strength of their friendships to withstand the horror of war. As Waugh points out, "It had never been in their hearts to hate the classmates they were fighting. Their lives and affections for one another had been indelibly framed and inextricably intertwined in their academy days. No adversity, war, killing, or political estrangement could undo that."[18] In his poem, "Meditation," Herman Melville, who visited the Virginia battlefront in the spring of 1864, celebrated their comradeship in the following verse:

> Mark the great Captains on both sides.
> The soldiers with the broad renown—
> They all were messmates on the Hudson's marge,
> Beneath one roof they laid them down;
> And, free from hate in many an after pass,
> Strove as in school-boy rivalry of the class.[19]

With some exaggeration, former West Pointer Morris Schaff wrote some forty years later that when "the graduates of both armies met as brothers" they symbolically "planted then and there the tree that has grown, blooming for the Confederate and blooming for the Federal, and under those whose shade we now gather in peace."[20] Our knowledge of the hatred and vengeance that Northerners and Southerners, including many West Pointers, felt toward each other and of the political conflicts attending Reconstruction might lead us to argue with the vision of West Pointers planting the tree of peace at Appomattox. But we cannot deny that, as their various diaries, letters, and memoirs document, that is what they thought they were doing.

Embattled Civility

A well-known paradox of the Civil War, writes Alan Nolan, was that "although fighting against each other with a devastating ferocity, the enlisted men and officers of the two sides tended to trust each other and did not see themselves in the manner of soldiers in most wars."[21] By the time Grant took command of the troubled Army of the Potomac in 1864, as Catton put it, "a fantastic sort of kinship"—"a queer combination of antagonism and understanding"—had grown up in regard to the Army of Northern Virginia. "There was no soft sentimentality about it, and the men would shoot to kill when the time for shooting came. Yet there was a familiarity and an understanding, at times something that verged almost on liking, based on solid respect." Now, on April 9, despite the fact that it was officially forbidden to prevent unpleasant contacts between members of the two armies, as soon as the surrender was announced there was quite a bit of visiting back and forth between the lines among Union and Confederate troops. Pvt. Charles Dunn of the 20th Maine reported that there was considerable trading that night.

> The two picket lines were within speaking distance, and we were on speaking terms with the "Johnnies" at once. There was nothing that resembled guard duty that night. It resembled a picnic rather than a picket line. They like ourselves were glad the war was over. We exchanged knicknacks with them, and were reminded of the days when at school we swapped jews-harps for old wooden toothed combs. The articles we exchanged that night were about the same value.[22]

Chamberlain wrote of receiving Confederate visitors all the next day. "Our camp was full of callers before we were up," he recalled. "The inundation of visitors grew so that it looked like a country fair, including the cattle-show."

J. Tracy Power notes that Confederates

were impressed by Federal soldiers who shared rations or money with them and carried on pleasant, and sometimes friendly, conversations about the end of the war. Maj. Richard Watson Jones of the 12th Virginia was visited by a Federal officer he had known before the war when they attended the same college. Sgt. James Whitehorne described the scene when the Federal entered the Confederate camp. "We saw him come up and hold out his hand—the Major did nothing for so long it was painful. Then he took the offered hand and I had a feeling the war was really over."[23]

It was in just such conduct that Bell Wiley, in his study of the common soldier, saw "undeveloped resources of strength and character that spelled hope for the country's future."[24] For his own part, Whitehorne declared, "After all, I never hated any one Yankee. I hated the spirit that was sending them to invade the south."

Two Sides but One Identity

In his moving tribute to the men in gray, Chamberlain asserted that "whoever had misled these men, we had not. We had led them back home." While it is true that Confederates had seceded from the Union politically, they had not left the Union culturally. A significant overarching factor in the reconciliation of the former combatants was the fact that the soldiers "were not alien foes but men of similar origin." The Civil War was not a conflict between Southern Cavaliers and New England Puritans, between a nation of warriors and a nation of shopkeepers, or, as abolitionist Wendell Phillips insisted, between a civilization based on democracy and one based on an aristocracy founded on slavery. Rather, it was, in the words of Walt Whitman, "a struggle going on within one identity." Robert Penn Warren concurs in his argument that the nation that went to war "share[d] deep and significant convictions and [was] not a mere handbasket of factions huddled arbitrarily together by historical happen-so."[25]

While it is true that Confederates had seceded from the Union politically, they had not left the Union culturally.

Whether consciously acknowledged by them or not, Northerners and Southerners shared significant elements of national identity that the war could not annihilate. By national identity I do not mean nationalism, to quote Merle Curti, "in the sense of both confidence in the strength of the federal government and devotion to the nation as a whole," which in the nineteenth century was only a hope, an aspiration. Rather, I mean shared nationality in the sense that, again, quoting Curti, rank-and-file Americans "[cherish] the Union as a precious symbol of a revered past and a bright future, identifying it with abundance, opportunity and ultimate peace."[26]

The social, cultural, philosophical, and ideological differences between the combatants have been fully documented. But, as Wiley concluded, "the similarities of Billy Yank and Johnny Reb far outweighed their differences. They were both Americans, by birth or by adoption, and they both had the weaknesses and the virtues of the people of their nation and time." Alan Nolan concurs: "They shared the same revolutionary experience, the same heroes, the same Founding Fathers; and, despite the south's departure from the Bill of Rights in the effort to protect slavery, they shared, at bottom, a sense of political values."[27]

America was becoming American. Johnny Reb and Billy Yank were creating a new kind of American and a new awareness of America.

A key element of the national identity that Northerners and Southerners shared was a vision of the nation as the promised land to which God had led his people to establish a new social order that was to be, as John Winthrop said in 1630, "a city upon a hill, the eyes of all people are upon us, so that if we shall deal falsely with our God in this work we have undertaken and so cause him to withdraw his present help from us, we shall be made a story and a by-word through the world."[28]

The sense of being on show and tested before God and the world was no less true of Civil War combatants than it was for the Puritans. And just as persistent was the corollary concern of Americans that they would fall short of the vision. Because of this "fear of falling away," as historian Rupert Wilkinson calls it, Northerners and Southerners alike were faced with two basic philosophical questions: Are we worthy of our revolutionary forebears? Are we undoing, by our divisiveness, all that they worked so hard to obtain? Both sides compared America with its past and found themselves wanting. Both invoked the Revolutionary-Constitution era in seeking redemption of the Republic.

Civil War combatants were also bound by their perception of the changes swirling around them in the wider society as well as within their armies. "Always the army reflected the nation," writes Catton. And the nation itself was changing. Increased immigration, factory production, and urbanization eroded and destroyed old unities—"unities of blood, of race, of language, of shared ideals and common memories and experiences, the very things which had always seemed essential beneath the word 'American.' In some mysterious way that nobody quite understood, the army not only mirrored the change but represented the effort to find a new synthesis."[29]

America was becoming American. Johnny Reb and Billy Yank were creating a new kind of American and a new awareness of America. As Warren points out,

> The War meant that Americans saw America. The farm boy of Ohio, the trapper in Minnesota, and the pimp of the Mackerelville section of New York City saw Richmond and Mobile. They not only saw America, they saw each other, and together shot it out with some Scot of the Valley of Virginia or ducked hardware hurled by a Louisiana Jew who might be a lieutenant of artillery, CSA.[30]

Out of the cauldron of hell into which were thrown Billy Yank, Johnny Reb, their immigrant comrades, as well as the black soldiers they all despised, came a pluralistic national community.

The Nationalization of Lee

In the decades following the war, as Americans became more American, so too did Robert E. Lee's image. By the turn of the century he was nationally elevated to a hero status shared by only a handful of individuals, such as Washington, Lincoln, and Jefferson. In their study of the transformation of Lee's image, Thomas Connelly and Barbara Bellows report: "A writer in *Harper's Weekly* proclaimed him 'the pride of a whole country.'. . . The *New York Times* praised Lee's 'grandeur of soul,' and the *Nation* called Lee 'great in gentleness and goodness.' "[31]

> The Americanization of Lee began long before he surrendered. When Brig. Gen. Samuel Crawford, in the 5th Corps of the Army of the Potomac, visited briefly with Lee the day after his surrender to Grant, he told Lee that, should he go North, he would find that he had "hosts of warm friends there." With tears in his eyes, Lee said, "I suppose all the people of the North looked upon me as a rebel traitor." Far from it. An unlikely contributor to his elevation was Julia Ward Howe, the abolitionist who wrote "Battle Hymn of the Republic":

> A gallant foeman in the fight,
> A brother when the fight was o'er,
> The hand that led the host with might
> The blessed torch of learning bore.
> No shriek of shells nor roll of drums,
> No challenge fierce, resounding far,
> When reconciling Wisdom comes
> To heal the cruel wounds of war.
> Thought may the minds of men divide,
> Love makes the heart of nations one,
> And so, the soldier grave beside,
> We honor thee, Virginia's son.[32]

The nationalization of Lee is a very American cultural practice: the elevation of worthy "native sons"—beyond the soil of their birth, beyond the privileges or lack of privileges of their class, beyond the dogma of their creed—to the position of national icon. In 1900 Virginia's son was inducted into the newly established Hall of Fame for Great Americans along with

Washington, Jefferson, John Adams, and Benjamin Franklin. In 1934, Virginia presented statues of Lee and Washington to Congress to be placed in Statuary Hall in the U.S. Capitol, which houses statues of outstanding citizens from each of the states. The Lee so honored—the Lee that won over the nation and was praised by every American president—was, as Connelly and Bellows describe him, "the man of basic American values of decency, duty, and honor, the devotee of unionism trapped in 1861 by conflicting loyalties." Lee was the postwar nationalist, driven by an unswerving determination to help restore the old Union.

In truth, America had never been united, but now it was on the road toward becoming American.

But Lee is the supreme paradoxical American hero. As McPherson insightfully points out, Lee's heroism has to be seen in terms of his gigantic role in prolonging the war longer than it might have been. When Lee took command of the Army of Northern Virginia in June 1862, the Confederacy was on the verge of collapse. In the previous four months, it had lost its largest city, New Orleans; much of the Mississippi Valley; and most of Tennessee; and Maj. Gen. George McClellan's Army of the Potomac had moved to within five miles of Richmond, the Confederate capital. McPherson cites the irony of Lee's command as follows:

> Within three months Lee's offensives had taken the Confederacy off the floor at the count of nine and had driven Union forces onto the ropes. Without Lee the Confederacy might have died in 1862. But slavery would have survived; the South would have suffered only limited death and destruction. Lee's victories prolonged the war until it destroyed slavery, the plantation economy, the wealth and infrastructure of the region, and everything else the confederacy stood for. That was the profound irony of Lee's military genius.[33]

The Significance of Appomattox

In an April 12 telegram to Grant, who had departed for Washington two days earlier, General Gibbon informed him that "the surrender of General Lee's army was finally completed today," then went on to comment on the meaning of Appomattox: "I have conversed with many of the surrendered officers, and am satisfied that by announcing at once terms and a liberal, merciful policy on the part of the Government we can once more have a happy, united country."[34]

This is what Lincoln wanted. In truth, America had never been united, but now it was on the road toward becoming American. And this is how it sounded: A Confederate offi-

cer at the head of his surrendering corps told Chamberlain, "General, this is deeply humiliating; but I console myself with the thought that the whole country will rejoice at this day." Another told him, "I went into that cause and I meant it. We had our choice of weapons and of ground, and we have lost. Now that is my flag (pointing to the flag of the Union), and I will prove myself as worthy as any of you."[35]

References

1. Bruce Catton, *The Centennial History of the Civil War: Never Call Retreat,* vol. 3 (New York: Doubleday and Co., 1965), 455–56.
2. James Robertson Jr., *Civil War Journal: Robert E. Lee: A History TV Network Presentation,* Time-Life Video (Alexandria, Va.: Time, 1994).
3. Bruce Catton, *A Stillness at Appomattox* (New York: Doubleday and Co., 1957), 340.
4. David Dixon Porter, quoted in Philip Van Doren Stern, *An End to Valor: The Last Days of the Civil Wa*r (Boston: Houghton Mifflin Co., 1858), 103–104.
5. Catton, *Stillness at Appomattox,* 341.
6. L.A. Hendrick, "Conferences of Commanding Officers," *Freeman's Journal and Catholic Register,* 22 April 1865. Quoted in Frank Cauble, *The Surrender Proceedings: April Ninth, 1865, Appomattox Court Hous*e (Lynchburg, Va.: H.E. Howard, 1987), 43–44.
7. Joshua Lawrence Chamberlain, *The Passing of the Armies: The Last Campaign of the Armie*s (Gettysburg, Pa.: Stan Clark Military Books, 1995 reprint ed.), 244.
8. Gary Gallagher, ed., *Fighting for the Confederacy: The Personal Recollections of General Edward Porter Alexander* (Chapel Hill, N.C.: University of North Carolina Press, 1989), 540.
9. William Styple, ed., *With a Flash of His Sword: The Writings of Maj. Holman S. Melcher, 20th Maine Infantry* (Kearny, N.J.: Belle Grove Publishing Co., 1994), 219.
10. J. Tracy Power, *Lee's Miserables: Life in the Army of Northern Virginia From the Wilderness to Appomattox* (Chapel Hill, N.C.: University of North Carolina Press, 1998), 282.
11. Thomas Connelly, *Marble Man: Robert E. Lee and His Image in American Society* (Baton Rouge, La.: Louisiana State University Press, 1978), 367.
12. Chamberlain, *Passing of the Armies,* 270.
13. Ulysses S. Grant, *Memoirs and Selected Letters: Personal Memoirs of U.S. Grant: Selected Letters 1839–1865* (New York: Library of America, 1990), 744.
14. Quoted in George Pappas, *To the Point: The United States Military Academy, 1802–1902* (Westport, Conn.: Praeger, 1993), 322.
15. James Longstreet, *From Manassas to Appomattox* [1896] (New York: Konecky and Konecky, 1992), 630.
16. Jeffrey Wert, *General James Longstreet: The Confederacy's Most Controversial Soldier* (New York: Simon and Schuster, 1994), 404.
17. Ronald Sharp, *Friendship and Literature: Spirit and Form* (Durham, N.C.: Duke University Press, 1986), 120.
18. John Waugh, *The Class of 1846: From West Point to Appomattox: Stonewall Jackson, George McClellan and Their Brothers* (New York: Warner Books, 1994), 500.
19. Herman Melville, *Battle-Pieces and Aspects of the War* [1866]. Quoted in Richard Dilworth Rust, ed., *Glory and Pathos:*

Responses of Nineteenth-Century American Authors to the Civil War (Boston: Holbrook Press, 1970), 177.

20. Morris Schaff, *The Spirit of Old West Point, 1858–1862* (Boston: Houghton-Mifflin, 1907), 140, 251–53.

21. Alan Nolan, *Lee Considered: General Robert E. Lee and Civil War History* (Chapel Hill, N.C.: University of North Carolina Press, 1991), 158.

22. Quoted in J.J. Pullen, *The Twentieth Maine* (Philadelphia: J.B. Lippincott Co., 1957), 270.

23. Quoted in Power, *Lee's Miserables,* 283.

24. Bell Wiley, *The Life of Johnny Reb and the Life of Billy Yank* [1943, 1952], reprint, Essential Classics of the Civil War (New York: Book-of-the-Month Club/Louisiana State University Press, 1994), 361.

25. Robert Penn Warren, *The Legacy of the Civil War* (New York: Random House, 1961), 83.

26. Merle Curti, *The Growth of American Thought* (New Brunswick, N.J.: Transaction Publishers, 1991), 423–24.

27. Nolan, *Lee Considered,* 157.

28. John Winthrop, "A Modell of Christian Charity," (1630), reprinted in Daniel Boorstin, ed., *An American Primer,* vol. 1 (Chicago: Chicago University Press, 1966), 22.

29. Catton, *Stillness at Appomattox,* 216.

30. Warren, *Legacy of the Civil War,* 13.

31. Thomas Connelly and Barbara Bellows, *God and General Longstreet: The Lost Cause and the Southern Mind* (Baton Rouge: Louisiana State University Press, 1982), 83.

32. Julia Ward Howe, "Robert E. Lee," in Lois Hill, ed., *Poems and Songs of the Civil War* (New York: Gramercy Books, 1990).

33. James McPherson, *Drawn With the Sword: Reflections on the American Civil War* (New York: Oxford University Press, 1996), 158.

34. Quoted in Bruce Catton, *Grant Takes Command* [1968] (New York: Book-of-the-Month Club, 1994), 473.

35. Chamberlain, *Passing of the Armies,* 266.

ANNE WORTHAM is associate professor of sociology at Illinois State University.

The American Civil War, Emancipation, and Reconstruction on the World Stage

Edward L. Ayers

Americans demanded the world's attention during their Civil War and Reconstruction. Newspapers around the globe reported the latest news from the United States as one vast battle followed another, as the largest system of slavery in the world crashed into pieces, as American democracy expanded to include people who had been enslaved only a few years before.[1]

Both the North and the South appealed to the global audience. Abraham Lincoln argued that his nation's Civil War "embraces more than the fate of these United States. It presents to the whole family of man, the question, whether a constitutional republic, or a democracy . . . can, or cannot, maintain its territorial integrity." The struggle. Lincoln said, was for "a vast future," a struggle to give all men "a fair chance in the race of life."[2] Confederates claimed that they were also fighting for a cause of world-wide significance: self-determination. Playing down the centrality of slavery to their new nation, white Southerners built their case for independence on the right of free citizens to determine their political future.[3]

People in other nations could see that the massive struggle in the United States embodied conflicts that had been appearing in different forms throughout the world. Defining nationhood, deciding the future of slavery, reinventing warfare for an industrial age, reconstructing a former slave society—all these played out in the American Civil War.

By no means a major power, the United States was nevertheless woven into the life of the world. The young nation touched, directly and indirectly, India and Egypt, Hawaii and Japan, Russia and Canada, Mexico and Cuba, the Caribbean and Brazil, Britain and France. The country was still very much an experiment in 1860, a representative government stretched over an enormous space, held together by law rather than by memory, religion, or monarch. The American Civil War, played out on the brightly lit stage of a new country, would be a drama of world history. How that experiment fared in its great crisis— regardless of what happened—would eventually matter to people everywhere.

More obviously than most nations, the United States was the product of global history. Created from European ideas, involvement in Atlantic trade, African slavery, conquest of land from American Indians and European powers, and massive migration from Europe, the United States took shape as the world watched. Long before the Civil War, the United States embodied the possibilities and contradictions of modern western history.

Slavery was the first, most powerful, and most widespread kind of globalization in the first three centuries after Columbus. While colonies came and went, while economies boomed and crashed, slavery relentlessly grew—and nowhere more than in the United States. By the middle of the nineteenth century, the slave South had assumed a central role on the world stage. Cotton emerged as the great global commodity, driving factories in the most advanced economies of the world. The slaves of the South were worth more than all the railroads and factories of the North and South combined; slavery was good business and shrewd investment.

While most other slave societies in the hemisphere gradually moved toward freedom, the American South moved toward the permanence of slavery. Southerners and their Northern allies, eager to expand, led the United States in a war to seize large parts of Mexico and looked hungrily upon the Caribbean and Central America. Of all the slave powers—including the giants of Brazil and Cuba, which continued to import slaves legally long after the United States—only the South and its Confederacy fought a war to maintain bondage.[4]

Ideas of justice circulated in global intercourse just as commodities did and those ideas made the American South increasingly anomalous as a modern society built on slavery. Demands for universal freedom came into conflict with ancient traditions of subordination. European nations, frightened by revolt in Haiti and elsewhere and confident of their empires' ability to prosper without slavery, dismantled slavery in their colonies in the western hemisphere while Russia dismantled serfdom.

Black and white abolitionists in the American North, though a tiny despised minority, worked with British allies to fight the acceptance of slavery in the United States. A vision of the South as backward, cruel, and power-hungry gained credence in many places in the North and took political force in the Republican party. The global economy of commodities and ideology, demanding cotton while attacking slavery, put enormous and contradictory strains on the young American nation.[5]

Meanwhile, a new urge to define national identity flowed through the western world in the first half of the nineteenth century. That determination took quite different forms. While some people still spoke of the universal dreams of the French and American Revolutions, of inalienable attributes of humankind, others spoke of historical grievance, ethnic unity, and economic self-interest. Many longed for new nations built around bonds of heritage, imagined and real.[6]

White Southerners, while building their case for secession with the language of constitutions and rights, presented themselves as a people profoundly different from white Northerners. They sought sanction for secession in the recent histories of Italy, Poland, Mexico, and Greece, where rebels rose up against central powers to declare their suppressed nationhood, where native elites led a "natural, necessary protest and revolt" against a "crushing, killing union with another nationality and form of society".[7]

As the South threatened to secede, the Republicans, a regional party themselves, emphasized the importance of Union for its own sake, the necessity of maintaining the integrity of a nation created by legal compact. It fell to the United States, the Republicans said, to show that large democracies could survive internal struggles and play a role in world affairs alongside monarchies and aristocracies.[8]

Once it became clear that war would come, the North and the South seized upon the latest war-making strategies and technologies. From the outset, both sides innovated at a rapid pace and imported ideas from abroad. Railroads and telegraphs extended supply lines, sped troop reinforcements, and permitted the mobilization of vast armies. Observers from Europe and other nations watched carefully to see how the Americans would use these new possibilities. The results were mixed. Ironclad ships, hurriedly constructed, made a difference in some Southern ports and rivers, but were not seaworthy enough to play the role some had envisioned for them. Submarines and balloons proved disappointments, unable to deliver significant advantages. Military leaders, rather than being subordinated by anonymous machinery, as some expected, actually became more important than before, their decisions amplified by the size of their armies and the speed of communication and transport.[9]

The scale and drama of the Civil War that ravaged America for four years, across an area larger than the European continent, fascinated and appalled a jaded world. A proportion of the population equal to five million people today died and the South suffered casualties at a rate equal to those who would be decimated in Europe's mechanized wars of the twentieth century.

The size, innovation, and destructiveness of the American Civil War have led some, looking back, to describe it as the first total war, the first truly modern war. Despite new technologies and strategies, however, much of the Civil War remained old-fashioned. The armies in the American Civil War still moved vast distances on foot or with animals. The food soldiers ate and the medical care they received showed little advance over previous generations of armies. The military history of the Civil War grew incrementally from world history and offered incremental changes to what would follow. Although, late in the war, continuous campaigning and extensive earthen entrenchments foreshadowed World War I, Europeans did not grasp the deadly lesson of the American Civil War: combining the tactics of Napoleon with rapid-fire weapons and trenches would culminate in horrors unanticipated at Shiloh and Antietam.[10]

Diplomacy proved challenging for all sides in the American crisis. The fragile balance of power on the Continent and in the empires centered there limited the range of movement of even the most powerful nations. The Confederacy's diplomatic strategy depended on gaining recognition from Great Britain and France, using cotton as a sort of blackmail, but European manufacturers had stockpiled large supplies of cotton in anticipation of the American war. British cartoonists, sympathetic to the Confederacy, ridiculed Abraham Lincoln at every opportunity, portraying him as an inept bumpkin—until his assassination, when Lincoln suddenly became sainted. Overall, the North benefited from the inaction of the British and the French, who could have changed the outcome and consequences of the war by their involvement.[11]

Inside the United States, the change unleashed by the war was as profound as it was unexpected. Even those who hated slavery had not believed in 1861 that generations of captivity could be ended overnight and former slaves and former slaveholders left to live together. The role of slavery in sustaining the Confederacy through humbling victories over the Union created the conditions in which Abraham Lincoln felt driven and empowered to issue the Emancipation Proclamation. The Union, briefly and precariously balanced between despair and hope, between defeat and victory, was willing in 1862 to accept that bold decision as a strategy of war and to enlist volunteers from among black Americans.[12]

The nearly 200,000 African Americans who came into the war as soldiers and sailors for the Union transformed the struggle. The addition of those men, greater in number than all the forces at Gettysburg, allowed the Union to build its advantage in manpower without pushing reluctant Northern whites into the draft. The enlistment of African Americans in the struggle for their own freedom ennobled the Union cause and promised to set a new global standard for the empowerment of formerly enslaved people. The world paid admiring attention to the brave and disciplined black troops in blue uniforms.[13]

The destruction of American slavery, a growing system of bondage of nearly four million people in one of the world's most powerful economies and most dynamic nation-states, was a consequence of world importance. Nowhere else besides Haiti did slavery end so suddenly, so completely, and with so little compensation for former slaveholders.[14] Had the United States failed to end slavery in the 1860s the world would have felt the difference. An independent Confederate States of America would certainly have put its enslaved population to effective use in coal mines, steel mills, and railroad building, since industrial slavery had been employed before secession and became more common during wartime. Though such a Confederacy might have found itself stigmatized, its survival would have meant the evolution of slavery into a new world of industrialization. The triumph of a major autonomous state built around slavery would have set a devastating example for the rest of the world, an encouragement to forces of reaction. It would have marked the repudiation of much that was liberating in Western thought and practice over the preceding two hundred years.[15]

Driven by the exigencies of war, Northern ideals of color-blind freedom and justice, so often latent and suppressed, suddenly if briefly bloomed in the mid-1860s. The Radical Republicans sought to create a black male American freedom based on the same basis as white male American freedom: property, citizenship, dignity, and equality before the law. They launched a bold Reconstruction to make those ideals a reality, their effort far surpassing those of emancipation anywhere else in the world. The white South resisted with vicious vehemence, however, and the Republicans, always ambivalent about black autonomy and eager to maintain their partisan power, lost heart after a decade of bitter, violent, and costly struggle in Reconstruction. Northern Democrats, opposing Reconstruction from the outset, hastened and celebrated its passing.[16]

If former slaves had been permitted to sustain the enduring political power they tried to build, if they had gone before juries and judges with a chance of fair treatment, if they had been granted homesteads to serve as a first step toward economic freedom, then Reconstruction could be hailed as a turning point in world history equal to any revolution. Those things did not happen, however. The white South claimed the mantle of victim, of a people forced to endure an unjust and unnatural subordination. They won international sympathy for generations to follow in films such as *Birth of a Nation* (1915) and *Gone With the Wind* (1939), which viewed events through the eyes of sympathetic white Southerners. Reconstruction came to be seen around the world not as the culmination of freedom but as a mistake, a story of the dangers of unrealistic expectations and failed social engineering. Though former slaves in the American South quietly made more progress in landholding and general prosperity than former slaves elsewhere, the public failures of Reconstruction obscured the progress black Southerners wrenched from the postwar decades.[17]

When the South lost its global monopoly of cotton production during the Civil War, governments, agents, and merchants around the world responded quickly to take the South's place and to build an efficient global machinery to supply an ever-growing demand in the world market. As a result, generations of black and white sharecroppers would compete with Indian, Brazilian, and Egyptian counterparts in a glutted market in which hard work often brought impoverishment. The South adapted its economy after the war as well. By the 1880s, the South's rates of urban growth, manufacturing, and population movement kept pace with the North—a remarkable shift for only twenty years after losing slavery and the Civil War—but black Southerners were excluded from much of the new prosperity.[18]

As the Civil War generation aged, younger men looked with longing on possible territorial acquisitions in their own hemisphere and farther afield. They talked openly of proving themselves, as their fathers and grandfathers had, on the battlefield. Some welcomed the fight against the Spanish and the Filipinos in 1898 as a test of American manhood and nationalism. The generation that came of age in 1900 built monuments to the heroes of the Civil War but seldom paused to listen to their stories of war's horror and costs.

The destruction of slavery, a major moral accomplishment of the United States Army, of Abraham Lincoln, and of the enslaved people themselves, would be overshadowed by the injustice and poverty that followed in the rapidly changing South, a mockery of American claims of moral leadership in the world. Black Southerners would struggle, largely on their own, for the next one hundred years. Their status, bound in an ever-tightening segregation, would stand as a rebuke to the United States in world opinion. The postwar South and its new system of segregation, in fact, became an explicit model for South Africa. That country created apartheid as it, like the American South, developed a more urban and industrial economy based on racial subordination.

Americans read about foreign affairs on the same pages that carried news of Reconstruction in the South. Even as the Southern states struggled to write new constitutions, Secretary of State William Henry Seward purchased Alaska in 1867 as a step toward the possible purchase of British Columbia. President Grant considered annexation of Santo Domingo, partly as a base for black Southern emigration; he won the support of black abolitionist Frederick Douglass, who wanted to help the Santo Domingans, but was opposed by Radical Republican Senator Charles Sumner.

Americans paid close attention to Hawaii in these same years. Mark Twain visited the islands in 1866, and Samuel Armstrong—the white founder of Hampton Institute, where Booker T. Washington was educated—argued that Hawaiians and former slaves in the South needed similar discipline to become industrious. At the same time, Seward signed a treaty with China to help supply laborers to the American West, a treaty that laid the foundation for a large migration in the next few decades. In 1871, American forces intervened militarily in Korea, killing 250 Korean soldiers. The leaders of the Americans admitted they knew little about their opponents, but brought the same assumptions about race to the conflict that they brought to their dealings with all non-Europeans everywhere, Koreans—like Hawaiians, Chinese, American Indians, and African Americans—needed to be disciplined, taught, and controlled.

No master plan guided Americans in their dealings with other peoples. In all of these places, the interests of American businessmen, the distortions of racial ideology, and hopes for partisan political advantage at home jostled with one another. As a result, the consequences of these involvements were often unclear and sometimes took generations to play out. Nevertheless, they remind us that Americans paid close attention to what was happening elsewhere, whether in the Franco-Prussian War (1870–1871), where the evolution of warfare continued to become more mechanized and lethal, or the Paris Commune (1871), where some thought they saw the result of unbridled democracy in chaos and violence—and wondered if Reconstruction did not represent a similar path.

Some people around the world were surprised that the United States did not use its enormous armies after the Civil War to seize Mexico from the French, Canada from the English, or Cuba from the Spanish. Conflict among the great powers on the European Continent certainly opened an opportunity and the United States had expanded relentlessly and opportunistically throughout its history. Few Americans, though, had the stomach for new adventures in the wake of the Civil War. The fighting against the American Indians on the Plains proved warfare enough for most white Americans in the 1870s and 1880s.[19]

The United States focused its postwar energies instead on commerce. Consolidated under Northern control, the nation's economy proved more formidable than ever before. The United States, its economic might growing with each passing year, its railroad network and financial systems consolidated, its cities and towns booming, its population surging westward, its mines turning out massive amounts of coal and precious minerals, its farms remarkably productive, and its corporations adopting new means of expansion and administration, became a force throughout the world. American engineers oversaw projects in Asia, Africa, and Latin America. American investors bought stock in railroads, factories, and mines around the globe. American companies came to dominate the economies of nations in Latin America.[20]

Americans became famous as rich, energetic, and somewhat reckless players amid the complexity of the world. As the Civil War generation aged, younger men looked with longing on possible territorial acquisitions in their own hemisphere and farther afield. They talked openly of proving themselves, as their fathers and grandfathers had, on the battlefield. Some welcomed the fight against the Spanish and the Filipinos in 1898 as a test of American manhood and nationalism. The generation that came of age in 1900 built monuments to the heroes of the Civil War but seldom paused to listen to their stories of war's horror and costs.

The American Civil War has carried a different meaning for every generation of Americans. In the 1920s and 1930s leading historians in a largely isolationist United States considered the Civil War a terrible mistake, the product of a "blundering generation." After the triumph of World War II

and in the glow of the Cold War's end, leading historians interpreted the Civil War as a chapter in the relentless destruction of slavery and the spread of democracy by the forces of modernization over the forces of reaction. Recently, living through more confusing times, some historians have begun to question straightforward stories of the war, emphasizing its contradictory meanings, unfulfilled promises, and unintended outcomes.[21]

The story of the American Civil War changes as world history lurches in unanticipated directions and as people ask different questions of the past. Things that once seemed settled now seem less so. The massive ranks, fortified trenches, heavy machinery, and broadened targets of the American Civil War once seemed to mark a step toward the culmination of "total" war. But the wars of the twenty-first century, often fought without formal battles, are proving relentless and boundless, "total" in ways the disciplined armies of the Union and Confederacy never imagined.[22] Nations continue to come apart over ancient grievances and modern geopolitics, the example of the United States notwithstanding. Coerced labor did not end in the nineteenth century, but instead has mutated and adapted to changes in the global economy. "A fair chance in the race of life" has yet to arrive for much of the world.

The great American trial of war, emancipation, and reconstruction mattered to the world. It embodied struggles that would confront people on every continent and it accelerated the emergence of a new global power. The American crisis, it was true, might have altered the course of world history more dramatically, in ways both worse and better, than what actually transpired. The war could have brought forth a powerful and independent Confederacy based on slavery or it could have established with its Reconstruction a new global standard of justice for people who had been enslaved. As it was, the events of the 1860s and 1870s in the United States proved both powerful and contradictory in their meaning for world history.

Notes

1. For other portrayals of the Civil War in international context, see David M. Potter, "Civil War," in C. Vann Woodward, ed., *The Comparative Approach to American History* (New York: Basic Books, 1968), pp. 135–451 Carl N. Degler, *One Among Many: The Civil War in Comparative Perspective*, 29th Annual Robert Fortenbaugh Memorial Lecture (Gettysburg, PA: Gettysburg College, 1990); Robert E. May, ed., *The Union, the Confederacy, and the Atlantic Rim* (West Lafayette, IN; Purdue University Press, 1995); Peter Kolchin, *A Sphinx on the American Land: The Nineteenth-Century South in Comparative Perspective* (Baton Rouge: Louisiana State University Press, 2003). My view of the workings of world history has been influenced by C. A. Bayly, *The Birth of the Modern World, 1780–1914: Global Connections and Comparisons* (Malden, MA: Blackwell, 2004). Bayly emphasizes that "in the nineteenth century, nation-states and contending territorial empires took on sharper lineaments and became more antagonistic to each other at the very same time as the similarities, connections, and linkages between them proliferated." (p. 2). By showing the "complex

interaction between political organization, political ideas, and economic activity," Bayly avoids the teleological models of modernization, nationalism, and liberalism that have dominated our understanding of the American Civil War.

2. Lincoln quoted in James M. McPherson, *Abraham Lincoln and the Second American Revolution,* reprint (New York: Oxford University Press: 1992, 1991), p. 28.

3. The seminal work is Drew Gilpin Faust, *The Creation of Confederate Nationalism: Ideology and Identity in the Civil War South* (Baton Rouge: Louisiana State University Press, 1988). For an excellent synthesis of the large literature on this topic, see Anne S. Rubin, *A Shattered Nation: The Rise and Fall of the Confederacy, 1861–1868* (Chapel Hill: University of North Carolina Press, 2005).

4. For a useful overview, see Robert W. Fogel, *Without Consent or Contract: The Rise and Fall of American Slavery* (New York: W. W. Norton, 1989).

5. David Brion Davis, *Slavery and Human Progress* (New York: Oxford University Press, 1984); Davis, The Problem of Slavery in the Age of Revolution, 1770–1823 (Ithaca, NY: Cornell University Press, 1975), and Davis, *Inhuman Bondage: The Rise and Fall of Slavery in the New World* (Oxford University Press, 2006).

6. For helpful overviews of the global situation, see Steven Hahn, "Class and State in Postemancipation Societies: Southern Planters in Comparative Perspective," *American Historical Review* 95 (February 1990): 75–98, and Hahn, *A Nation Under Our Feet: Black Political Struggles in the Rural South From Slavery to the Great Migration* (Cambridge, MA: Belknap Press of Harvard University Press, 2003).

7. Quoted in Faust, *Creation of Confederate Nationalism,* p. 13.

8. There is a large literature on this subject, not surprisingly. A useful recent treatment is Susan-Mary Grant, *North Over South: Northern Nationalism and American Identity in the Antebellum Era* (Lawrence: University of Kansas Press, 2000). Peter Kolchin also offers penetrating comments on nationalism in *A Sphinx on the American Land,* 89–92.

9. Brian Holden Reid, *The American Civil War and the Wars of the Industrial Revolution* (London: Cassell, 1999), 211–13; John E. Clark Jr., *Railroads in the Civil War: The Impact of Management on Victory and Defeat* (Baton Rouge: Louisiana State University Press, 2001); Robert G. Angevine, *The Railroad and the State: War, Politics, and Technology in Nineteenth-Century America* (Stanford, CA: Stanford University Press, 2004).

10. For a range of interesting essays on this subject, see Stig Forster and Jorg Nagler, eds., *On the Road to Total War: The American Civil War and the German Wars of Unification, 1861–1871* (Washington, DC: The German Historical Institute, 1997).

11. See D. P. Crook, *The North, the South, and the Powers, 1861–1865* (New York: Wiley, 1974), R. J. M. Blackett, *Divided Hearts: Britain and the American Civil War* (Baton Rouge: Louisiana State University Press, 2001), James M. McPherson, *Crossroads of Freedom: Antietam* (Oxford: Oxford University Press, 2002), May, ed., *The Union, the Confederacy, and the Atlantic Rim,* and Charles M. Hubbard, *The Burden of Confederate Diplomacy* (Knoxville: University of Tennessee Press, 1998).

12. See Allen C. Guelzo, *Lincoln's Emancipation Proclamation: The End of Slavery in America* (New York: Simon and Schuster. 2004).

13. See Joseph T. Glatthaar, *Forged in Battle: The Civil War Alliance of Black Soldiers and White Officers* (New York: Free Press, 1990).

14. See Leon Litwack, *Been in the Storm So Long: The Aftermath of Slavery,* 1st Vintage ed. (New York: Vintage, 1980, 1979) and the major documentary collection edited by Ira Berlin, Leslie S. Rowland, and their colleagues, sampled in *Free At Last: A Documentary History of Slavery, Freedom, and the Civil War* (New York: The New Press, 1992).

15. See Davis, *Slavery and Human Progress,* for a sweeping perspective on this issue.

16. The classic history is Eric Foner, *Reconstruction: America's Unfinished Revolution, 1863–1877* (New York: Harper and Row, 1988), I have offered some thoughts on Reconstruction's legacy in "Exporting Reconstruction" in *What Caused the Civil War? Reflections on the South and Southern History* (New York: W. W. Norton, 2005).

17. On the legacy of Reconstruction, see David W. Blight, *Race and Reunion The Civil War in American Memory* (Cambridge, MA: Belknap Press of Harvard University Press, 2001).

18. For a fascinating essay on the South's loss of the cotton monopoly, see Sven Beckert, "Emancipation and Empire: Reconstructing the Worldwide Web of Cotton Production in the Age of the American Civil War," *American Historical Review* 109 (December 2004): 1405–38. On South Africa: John W. Cell, *The Highest Stage of White Supremacy: The Origins of Segregation in South Africa and the American South* (Cambridge: Cambridge University Press, 1982) and George M. Fredrickson, *White Supremacy: A Comparative Study in American and South African History* (New York: Oxford University Press, 1981).

19. See the discussion in the essays by Robert E. May and James M. McPherson in May, ed., *The Union, the Confederacy, and the Atlantic Rim.*

20. For the larger context, see Eric J. Hobsbawm, *The Age of Empire, 1875–1914* (New York: Pantheon, 1987) and Bayly, *Birth of the Modern World.*

21. I have described this literature and offered some thoughts on it in the essay "Worrying About the Civil War" in my *What Caused the Civil War?*

22. Reid, *American Civil War,* p. 213.

Bibliography

Surprisingly, no one book covers the themes of this essay. To understand this era of American history in global context, we need to piece together accounts from a variety of books and articles. For recent over-views of different components of these years, see Jay Sexton, "Towards a Synthesis of Foreign Relations in the Civil War Era. 1848–1877," *American Nineteenth-Century History* 5 (Fall 2004): 50–75, and Amy Kaplan, *The Anarchy of Empire in the Making of U. S. Culture* (Cambridge, MA; Harvard University Press, 2002).

Robert F. May, in the introduction to the book he edited, *The Union, the Confederacy, and the Atlantic Rim* (West Lafayette, IN: Purdue University Press, 1995), provides a useful summary of the larger context of the war. Though it is older, the perspective of D, P. Crook, *The North, the South, and the Powers, 1861–1865* (New York: Wiley, 1974) brings a welcome worldliness to the discussion. On the crucial debate in Britain, see Howard Jones, *Union in Peril: The Crisis Over British Intervention in the Civil War* (Chapel Hill: University of North Carolina Press, 1992) and R. J. M. Blackett, *Divided Hearts: Britain and the American Civil War* (Baton Rouge: Louisiana State University Press, 2001).

James M. McPherson offers characteristically insightful, and hopeful, analysis in several places. Perhaps the single best focused portrayal of the interplay between events in the United States and in the Atlantic World is in his *Crossroads of Freedom: Antietam* (Oxford: Oxford University Press, 2002). McPherson's essay, " 'The Whole Family of Man': Lincoln and the Last Best Hope Abroad," in May, ed., *The Union, the Confederacy, and the Atlantic Rim,* makes the fullest case for the larger significance of the war in encouraging liberal movements and belief around the world.

Peter Kolchin's, *A Sphinx on the American Land: The Nineteenth-Century South in Comparative Perspective* (Baton Rouge: Louisiana State University Press, 2003), offers an elegant and up-to-date survey that puts the conflict in the larger context of emancipation movements. A useful overview appears in Steven Hahn, "Class and State in Postemancipation Societies: Southern Planters in Comparative Perspective," *American Historical Review* 95 (February 1990): 75–98.

Another pioneering work is Drew Gilpin Faust, *The Creation of Confederate Nationalism: Ideology and Identity in the Civil War South* (Baton Rouge: Louisiana State University Press, 1988). Faust changed historians' perspective on nationalism in the South, which had been considered largely fraudulent before her account. Building on Faust are two recent books that offer fresh interpretations: Anne S. Rubin, *A Shattered Nation: The Rise and Fall of the Confederacy, 1861–1868* (Chapel Hill: University of North Carolina Press, 2005) and Susan-Mary Crant, *North Over South: Northern Nationalism and American Identity in the Antebellum Era* (Lawrence: University of Kansas Press, 2000).

On the much-debated issue of the relative modernity and totality of the Civil War, see Stig Förster and Jörg Nagler, eds., *On the Road to Total War: The American Civil War and the German Wars of Unification, 1861–1871* (Washington, DC: The German Historical Institute, 1997); the essays by Stanley L. Engerman and J. Matthew Gallman, Farl J. Hess, Michael Fellman, and Richard Current are especially helpful. Brian Holden Reid, in *The American Civil War and the Wars of the Industrial Revolution* (London: Cassell, 1999), offers a concise but insightful portrayal of the war in larger military context.

For a powerful representation of the role of slavery in this history, David Brion Davis's works are all helpful. His most recent account synthesizes a vast literature in an accessible way: *Inhuman Bondage: The Rise and Fall of Slavery in the New World* (Oxford University Press, 2006).

Excellent examples of what might be thought of as the new global history appear in Sven Beckert, "Emancipation and Empire: Reconstructing the Worldwide Web of Cotton Production in the Age of the American Civil War," *American Historical Review* 109 (December 2004): 1405–38; and Gordon H. Chang, "Whose 'Barbarism'? whose 'Treachery'? Race and Civilization in the Unknown United States-Korea War of 1871," *Journal of American History* 89 (March 2003): 1331–65.

EDWARD L. AYERS is Dean of the College of Art and Sciences at the University of Virginia, where he is also the Hugh P. Kelly Professor of History. He has published extensively on nineteenth-century Southern history, his most recent publication being *In the Presence of Mine Enemies: War in the Heart of America, 1859–1863 (2003),* which received the Bancroft Prize. An earlier book, *The Promise of the New South (1992),* was a finalist for both the Pulitzer Prize and the National Book Award. In addition, Ayers has created and directs a prize-winning Internet archive, "Valley of the Shadow: Two Communities in the American Civil War," containing original sources related to two towns at either end of the Shenandoah Valley, one in Virginia and the other in Pennsylvania.

Test-Your-Knowledge Form

We encourage you to photocopy and use this page as a tool to assess how the articles in *Annual Editions* expand on the information in your textbook. By reflecting on the articles you will gain enhanced text information. You can also access this useful form on a product's book support Web site at *http://www.mhcls.com/online/*.

NAME:

DATE:

TITLE AND NUMBER OF ARTICLE:

BRIEFLY STATE THE MAIN IDEA OF THIS ARTICLE:

LIST THREE IMPORTANT FACTS THAT THE AUTHOR USES TO SUPPORT THE MAIN IDEA:

WHAT INFORMATION OR IDEAS DISCUSSED IN THIS ARTICLE ARE ALSO DISCUSSED IN YOUR TEXTBOOK OR OTHER READINGS THAT YOU HAVE DONE? LIST THE TEXTBOOK CHAPTERS AND PAGE NUMBERS:

LIST ANY EXAMPLES OF BIAS OR FAULTY REASONING THAT YOU FOUND IN THE ARTICLE:

LIST ANY NEW TERMS/CONCEPTS THAT WERE DISCUSSED IN THE ARTICLE, AND WRITE A SHORT DEFINITION:

We Want Your Advice

ANNUAL EDITIONS revisions depend on two major opinion sources: one is our Advisory Board, listed in the front of this volume, which works with us in scanning the thousands of articles published in the public press each year; the other is you—the person actually using the book. Please help us and the users of the next edition by completing the prepaid article rating form on this page and returning it to us. Thank you for your help!

ANNUAL EDITIONS: United States History, Volume 1, 20/e

ARTICLE RATING FORM

Here is an opportunity for you to have direct input into the next revision of this volume.
We would like you to rate each of the articles listed below, using the following scale:

1. **Excellent: should definitely be retained**
2. **Above average: should probably be retained**
3. **Below average: should probably be deleted**
4. **Poor: should definitely be deleted**

Your ratings will play a vital part in the next revision.
Please mail this prepaid form to us as soon as possible.
Thanks for your help!

RATING	ARTICLE	RATING	ARTICLE
	1. America's First Immigrants		21. The Best of Enemies
	2. 1491		22. Cliffhanger
	3. How Cruel Were the Spaniards?		23. The Revolution of 1803
	4. America, the Atlantic, and Global Consumer Demand, 1500–1800		24. Saving New Orleans
	5. The Birth of America		25. Women in the Early Republic
	6. The Root of the Problem		26. African Americans in the Early Republic
	7. Blessed and Bedeviled		27. Liberty is Exploitation
	8. American Indians, Witchcraft, and Witch-hunting		28. From Detroit to the Promised Land
	9. Slavery in the North		29. Andrew Jackson Versus the Cherokee Nation
	10. Were American Indians the Victims of Genocide?		30. Storm over Mexico
	11. Dirty Little Secret		31. Free at Last
	12. Midnight Riders		32. A Day to Remember
	13. God and the Founders		33. New York City's Secession Crisis
	14. The Rocky Road to Revolution		34. Lincoln and the Constitutional Dilemma of Emancipation
	15. A Day to Remember: July 4, 1776		35. A Gallant Rush for Glory
	16. Washington Takes Charge		36. How the West Was Lost
	17. Winter of Discontent		37. America's Birth at Appomattox
	18. Evacuation Day		38. The American Civil War, Emancipation, and Reconstruction on the World Stage
	19. The Necessity of Refusing My Signature		
	20. Remembering Martha		